D1118982

WITHDRAWN
UTSA LIBRARIES

OUT OF WHAT BEGAN

GREGORY A. SCHIRMER

OUT OF

WHAT

BEGAN

A HISTORY OF IRISH
POETRY IN ENGLISH

CORNELL UNIVERSITY PRESS

ITHACA AND LONDON

Copyright © 1998 by Cornell University

All rights reserved. Except for brief quotations in a review, this book, or parts thereof, must not be
reproduced in any form without permission in writing from the publisher. For information,
address Cornell University Press, Sage House, 512 East State Street, Ithaca, New York 14850.

First published 1998 by Cornell University Press.

Printed in the United States of America.

LIBRARY OF CONGRESS CATALOGING-IN-PUBLICATION DATA
Schirmer, Gregory A.
    Out of what began : a history of Irish poetry in English / Gregory
A. Schirmer.
        p.   cm.
    Includes bibliographical references and index.
    ISBN 0-8014-3498-X (cloth : alk. paper)
    1. English poetry—Irish authors—History and criticism.
    2. Ireland—Intellectual life.   3. Ireland—In literature.
    I. Title.
    PR8761.S35   1998
    821.009′9417—dc21   98-8409

Cornell University Press strives to use environmentally responsible suppliers and materials to the
fullest extent possible in the publishing of its books. Such materials include vegetable-based,
low-VOC inks and acid-free papers that are also recycled, totally chlorine-free, or partly
composed of nonwood fibers.

Cloth printing   10 9 8 7 6 5 4 3 2 1

Library
University of Texas
at San Antonio

FOR JANE

Those masterful images because complete
Grew in pure mind, but out of what began?

— W. B. YEATS,
"The Circus Animals' Desertion"

CONTENTS

PREFACE

By the knowledge of the acts, opinions, and condition of our ancestors . . . we can extend the three score and ten years, which is our immediate portion in time, back and back as far as facts exist, for the support of speculation. It is this enlarging of our portion of space, of time, of feeling, that is the true source of all intellectual pleasure.
—Samuel Ferguson, *Dublin University Magazine* (1840)

Ferguson's statement might be taken as sufficient justification for a history of any kind. There are, however, more specific arguments to be made on behalf of a history of Irish poetry in English. For one, although a number of general histories of Irish writing, and several more specialized historical accounts of Irish fiction and Irish drama, have appeared within the past two decades, to date no history of Irish poetry written in English has been published, even though such a genre can be identified as a significant part of the Irish literary and cultural landscape at least as far back as the early decades of the eighteenth century. (That two of Ireland's four Nobel Prize winners in this century are poets might be said to testify to the continuing importance of Irish poetry to literature written in English as well as to Irish writing.) This book attempts to provide such a history, to chart the development of Irish poetry in English from the work of Jonathan Swift at the beginning of the eighteenth century to that of John Montague near the end of the twentieth, to establish the distinctive aesthetic and cultural qualities of the genre, to consider its complex relationship to the traditions of English poetry and of poetry written in Irish, and to make clear the ways in which it both reflected and contributed to the social, political, and cultural history of Ireland.

All the principal terms of a phrase like "a history of Irish poetry" are, I realize, open to question. In the first place, the writing of any *history* inevitably entails exclusions and simplifications, inevitably constitutes a narrative that is grounded in and itself generates values, attitudes, and assumptions that profoundly, and often covertly, affect the historian's attempt to discover and represent the past. While trying to be sensitive to this problem, and wary especially of the tendency of literary histories to engender their own critical criteria, I have relied on a relatively conventional approach in writing this history, following a chronological structure, and organizing the narrative around individual poets rather than themes, issues, or poetic styles. This focus on specific writers reflects in part my own belief in the centrality of the author; it also encourages the bringing to light of numerous writers, including a considerable number of women poets, who have fallen into undeserved neglect over the past two-and-a-half centuries. In considering the question of what constitutes *"Irish* poetry," I have tried to define the tradition in such a way as to reflect the variety and diversity of Irish culture as it has developed from the beginning of the eighteenth century to the present. Thus, this book is as interested in an Ulster Protestant like Louis MacNeice, whose work on the whole belongs more to English poetry than to Irish but who wrote seriously about Irish issues and conditions, as it is in a Dublin Catholic like James Clarence Mangan, whose work is thoroughly and intimately bound up with Irish culture. At the same time, this book does not attempt to provide a history of poetry written in Irish, a tradition that is in fact far older, and arguably richer, than that of Irish poetry written in English. This is, in my view, a subject for another full-length study, but I have tried to represent to some degree the complex relationship between the two traditions, principally in considering the development of translation as a distinct and significant poetic mode in Ireland. Finally, this history defines "Irish *poetry"* in ways that, for the most part, exclude popular ballads and songs. This decision is not meant to suggest that these forms are not worthy of serious analysis—indeed, it might be argued that in the long run popular ballads and songs have been more important to the development of Irish culture, at least from the middle of the nineteenth century on, than Irish poetry has been —but instead to suggest that they deserve separate consideration, attentive to their distinctive purposes, aesthetic qualities, and audiences.

"There is no History, just histories," the Irish critic Declan Kiberd has said. This book was written in the understanding that it represents just one possible account of its subject, that it is *a* history of Irish poetry in English, not *the* history of Irish poetry in English. At the same time, it was written in the spirit of Samuel Ferguson's faith in the liberating power of history, and so represents one more attempt at that "enlarging of our portion of space, of time, of feeling."

GREGORY A. SCHIRMER

ACKNOWLEDGMENTS

I am grateful to the Office of Research and the Department of English at the University of Mississippi, and to the School for Irish Studies Foundation in Dublin, for their generous support of this project. I would also like to acknowledge the staffs of the National Library of Ireland, the Trinity College Dublin Library, the Bancroft Library at the University of California, Berkeley, and the University of Mississippi Library for their cooperation and assistance. In Ireland, conversations with the late Sean White and the late Augustine Martin were, as always, inspiring as well as informative. Finally, the bulk of this book was written in Ireland, and I am most grateful to Jack and Barbara O'Connell of Schull Books for their invaluable assistance and to Dan and Jane O'Donovan, whose hospitality and generosity contributed to this work in ways too numerous to mention.

Grateful acknowledgment is given for the use of the following material:

Eavan Boland, lines from "Mise Eire," from *The Journey* (Manchester: Carcanet Press, 1986); "Tirade for the Mimic Muse," from *Selected Poems* (Manchester: Carcanet Press, 1989). Reprinted by permission of Carcanet Press Limited. "Tirade for the Mimic Muse," copyright © 1990 Eavan Boland, "Mise Eire," copyright © 1987 Eavan Boland, "The Emigrant Irish," copyright © 1987 by Eavan Boland, from *An Origin Like Water: Collected Poems 1967–1987* by Eavan Boland. Reprinted by permission W. W. Norton & Company, Inc.

Austin Clarke, lines from "The Cattledrive in Connaught," "Pilgrimage," "Tenebrae," "The Scholar," "The Straying Student," "Three Poems about Children," "Celebrations," "The Loss of Strength," "Mabel Kelly,"

"O'Rourke's Feast," from *Collected Poems* (Dublin: Dolmen Press, 1974). Reprinted by permission of R. Dardis Clarke, 21 Pleasants Street, Dublin 8.

Rhoda Coghill, lines from "Dead" and "The Young Bride's Dream," from *The Bright Hillside* (Dublin: Hodges, Figgis, 1948). Reprinted by permission of Rhoda Coghill.

Padraic Colum, lines from "A Man Bereaved," from *Old Pastures* (New York: Macmillan, 1930); "Fore-piece," from *The Poet's Circuits: Collected Poems of Ireland* (London: Oxford University Press, 1960). Reprinted by permission of Máire Colum O'Sullivan.

Denis Devlin, lines from "Lough Derg," "Liffey Bridge," "Est Prodest," "Meditation at Avila," "The Heavenly Foreigner," "The Tomb of Michael Collins," from *Collected Poems of Denis Devlin,* ed. J. C. C. Mays (Winston-Salem, N. C.: Wake Forest University Press, 1989). Reprinted by permission of Wake Forest University Press and The Dedalus Press.

Padraic Fallon, lines from "Yeats's Tower at Ballylee," "Yeats at Athenry Perhaps," "Letter from Ballylee," "For Paddy Mac," "Peasantry," from *Collected Poems of Padraic Fallon,* ed. Brian Fallon (Oldcastle, Co. Meath: Gallery Press, 1990). Reprinted by permission of Carcanet Press Limited.

Oliver St. John Gogarty, lines from "The Crab Tree," "Leda and the Swan," "High Tide at Malahide," "Ringsend," from *Collected Poems of Oliver St. John Gogarty* (New York: Devin-Adair, 1954). Copyright by Devin-Adair, Publishers, Inc., Old Greenwich, Connecticut 06870. Permission granted to reprint *Collected Poems of Oliver St. John Gogarty,* 1954. All rights reserved.

Seamus Heaney, lines from "Casualty," from *Field Work* (New York: Farrar, Straus & Giroux, 1979). Copyright © by Seamus Heaney. Reprinted by permission of Farrar, Straus & Giroux, Inc., and Faber and Faber Ltd.

John Hewitt, lines from "The Colony," "Once Alien Here," "The Glens," from *Collected Poems of John Hewitt* (Belfast: Blackstaff Press, 1991). Reprinted by permission of Blackstaff Press.

Patrick Kavanagh, lines from "Inniskeen Road: July Evening," "Kerr's Ass," "The Great Hunger," "Canal Bank Walk," "Prelude," "Auditors In," from *Collected Poems of Patrick Kavanagh* (New York: W. W. Norton, 1964). Reprinted by permission of the Trustees of the Estate of Patrick Kavanagh, c/o Peter Fallon, Literary Agent, Loughcrew, Oldcastle, Co. Meath, Ireland. Also, copyright by Deven-Adair Publishers, Inc., Old Greenwich, Connecticut, 06870. Permission granted to reprint *The Collected Poems of Patrick Kavanagh,* 1964. All rights reserved.

Thomas Kinsella, lines from "Nightwalker," "Downstream," "A Country Walk," from *Poems 1956–1973* (Winston-Salem, N. C.: Wake Forest University Press, 1979). Reprinted by permission of Thomas Kinsella.

Máire MacEntee, lines from "Duibhe Id Mhailghibh," "Mo-Chion Dár Lucht Abarthaigh," from *A Heart Full of Thought* (Dublin: Dolmen Press, 1959). Reprinted by permission of Máire MacEntee.

Thomas MacGreevy, lines from "The Six Who Were Hanged," "Aodh Ruadh Ó Domhnaill," "Crán Tráth na nDeith," from *Collected Poems of Thomas MacGreevy*, ed. Susan Schreibman (Washington, D.C.: Catholic University of America Press; Dublin: Anna Livia Press, 1991). Reprinted by permission of Catholic University of America Press.

Louis MacNeice, lines from "Carrickfergus," "Belfast," "Eclogue from Iceland," "Autumn Journal," "Western Landscape," "Dublin," "Valediction," from *Collected Poems of Louis MacNeice,* ed. E. R. Dodds (London: Faber and Faber, 1966, 1979). Reprinted by permission of David Higham Associates.

Derek Mahon, lines from *The Hudson Letter* (Oldcastle, Co. Meath: Gallery Press, 1995). Reprinted by permission of Gallery Press and Wake Forest University Press. Lines from "The Sea in Winter," "Afterlives," "In Carrowdore Churchyard," from *Selected Poems* (London: Penguin; Oldcastle, Co. Meath: Gallery Press, 1991). Reprinted by permission of Oxford University Press.

John Montague, lines from "The Rough Field," "Old Rhyme," "Epilogue," from *The Rough Field* (Dublin: Dolmen Press, 1972); "Speech for an Ideal Irish Election," "The Siege of Mullingar," "The Sean Bhean Bhoct," from *John Montague: Collected Poems* (Oldcastle, Co. Meath: Gallery Press; Winston-Salem, N. C.: Wake Forest University Press, 1995). Reprinted from *John Montague: Collected Poems* with the permission of Wake Forest Univerity Press and Gallery Press.

Paul Muldoon, "As for Quince," translation of Nuala Ní Dhomhnaill, "An Crann," from *The Penguin Book of Contemporary Irish Poetry,* ed. Peter Fallon and Derek Mahon (London: Penguin; New York: Viking Penguin, 1990). Reprinted from Nuala Ní Dhomhnaill, *Pharoah's Daughter* (Oldcastle, Co. Meath: Gallery Press; Winston-Salem, N. C.: Wake Forest University Press, 1991), by permission of Gallery Press and Wake Forest University Press.

Richard Murphy, lines from "The Last Galway Hooker," "The Woman of the House," "Sailing to an Island," from *Sailing to an Island* (London: Faber and Faber, 1963); "Christening," "Legend," "History," "Orange March," from *New Selected Poems* (London: Faber and Faber, 1989). Reprinted by permission of Richard Murphy.

W. R. Rodgers, lines from "The Net," "The Character of Ireland," "The Swan," from *Collected Poems* (London: Oxford University Press, 1971). Reprinted from *Poems* (Oldcastle, Co. Meath: Gallery Press, 1993) by permission of Gallery Press.

Blanaid Salkeld, lines from "The Fox's Covert," from *The Fox's Covert* (London: J. M. Dent, 1933). Reprinted by permission of Orion Publishing Group Ltd.

Eithne Strong, lines from "Symbols," "A Woman Unleashed," "Synthesis—Achill 1958," from *Songs of the Living* (Monkstown: Runa Press, 1961). Reprinted by permission of Eithne Strong.

Sheila Wingfield, lines from "Beggarman," "Clonmacnoise," from *Collected Poems: 1938–1983* (London: Enitharmon Press, 1939). Reprinted by permission of David Pryce-Jones.

William Butler Yeats, lines from "The Circus Animals' Desertion," "Easter, 1916," "Meditations in Time of Civil War," "The Tower," "In Memory of Eva Gore-Booth and Con Markiewicz," "Coole Park, 1929," "Coole and Ballylee, 1931," "Blood and Moon," "An Irish Airman Foresees His Death," "To the Rose upon the Rood of Time," "Upon a House Shaken by the Land Agitation," "To Ireland in the Coming Times," "The Wanderings of Oisin," "Fergus and the Druid," "The Lake Isle of Innisfree," "The Valley of the Black Pig," "The Heart of the Woman," "The Song of the Old Mother," "The Ballad of Father Hart," "In Memory of Major Robert Gregory," "The Fisherman," "September 1913," "The Man and the Echo," "Come Gather Round Me, Parnellites," *Variorum Edition of the Poems of W. B. Yeats,* ed. Peter Allt and Russell K. Alspach (New York: Macmillan, 1957). Reprinted with the permission of Simon & Schuster from *Collected Works of W. B. Yeats, Vol. I: The Poems,* revised and edited by Richard J. Finneran. Copyright 1919 by Macmillan Publishing Company, renewed 1947 Bertha Georgie Yeats. Also reprinted by permission of A. P. Watt Ltd. on behalf of Michael Yeats.

Every effort has been made to trace copyright holders. I would be grateful to hear from any copyright holder not acknowledged here.

PART ONE

The Eighteenth Century

INTRODUCTION

The very concept of eighteenth-century Irish poetry in English is shrouded in ambiguity. For one thing, the overwhelming presence of Swift casts into shadow, if not oblivion, the work of lesser poets, many of whom have indeed been forgotten. Then there is the more oblique but nearly as powerful presence of Yeats, whose rewriting of eighteenth-century Anglo-Ireland into a remarkable moment of high culture, a civilization of "high laughter, loveliness and ease," posited a more-or-less monolithic literary environment that has only recently been called into serious question.[1] From various nationalist points of view, almost all the writing produced in Ireland during the eighteenth century belongs more to the English tradition than to an Irish one. Although there is something to be said for all these versions of Irish writing, none of them does justice to the complex realities of eighteenth-century Ireland, or to the literature, especially the poetry, that came out of it. Ireland in the eighteenth century was, in fact, marked by considerable cultural, political, and sectarian diversity; the conventional, principally nationalist, model of a society divided into a prosperous class of Anglo-Irish Protestant gentry and an oppressed class of Irish Catholic peasants ignores, among other things, the importance of Presbyterian dissenters in Ulster and of a sizable Catholic and Protestant middle class scattered throughout the island. Eighteenth-century Ireland also had its fair share of recurrent and serious disruptions—the agrarian violence of the 1760s and 1770s, for instance, and the 1798 insurrection. The condition of Ireland during these years was, as one literary historian has put it, one of "tense coexistence" among several different kinds of Irish, compounded by the inevitable and always uneasy relationship with the politics and culture of England.[2] This relatively unstable and culturally complex society produced a large and varied body of poetry written in English that was at times quite distinctively Irish in

3

its concerns, if English in its forms. There were more publishers in Dublin during the eighteenth century than in any other English-speaking city outside London, and most Irish poets writing during the eighteenth century, unlike many of their later counterparts, published their poems first in Dublin, not London. And if this poetry was written and read almost exclusively by members of the Anglo-Irish governing class, at its best it both reflected the diversity of eighteenth-century Irish society and was energized by it, often demonstrating the extent to which the Anglo-Irish were conscious, often uneasily, of the complexity and instability of the society that they presumed to govern and of the cultural and political ambiguity of their own position within that society.

Swift, an Anglo-Irishman enmeshed in one love-hate relationship with his native country and in another with his adopted country, England, embodied many of these pressures in his work. Indeed, Swift's art might be said to be governed almost entirely by the principle of division: between England and Ireland, between Anglo-Ireland and native Ireland, between an Irish audience and an English one, between affection for Ireland and hatred of it, between political liberalism and religious conservatism. The general restlessness and satirical energy that mark the best of his writing grew out of this condition. Many important social and cultural issues were not reflected in Swift's writing, however, but were examined by other Irish poets writing in the eighteenth century. Swift's literary circle in Dublin included, for example, several women poets who explored the situation of women in eighteenth-century Anglo-Irish society, at times drawing distinctly nationalist parallels between the condition of women as an oppressed class and that of Ireland in its relationship to England. Also, the work of Thomas Parnell, Swift's contemporary, included poems marked by a lyricism and melancholy that anticipate the development of an Irish Gothic tradition in the nineteenth century. The vexing question of Irish rural life, and specifically of the politics and economics of the tenant-landlord system—carrying powerful and potentially explosive implications for the relationship between Anglo-Ireland and native Ireland, and between Ireland and England as well—was explored not only in the 1760s and 1770s in Goldsmith's critiques of the rise of commercialism and the threatened demise of the rural way of life, but also earlier, and with considerable force, in the work of the lesser-known Laurence Whyte, writing sympathetically about tenant farmers in his native Westmeath. Goldsmith also developed Swift's sense of cultural ambiguity into an extended meditation on the condition of exile, introducing into Irish poetry in English a theme that was to preoccupy Irish writing through the nineteenth and twentieth centuries. The first traces of romanticism, a phenomenon that, because of its associations with the English tradition, was particularly problematic for Irish writers, also could be found in the work of several late-eighteenth-century Irish poets. Although the poems of Samuel Whyte and Thomas Dermody did not attempt the fusion of romanticism and nationalism that was to inspire so much Irish writing in the nineteenth century, Dermody's writing especially was characterized by a formal unconventionality that anticipated later efforts to free Irish poetry from the inhibiting effect of forms inherited from the English tradition. At the same time, in the politically charged closing years of the century, a popular political poetry began to appear; much of this work, coming at the time of the French Revolution and, in Ireland, of the events leading up to the insurrection of 1798, advanced more radically nationalist positions than those taken earlier in the century by Swift. Finally, although many Anglo-Irish writers in the eighteenth century were contentedly ignorant of the Gaelic culture that lay for the most part beyond the English pale, and indeed were part of a political enterprise destined, if not intended, to destroy it, and although a relatively sophisticated antiquarian movement to recover the culture of the colonized would not emerge until the nineteenth century, there were some significant points of contact in eighteenth-century poetry between the two cultures, including the first collection of translations of Irish poems into English—the work of an Anglo-Irish Protestant woman.

It might be said that the entire Anglo-Irish cultural enterprise, from the poems of Swift to the splendid architecture of Georgian Dublin, rested on an unjust base of exclusion and oppression, a base that was, therefore, fundamentally unstable. The Anglo-Irish Ascendancy responsible for most of the Irish poetry written in English during the eighteenth century was, in fact, suspended between two uneasy relationships. On the one hand, it was dependent on England—culturally, politically, economically, and, because of the perceived threat of a Jacobite uprising, militarily. At the same time, it was also intent on establishing a reasonable degree of independence from English political control, as evidenced in Swift's attack on the Woods coinage scheme in the 1720s and in the movement for legislative independence that resulted in the constitution of 1782 and Grattan's parliament. The Anglo-Irish were also dependent on the native Irish population that they considered themselves essentially separate from, if not superior to; it was native Irish labor that drove much of the economy that supported them in relative comfort, it was native Irish culture that provided them with one important means of differentiating themselves from the English, and it was native Irish hostility that nagged at them with the worrying threat of insurrection. The implications of this instability for eighteenth-century Irish writing were far-reaching. For one thing, the ambiguous position of the Anglo-Irish inevitably generated a disjunction between language and reality,[3] often taking the form of anxieties about writing about Irish experience in the English language or of using poetic forms and conventions taken more or less wholesale from the English tradition. The state of cultural limbo in which most eighteenth-century Anglo-Irish poets found themselves also tended to produce a sense of exile and alienation, of homelessness, expressed with particular force in the work of Goldsmith, but also in that of several lesser poets. And finally, writing from a position defined by ambiguity often led to an unusual degree of self-consciousness, of writing anxiously concerned with the poet's place and function in society. That all these issues are familiar to readers of Irish literature written in the nineteenth and twentieth centuries only attests to the significance of eighteenth-century Irish poetry to the tradition of Irish writing as a whole.

SWIFT AND HIS WORLD

Any number of reasons might be given for placing Jonathan Swift (1667–1745) at the beginning of this history. It might be argued, for example, that he was the first Irish poet writing in English out of significant Irish interests.[1] More specifically, Swift might be described (as he often has been, and as he was in his own day) as Ireland's first patriot-poet writing in the English language. This view of Swift's Irishness appealed particularly to nineteenth-century Irish poets committed to reading Irish literature as a history of nationalist writing; thus, Denis Florence MacCarthy, a poet associated with the Young Ireland movement of the 1840s, described Swift as "the first great Anglo-Irish writer who felt that he was an Irishman, and that his injured and despised country was worthy even of the affection of patriotism."[2] It might further be argued that Swift had at least some knowledge of and interest in the Gaelic tradition; he did publish one version of a poem taken from the Irish, and there are other instances in his work in which the English literary tradition intersects, albeit somewhat inaccurately, with the Gaelic tradition. More generally, it might be pointed out that, especially in comparison with his English contemporaries, such as Dryden and Pope, Swift's writing manifests a rugged, rough aggressiveness and energy that could be said to register the influences of his experiences in Ireland on his neo-classical aesthetics. More important than any of these arguments, however, is the quality of ambiguity and doubt, of insecurity and restlessness, that characterizes the best of Swift's writing. No Irish poet writing in English before Swift, and very few after him, so consistently or so powerfully embodies the tensions and pressures arising from cultural displacement and instability that have come to define so much Irish writing in general, and very few Irish poets have been so profoundly, even obsessively, self-reflexive in their work, so blatantly anxious about the poetic self and its relation to society.

The most obvious manifestation of this is the difference felt in Swift's life
and art between England and Ireland. His family came to Ireland as part of the
Act of Settlement in 1662, and Swift was born in Dublin five years later. But
his father, an attorney, had died before Swift was born, and Swift spent the early
years of his childhood in England before returning to Ireland to be educated (at
Kilkenny School and Trinity College). It was, moreover, in England that Swift
first made his mark as a public figure and a writer, and he devoted considerable
energy to remaining there. When, in 1714 (after the death of Queen Anne and
the fall of the Tory ministry with which Swift had been closely associated),
Swift returned to Ireland to become the Dean of St. Patrick's in Dublin, he
went with great reluctance, seeing Ireland as a provincial, backward nation, a
place fit only for outcasts from the glitter of London life, and, as he took every
opportunity of saying, a land of slaves. He never really abandoned this view.
In 1732, after nearly two decades of living in Ireland, and nearly a decade after
the triumph of his *Drapier's Letters,* Swift gave this account of Ireland to a
newcomer:

> Tipperary . . . is like the rest of the whole kingdom, a bare face of nature,
> without houses or plantations; filthy cabins, miserably tattered, half-starved
> creatures, scarce in human shape; one insolent ignorant oppressive squire to
> be found in twenty miles riding; a parish church to be found only in a summer-
> day's journey, in comparison of which, an English farmer's barn is a cathedral;
> a bog of fifteen miles round; every meadow a slough, and every hill a mixture
> of rock, heath, and marsh; and every male and female, from the farmer,
> inclusive to the day labourer, infallibly a thief, and consequently a beggar,
> which in this island are terms convertible.[3]

Much of Swift's satire written in the 1730s squarely places the blame for
Ireland's suffering not on the English but on Anglo-Irish absentee landlords
and a corrupt Irish parliament. It is also true, however, that in the end Swift
spent sixty-four of his seventy-seven years in Ireland, and that his sympathies
often lay with the Irish in opposition to the England to which he yearned to
return. The Woods halfpence controversy in the 1720s, the occasion for Swift's
most effective political satire and, in some ways, the triumph of his career
(after the *Drapier's Letters,* Samuel Johnson said, the Irish "reverenced him as
a guardian, and obeyed him as a dictator"[4]), drove Swift into a strongly anti-
English position. And when finally, in 1732, Swift was offered the English
living to which he had so long aspired, he turned it down with hardly a second
thought, preferring to live out his days in Ireland. The truth is that Swift never
resolved the Ireland-England conflict within himself. Near the end of his life,
when he was afflicted with various maladies, mental as well as physical, he
started telling people that he had been born not in Dublin of an attorney but in

Leicester (where his mother in fact spent most of her life) of a clergyman. Johnson's comment on this extraordinary bit of deception is apt: "The question may, without much regret, be left in the obscurity in which he delighted to involve it." [5]

The obscurity of Swift's position went considerably beyond questions of his divided loyalties to Ireland and England. Not only did Swift, living in Dublin, feel himself in exile from the country of his preference, but also, as an Anglo-Irishman, he could not help but feel alienated from the culture of the native Irish, from which he was decidedly separated by social class and religion, but with which he apparently felt some genuine sympathy. In a letter written in 1732, he said that the English ought to be "ashamed of the Reproaches they cast on the Ignorance, the Dulness, and the Want of Courage, in the *Irish* Nations; those Defects, wherever they happen, arising only from the Poverty and Slavery they suffer from their inhuman Neighbors." [6] Nevertheless, Swift's sympathies could extend only so far. The native Irish culture was, if visible, finally out of reach; moreover, Swift's attitude toward it—like that of many of the Anglo-Irish, especially those arriving as part of the post-Cromwellian settlement—had to be tinged with some guilt. Also, as he well knew, his defense of Irish independence during the Woods controversy was a defense of the independence of the Irish parliament, from which Irish Catholics were excluded. And there is evidence that his status as an Irish patriot rested uneasily on his shoulders. According to Johnson, at one point late in his life, when he was told that "the usual bonfires and illuminations" were being prepared around the city to celebrate his birthday, Swift said, "It is all folly; they had better let it alone." [7]

Swift's private life was also marked by ambiguity. The two women in Swift's life—Stella (Esther Johnson) and Vanessa (Hester Vanhomrigh)—seemed to represent, for Swift at least, two different aspects of the feminine: Stella was the passive pupil perfectly willing to be created in Swift's own image, while Vanessa was much more aggressive and independent. Swift's inability or un-willingness to choose finally one or the other, however much he was tormented by this dual presence in his life, suggests the extent to which he needed both, yet needed to be free from both. Furthermore, each of the two relationships was characterized by paradox. If Stella and Swift were, as seems likely, secretly married, the marriage was not only never publicly acknowledged but also probably never consummated; as Johnson put it, Stella "never was treated as a wife, and to the world she had the appearance of a mistress." [8] And if Vanessa can be seen, in some ways, as Swift's mistress, the betrayal enacted by their passion is itself incomplete, since the marriage being betrayed had never been consummated. Moreover, it seems likely that Swift's relationship with Vanessa, although considerably more sexual than that with Stella, also was not consum-mated, presumably by Swift's choice. [9] All the various contending forces behind and between these two relationships—including the central one of chastity versus sexuality, often projected by Swift into lasting spiritual virtue versus transient physical indulgence—inform the best of what might be called Swift's love poems, including the birthday poems to Stella and "Cadenus and Vanessa."

Standing behind all these contradictions and paradoxes, public and private, in Swift's life and art, are broader, more far-reaching dichotomies. Swift's political and religious views, and the ambiguities surrounding his position as an Anglo-Irish writer, reflect a deep-seated conflict between tradition and revolution, moral discipline and liberal license, authoritarianism and libertarianism. Swift's *Drapier's Letters,* for example, may have had the effect of a call for freedom that could be read as revolutionary, but Swift's arguments themselves carefully skirt political radicalism, resting firmly on appeals to precedent and tradition, on the strength of the monarchy as an institution, and on the constitutional validity of the legislative bodies.[10] More generally, Swift's work manifests an unresolved tension between stability and disorder, evident in the difference between the harmonizing principles of the English Enlightenment and the unstable reality of everyday, variegated life that Swift saw around him in an Ireland that must have seemed largely indifferent to those principles. Although Swift almost always wrote in defense of stability, his work is marked by an unsettling awareness that chaos is just around the corner. That awareness often makes itself felt in the rhetorical and formal qualities of Swift's poetry: the defense of an essentially conservative position is usually made by means of an unconventional assortment of paradoxes, allegories, personae, masks, fantasies, exaggerations, grotesqueries, puns, word-plays, and the like. Finally, for Swift, the surface of life, the evidence of the senses, is never to be wholly trusted; there is always an underside that contradicts the surface and threatens to destroy it. Moreover, that underside, no matter how distressful, may well contain truth, the surface only illusion; much of Swift's satire takes the form of a stripping away of the surface to expose the often unsettling realities that lurk just below.

It is hardly surprising, given the cultural and political ambiguities surrounding Swift's position as an Irish writer, that one of the established figures that comes under question in Swift's work is the poet himself. A remarkable number of Swift's poems, especially among those written relatively late in his life, consider critically both Swift's own career as a writer and the broader question of the artist's place and function in society. Characteristically, Swift addresses these issues by means of an array of varying masks, tones, and points of view. Nevertheless, the picture of the poet that emerges is fairly consistent: a figure of exile and alienation, of someone excluded, as Swift considered himself to be, from the mainstream of society, doomed to observing, often through the lens of irony and satire, all that he could not have.

As Johnson once said, "Swift was not one of those minds which amaze the world with early pregnancy." [11] What is generally considered to be Swift's early poetry was written when he was in his thirties and forties, which may explain why even Swift's earliest poems often embody the same qualities and express the same themes that characterize his later work. The two well-known "description" poems, for example—"A Description of the Morning" (1709) and "A Description of a City Shower" (1710)—depend upon and exploit a variety of conflicts and reversals of convention: pastoral idealism versus urban realism; conventional notions of the dawn and of water as life-giving sources versus perceptions of the morning as the revealer of the night's sins and the day's coming drudgery and of water as the bearer of evidence of the city's ugliness and inhumanity; poetry as a form of heightened discourse attached to the classical tradition and governed by certain conventions versus poetry as more-or-less ordinary language meant to describe things as they are. What is perhaps most remarkable about these poems is the way in which Swift manipulates tone and voice to dramatize these tensions, foreshadowing the extraordinary powers of ventriloquism with which, throughout his career, he negotiated the unresolvable conflicts that are central to his art. In "A Description of a City Shower," for example, Swift welds together in a single sentence two radically different forms of discourse, allowing high and low culture to coexist in an uneasy relationship:

> Mean while the South rising with dabbled Wings,
> A Sable Cloud a-thwart the Welkin flings,
> That swill'd more Liquor than it could contain,
> And like a Drunkard gives it up again. [12]

When Swift finally took up his pen to write on behalf of Ireland, he was fifty-three years old. He had vowed, when he arrived in Ireland six years earlier, in 1714, to steer clear of Irish politics. This vow was no doubt motivated by the bitter disappointments that he suffered in seeking some reward—specifically, an ecclesiastical position in England—for his four years of service to the Tory ministry during the reign of Queen Anne. In fact, as is suggested in a poem entitled "In Sickness" that Swift wrote upon his arrival in Ireland, he seemed at that point to have considered his useful life to be at an end, and ready to embrace, almost eagerly, the role of sick and dying victim:

> 'Tis true,—then why should I repine,
> To see my Life so fast decline?
> But, why obscurely here alone?
> Where I am neither lov'd nor known.
> My State of Health none care to learn;
> My Life is here no Soul's Concern. [13]

It took the Declaratory Act of 1720, which stated that the English parliament had full authority to make laws "of sufficient force and validity to bind the kingdom and people of Ireland," to draw him out of this gloom. Swift's immediate response, expressed in the pamphlet "A Proposal for the Universal Use of *Irish* Manufacture" (1720), took precisely the opposite view. Indeed, one of the pillars of Swift's political position throughout the closing decades of his life was that the relationship between the English parliament and its counterpart in Dublin should be one of equality, both parliaments existing side by side and in the service of the monarchy. This theory inspired *The Drapier's Letters,* as Swift made clear in the third of them:

> Were not the People of *Ireland* born as *free* as those of *England?* . . . Is not their *Parliament* as fair a *Representative* of the *People,* as that of *England?* . . . Does not the same *Sun* shine over them? And have they not the same *God* for their *Protector?* Am I a *Free-man* in *England,* and do I become a *Slave* in six hours by crossing the *Channel?*[14]

Of course, as Swift well knew, the Irish parliament was not a fair representative of the Irish people, but was in fact constructed on the principle of exclusion: of Catholics, about whom Swift does not seem to have been very worried, and of dissenters, whose aggressive characteristics and history (specifically, the Puritan revolution) did worry him considerably. At the same time, he seems to have been reasonably aware of the poverty and suffering experienced by the native Irish. "Whoever travels this Country," he said in "A Proposal for the Universal Use of *Irish* Manufacture," "and observes the *Face* of Nature, or the *Faces,* and Habits, and Dwellings of the *Natives,* will hardly think himself in a Land where either *Law, Religion,* or *common Humanity* is professed." [15] The way to reform, in Swift's view, lay inside existing political and cultural institutions— the *"Law, Religion,* or *common Humanity"*—rather than through revolution. Moreover, from his position as a person of Irish birth who saw himself as betrayed by the English political system, Swift could blame England for much of the suffering of the Irish. As a person who considered himself one of the king's loyal subjects, however, he also could argue that the Irish themselves bore some responsibility for their oppressed condition. Swift did not exclude the Irish parliament from his list of the accused. Indeed, one of his most vitriolic satirical poems is "A Character, Panegyric, and Description of the Legion Club" (1736), an attack on members of the Irish parliament. Swift's view is summed up neatly in these lines, from "A Libel on D——D——and a Certain Great Lord" (1730), concerning the Lord Lieutenant of Ireland, Lord Carteret:

> And what Condition can be worse?
> He comes to *drain* a *Beggar's Purse:*

He comes to tye our Chains on faster,
And shew us, E——is our Master:
Caressing Knaves and Dunces wooing,
To make them work their own undoing.[16]

Although many of Swift's satirical poems about Ireland are marred by shrill-
ness or oversimplification, at their best his Irish satires, by manipulating various
voices and personae, and by entertaining more than one competing view of a
given question, effectively embody the complexities of eighteenth-century Irish
political and cultural life. Not long after the anonymous publication of "A
Proposal for the Universal Use of *Irish* Manufacture," the printer, a Mr. Waters,
was prosecuted, inspiring Swift's "An Excellent new Song on a seditious
Pamphlet" (1720). In this poem, the satire is delivered through the persona of
an Irish shopkeeper who, unlike the narrator of *The Drapier's Letters,* is not
sympathetic to Swift's position:

Brocado's, and Damasks, and Tabbies, and Gawses,
    Are by *Robert Ballentine* lately brought over;
With Forty Things more: Now hear what the Law says,
    Whoe'er will not were them, is not the King's Lover.
        Tho' a Printer and Dean
        Seditiously mean
    Our true *Irish* Hearts from old *England* to wean.[17]

While remaining true to the shopkeeper's point of view, largely by means of
colloquial rhythms and diction, these lines ironically undermine that position
by exposing the assumption that stands behind the case against Swift: that the
ideal relationship between Ireland and England is that of infant suckling and
mother. Later, Swift uses the voice of the shopkeeper both to expose the English
fear that lies behind the fierce reaction to Swift's pamphlet and to flirt with,
without actually embracing, a relatively revolutionary sentiment:

Whoever our Trading with *England* would hinder,
    To *inflame* both the Nations do plainly conspire;
Because *Irish* Linen will soon turn to Tinder;
    And Wool it is greasy, and quickly takes Fire.[18]

This is Swift's most effective mode of satire, governed by and exploiting the
multiple ambiguities that defined the political and cultural context in which he
was writing. It enabled him to gesture, when rhetorically necessary, toward
relatively extremist views (and thereby encouraged the nineteenth-century reading of him as Ireland's first great nationalist poet), while his sense of the

complexity of Irish life prevented him from embracing without qualification any one position. For example, the view that England was the principal cause of Ireland's deprivation, and the related, essentially nationalist argument for severing Ireland's relationship with England, might be inferred from some of Swift's poems about the Woods halfpence controversy. The conclusion of a version of an Horatian ode that Swift adapted to this purpose ("Horace. Book I. Ode XIV") certainly invites that kind of reading:

> Beware, and when you hear the Surges roar,
> Avoid the Rocks on *Britain's* angry Shore:
> They lye, alas, too easy to be found,
> For thee alone they lye the Island round.[19]

But Swift's view of Ireland's condition is considerably wider than this interpretation suggests. The theme of this ode, as of much of Swift's writing about Ireland, is betrayal, but for Swift the Irish themselves are as guilty of this crime as are the English. Moreover, the principal victim of the betrayal attributed to the Irish is (and here Swift anticipates many modern Irish writers) the writer himself:

> As when some Writer in a public Cause,
> His Pen to save a sinking Nation draws,
> While all is Calm, his Arguments prevail,
> The People's Voice expands his Paper Sail;
> 'Till Pow'r, discharging all her stormy Bags,
> Flutters the feeble Pamphlet into Rags.
> The Nation scar'd, the Author doom'd to Death,
> Who fondly put his Trust in pop'lar Breath.[20]

Swift's ambiguous position as an Anglo-Irishman who considered himself alienated from both England and Ireland stands behind this condemnation of both English "Pow'r" and the "pop'lar Breath" of the Irish on whose behalf he is writing. This self-reflexive, autobiographical stance is characteristic of much of Swift's writing about Ireland. Not until Yeats is there an Irish poet so obsessed as Swift with creating and exploring various images of self, and these self-conscious self-presentations reflect not only Swift's own personal, political, and cultural insecurities but also the complexity and instability of the eighteenth-century Ireland in which he was working. In "My Lady's Lamentation and Complaint against the Dean" (1728), for example, Swift's ironies generate a complexity that gives this self-portrait considerable psychological authenticity, and describes the ambiguous, unstable relationship between the Anglo-Irish and the native Irish. Swift's ability to negotiate between these two

divided groups and between their stereotyped perceptions of each other—
one of the principal causes of their mutual alienation—can be seen when the
Anglo-Irish narrator disparagingly describes Swift's relationship with those
below him on the social ladder:

> He's all the day saunt'ring,
> With labourers bant'ring,
> Among his colleagues,
> A parcel of Teagues,
> (Whom he brings in among us
> And bribes with mundungus.)
> Hail, fellow, well met,
> All dirty and wet:
> Find out, if you can,
> Who's master, who's man.[21]

This method of projecting his self-image through other characters reaches its
most ambitious point in "Verses on the Death of Dr. Swift" (1731), in which
multiple voices of evaluation are filtered through a first-person narrator, and in
which Swift sets out his views on the poet and his position in society. In the
self-reflexive argument of this poem—and in Swift's experience, as he saw it
—the writer is certain to be a figure of alienation whom society punishes with
obscurity for telling the truth: "Had he but spar'd his Tongue and Pen,/He
might have rose like other Men." [22] Nonetheless, the writer has a moral obligation to address political and social issues, even if the result is enforced or
effective silence. Moreover, all writing, but particularly satire, can be justified
only if it is written out of a moral vision, not out of spite. "Malice never was
his aim," says the narrator speaking on Swift's behalf.[23] All kinds of ironies
and paradoxes hover around this self-image. Swift was not, at least in Ireland,
the outcast figure that he often projected himself to be. And malice was quite
frequently his aim; much of his satire is marred by a bitterness and invective
that he could not or would not control. Finally, the idea that the successful
satirist is doomed to an ineffectual alienation is belied by the very poem that
makes the argument; "Verses on the Death of Dr. Swift" was widely regarded
at the time as a powerful and effective satire on Irish society. Nonetheless,
through all the mirrors and ironies, the poem does present an aesthetics of
alienation that clearly defined Swift's view of himself as an Irish poet and that
governed much of his writing.

Swift was aware, to some extent at least, of the other culture that surrounded
him but was essentially foreign to him: the Gaelic tradition that during Swift's
lifetime suffered a continual decline from which it has never recovered. The
most obvious evidence for this is Swift's "The Description of an *Irish-Feast*"

(1720), an English version of an eighteenth-century Irish poem, "Pléaráca na Ruarcach," which tells of a famous feast given by a Co. Leitrim chieftain named Brian O'Rourke in the sixteenth century. Believed to be the work of Aodh Mac Gabhráin (Hugh MacGauran), an Irish poet who flourished in the early decades of the eighteenth century, the poem was set to an air, "O'Rourke's Feast," by the blind Irish harper Turlough Carolan. How it came to Swift's attention is not known—Carolan's air may well have had something to do with it[24]—but Swift's version, written in a thumping iambic/anapaestic dimeter, is not at all faithful to the subtle rhythms of the original (a far more sensitive version was written by Austin Clarke in the twentieth century [25]). Nonetheless, the poem is informed by a rough, driving energy that is true to the occasion that it describes, and by an unblinking realism true to the nature of Gaelic poetry in general, as is evident in this description of the brawl that follows the eating and drinking:

> What Stabs and what Cuts,
>   What clatt'ring of Sticks,
> What Strokes on Guts,
>   What Bastings and Kicks![26]

However much Swift has imposed an alien poetic form on this Irish material, there are a few places in his version where he seems to echo the complex assonantal patterns that are the trademark of much Gaelic verse, specifically a standard Gaelic pattern of linkages between terminal and medial positions:

> O'Rourk's noble *Fare*
>   Will *ne'er* be forgot,
> By those who were *there,*
>   Or those who were not.
>
>   .   .   .
>
> O there is the *Sport,*
>   We rise with the *Light,*
> In dis*or*derly *Sort,*
>   From *sno*ring all Night.[27] (emphasis added)

Swift was, of course, perfectly capable of seeing his own interest, and that of his class, in Ireland's Gaelic past in the context of his own characteristic division between affection for Ireland and exasperation with it. On the surface, his poem entitled "Verses occasioned by the sudden drying up of St. Patrick's Well" (1729) can be read as contrasting the glories of Ireland's cultural past with the debasement and corruption of its present. The claims for Ireland's native culture are made, appropriately enough, by St. Patrick himself, who narrates the poem:

> Ierne, to the World's remotest Parts,
> Renown'd for Valour, Policy and Arts.
>   Hither from Colchos, with the fleecy Ore,
> Jason arriv'd two thousand Years before.
> Thee, happy Island, Pallas call'd her own,
> When haughty Britain was a Land unknown.[28]

The ironies that lurk here within St. Patrick's unqualified enthusiasm (the kind of enthusiasm that led many nineteenth-century nationalists to make extravagant claims for Ireland's culture and history) are reinforced in extensive footnotes that Swift attached to the text of the poem, citing in strictly scholarly form but with obvious ironic intent a host of classical and English authorities to support St. Patrick's assertions of former glories for Ireland, including Virgil, the text of a Greek poem about the Argonaut, and even the venerable Bede.

In September of 1727, Swift was literally suspended between England and Ireland, forced by unfavorable winds to lay up at Holyhead while on a journey back to Ireland. Swift was irritated by the delay; he knew that Stella was ill, and he was eager to be with her. In his anxiety and frustration, he scratched out the angry lines of "Holyhead," ending with a scathing denunciation of Ireland:

> I never was in hast before
> To reach that slavish hateful shore
> Before, I always found the wind
> To me was most malicious kind
> But now, the danger of a friend
> On whom my fears and hopes depend
> Absent from whom all Clymes are curst
> With whom I'm happy in the worst
> With rage impatient makes me wait
> A passage to the land I hate.
> Else, rather on this bleaky shore
> Where loudest winds incessant roar
> Where neither herb nor tree will thrive,
> Where nature hardly seems alive,
> I'd go in freedom to my grave,
> Than Rule yon Isle and be a Slave.[29]

This fantasy did not come true; Swift is buried, with Stella, in St. Patrick's Cathedral. Moreover, Swift did, as its leading literary figure, rule "yon Isle" for years while remaining, despite and because of this, its slave. A significant tradition of Irish writing might be said to rest on that Swiftian paradox.

Satire and Song in the Shadow of Swift

Most of the writers in Dublin in the early decades of the eighteenth century had some kind of relationship, sympathetic or hostile, with Swift, and most were arguably inhibited by Swift's powerful and singular poetic voice, much as many of the poets associated with the Irish literary revival were overshadowed by Yeats nearly two centuries later. Swift's contemporaries also tended to rely on the neo-Augustan poetic conventions that dominated poetry in England at the time but, when applied to Irish materials, often produced problematic results. Nevertheless, these poets embody in their work aspects of eighteenth-century Irish culture not always evident in Swift's work, and they anticipate several important aspects of the tradition of Irish poetry as it develops in the nineteenth and twentieth centuries.

Two political satirists working very much under the shadow of Swift were Jonathan Smedley (1671–c. 1729) and John Winstanley (c. 1677–1750). Born in Dublin just four years after Swift, Smedley followed Swift to Trinity College and then into the Church of Ireland, becoming dean of Killala in 1718 and dean of Clogher in 1724. Unlike Swift, however, Smedley was an ardent supporter of the Whigs in Dublin, and so saw Swift's going over to the Tories in 1710 as the unforgivable act of a traitor. Like Swift, Smedley had a gift for sharp-edged satire. The difference is that Smedley directed his satire less toward political and social issues than toward individuals, including, in perhaps his best-known poem, Swift himself. "Verses, *Fix'd on the Cathedral Door, the Day of* Dean Gulliver's *Installment*" depicts Swift as a man of neither political principle nor religious faith:

> Today, this Temple gets a *Dean,*
> Of Parts and Fame, uncommon;
> Us'd, both to Pray, and to Prophane,
> To serve both *God* and *Mammon*
>
> . . .
>
> This Place He got by Wit and Rhime,
> And many Ways most odd;
> And might a Bishop be, in Time,
> Did he believe in God.
>
> . . .
>
> Look down, St. *Patrick,* look, we pray,
> On thine own *Church and Steeple;*

Convert thy *Dean,* on this *Great Day;*
Or else God help the People![30]

Given the evidence, Smedley's claim that Swift was not a believer went close to the mark.[31] But Swift did, of course, reply—"Ah never lay thy Head to Rest!/That Head so well by Wisdom fraught!/That writes without the Toil of Thought"[32]—and Smedley was included as one of the dunces in Pope's *The Dunciad.*

For many in Swift's circle, rural Ireland and the Gaelic culture that lay beyond the English pale were hardly worth thinking about. This prejudice, based on a willed ignorance and usually manifesting itself in condescension, is exemplified in Smedley's "A Familiar Epistle to the Earl of Sunderland," a poem in which Ireland outside Dublin is viewed as a cultural wasteland: "Cloudy's the Climate, *Poor* the Land;/Verse thrives not on the barren Sand." [33] Smedley's stance illustrates how the neo-classical affinity for urban culture in general could be put to particular political use in Ireland, making it possible to see the native Irish as savages in need of Anglo-Irish if not English civilization.

Winstanley's work is considerable in bulk: his poetry was collected in two thick volumes, one published in 1742 and one in 1751.[34] But his verse is generally more limited than is Smedley's by neo-Augustan conventions and a voice too strongly imitative of Swift. There is also a tendency toward low farce and vulgarity. At times, however, this son of a Dublin lawyer is capable of writing with convincing realism about aspects of eighteenth-century Dublin ignored by much of the relatively polite or politically focused verse of the period. In "An Elegy on Capt. Molineux," for example, Winstanley gets much closer than a poet like Smedley ever does to the seamy underside of the city's nightlife:

'Twas twelve at Night; patrolling were the *Watch,*
Poor strolling *Strums,* or bosky *Cits* to catch;
While roaring *Bullies* pass them boldly by,
And *Rogues* and *Robbers* sculk, or from them fly;
When luckless *Molineux* just made a sally,
From guz'ling Belch and Brandy in *Smock-Ally*
With *Bawds, Pimps, Bullies, Pickpockets,* and *Whores,*
Who made him drunk, then kick'd him out of Doors.[35]

This passage echoes Swift's early descriptive poems about urban life, but with a specifically Dublin focus, and Winstanley's work in this vein anticipates the urban realism of twentieth-century Dublin poets such as Seamus O'Sullivan and James Stephens. But in the end, "An Elegy on Captain Molineux" dissipates its energies in a vulgar farce in which the hero is strangled by his mistress using his own wig.

At the opposite end of the spectrum from Winstanley is the work of Thomas Parnell (1679–1718), the most polished and probably most accomplished of the early-eighteenth-century Dublin poets. Next to Swift, Parnell was the best-known Irish poet in his age (his poems stayed in print through most of the eighteenth century, Goldsmith wrote a biography of him, and Samuel Johnson included him in *The Lives of the Poets),* and his work has survived into the twentieth century better than that of most of his contemporaries (the Cuala Press published a selection of his poems, edited by Lennox Robinson, in 1927, and a new collected edition was published in 1989). The son of a Chesire gentleman who had supported Cromwell and, following the Restoration, gone to ground in Ireland, Parnell entered Trinity College at the precocious age of thirteen, taking a Master's degree in 1700. He entered the church, and in 1705 was made archdeacon of Clogher, the church of which Smedley later became dean. His life was divided between his duties in Ireland and his friends in London, notably the members of the distinguished if somewhat maverick Scriblerus Club (Pope, Swift, Dr. John Arbuthnot, John Gay, and the Earl of Oxford among them). Parnell was particularly close to Pope; he wrote the preface for Pope's translation of the *Iliad,* and Pope, it has been said, revised many of Parnell's poems.

Given his background, education, and associations, it is hardly surprising that so much of Parnell's writing bears the marks of the neo-classical fashion that dominated the English literary scene to which he aspired. "He appears to me," Goldsmith wrote, "to be the last of that great school that had modelled itself upon the ancients, and taught English poetry to resemble what the generality of mankind have allowed to excel." [36] He also had something to teach eighteeenth-century Irish poetry in English, most notably the high pitch of lyricism to be found in his love poems. Dr. Johnson praised "the easy sweetness of his diction," [37] and in this "Song," that quality combines with a pleasantly casual, partly anapaestic rhythm to generate the lyric quality for which Parnell was so admired:

> When thy Beauty appears
> In its Graces and Airs,
> All bright as an Angel new dropt from the Sky;
> At distance I gaze, and am aw'd by my Fears,
> So strangely you dazzle my Eye!
>
> But when without Art,
> Your kind Thoughts you impart,
> When your Love runs in Blushes thro' ev'ry Vein;
> When it darts from your Eyes, when it pants in your
> Heart,
> Then I know you're a Woman again. [38]

Although it seems unlikely that Parnell was well acquainted with the traditions of Irish verse, the rhythms here resist the iambic rigors of much eighteenth-century English poetry,while seeming to anticipate the connections made later, most notably by Thomas Moore at the beginning of the next century, between poetry in English and the Irish song tradition.

By all accounts, Parnell was emotionally unstable, subject to fits of acute depression. He reportedly spent the last years of his life, after the death of his wife and the failure of his political ambitions in London (similar to those in which Swift was disappointed), in the throes of alcoholism. When he fell into a melancholic mood, he retreated, Goldsmith says, "to the remote parts of Ireland, and there made out a gloomy kind of satisfaction, in giving hideous descriptions of the solitude to which he retired." [39] Some of these found their way into his verse, sounding the note of melancholy characteristic of much Irish writing and often identifying his own despair with the condition, or at least the landscape, of Ireland, a practice brought to its romantic fruition in the work of James Clarence Mangan more than a century later. One of Parnell's best-known poems, "A Nightpiece on Death," which Goldsmith described as a poem that "with very little amendment might be made to surpass all those night pieces and church yard scenes that have since appeared," [40] exemplifies both Parnell's melancholy and his empathic use of Irish scenery, here with characteristics that anticipate Irish Gothicism:

> The slumb'ring Breeze forgets to breathe,
> The Lake is smooth and clear beneath,
> Where once again the spangled Show
> Descends to meet our Eyes below.
> The Grounds which on the right aspire,
> In dimness from the View retire:
> The Left presents a place of Graves,
> Whose Wall the silent Water laves.
> That Steeple guides thy doubtful sight
> Among the livid gleams of Night.
>   . . .
> Now from yon black and fun'ral Yew,
> That bathes the Charnel House with Dew,
> Methinks I hear a *Voice* begin;
> (Ye Ravens, cease your croaking Din,
> Ye tolling Clocks, no Time resound
> O'er the long Lake and midnight Ground)
> It sends a Peal of hollow Groans,
> Thus speaking from among the Bones. [41]

This Gothic gloom gives way, by the end of the poem, to religious consolation, although a considerable amount of poetic force is lost in the transition. Parnell was seriously committed to writing poetry of religious belief. In this, he stands somewhat apart from most writers in Swift's circle, and certainly from Swift himself, who treated religion almost exclusively in terms of its political and cultural significance. Parnell's religious verse is not among his best writing, but at times it embodies a nearly romantic view of the relation between the natural world, God, and the poet, as in this passage from "A Hymn on Contentment":

> The Sun that walks his airy Way,
> To light the World, and give the Day;
> The Moon that shines with borow'd Light,
> The Stars that gild the gloomy Night,
> The Seas that roll unnumber'd Waves,
> The Wood that spreads its shady Leaves,
> The Field whose Ears conceal the Grain,
> The yellow Treasure of the Plain;
> All of these, and all I see,
> Wou'd be sung, and sung by me.
> They speak their *Maker* as they can,
> But want and ask the Tongue of Man.[42]

Parnell died in Chester, at the age of thirty-eight, while en route from London to Ireland. Like many Anglo-Irishmen of his day, he lived a life that was deeply divided in its national loyalties and cultural interests. If, as Lennox Robinson said of him, "he belonged completely to neither country," [43] it might also be said that, because of his poetry, he belongs still to both.

While Parnell's reputation depended to some extent on his being friends with Pope and Swift, that of Matthew Concanen (1701–1749) depended to more or less the same extent on his being their enemy. Believed to be a native of Dublin, Concanen went to London in the 1720s, taking up journalism on behalf of the Whigs. Among those whom he attacked was Pope, who promptly included him in *The Dunciad* of 1729 in highly unflattering terms: "True to the bottom see Concanen creep,/A cold, long-winded native of the deep." [44] Swift denigrated him in "On Poetry: A Rhapsody" four years later. It seems unlikely that this Irish-born poet who did not attend Trinity College and did not become a Church of Ireland clergyman (and who may have had Catholics of Gaelic origin in his background) deserved all this vituperation. His literary credentials were quite impressive. His first successes as a writer came at an astonishingly early age; his play *Wexford Wells* was staged at Dublin's Smock Alley Theatre in 1720, when Concanen was just nineteen. Two years later he was well enough regarded in literary circles to be asked to write the prologue and epilogue for Thomas Betterton's *The Amorous Widow,* also put on at Smock Alley. Concanen had by then already published the long, mock-heroic poem that established his reputation, "A Match at Foot-ball" (1721), and in 1722, when he was twenty-one, his *Poems upon Several Occasions* appeared. In 1724, he published *Miscellaneous Poems,* generally regarded as the first anthology of Irish poetry in English, which included several poems by Swift and Parnell, among others. However, this career that started so early ended early as well; Concanen seems to have given up poetry once he became established as a London journalist, and he spent his mature years in public service (he was appointed attorney general to Jamaica in 1732) and in amassing a sizable private fortune.

The poetry, then, is the work of a young man. The best of it is closer to the traditions of popular song than it is to that of the English neo-classicism that inspired those Anglo-Irish poets who were products of Trinity College. Although Concanen's poetry in this vein bears few if any marks of the tradition of Gaelic airs that shaped Thomas Moore's poetry nearly a century later, Concanen did at times use the forms of popular song to deliver political messages. In "A Ballad," for example, a song from *Wexford Wells,* the popular drinking song becomes a vehicle for sharply anti-English views:

> Let others raise
> Their Voice to praise
> The *Rhenish* or the *Sherry,*
> The sparkling *White,*
> *Champaign* so bright,
> The *Claret* or *Canary.*
> 'Tis true, they'll thaw the freezing Blood,
> And hinder our being sober;
> But what for that was e'er so good
> As lovely brown *OCTOBER?*

> What Knaves are they
> Who cross the Sea.
> To bring such Stuff among us?
> How blind are we,
> Who will not see
> How grievously they wrong us?

> They spoil the Products of the Land,
> And of her Coin disrobe her;
> But yet their Dregs can never stand
> Against our brave *OCTOBER.*[45]

This poem was sung on a Dublin stage the same year that Swift's pamphlet "A Proposal for the Universal Use of *Irish* Manufacture" was published, and it echoes Swift's argument for supporting Irish-made products and boycotting foreign ones. Concanen's poem is certainly less blatant in its revolutionary sentiments than is Swift's pamphlet—the shift from "lovely brown OCTO-BER" to "our brave OCTOBER" is perhaps the most politically daring part of the poem—but it is nonetheless effective, and deserves a place in the rich tradition of Irish songs with political subtexts.

"A Match at Foot-ball," Concanen's best-known poem, illustrates all too well a problem faced by many eighteenth-century Irish poets writing in English: the difficulty of writing about Irish material in forms essentially alien to it. "A Match at Foot-ball" is a mock-heroic epic, modelled on Pope's "The Rape of the Lock" (written a decade earlier), and part of its business is to parody satirically many of the poetic conventions then in vogue. But Concanen's poetic vehicle is not English social life but a football match between two Irish teams, and whatever Concanen's own position might have been—and it does seem less thoroughly Anglo-Irish than that of someone like Smedley or Parnell, writing from inside the Anglo-Irish Protestant establishment—the disjunction between the poem's form (part of the world of English poetics and manners) and its subject-matter (part of the world of native Irish life) encourages an attitude of condescension, as can be seen in this portrait of one of the players:

> The next to these in Place was sturdy *Hugh,*
> His Sinews tougher than the twanging Yew,
> For hence on *Wicklow's* steepy Mountains bred,
> With strengthening Pig-nuts and Potato's fed.[46]

This tendency seems endemic to Anglo-Irish poetry in Concanen's day, and can be found even in poems apparently intended to celebrate native Irish culture. Like many of the poets writing in Ireland at this time, Matthew Pilkington (c. 1701–1774) was educated at Trinity College and ordained into the Church of Ireland. He was also a classical scholar and a musician. His "The Progress of Music in *Ireland*" (1725) is a kind of cultural history in verse, and represents an attempt to recognize the significance and validity of Ireland's Gaelic past. For example, the poem contains a tribute to Turlough Carolan, the Irish harper who inspired a number of Irish poets writing in English in the eighteenth century:

> The Vagrant *Bard* his circling Visits pays,
> And charms the Villages with venal Lays.
> The solemn *Harp,* beneath his Shoulder plac'd,
> With both his Arms is earnestly embrac'd,
> Sweetly irregular, now swift, now slow,
> With soft Variety his Numbers flow,
> The shrill, the deep, the gentle, and the strong,

With pleasing Dissonance adorn his Song;
While thro' the Chords his Hands unweary'd range,
The Music changing as his Fingers change.[47]

There certainly seems to be no conscious condescension in these lines, or, for that matter, in most of this lengthy poem, but the heroic couplet, a trademark of neo-Augustan English verse, keeps the poem at a considerable distance from its subject matter. In this passage, for example, the regulated rhythm of the heroic couplet is inappropriate to a description of the "Sweetly irregular" rhythms of Carolan. It is a significant measure of the hold that English poetry had on eighteenth-century Irish poets that it is not until a century after the time of Swift and his contemporaries that Irish poets writing in English began to incorporate into their verse some of the sweetly irregular music of poetry written in Irish.

Issues of Gender

In his last active years, during the 1730s, Swift was surrounded by a circle of admirers, including three Anglo-Irish women intent on making their marks as poets in a male-dominated literary world: Mary Barber, Constantia Grierson, and Laetitia Pilkington. Whatever his motives—and The Earl of Orrery, for one, found the situation a little odd: "You would have smiled," he wrote to a friend, "to have found his house a constant seraglio of very virtuous women, who attended him from morning till night, with an obedience, an awe and an assiduity,"[48]—Swift used his considerable influence to help all three get their work published. The particular difficulties that these women faced as aspiring poets were unwittingly identified by Swift in a letter that he wrote to that same Earl of Orrery in 1733, recommending the poetry of Mary Barber. "She seemeth to have a true political Genius," Swift wrote, "better cultivated than could well be expected, either from her Sex, or the Scene she hath acted in, as the Wife of a Citizen."[49] For these women, the attitudes revealed in these remarks compounded significantly the cultural and political ambiguities surrounding Anglo-Irish writers in the eighteenth century in general. And the work of all three of these writers is distinctively marked by this situation: not only is their writing more gender-conscious than is that of their male counterparts, but also their satire is frequently directed at oppressive male attitudes and a society seen to be governed by them. All three women poets led lives that were, for their time, unconventional. Barber lived apart from her husband for years while she was trying to make her way as a writer, Grierson came from a relatively poor family who expected her to become a midwife, and Pilkington was charged by her poet-husband Matthew with adultery and eventually divorced, amid considerable scandal. (Swift banished both husband and wife from his circle, reportedly remarking: "He proved the falsest rogue and she the most profligate whore in either kingdom." [50]) It is hardly surprising that these writers tended to see themselves as alienated, or that their work tends to be preoccupied with defining and defending their positions as women who write, a concern that characterizes Irish women writers from the eighteenth to the twentieth century.

It is ironic that Mary Barber (1690–1757), [51] who depicted herself in her poetry as a prisoner of the domestic role that her society expected her to play, should have begun her poetic career by writing poems aimed at helping her children remember the moral precepts that she was teaching them. The wife of a Dublin woolen draper described by one of Barber's friends as a man who "drinks his claret, smokes his pipe and cares not a pin for any of his family who, if they had not met with better friends than himself, might have starved," [52] she emerged into the public literary eye as a result of her attempt to help an officer's widow get satisfaction in her stalled petition for support from the government. Barber wrote a petition in the form of a poem addressed to Lady Carteret, wife of the Lord Lieutenant of Ireland at the time (1724), and the poem, "The Widow Gordon's Petition," made such an impression that it led to an introduction to Swift. Ten years later, after much struggle, she published *Poems on Several Occasions,* which ran to a second edition in 1735 and a third in 1736. For most of the rest of her life, plagued by illness and her apparently indifferent husband, Barber struggled to establish her independence as a writer, even when that required the scandalous act of keeping house separately from her husband.

"The Widow Gordon's Petition" constructs a relatively sophisticated rhetorical appeal on behalf of the widow, first making the emotional claim of one mother speaking to another and then arguing that a woman of Lady Carteret's reputation for generosity could do no less than help. With at times remarkable success, the poem employs an appropriately melodramatic voice to present the widow as lonely and helpless, a woman adrift without the support of a man in a male-controlled society. This image becomes an emblem of Barber's own position as a woman poet:

> No friendly Voice my lonely Mansion cheers;
> All fly th'Inflection of my Widow's Tears:
> Even those, whose Pity eas'd my Wants with Bread,
> Are now, O sad Reverse! my greatest Dread.
> My mournful Story will no more prevail,
> And ev'ry Hour I dread a dismal Jail:
> I start at each imaginary Sound,
> And *Horrors have encompass'd me around.* [53]

This ability to manipulate dramatic voice is characteristic of the best of Barber's work. No doubt it owes more than a little to the influence of Swift, but this kind of poetic ventriloquism also derives from and embodies the cultural inse-curities that define Barber's position as an Anglo-Irish woman in the eighteenth century. At times, this dramatic mode works through irony to expose the forces responsible for that position. In a poem entitled "Conclusion of a Letter to the Rev. Mr. C———," Barber uses a male fictional voice to satirize male attitudes toward women:

> I pity poor *Barber,* his Wife's so romantick:
> A Letter in Rhyme!—Why, the Woman is frantick!
> This Reading the Poets has quite turn'd her Head!
> On my Life, she should have a dark Room, and Straw-Bed.[54]

Later, ironic mask firmly in place, the narrator outlines what he considers to be the qualities of an ideal wife:

> If ever I marry, I'll choose me a Spouse,
> That shall *serve* and *obey,* as she's bound by her Vows;
> That shall, When I'm dressing, attend like a Valet;
> Then go to the Kitchen, and study my Palate.
> She has Wisdom enough, that keeps out of the Dirt,
> And can make a good *Pudding,* and cut out a *Shirt.*
> What Good's in a Dame, that will pore on a Book?
> No!—Give me the Wife, that shall save me a Cook.[55]

In "To a Lady who invited the Author into the Country" (1728), Barber converts the conventional, polite form of a verse letter into a vehicle for her frustration:

> O! would kind Heav'n reverse my Fate,
> Give me to quit a Life I hate,
> To flow'ry fields I soon would fly:
> Let others stay—to *cheat* and *lie.*
> There, in some blissful Solitude,
> Where eating Care should ne'er intrude,
> The Muse should do the Country Right,
> And paint the glorious Scenes *you* slight.[56]

This poem reverses the eighteenth-century convention associating the city with cultural fertility and the country with barrenness, a convention more English than Irish; the city is seen as the place of the woman's imprisonment, the place where she is made to conform to society's expectations of what a woman should be, while the countryside is perceived as a place where she could fulfill herself as an artist precisely because there she could be liberated from those expectations.

As is particularly evident in some of the nationalist poetry written by women in the nineteenth century, the image of Ireland as a woman (Cathleen Ní Houlihan, the Shan Van Vocht) victimized by male England often occludes issues of gender in the interest of a political ideology committed to eliminating or absorbing difference. Barber's writing, however, tends to resist the tendency to make gender issues subservient to nationalist ones. As a middle-class Anglo-Irish woman trying to establish herself as a poet in a male-dominated society, Barber draws correspondences between her position and Ireland's difficulties in establishing its independence and prosperity, but she does so in ways that insist on the validity of both gender and nationalist issues. In "To the Right Hon. Lady Dowager Torrington," Barber yearns for a poetic release from her position both as a woman and as a woman living in Ireland:

> A Life of unsuccessful Care
> Too often sinks us to Despair.
> From such a Life as this, I chuse
> To snatch some Moments for the Muse;
> To slight Mortality, and soar
> To Worlds where Anguish is no more;
> Forget IERNE'S wretched State,
> Tho' doomed to share her cruel Fate;
> Destin'd to pass my joyless Days,
> Where Poverty, relentless, preys;
> And form'd, unhappily, to grieve
> For Miseries I can't relieve.[57]

The sophistication of Barber's writing can, to some extent, be measured by comparing it with that of her contemporary and friend, Constantia Grierson (c. 1706–1733). Born into a relatively disadvantaged family in Co. Kilkenny, Grierson managed to pick up considerable learning from the minister of her parish, including knowledge of Greek and Roman literature. She married a man who was given a patent as a king's printer, but the relatively few poems that she wrote in her short life—she died when she was twenty-seven—were never collected in a single volume; several were included in Barber's *Poems on Several Occasions* and in an anthology entitled *Poems by Eminent Ladies* (1755). Barber praised Grierson's poems for doing "Honour to the Female Sex in general, as they are a strong Proof that Women may have so much Virtue," [58] but in truth Grierson's poetry, consisting chiefly of light satire on the comings

and goings of Dublin's smart society, does not seriously explore issues of
gender or of nationalism, as Barber's work does. Indeed, when Grierson turns
her attention to the matter of Ireland, she tends to fall into the condescension
that characterizes so much Anglo-Irish writing of the period. Even when she is
writing from a position sympathetic to the plight of Irish Catholics, as in this
attack on absentee landlords, she cannot keep out a note of class superiority:

> Let others still near *Albion's* Court reside,
> Who sacrifice their Country to their Pride;
> And squander vast Estates at Balls and Play,
> While public Debts increase, and Funds decay,
> While the starv'd Hind with Want distracted lives,
> Nor tastes that Plenty, which his Labour gives.[59]

The economic and social analysis here may be perfectly sound, but that
"starv'd Hind" betrays a whole range of attitudes and values based on class
prejudice.

The work of Laetitia Pilkington (1712–1750) is also marred in places by the
artificial quality observable in Grierson's writing; moreover, there is very little
of Pilkington's poetry that focuses directly on the political and social realities
of eighteenth-century Ireland. Nevertheless, at its best, her poetry brings to the
vexed question of the relationship between men and women in eighteenth-
century Ireland an emotional forcefulness and freedom from inhibition not to
be found in other poets of her day. Her life was no doubt a source for much of
this; many of her poems were published in her two-volume *Memoirs,* and so
placed specifically in the context of her life. The unconventional, rebellious
nature of that life—"To give me my due I was pretty pert," she says, with
uncharacteristic understatement[60]—is unusually well documented because of
the *Memoirs.* The precocious daughter of a Dutch doctor, Laetitia married
Matthew Pilkington, parson and aspiring poet, when she was eighteen. The
marriage was undermined in part, according to Laetitia, by Matthew's jealousy
of her work. Her husband also seems to have had suspicions about her appeal
to other men, and after allegedly finding her in bed with another man, sued
successfully for divorce in 1738. Separated from her husband, cut off from her
children, and turned away from Dublin society (including that of Swift, with
whom she was close during most of the 1730s), Pilkington was forced to be
independent. She suffered greatly, if the *Memoirs* are to be believed; at one
point she was imprisoned for failing to pay her debts. But she did manage to
continue working; and at her untimely death at the age of thirty-nine, she had
completed her *Memoirs* and two plays, as well as a substantial body of poetry.

Not surprisingly, the view of men that emerges in this poetry is not very
flattering. In a lengthy narrative poem entitled "The Statues or, the Trial of

Constancy," Pilkington reverses the conventional fairy-tale motif of the beautiful but inconstant young woman, telling instead a story of a queen who finds a
beautiful young man asleep on her shore and puts him to a test of constancy,
which he fails. Near the end of the poem, the queen delivers to the young man
this blanket denunciation of his sex:

> Thy changeful Sex in Perfidy delight,
> Despise Perfection, and fair Virtue flight;
> False, fickle, base, tyrannic, and unkind,
> Whose Hearts nor Vows can chain nor Honour bind:
> Mad to possess, by Passion blindly led;
> And then as mad to stain the nuptial Bed.[61]

More subtle and psychologically authentic is the voice in "Sorrow," written
during the time that Pilkington's husband was suing for divorce. The poem's
presumably autobiographical narrator describes with considerable force the
position of alienation and exile in which she finds herself:

> Encompassed round with Ruin, Want, and Shame,
> Undone in Fortune, blasted in my Fame;
> Lost to the soft endearing Ties of Life,
> And tender Names of Daughter, Mother, Wife.[62]

The poem's conclusion brings together the two principle themes of Pilkington's
poetry, the infidelity of men and a melancholy longing for release from the
afflictions of life:

> And thou once my Soul's fondest dearest Part,
> Who schem'd my Ruin with such cruel Art,
> From human Laws no longer seek to find,
> A pow'r to loose that Knot which God has join'd,
> The Props of Life are rudely pull'd away,
> And the frail Building falling to Decay;
> My Death shall give thee thy desir'd Release,
> And lay me down in everlasting Peace.[63]

At such moments, Pilkington's work anticipates some facets of romanticism;
and more than half a century after "Sorrow" was published, Wordsworth
included it in a collection of poems that he put together for the reading pleasure
of a woman of his acquaintance.

    That yearning for the "everlasting peace" of death represents a streak of
melancholy that runs through a number of Pilkington's poems, as it does

through the work of that other member of Swift's circle given to melancholy, Thomas Parnell. In Pilkington's hands, however, this theme is developed specifically in terms of Pilkington's own disastrous experiences as an eighteenth-century Anglo-Irish woman who refused to conform to social conventions regarding gender. In a lyric entitled "Expostulation," Pilkington boldly questions the justice of a God who created woman only to afflict her with suffering:

> Thro' ev'ry Scene of Life distress'd,
> As Daughter, Mother, Wife;
> When wilt thou close my Eyes in Rest,
> And take my weary Life.[64]

There is a tension here between resignation and energy, between the desire to end the difficulties and frustrations of her life and a rebellious spirit, manifest in the quality of the verse itself, that keeps the writer alive and writing.

That spirit of rebellion informs the work of Dorothea Du Bois (1728–1774), an Anglo-Irish woman writing in the second half of the century. Du Bois's work is thoroughly monarchist; she wrote an ode on the death of George II and another on the marriage of George III, and when the Earl of Northumberland visited Ireland in 1763, she wrote a poem expressing the hope that his presence would put to rest the various subversive challenges to the authority of the English in Ireland that always threatened Du Bois's class:

> And mays't thou, *Percy,* all our Fears remove
> Lull busy Faction into soft Repose,
> Or rather crush this horrid, worst of Foes.[65]

But on matters of gender, Du Bois took her cue from Irish women poets working earlier in the century, writing with an irony worthy at times of Swift. Her most accomplished piece of work in this vein, on the vexed question of male attitudes toward women, is "The Amazonian Gift":

> Is Courage in a Woman's Breast,
> Less pleasing than in Man?
> And is a smiling Maid allow'd
> No weapon but a Fan?
>
> 'Tis true, her Tongue, I've heard 'em say,
> Is Woman's chief Defence;
> And if you'll b'lieve me, gentle Youths,
> I have no Aid from thence.

And, some will say, that sparkling Eyes,
　　More dang'rous are, than Swords;
But I ne'er point my Eyes to kill,
　　Nor put I trust in Words.

Then, since the Arms that Women use,
　　Successless are in me;
I'll take the Pistol, Sword or Gun,
　　And thus equip'd, live free.

The Pattern of the *Spartan* Dame,
　　I'll copy as I can;
To Man, degen'rate Man, I'll give
　　That simple Thing, a *Fan*.[66]

The lightness of the tone here betrays the very real suffering that Du Bois and her mother seem to have endured at the hands of Du Bois's father, Richard Annesley, Lord Altham. When Du Bois was twelve, her father turned out the entire family, claiming that his marriage was invalid. Years later, when he was on his deathbed, Du Bois visited him, in Co. Wexford, in an effort to get him to change his mind; she was rudely repulsed by the woman then claiming to be his wife, and in the following year, her mother died without ever having satisfied her claim. This grim story of the victimization of women is told in a long narrative poem, "A True Tale," that Du Bois included in *Poems on Several Occasions* (1764). The note of playful irony that marks many of her lyrics gives way here to one of pain and outrage, as in this passage describing the character representing Du Bois's mother just after she has been abandoned by her husband:

The faithful Wife, the tender Mother view,
Now exil'd from her Lord, and Children too;
To his Inconstancy a Victim made,
Forsaken, comfortless, to Want betrayed.[67]

It will be a long time in Irish writing—after the rise of nationalist poetry in the nineteenth century, with its tendency to absorb issues of gender into political ideology, and after the emergence of the literary revival at the turn of the twentieth century—before women poets in Ireland are able to write about relationships between men and women with such directness and such force.

CHAPTER TWO

DIVERGENT DIRECTIONS:
BEYOND AND WITHIN THE PALE

Swift was such a Brobdignagian figure on the landscape of eighteenth-century Irish writing primarily because he managed to embody in his work so many of the competing and conflicting dimensions of the Irish experience. Apart from women such as Mary Barber and Laetitia Pilkington, Swift's contemporaries and most of the poets of the next generation were unable to break important new ground in describing that experience. Two poets in the generation after Swift, however, significantly developed divergent aspects of eighteenth-century Irish culture that were embedded in Swift's work but were not given much detail or emphasis there. Moreover, the work of Laurence Whyte and William Dunkin, both schoolteachers by profession and both admirers of Swift, drew into sharp relief a set of political and cultural differences that was to shape Irish life, and Irish poetry in English, well into the nineteenth century. Whyte's poetry represents an important first step, albeit a somewhat stumbling one, toward recognizing the life of rural Ireland, including the Irish language and Gaelic culture, as fit subject matter for Irish poets writing in English. Dunkin's poetry, formally more accomplished than Whyte's, represents an attempt to maintain the cultural and political superiority of the Anglo-Irish governing class and of the English poetic tradition.

When Whyte (c. 1700–c. 1753) published his *Poems on Various Subjects, Serious and Diverting* in 1740, the list of subscribers included numerous people from Whyte's native Ballymore, in Co. Westmeath.[1] It was an unusual list in that it cut across so many divisions; there were Catholics and Protestants, members of old Gaelic families, descendants of Anglo-Normans, and Cromwellian planters. It was also indicative of Whyte's life and art. Born in the vicinity of Ballymore, Whyte seems to have been the son or possibly grandson of a man named Henry White, whose family had been transplanted to Connacht under the Cromwellian settlement. There was also in the family a Captain Thomas White, who raised a company of horse in King James II's army during the Williamite wars, and some of Whyte's work is unabashedly Jacobite. On the other hand, if, as Whyte suggests in his poem "The Parting Cup," his father's family was "of *Milesian* Race," his mother's side of the family was of Norman descent, or, as Whyte says, "of the strongbonian Race." [2] Whyte seems to have changed the spelling of his name to make it fit more closely with English practice, and there is some reason to believe that at some point in his life he may have converted from the Catholicism of his upbringing to the Church of Ireland.[3] There are other interesting paradoxes about Whyte. Although he wrote quite plainly out of the English tradition, favoring the galloping tetrameter of Samuel Butler in particular, he also had some knowledge of the Irish language and some acquaintance with its literature. And although he spent most of his adult life as a schoolteacher in Dublin, he frequently wrote about life in his native Westmeath.

Whyte's *Poems on Various Subjects* contains several quatrains in Irish accompanied by translations that are presumably Whyte's. His sympathies with the Irish tradition are most evident in his poem "A Dissertation on *Italian* and *Irish* Musick," which, like Matthew Pilkington's "The Progress of Music in *Ireland*," is essentially a defense of Ireland's native culture. Whyte's poem attacks the Irish for allowing foreign music to dominate their lives, a cultural version of Swift's argument about foreign versus Irish goods in "A Proposal for the Universal Use of *Irish* Manufacture"; but it argues that the Irish tradition is strong enough to survive. Whyte casts in specifically cultural terms the conventional notion of Ireland's invaders becoming part of the race that they sought to conquer:

> Sweet *Bocchi* thought it worth his while,
> In doing honour to our *Isle,*
> To build on *Carallan's* Foundation,
> Which he perform'd to Admiration.[4]

The reference to the Irish harper Turlough Carolan, who died in 1738, is taken up again at the end of the poem in a lament for the passing of one of the principal figures of the Irish musical tradition:

> The greatest *Genius* in his way,
> An *Orpheus,* who cou'd sing and play,
> So great a Bard where can we find,
> Like him illiterate, and blind.[5]

The tone in this poem is uneven and the tetrameter measure often inappropriate to the subject matter, but Whyte's spirited defense of the Irish tradition beyond the pale, and his assumptions about the validity and value of that tradition, anticipate the work of nineteenth-century poet-translators such as James Clarence Mangan and Samuel Ferguson, and, later, the Irish literary revival.

Much of Whyte's writing about Irish rural life is marred by sentimentality. This is especially true of the poem for which he was probably best known, "The Parting Cup," a lengthy account of a tenant-farmer family that was apparently based on his own family in Ballymore. In the preface to this poem, Whyte says that it "sets forth the great Hospitality and good Entertainment formerly met with in Irish families,"[6] and the poem goes overboard in portraying the goodness of its protagonists and the harmony of their social and cultural environment. The tenant-farming couple represents a dramatization of the kind of political and sectarian reconciliation that Whyte saw as Ireland's only hope, but the poem's unqualified idealization of this family and its community—the other side of the sneering condescension visible in poems about the native Irish by writers like Jonathan Smedley and Matthew Concanen—tends to undermine its authenticity and power of conviction. There is, however, another side to Whyte's writing about the rural Irish, and here "The Parting Cup" looks ahead to the concreteness and authority of that other eighteenth-century poem about rural Ireland, Goldsmith's "The Deserted Village," and to the social realism of William Allingham's narrative account of nineteenth-century rural Ireland, *Laurence Bloomfield in Ireland*. This more realistic side of Whyte emerges when he turns to the devastating effects on tenant farmers of the changeover from tillage to pasturage that started in the early decades of the eighteenth century:

> Their *Flocks* do range on ev'ry *Plain*,
> That once produc'd all kinds of *Grain*.
> Depopulating ev'ry *Village*,
> Where we had *Husbandry* and *Tillage*,
> Fat *Bacon, Poultry* and good *Bread*,
> By which the *Poor* were daily fed.[7]

Whyte clearly understands the economics of the situation and, having witnessed the horrors of the famine of 1727–1730, is able to write without a trace of sentimentality about what was happening to the Irish rural way of life:

> But now the Case is quite reversed,
> The *Tenants* ev'ry Day distress'd,
> Instead of living well and thriving,
> There's nothing now, but *leading, driving,—*
> The *Lands* are all *monopoliz'd*,
> The *Tenants* rack'd and sacrific'd,

> Whole *Colonies* to shun the Fate,
> Of being oppres'd at such a Rate
> By *Tyrants* who still raised the Rent,
> Sailed to the *Western Continent*.[8]

If, as Whyte once said of himself, he was a man "Whose Head cou'd never Politicks distil,"[9] his writing about rural Ireland carried political implications that would not be fully realized until the famine of the late 1840s, nearly a century after his death.

Whyte was one of a handful of Irish poets writing in English in the first half of the eighteenth century who did not attend Trinity College. William Dunkin (c. 1709–1765) seems never to have left it.[10] By far the most learned and scholarly of the poets of his day, Dunkin entered Trinity College in 1725 and took his doctorate of divinity in 1744. Although he was ordained, he does not seem to have spent much time as a minister; instead, he taught school in Dublin until 1746, when he was appointed headmaster of a school in Enniskillen, where he remained until he died. There is a donnish quality to much of Dunkin's writing (many of his poems were published in side-by-side Latin and English versions), and in the end, Dunkin's scholarly nature, combined with a relatively narrow view of Ireland—essentially that from within the Anglo-Irish Protestant bastion of Trinity College—inhibited his ability to write with authority about the complex political and cultural realities of eighteenth-century Ireland. Nevertheless, Swift recognized Dunkin as a gifted scholar and poet, "a Gentleman of much Wit and the best English as well as Latin Poet in this Kingdom."[11] Dunkin often returned the compliment; he wrote a number of poems praising Swift, including "An Epistle to R[o]b[er]t N[u]g[en]t," a moving portrait of Swift in old age. Dunkin certainly stands much closer to Swift than he does to Whyte. His political convictions were significantly shaped, as were Swift's, by a fierce loyalty to the Church of Ireland and a corresponding distrust of both Catholicism and the dissenting tradition. Like Swift, Dunkin preferred the ancients to the moderns in literature, and had a penchant for sharp-edged satire.

Dunkin's poetry—and here he generally parts company with Swift—is very often driven by the principle of exclusion. For Dunkin, Anglo-Irish Protestantism represented order and stability, and Irish Catholicism chaos and lawlessness, an assumption upon which much of England's colonization of Ireland, especially after 1690, rested; and in Dunkin's poetry, Irish Catholics are almost always stereotyped as primitives. In "The Poetical Mirror," a lengthy blank-verse poem written in Latin and English, Dunkin presents William III as a god-like figure redeeming the provinces, including Ireland, from barbarism, and the poem's portrait of the conquest of Ireland is notably anti-Catholic:

> There lawless fury, sanctify'd misrule,
> That raged with havock through Hibernian towns,
> And her twin-sister superstition sad,
> And arm'd with snakes imbosom'd, murm'ring fled
> Appall'd, and routed to the Stygian shades.[12]

Dunkin is not at his most inventive in this kind of didactic poem. A better representative of his poetic accomplishment is "The Art of Gate-Passing: or, The Murphaeid," a long mock-epic poem set at Trinity College. The reductive subject-matter of "The Murphaeid" (the title echoes Pope's "The Dunciad") is the conflict between students and the gate porter, a man named Murphy famous for his strictness in preventing students from leaving the college grounds unlawfully. It is, in some ways, very much an undergraduate poem (and Dunkin wrote it while at Trinity), but it is also, especially in comparison with Matthew Concanen's far cruder mock-epic, "A Match at Foot-ball," a relatively sophisticated and accomplished piece of writing. In this passage, for example, describing some students who manage to get past the ever-watchful Murphy to enjoy the pleasures of Dublin and the surrounding countryside, Dunkin expertly invokes the tropes and language of the pastoral tradition while maintaining, through sexual imagery, the poem's ironic tension between convention and reality:

> Whether each winding street they traverse o'er,
> Eblana, rifling thy promiscuous store,
> Or, more transported with a rural scene,
> They court calm pleasures on the flow'ry plain,
> Supinely stretch'd along the tender grass,
> Or, if they trust to painted gallies gay,
> And painted nymphs with painted loose array,
> And, gliding down the Liffey's glassy tide,
> With bending oars the curling waves divide;
> And soft, to fan the lover's youthful fire,
> The sails, light gales, and lighter nymphs conspire.[13]

Dunkin is equally capable of a far more vulgar, heavy-handed irony, especially when the subject is the native Irish. The plot of "The Murphaeid"—how to get past Murphy—depends on seeing Murphy as a stage Irishman, and the way to defeat Murphy's vigilance is to find some native Irish people and get them to distract him with a discussion, in Irish, about his genealogy:

> If haply therefore you should spy a pair
> Of friends, distinguish'd by their awkward air,

Their Teaguish tone and clannly garb, engage
These, thy best actors for the doubtful stage.
In Attic Irish let them greeting pray
To know with favour but the time of day:
By compliments like these, when grown more free,
Let them cull out his birth and pedigree,
Assume his name, recount their fathers o'er
And sons, descended from O MURPHY-MORE,
O MURPHY-MORE, who held the regal reins
Of Munster fair, and rul'd the vassal swains,
Who daily slaughtered, for his guests to dine,
Thrice ten fat wethers, and as many swine,
His whisky burn'd with purifying flame,
And pour'd, like water from the running stream.[14]

Dunkin was not above exploiting the worst stage-Irish dialogue for purposes of caricaturing the native Irish. In "The Parson's Revels," a lengthy burlesque that includes a violent quarrel between a Catholic and a dissenter, Dunkin has a character named Father Fagan speak in an unspeakable brogue:

"Gaad blish king Gaarge and hish Lutterians,
But cursh upon dhe Proshpiterians,
The knaaves are oogly Nolliverians,
             and apish—" [15]

This is precisely the kind of writing that a poet like Whyte sought to avoid in his own work and to counter in that of others. As it turned out, however, the gap between the two different views of eighteenth-century Ireland represented by Whyte's sympathetic accounts of rural Irish life and Dunkin's unsympathetic burlesques and parodies is one that proved extremely difficult, if not impossible, to bridge.

Dunkin's burlesqued portrayal of the native Irish as savages hardly stands alone; it is, in fact, part of a tradition of writing in Ireland that goes back at least as far as Edmund Spenser's *A View of the Present State of Ireland* at the end of the sixteenth century. In most cases, and certainly in Dunkin's, this project was politically motivated; to present the Irish in this way was both to insist on the superiority of English (and Anglo-Irish) Protestant culture, and so to reinforce culturally the political authority established by conquest, and to justify morally the English presence in Ireland (and the Anglo-Irish governing of Ireland) by defining it as a colonial mission intended to civilize the uncivilized. This position can be seen with particular clarity in the work of several important anonymous poems written during the age of Swift that are of interest chiefly for what they reveal about the culture that produced them. The earliest, *The Irish Hudibras, Or, Fingallian Prince,* is a late-seventeenth-century poem that satirizes the Irish peasant by means of an elaborate reductive parody of Virgil's *Aeneid.* As its title indicates, the poem's satire also relies on the tone and metrics of Samuel Butler, and therefore much of the poem's irony is generated by a calculated distance between English literary culture, including its neo-classical interests, and the presumed cultural barrenness of the world that it is describing. The third version of the poem, published in 1689, begins and ends with stereotypes, and its irony is anything but subtle. Here, for example, is a description of the mourners at the wake of a local piper who, like his prototype Misenus in *The Aeneid,* has drowned:

> Some for their pastime count their Beads,
> Some scratch their Breech, some louse their Heads;
> Some sit and chat, some laugh, some weep;
> Some sing *Cronans,* and some do sleep;
> Some pray, and with their prayers mix curses;
> Some Vermin pick, and some pick Purses;
> Some court, some scold, some blow, some puff,
> Some take Tobacco, some take Snuff.[16]

Published the year before the Battle of the Boyne, the poem also forecasts the conquest of Ireland by English forces ("The *Liffy* shall be chang'd to Blood,/ Besmear'd with Gore, instead of Mud . . . Thy flying Hosts *Dutch*-Troops shall rack 'em,'/With Thousand *English* Braves to back 'em" [17]), and contains its fair share of satirical representations of Catholic figures. The poem also critiques Irish nationalists, who are discovered by the poem's Aeneas-like voyager when he arrives in purgatory. The author takes particular pains to identify the rebellious Irish as victims of French manipulation:

> Here all that fought in Vindication
> Of *Shamrog-shire,* made Habitation.
> The Champion of the *Irish* Cause,
> A numberous train of *Mac's* and *O's,*
> Whom the *Monsieur,* by treacherous Art,
> Hath cram'd into this Malapert.[18]

'Hesperi-neso-Graphia: or, a Description of the Western Isles' (c. 1716) constructs its politically potent portrait of the native Irish out of an entire array of stereotypes. The poem's protagonist, an Irish peasant named Gillo (a play on the Irish word for servant or attendant, "giolla"), is introduced in a canto-long recitation of his ancestry, in the course of which a series of conventional notions

about the Irish are brought to the surface. Among Gillo's ancestors is a man famous for killing a political enemy in an ambush ("to his great and endless glory"), a man widely known for his primitive strength ("With's head instead of hammer cou'd,/Knock nail into a piece of wood,/And with his teeth, without least pain,/Could pull the nail from thence again"), and a man falsely admired for his learning ("And, without doubt had so much sense,/To form a verb through mood and tense;/Nay, some do say that he was able/To moralize on *Aesop*'s fable!").[19] The poem also goes to considerable lengths to connect Gillo's presumed ignorance of reason and civilization with his Catholicism:

> . . . You may guess
> What faith this *Gillo* did profess;
> A faith St. *Paul* did never teach,
> Altho' to *Romans* he did preach;
> A faith that makes you to deny,
> The testimony of your eye;
> A faith obliges you to pray,
> Altho' you know not what you say.[20]

The argument for the theological superiority of Protestantism is complemented by an attack on the Gaelic literary tradition. Referring to the reported practice of the ancient Irish *filí* of composing while lying down in the dark, the author of *Hesperi* burlesques this into another example of the primitive irrationality of the Irish, while at the same time associating it, through a parody of religious asceticism, with Irish Catholicism.

> When e'er he verses wou'd compose,
> Above all postures this he chose;
> On's back he did extended lye,
> Gazing upon the vaulted skie:
> On's belly by a ponderous stone,
> Which made him pant, and puff, and groan,
> And often made him cry, O hone.[21]

This kind of stereotyping itself stereotypes eighteenth-century Anglo-Irish attitudes, which were in fact, as evidenced in the work of Swift, by no means monolithic. Another anonymous poem of this period, and one almost certainly written by an Anglo-Irish Protestant, expresses a much more sympathetic view of rural Ireland than that found in *The Irish Hudibras* or *Hesperi-neso-Graphia*. This poem, entitled "The County of Kerry," first published in 1726 and later included in a pamphlet-sized group of poems called *The Petition of Murrough O Connor to the Provost and Senior Fellows of Trinity College, near Dublin,* contains the apparently inevitable and always derogatory brawl scene—much of *Hesperi-neso-Graphia* is given over to a fight in Gillo's house—and there are passages that clearly mock the native Irish. Yet it also includes some descriptions of the Kerry landscape that come closer to Wordsworth's admiration of the inspirational qualities of the Lake District than to the conventional Anglo-Irish view of rural Ireland as a setting inimical to the muse and civilization in general:

> Sure there are poets who did never dream,
> On Brandon hill, nor taste the gentle stream,
> Which from the glitt'ring summit daily flows:
> And the bright pebbles in its fair bosom shews:
> From thy clear height I take my lofty flight,
> Which opens all the country to my sight.[22]

A more politically aggressive view of the land is offered in other sections of *The Petition of Murrough O Connor,* which concern O Connor's efforts to prevent his land from being taken from him. One of these consists of a conversation, modeled on the Virgilian eclogues but without the ironic deflation of the *Aeneid* parallel in *The Irish Hudibras,* between O Connor and his friend Owen Sullivan; at one point, Sullivan, whose land in Kerry has been given to an army officer, complains:

> But shall this foreign captain force from me,
> My house, my land, my wayers, my fishery?
> Was it for him I those improvements made?
> Must his long sword turn out my lab'ring spade?[23]

This question may be considerably less aggressive than the poetry of political protest that dominated the nineteenth century and considerably less accomplished than Goldsmith's poetry of lament in the second half of the eighteenth century. But it clearly anticipates the concerns of both, sounding a lament that was to echo through Irish writing for nearly two succeeding centuries.

CHAPTER THREE

GOLDSMITH AND THE
BEGINNINGS OF ROMANTICISM

In January of 1759, Oliver Goldsmith, aged twenty-nine, living in London while trying to make a literary name for himself, wrote to his brother Henry back in his native Co. Westmeath. He complained about feeling detached from English and Irish society, and of a strong streak of melancholy. And then he added: "Whence this romantic turn that all our family are possessed with, whence this love for every place and every country but that in which we reside?" [1] It is a familiar note to the reader of Irish literature: the voice of alienation, of homelessness, of the Irishman unable or unwilling to live in his native land but still powerfully drawn to it. Apart from its somewhat melodramatic tone, that sentence could as well have been written 150 years later by Joyce to his brother back in Ireland as by Goldsmith to his.

The idea of cultural displacement takes a variety of forms in the work of several writers in Swift's half of the eighteenth century (the displaced woman, for example, in Mary Barber's poems and the displaced countryman in some of Lawrence Whyte's). But it is with Goldsmith (1728–1774) that the condition of exile first emerges as an overwhelming preoccupation in Irish poetry. Almost everything that Goldsmith wrote is inseparable from it: his bittersweet melancholy (sometimes considered a particularly Irish quality of his work), his cautious attitude toward nationalism, and the emotional force of his writing on the collapse of moral virtues and values. Goldsmith's experience of exile was first-hand and profound. He attended Trinity College, taking a B.A. degree in 1750, but failed to obtain ordination in the Church of Ireland. He considered emigration to America and a career in law before enrolling at the University of Edinburgh, in 1752, to study medicine. During a year (1755) spent traveling and studying on the continent, he began work on his long poem "The Traveller," not published until 1764. He then he turned up in London, where he assumed a wide variety of posts, including assistant to an apothecary, a practicing physician, a proof-reader, and an usher. Goldsmith did eventually establish himself as a literary figure to be reckoned with—he knew Samuel Johnson well, and was one of the founding members of The Club—but there is something unfocused, scattered, about his literary output: there are numerous journalistic pieces and essays, several biographies and histories, a considerable amount of poetry, one novel, and two plays. As Johnson said of him, he "left scarcely any kind of writing untouched." [2] As an Anglo-Irishman living in London, suspended between two cultures, neither of which he could call fully his own, Goldsmith experienced exile in ways that went beyond physical displacement. "I should actually be as unfit for the society of my friends at home," he complained to his brother in the 1759 letter, "as I detest that which I am obliged to partake of here." [3] To Goldsmith, the London literary world that he aspired to partake of seemed always a foreign and alienating place, and it in turn inevitably viewed him as an outsider because of his Irish background. At the same time, he seems to have had little respect for his own class; in a letter written in 1757, he said of the Anglo-Irish: "All their productions in learning amount to perhaps a translation, or a few tracts in divinity; and all their productions in wit, to just nothing at all." [4] His attitude toward the native Irish was somewhat more ambiguous; in an essay entitled "A Description of the Manners and Customs of the Native *Irish*" (1759), he wrote: "The original Irish are . . . frequently found fawning, insincere, and fond of pleasure, prodigality makes them poor, and poverty makes them vicious, such are their faults, but they have national virtues to recompence these defects. They are valiant, sensible, polite, and generally beautiful." [5] It is hardly surprising that readers of Goldsmith's best-known poem, "The Deserted Village," are still divided as to whether the fictional village of Auburn refers to an English village or to Lissoy in Co. Roscommon, where Goldsmith grew up. All that can be said for sure is that the uncertainty itself defines Goldsmith as an Anglo-Irish writer.

If the centrality of exile in his work is one reason for Goldsmith's importance to the history of Irish poetry in English, another of at least equal significance is the importance of the land in his work. Goldsmith is the first Irish poet writing in English to recognize fully the political, economic, social and moral significance of Irish rural life, a question of little or no interest to Swift, and a subject for condescension in the hands of most of his contemporaries.[6] Moreover, Goldsmith's view of the rural community as embodying admirable moral values under siege from the rising forces of commercialism and materialism anticipates not only later critiques of capitalism generally but also, in Ireland, the identification of the Irish peasant with nationalist ideals in patriotic writing and the glorification of Irish peasant culture generally. Goldsmith has been accused of romanticizing Irish rural life, of transforming it into an Edenic vision that

ignores the ugly realities of famine, eviction, and prejudice that in fact constituted life for most Irish peasants and farm laborers in the eighteenth century.[7]
But this is to misread Goldsmith's argument about the destruction of the countryside, and to underestimate the significance of that argument for the project
of defining Ireland's relationship to England. Whether the Auburn of "The
Deserted Village" refers to an English or an Irish village or, what is more
likely, to both, the poem lays the blame for the demise of the rural way of life
and of the moral values that it embodies squarely at the door of the competitive
principle in general, and specifically of the political and economic institutions
that competition thrives on and encourages. In the context of the relationship
between England and Ireland, this critique embodies and anticipates the dichotomy, put to specifically nationalist purposes in the nineteenth century, between
a traditional Ireland perceived as morally and spiritually sound although materially impoverished and a modern, capitalist England materially prosperous but
morally and spiritually bankrupt. This analysis is the principal concern of
both of Goldsmith's major poems, "The Traveller" (1764) and "The Deserted
Village" (1770). The poems differ in their rhetorical modes—"The Traveller"
is more didactic—and in the specific ways in which they deliver their common
theme, "The Traveller" principally through a consideration of the condition of
exile, and "The Deserted Village" through an analysis of the land question.
But taken together, and read in the sequence in which they were composed and
published, they constitute a developing critique of the principles of capitalism
that has much to say about the Irish situation.

The opening of "The Traveller" evokes the speaker's sense of exile, built
up through a succession of images of barrenness and loss:

> Remote, unfriended, melancholy, slow,
> Or by the lazy Scheld or wandering Po;
> Or onward, where the rude Carinthian boor
> Against the houseless stranger shuts the door;
> Or where Campania's plain forsaken lies,
> A weary waste expanding to the skies.
> Wher'er I roam, whatever realms to see,
> My heart untravell'd fondly turns to thee;
> Still to my brother turns, with ceaseless pain,
> And drags at each remove a lengthening chain.[8]

A detailed description of the home and hearth of Goldsmith's brother Henry in
Ireland follows. What is most striking about this is how much attention is
lavished on home and how little reason given for staying away from it—only
a vague, melancholy sense of being compelled to wander:

> But me, not destin'd such delights to share,
> My prime of life in wand'ring spent and care:
> Impell'd with steps unceasing, to pursue
> Some fleeting good, that mocks me with the view;
> That, like the circle bounding earth and skies,
> Allures from far, yet, as I follow, flies;
> My fortune leads to traverse realms alone
> And find no spot of all the world my own.[9]

The alienation experienced in this exile is not merely a point of view from which Goldsmith's world-weary traveler surveys the countries that he has visited and, in one way or another, found wanting. It is, in fact, essential to the emotional force of Goldsmith's critique of capitalist enterprise.

That critique is spelled out most clearly when the poem's speaker comes to consider Britain, the most powerful center of the competitive principle that Goldsmith's traveler has seen:

> That independence Britons prize too high,
> Keeps man from man, and breaks the social tie;
> The self dependent lordlings stand alone,
> All claims that bind and sweeten life unknown;
> Here by the bonds of nature feebly held,
> Minds combat minds, repelling and repell'd;
> Ferments arise, imprison'd factions roar,
> Represt ambition struggles round her shore.[10]

The dire consequences of organizing human society around this kind of "independence," in which "nature's ties" are replaced by "fictitious bonds, the bonds of wealth and law," are then forecast in a moment marked by the highest pitch of intensity that the poem achieves:

> Till Time may come, when stript of all her charms,
> The land of scholars, and the nurse of arms;
> Where noble stems transmit the patriot flame,
> Where kings have toil'd, and poets wrote for fame,
> One sink of level avarice shall lie,
> And scholars, soldiers, kings unhonor'd die.[11]

Goldsmith does not, however, leave it at that. Instead, he calls up a scene of forced emigration, or, as he puts it, "stern depopulation":

> Have we not seen, at pleasure's lordly call,
> The smiling long-frequented village fall?
> Beheld the duteous son, the sire decay'd,
> The modest matron, and the blushing maid,
> Forc'd from their homes, a melancholy train,
> To traverse climes beyond the western main?[12]

The political argument here, developed further in "The Deserted Village," is that the destruction of a social community, in part through forced emigration, is too high a price to pay for economic prosperity, especially of the few. The considerable emotional force that Goldsmith manages to generate in this critique depends significantly on a projection of the feelings of alienation and loss evoked in the individual traveler described at the beginning of the poem onto the larger canvas of the "stern depopulation" of an entire class that this passage describes. That image of emigration also inevitably associates Goldsmith's critique of capitalism with the economic and political exploitation of Ireland by England; after all, emigration—as Goldsmith knew from hard personal experience—was all too common a destructive influence on the communal life of Ireland, and one for which England often could be held responsible.

While the narrator of "The Traveller" seems a perennial, almost involuntary wanderer, the speaker of "The Deserted Village" is a wanderer fully ready to return home but with no home to return to. The two types represent, as John Montague has said, "two of the permanent themes of our island's literature, from Colmcille to James Joyce."[13] Moreover, the reason that "Sweet Auburn, loveliest village of the plain" has all but disappeared is the same that is given in "The Traveller" for the prophesied collapse of the moral and social order of western civilization: the economic tyranny of a rising commercialism fueled by capitalist competition. The practice of enclosure that was breaking up small farms in both England and Ireland during the eighteenth century was felt with particular force in the overwhelmingly agricultural economy of Ireland. In 1759, eleven years before "The Deserted Village" was published, restrictions on the import of Irish cattle into England were lifted, and pasturage was immediately and significantly extended; commons were enclosed, entire villages disappeared, and agrarian violence erupted. Goldsmith considered the rural way of life as providing the moral foundation of society, so any erosion of its practices and traditions constituted an extremely serious threat. "Those who constitute the basis of the great fabric of society should be particularly regarded," Goldsmith once said, "for in policy, as in architecture, ruin is most fatal when it begins from the bottom."[14] Goldsmith's account of the demise of Auburn can therefore be read as prophesying the potential destruction of civilization, making "The Deserted Village," as Montague has argued, "one of the first statements of a great modern theme: the erosion of traditional values and natural rhythms in a commercial society . . . a sort of rural *Wasteland*."[15]

The destruction of Auburn not only implies the collapse of the social order in general, but it also has specific implications for the relationship between a generally prosperous, increasingly urban England and a generally unprosperous, stubbornly rural Ireland. One way in which Goldsmith's poem draws out this politically charged distinction between the two countries, and suggests the victimization of one by the other, is through the use of imagery taken from the tradition of Irish nationalist thinking, specifically the identification of Ireland, and the Irish landscape itself, with the figure of a betrayed woman. In describing the rise of men of wealth and the corresponding replacement of economic and social proportion with disproportion, Goldsmith presents the demise of the rural way of life in the image of an innocent country girl forced to the city for economic reasons, and there inevitably falling into evil ways:

> . . . Ah, turn thine eyes
> Where the poor houseless shivering female lies.
> She once, perhaps, in village plenty blest,
> Has wept at tales of innocence distrest;
> Her modest looks the cottage might adorn,
> Sweet as the primrose peeps beneath the thorn;
> Now lost to all; her friends, her virtue fled,
> Near her betrayer's door she lays her head.[16]

As Goldsmith no doubt was aware, London in 1770 was full of Irish country girls in this position; in any case, the symbolic suggestiveness of that final image, in terms of the geography of Ireland and England, is difficult to overlook. "The Deserted Village" also has its scene of emigration, a problem particularly associated with Ireland, rendered in explicit, if overly stylized, details that interpret the experience in terms of the destruction of innocence and social order:

> The good old sire, the first prepared to go
> To new found worlds, and wept for others woe.
> But for himself, in conscious virtue brave,
> He only wished for worlds beyond the grave.
> His lovely daughter, lovelier in her tears,
> The fond companion of his helpless years,
> Silent went next, neglectful of her charms,
> And left a lover's for a father's arms.[17]

The debate over whether Auburn is based on an English village or the Lissoy of Goldsmith's boyhood probably will never be resolved, in part because there is convincing evidence, some of it provided by Goldsmith himself, on both sides. Goldsmith's letter-to-the-editor, "The Revelation in Low Life," published in 1762, strongly suggests that the deserted village is English, "distant about fifty miles from town."[18] But Goldsmith is also on record as having said of the land clearances that the poem describes, "I remember it in my own country, and I have seen it in this."[19] Moreover, the man who succeeded Goldsmith's brother in the curacy of Kilkenny West has left behind the story of one General Robert Napper who bought an extensive tract of land surrounding Lissoy, "in consequence of which many families . . . were removed, to make room for the intended improvements of what was now to become the wide domain of a rich man."[20] In any case, the argument is significant only in so far as it demonstrates the extent to which Goldsmith belongs to both the English and the Irish traditions, and therefore the extent to which his work represents and embodies the need for eighteenth-century Irish writers to negotiate between the two. In "The Deserted Village," there is a description of a public house in Auburn:

> Imagination fondly stoops to trace
> The parlour splendours of that festive place;
> The white-washed wall, the nicely sanded floor,
> The varnished clock that clicked behind the door.[21]

This looks like no rural pub in Ireland that Goldsmith could ever have seen. In fact, writing to his brother Henry, Goldsmith once asked for his opinion of a very different description of a pub, one, he says, "taken from Nature":

> The sandy floor that grits beneath the tread,
> The humid wall with paltry pictures spread;
>   .   .   .
> A rusty grate unconscious of a fire.[22]

As Frank O'Connor has argued, these two passages nicely illustrate the problem of most Irish writers, Goldsmith included: "To make his experience relevant to his English readers he has to alter it to fit their experience, but to make his experience relevant to his brother, Goldsmith has to translate himself back into Irish poetry."[23] For Goldsmith, this represented both a difficulty and a source of strength.

At one point in "The Deserted Village," Goldsmith recalls his youthful innocence in Auburn in terms that seem remarkably romantic:

> To me more dear, congenial to my heart,
> One native charm, than all the gloss of art;
> Spontaneous joys, where Nature has its play,
> The soul adopts, and owns their first born sway.[24]

And Goldsmith concludes his poem with a view of the artist that strikes a particularly romantic note, seeing poetry as one of the virtues driven away by the crass commercialism responsible for the decline of rural life. If Goldsmith's work contains some seeds of English romanticism ("The Deserted Village" was published less than three decades before the appearance of Wordsworth's and Coleridge's *Lyrical Ballads*), those seeds are also to be found in several other Irish poets writing in English in the latter decades of the eighteenth century. What is perhaps most striking about the writers who fall into this category, including Samuel Whyte and Thomas Dermody, is how undifferentiated their work is from the English tradition, how little their romanticism resembles the specifically Irish romanticism of the nineteenth century, with its fusion of romantic principles and nationalist ideology. The Anglo-Irish Protestant backgrounds of these writers—combined, in the case of Whyte at least, with a virulent anti-Catholicism—cut them off from the Gaelic culture that fed both the romanticism and nationalism of many nineteenth-century Irish writers. Also, the antiquarian movement that made much of that culture broadly accessible in the nineteenth century was still in its infancy at the time that Whyte and Dermody were writing. Finally, both Whyte and Dermody tended to steer clear of the political and social ramifications of romanticism, focusing instead on aesthetic and broadly metaphysical concerns. Still, there are specifically Irish elements in the work of both these poets—especially in that of Dermody, the more significant of the two—and they both bring to light romantic views that were to become increasingly important, and increasingly political, in Irish poetry during the following century.

Samuel Whyte (1733–1811) (possibly a cousin of Laurence Whyte) was a fairly prolific poet, with two thick volumes of verse to his credit: *The Shamrock: or Hibernian Cresses* (1772) and *Poems on Various Subjects* (1795). He was also a schoolmaster for most of his life; in 1758, when he was twenty-five, he opened his "seminary" in Dublin, and devoted more than half a century to it. (Among his students were Richard Brinsley Sheridan and Thomas Moore.) There is a chalky stuffiness to much of Whyte's writing, the work of a man used to discoursing at length to a captive audience, and one critic's blunt characterization of *The Shamrock* as "insufferably dull" is not far off the mark.[25] There are, however, moments in Whyte's writing in which he challenges, explicitly or implicitly, the conventions of neo-classicism, and in which he entertains romantic ideas and attitudes. "The Farewell: A Pastoral Ballad," for example, describes the area around Mallow in Co. Cork in terms that both transcend the conventions of eighteenth-century descriptive poetry and transform a specifically local landscape into a romantically poetic one:

> O'er thy green Hills high-bosom'd in Wood,
> O'er thy sweetly diversified Ground,

> How oft, as my Walk I pursued,
>   Have I gaz'd in wild Transport around!
> Invoking the Powers that preside
>   O'er the stream, o'er the Grove, or the Hill,
> With their Presence my Fancy to guide
>   With their Fire my rapt Bosom to fill.[26]

The transition from neo-classicism to romanticism can itself be traced in Whyte's "Powerscourt," a poem addressed to Richard Wingfield, who built the Powerscourt estate in Co. Wicklow in the 1730s. The poem begins by arguing, in neo-classical fashion, for the moral force of "Taste," of the imposition on nature of man's civilizing hand:

> If Public Spirit shines, 'tis just at least,
> To give some Glory too to *Public Taste,*
> Which bids proud Art the pillar'd Fabric raise;
> Scoops the rough Rock, and levels vast High-ways!
> Plans future Woods for Prospect and Defence;
> And forms a Bower a hundred Summers hence.[27]

But when the narrator's attention turns to the famous Powerscourt waterfall, the poem is overtaken by romantic impulses. "Proud Art" pales in the face of the transcendent power of raw nature: "Her rudest Prospects bid the Fancy start,/And snatch the Soul beyond the Works of Art." [28] Whyte's description of the waterfall is closer, in tone and intensity, to Shelley's "Mont Blanc" than to most eighteenth-century descriptive poetry, in Ireland or England:

> Lo, down the Rock which Clouds and Darkness hide,
> In wild Meanders spouts a silver Tide;
> Or sprung from dropping Mists, or Wintry Rills,
> Rolls the large Tribute of the Cloud-topp'd Hills;
>
>   .   .   .
>
> From Rock to Rock its boiling flood is broke,
> And all below the Waters surge in Smoke—
> So vast the Height, no Distance seems between
> The Mountain's Summit, and the blue *Serene.*
> So wondrous fierce the sloping Torrents roll!
> Such still Amazement fixes all the Soul![29]

Whyte's excursions into this kind of romantic territory are usually impeded by an inability to get beyond, or at least significantly modify, eighteenth-century conventions and forms. Whyte's work is also limited by its ignorance of rural

Ireland. Indeed, Whyte's attitudes toward the native Irish are characterized by the same kind of condescension and ignorance found in the work of that other Anglo-Irish Protestant schoolteacher, William Dunkin. Whyte's "The Hone: A Piece of Irish Mythology," for example, describes the native Irish as "The rude, unletter'd natives of this land,"[30] and only an occasional, not to say willfully uninformed, visitor to the Irish countryside in the 1770s could have written these lines:

> Let wealth regale itself on costly plate,
> Cares will intrude and happiness prevent;
> But peasants, who off humble trenchers eat,
> With rosy health enjoy supreme content.[31]

Whyte's ability to see things this way at a time when Ireland was experiencing the most sustained and violent agrarian unrest of the century (the Whiteboy movement was in its ascendancy) indicates how far removed Whyte was from the realities of Irish rural life and from the forces that eventually would shape much romantic and post-romantic writing in Ireland.

The romanticism of Thomas Dermody (1775–1802) was far less ambiguous than that of Whyte, although equally divorced from a specific Irish context. Characterized in one biographical account as "the Chatterton of Ireland,"[32] Dermody seems to have been committed to living up to all the stereotypes of the romantic artist. He was a child prodigy, allegedly writing accomplished verse before the age of ten and actually publishing his first collection of poems at fourteen. As Dermody himself once put it, in a poem entitled "My Own Character," "my summer of genius arriv'd ere its spring."[33] He ran away from the home of his father, an Ennis schoolteacher, and was taken up in Dublin by various people interested in promoting his poetic genius. His first book was published, in 1789, with the help of several patrons, followed by a collection in 1792 astonishingly entitled, *Poems, Consisting of Essays, Lyric, Elegaic, etc. Written between the 13th and 16th Year of His Age.* He published two more collections of verse in his short life. But Dermody was, by all accounts, bent on self-destruction. He apparently never overcame an early addiction to alcohol; several attempts to have him educated at Trinity College failed, and he eventually enlisted in the army as a private. He died in a hovel in Kent at the age of twenty-seven. In his preface to the two-volume edition of Dermody's poetry published posthumously in 1807, Dermody's biographer summed up his life in appropriately melodramatic terms: "The annals of literature cannot, perhaps, furnish a more extraordinary example of the willful debasement of Transcendent genius, than in the varied and extraordinary life of the unfortunate author of the following poems."[34]

Dermody was born more than forty years after Whyte, and his work consistently embodies a whole range of qualities and concerns that might be described as romantic, a preoccupation with nature perceived as an active source of spiritual power and fulfillment; a trust in rural solitude and a corresponding distrust of urban society; a belief, at times running to Gothic proportions, in the sensual and emotional force of art; a faith in the redemptive powers of the creative imagination; and the conviction that the rising tide of materialism and commercialism threatened the survival of art, and so of man's moral being. Unlike most of Whyte's writing, Dermody's poetry, in an effort to accommodate these romantic themes, actively resists the constraints of eighteenth-century poetic forms and conventions. This quality is especially evident in his poetry centering on nature; these lines from a poem entitled "The Enthusiast," for example, might be compared with Whyte's more convention-bound description of the waterfall in "Powerscourt":

> High o'er the headlong torrents' foamy fall,
> Where waters howl along the rugged steep,
> On the loose-jutting rock, or mould'ring wall,
> See where gaunt Danger lays him down to sleep![35]

It is to the hidden power behind all this energy that the poet, in Dermody's romantic view, owes his allegiance, and from which he derives his inspiration. His image of the poet in "The Pleasures of Poesy" is remarkably Wordsworthian in spirit if not always in tone:

> My nature will no courtly shackles bind;
> No servile flatt'ry, varnish'd o'er with art;
> While, on yon mountain's misty summit shrin'd,
> Majestic sitting from the world apart,
> I to great Nature pour the homage of my heart.
>
> . . .
>
> To airy regions may my spirit roam,
> Wafted on wild Imagination's wing:
> There can I find and fix my viewless home,
> And reign o'er magic realms creative king.[36]

Most of Dermody's poems could as well be set in the Lake District as in his native country. The truth is that Dermody does not seem very well informed about Ireland. Dermody's romantic rewriting of Goldsmith's "The Deserted Village," a poem entitled "The Fragmented Village," transforms sweet Auburn into an Edenic place that betrays a remarkable naivete on Dermody's part:

Would the rich man but thank the lab'rers toil,
And cheer the brow of anguish with a smile,
Inglorious sloth would shortly leave the land,
And fly pernicious to some alien strand.

            .   .   .

O'er cultur'd grounds the master walk with joy,
And see mute gladness in the farmer's eye.[37]

Although Dermody's romanticism does not seem much grounded in the Irish experience, at least by the standards of nineteenth-century Irish romanticism, there is nonetheless some evidence, in the rhythms of his verse, that he was influenced by the Gaelic tradition. The opening of "Another," for example, might be said to anticipate the lyrics of Thomas Moore:

When I sat by my fair, and she tremblingly told
The soft wishes and doubts of her heart,
How quickly old Time then delightfully roll'd,
For Love lent the plume from his dart![38]

And "The Grave of Morno," a lyric poem about a legendary Gaelic hero, employs a heavily stressed rhythm that owes little to the English tradition:

Heard ye not the moan profound
Bursting from yon blighted mound,
Where, amid the murky air,
The wild ash waves its branches bare?
There, in dark-brown dust array'd,
Morno's giant limbs are laid.[39]

Dermody left Ireland in 1794 at the age of nineteen, going with his regiment to England. He wrote a poem on the occasion, "Farewell to Ireland," and in it he defines the condition of exile in specifically romantic terms. There is, on the one hand, a Swiftian bitterness about Ireland:

Rank nurse of nonsense, on whose thankless coast
The base weed thrives, the nobler bloom is lost:
Parent of pride and poverty, where dwell
Dullness and brogue and calumny:—farewell![40]

Dermody cannot, however, leave it at that. Seeing himself as bearing an "injured breast" (shades of Joyce's Stephen Dedalus), he pleads with Ireland to "raise thy pale, thy drooping sons," and, above all, "Thy artists cherish," and, finally, not to forget him: "And haply when some native gem you see/Unknown, unfriended, lost—oh, think on me!" [41] This cry of the Irish exile, perceiving himself as both victim and potential savior, outcast and loyal son, would be voiced, in equally romantic strains, by many Irish writers over the next two centuries.

POLITICAL POETRY AT THE
END OF THE CENTURY

The last quarter of the eighteenth century in Ireland was a time of high political voltage. The rise of the Volunteers in the late 1770s, the drive for legislative independence culminating in the constitution and reforms of 1782 and Grattan's parliament, the beginning of the French Revolution in 1789, the founding two years later of Theobold Wolfe Tone's United Irishmen with its commitment to alliance with the French and separation from England, the doomed but crucial insurrection of 1798, and the act of Union that followed two years later—all these events put pressures on Irish writers that could not easily be ignored. The Irish poetry that emerged in response to these events, and that contributed to them, was significantly political in ways that distinguished it sharply from the political verse of Swift and his contemporaries writing a half-century earlier. Much of the verse written near the end of the century took the form of popular ballads and other forms designed to appeal to a broad, even illiterate, readership, as opposed to the satirical verse of such writers as Swift and Jonathan Smedley, which was plainly intended for a small, educated readership. The political concerns of a writer such as Swift were largely legislative and targeted primarily at Anglo-Irish Protestants, whereas the nationalist ambitions of writers associated with Tone and his United Irishmen, inspired by the French Revolution, were far broader and more radical. Poets writing in this charged atmosphere tended to be intimately and often quite practically involved in political action. James Orr, for example, took an active part in the 1798 insurrection, and, like a number of nationalist poets in the following century, was imprisoned and sent into exile for his efforts. William Drennan is believed to have written the original prospectus for the United Irishmen, and was tried for sedition. Finally, some of the political verse written in this period was influenced by romanticism, and so anticipated the radical redefinition of the nationalist project that took place in the nineteenth century with the creation of an idealized, transhistorical concept of Irish nationhood and a concurrent emphasis on political martyrdom and blood-sacrifice.

One important exception to most of these generalizations was the work of Mary O'Brien (fl. 1783–1790), the most Swiftian of the political poets of the period. Little is known about her life, and she published just one slim volume of poems, *The Political Monitor; or Regent's Friend* (1790), almost all of which have to do with the regency crisis of 1788–89. But O'Brien is an accomplished satirist with a sophisticated sense of irony and a Swiftian gift for manipulating a variety of dramatic personae. O'Brien's position in the regency crisis was that of most Irish political leaders at the time: that the Prince of Wales should be appointed regent for as long as George III was judged to be incompetent to rule. O'Brien also shared the hope of many Irish politicians that a regency would lead to the removal of William Pitt as prime minister. What is most striking about several of O'Brien's poems attacking Pitt's actions during this crisis (he managed to delay matters until the king recovered) is the way in which they turn condescending stereotypes of the Irish back against the English. "Paddy's Opinion. An Irish Ballad," for example, is written from the point of view of an Irishman who addresses Pitt with all the obsequiousness attributed to the stereotyped Irish peasant, and it ends with an insult that depends on applying to the English the same kind of reductive condescension that stands behind Paddy's name:

> But beware now, dear *crature,*
> > Since wisdom may fail ye,
> To smoke out our brains,
> > In the land of Shillelah;
>
> Lest Hibernia's high notions
> > To anger should rise,
> And smoke out your taxes,
> > And blast your excise.
>
> Arrah, then, my dear Billy,
> > It might prove in the pull,
> Paddy's not quite so silly
> > As your Jacky Bull.[1]

There is a real, and notably Swiftian, venom in that "Jacky Bull," and in much of O'Brien's political verse, but in the end the significance of O'Brien's work is limited by its narrow focus on a specific political occasion.

O'Brien's verse also demonstrates little evident interest in reaching a popular audience. The work of Edward Lysaght (1763–1810), on the other hand, is very much part of the movement at the end of the eighteenth century toward popular political verse. Lysaght would seem to be an unlikely poet for this role. He was born into a Protestant family in Co. Clare with distinguished ancestors on both sides, and educated first at a highly regarded Catholic seminary in Cashel and then at Trinity College and Oxford University. At the age of twenty-five, he was called to both the English and the Irish bar, and he took up the practice of law first in England and then in Ireland. Poetry seems to have come relatively easy to him, and his love poetry is marked by a flair for lyricism similar to that observed earlier in the work of Thomas Parnell, as is evident in the opening of a poem entitled "To Miss N****":

> Oh, free were I as air that blows
> On flow'ry heath, or mountain rose,
> The tenderest feeling I'd disclose
> To lovely, gentle Bessy.[2]

And into the six lines of this brief lyric, entitled "Fragment," Lysaght manages to compress a considerable degree of feeling and, at the same time, to celebrate a side of Swift not always remembered:

> Did I enjoy the muses' gift
> Of inspiration, such as Swift
> Was filled with, when he sang of Stella,
> I'd celebrate the brighter charms
> (Although they bless another's arms)
> And sing of lovely ISABELLA![3]

Like many Irishmen of his class at the time, Lysaght actively supported the Volunteers and Henry Grattan's movement for legislative independence. When he turned to writing political verse, his sensibility found its home in the tradition of the popular political ballad. On the whole, Lysaght's contributions to this genre were not particularly distinguished, but he did write one poem, "The Man Who Led the Van of Irish Volunteers," that is still occasionally anthologized, and that, in its praise of Grattan, exemplifies the appeal and energy of the popular ballad:

> The gen'rous sons of Erin, in manly virtue bold,
> With hearts and hands preparing our country to uphold,
> Tho' cruel knaves and bigot slaves disturbed our isle some years,
> Now hail the man, who led the van of Irish Volunteers.
>
> .   .   .
>
> He sows no vile dissensions; good will to all he bears:
> He knows no vain pretensions, no paltry fears or cares;

> To Erin's and to Britain's sons his worth his name endears;
> They love the man, who led the van of Irish Volunteers.[4]

Lysaght also wrote a number of poems expressing fierce opposition to the Union, a few of which exhibit a Swiftian sense of irony, such as this brief satire, one of two "Fragments":

> No more at city feasts can you boast of independency,
> Nor shall Catholics be rode down by Protestant ascendancy;
> The U——, like the grave, all distinctions soon will level,
> And send you all most lovingly together to the devil.[5]

Lysaght was known to his friends as "Pleasant Ned," and the epithet describes much of his poetry all too well. But in terms of at least one direction that Irish poetry was to take in the next century, it is significant that this man, whose Anglo-Irish pedigree and classical education were every bit the equal of William Dunkin's, should devote his poetical energies to writing nationalist ballads for the people.

While Lysaght inevitably found himself observing much of Irish life from the distance of his privileged class and education, which often robbed his popular ballads of specificity and vitality, the work of James Orr (1770–1816), born in a village in Co. Antrim and in his early life following the trade of a journeyman weaver, was written very much from the inside of lower-middle-class, provincial life. It was also written, in a way that Lysaght's poetry was not, from inside the world of insurrectionary nationalism. When *The Northern Star,* a newspaper founded by the United Irishmen in Belfast, first appeared in 1791, Orr began contributing poems of a more-or-less nationalist stripe to it; by 1798, the year of the insurrection, he was so deeply committed to the cause of separation from England that he joined the fighting, taking part in the battle of Antrim in June, for which he was later imprisoned and then sent to America. In this, Orr anticipates an entire tradition of nineteenth-and twentieth-century Irish writing—Young Ireland, the Fenian poets, and the poets of the Easter Rising of 1916, most notably—constructed on the principle that there is a vitalizing link between poetry and political action. At the same time, the impulse toward social realism that defines some of Orr's writing about his native Ulster, combined with his class background, produced a sympathetic provincial focus on the specific cultural qualities of Ulster, a part of the Irish tradition that is often under-represented because of the increasing tendency in Irish nationalist writing to associate Gaelicism with the west and south of Ireland. In "The Irish Cottier's Death and Burial," Orr reproduces the dialect of Co. Antrim without any trace of the condescension that marks the portrayal by other eighteenth-century poets of provincial Irish culture:

While thus they sit, the widow lifts the sheet,
    To kiss the corps that worms will shortly gnaw;
Some argue Scripture—some play tricks—some greet;
    Here they're asleep—an' there they slip awa'.
Folk wha lay list'ning' till the cock wad craw,
Now rise frae rest, an' come to sit a while;
    Salute their frien's, and speer for their folk a',
An' to the fire step ben, frae which a file
O' warmer rustics rise, polite in simplest stile.[6]

Orr was by no means unaware of the political implications of his writing in this vein; like Goldsmith, he believed that Ireland's moral foundation and virtues were embodied in the life of its ordinary people. In general, however, Orr's political poems are marred by the penchant for abstraction and stereotype that also characterizes much nationalist writing in the nineteenth century, a tendency to minimize local details and eliminate issues of difference in a desire to construct a sense of national identity. But one of Orr's political poems, having to do with emigration, that dominant issue of nineteenth-century nationalist verse, contains a remarkably detailed and concrete account of the conditions on board a ship sailing to America. The poem, entitled "Song: Composed on the Banks of Newfoundland," seems written out of Orr's own experience of forced exile:

How hideous the hold is!—Here, children are screaming,
    There dames faint, thro' thirst, with their babes on their knee;
Here, down ev'ry hatch the big breakers are streaming,
    And, there, with a crash, half the fixtures break free:
Some court—some contend—some sit dull stories telling—
    The mate's mad and drunk, and the tar's task'd and yelling:
What sickness and sorrow, pervade my rude dwelling!—
    A huge floating lazar-house, far, far at sea.[7]

At the end of this poem, which represents Orr's most effective political writing, the narrator imagines returning one day to an Ireland altered almost beyond recognition, a version of Goldsmith's deserted Auburn:

How chang'd all may be when I seek the sweet village!
    A hedge-row may bloom where its street us'd to be;
The floors of my friends may be tortur'd by tillage,
    And the upstart be served by the fallen grandee:
The axe may have humbled the grove that I haunted,
    And shades be my shield that as yet are unplanted;

> Nor one comrade live, who repin'd when he wanted
>   The sociable suff'rer, that's far, far at sea.[8]

Orr is less in control of his material here than is Goldsmith in "The Deserted Village," and his writing is occasionally marred by awkwardness, carelessness, or sentimentality, but one can find in his work traces of the romantic identification between personal suffering and the condition of Ireland that governs much of the poetry of James Clarence Mangan a half-century later. The comparison is particularly striking in "The Poor House: An Elegy," in which Orr, writing in the service more of social criticism than of any specific nationalist ideology, achieves both a remarkable quality of realism and a sense of individual melancholy that might be taken to represent Ireland's situation:

> What ghastly groups, diseas'd, around me stand!
>   Dull headache droops, spleen frets, consumption wastes,
> And dotage wildly stares, while palsy's hand
>   Flings o'er his head the meal he seldom tastes.
>
> The beldame pants, that's gasping asthma's prey,
>   The rheum-rack'd soldier pines, but ne'er complains;
> The tar crawls by, whose limbs felt frosts stern sway—
>   Hark how they talk of shipwrecks and campaigns!
>   .   .   .
> My heart forebodes that I, ere life shall cease,
>   A poor old man, the last of all my race,
> Coughing along, and shouldering the breeze,
>   May seek sad refuge in some kindred place.
>
> There, far remov'd from every hope and fear;
>   Recite the scenes of youth, so like a dream,
> Till death conclude the winter of my year,
>   And give the dust my weary, willing frame.[9]

Like Orr, William Drennan (1754–1820) was an Ulsterman and an active member of the United Irishmen. He is credited with having written the original prospectus for the group in 1791, and three years later was tried, unsuccessfully, on charges on sedition. The similarities between these two Ulster poets end there, however. For one thing, Drennan, like Lysaght, belonged to the professional classes. The son of a Belfast Presbyterian minister, he was educated at Glasgow and Edinburgh Universities, receiving an M.D. degree from Edinburgh, and he practiced medicine first in Newry and then, from 1789 to 1807, in Dublin, where he knew Lysaght. More important, Drennan's nationalism, although relatively militant, was considerably less informed by romanticism

than was Orr's; Drennan's political convictions were drawn chiefly from eighteenth-century Enlightenment thinking, and the poetry that he wrote out of
those convictions gave voice to a rationalistic nationalism that was all but
extinguished by the romantic politics of the nineteenth century. Drennan also
expressed more clearly than did Orr the nationalist dimension inside Ulster's
dissenting tradition.[10] And finally, Drennan's anti-sectarian thinking anticipated
some of the positions advanced by Thomas Davis and the Young Ireland movement of the 1840s, although it eschewed, for the most part, the romantic
impulses behind that movement. It is no accident that of the four political poets
considered here, Drennan is the only one represented in *The Spirit of the
Nation,* Young Ireland's anthology of nationalist verse.

Drennan's work is not untouched by romanticism or its implications for Irish
nationalism. But the romantic urgency and tone of a poem such as Orr's "The
Poor House" is, in Drennan's hands, sharply contained, in part through a
strictly controlled use of poetic forms taken from the English neo-Augustan
tradition. Drennan's best-known poem, "The Wake of William Orr," may suggest the political significance of martyrdom, but it stops considerably short of
embracing that romantic notion. Written in response to the execution in 1797
of a member of the United Irishmen (apparently no relation to James Orr) for
administering an illegal oath, the poem moves with a dignity and restraint that
help resist any temptation to romanticize the event:

> Here our brother worthy lies,
> Wake not him with women's cries;
> Mourn the way that mankind ought;
> Sit, in silent trance of thought.[11]

At one point, Drennan specifically draws a parallel between Orr's death and
that of Christ, opening up the poem to the concept of political martyrdom:

> Why cut off in palmy youth?
> Truth he spoke, and acted truth—
> "Countrymen, Unite!" he cried,
> And died, for what his Saviour died!
>
> God of Peace, and God of Love,
> Let it not thy vengeance move!
> Let it not thy lightnings draw,
> A nation guillotin'd by law![12]

The romantic identification of revolution with redemption is unmistakable here,
but the poem does not pursue this idea to its conclusion. Instead, it ends by

returning to the soberness of the opening stanzas and to the relatively vague
faith that the darkness of Orr's death will produce some kind of light:

> Here we watch our brother's sleep;
> Watch with us, but do not weep:
> Watch with us thro' dead of night—
> But expect the morning light.
>
> Conquer fortune—persevere—
> Lo! it breaks—the morning clear!
> The chearful cock awakes the skies;
> The day is come—Arise, arise![13]

Drennan's commitment to rationalism as opposed to romanticism is perhaps
most effectively expressed in a long, anti-Union poem entitled "Glendalloch,"
first published in 1802, that consists of an account of Ireland's history, going
back to pre-Christian times. It is, as Terence Brown has said, "a sceptical
exposition of Irish history," not a romantic, mythologizing account.[14] Essentially, it tells a story of repeated conquest and betrayal, with just one moment
of true freedom and hope: 1782, the year of Grattan's parliament and, as
Drennan sees it, the culmination of Enlightenment patriotism: "Gain'd by a
nation, rais'd, inspir'd,/By eloquence and virtue fir'd."[15] For Drennan, this is
what was destroyed by the Union of 1800, and his poem concludes with an
image of the famous tower at Glendaloch as a symbol of its ruin:

> Here be the mausoléum plac'd;
> In this vast vault, this silent waste;—
> Yon mould'ring pillar, 'midst the gloom,
> Finger of Time! shall point her tomb;
> While silence of the evening hour
> Hangs o'er Glendalloch's ruin'd tow'r.[16]

As Drennan seems to have understood, and as the next generation of nationalist
poets confirmed, the moment of Enlightenment liberty mourned here had
passed forever, its demise occurring almost precisely as the eighteenth century
ended and the nineteenth began.

EPILOGUE:

THE OTHER IRELAND

Thirteen years before the publication in Belfast of Drennan's "Glendalloch," with its gloomy view of Ireland's past, present, and future, a strikingly different prognosis for Ireland's cultural and political life appeared in Dublin, in the pages of a most unlooked-for book from the hand of a most unlooked-for author. Charlotte Brooke (1740–1793) was the last of twenty-two children born to Henry Brooke (1703–1783), an extremely prolific writer as well as father, with numerous poems, plays, novels and political pamphlets to his credit. As a poet, Henry Brooke tended to be ponderous and pedantic, although his lengthy treatise in verse, *Universal Beauty* (1735), won him the attention of Swift and Pope. Until relatively late in his life, Brooke was virulently anti-Catholic; he feared most of all a Jacobite rebellion in Ireland, predicting at one point that were such an event to succeed, "the Consequence to us would be the same, as if this whole Frame of Heaven and Earth was to be broken, and thrown into its first Darkness and Confusion." [1] Like Maria Edgeworth a generation later, Charlotte Brooke seems to have devoted most of her life to her father and his writings, and he in turn educated her. Six years after Henry Brooke died, Charlotte Brooke published a work, carrying the modest, scholarly title of *Reliques of Irish Poetry: Consisting of Heroic Poems, Odes, Elegies, and Songs,* that was to make her name of more significance to the history of Irish literature than were all her father's many works combined. Brooke's book was the first attempt to publish in one volume translations of poetry from Ireland's Gaelic tradition. Although very much a product of an eighteenth-century sensibility, it stands on the brink of the development in the nineteenth century of an Irish poetry written in English but profoundly aware of Gaelic Ireland.

The translations themselves were not very accomplished, and certainly not faithful to the poetic texture of the originals, a point that Brooke was perfectly

63

willing to concede. Unlike James Macpherson, the author of the enormously popular but fraudulent "translations" of Ossian that appeared in the 1760s, Brooke included in her collection copies of her original sources, as part of an effort to restore to the enterprise of translation from the Irish some of the scholarly authority undermined by Macpherson. The difficulties of providing translations that were poetically faithful to the originals had to do in part with the incongruity of English and Irish verse forms. The imposition of English forms and rhythms on Irish originals produced translations in Brooke's book that at times bordered on the ludicrous, and that, even at their best, were crippled by Brooke's inability to get into her translations any of the rhythmic and assonantal complexities of the Gaelic originals. The effect of this can be seen by comparing Brooke's version of a lyric by Turlough Carolan with a version by the nineteenth-century poet-translator Samuel Ferguson. Brooke's translation relies on iambic tetrameter quatrains, taken whole from the English tradition, and on an artificial poetic diction common to much eighteenth-century verse:

> The youth whom fav'ring Heav'n's decree
> To join his Fate, my Fair! with thee;
> And see that lovely head of thine
> With fondness on his own recline:
>
> No thought but joy can fill his mind,
> Nor any care can entrance find,
> Nor sickness hurt, nor terror shake,—
> And Death will spare him, for thy sake!
>
> For the bright flowing of thy hair,
> That decks a face so heavenly fair;
> And a fair form, to match that face,
> The rival of the Cygnet's grace.[2]

Ferguson's version employs a more open stanzaic form and a more flexible, anapaestic line, in an effort to reproduce some of the un-English rhythmic qualities of Carolan's poem:

> Whoever the youth who by Heaven's decree
>   Has his happy right hand 'neath that bright head of thine,
>   Tis certain that he
>   From all sorrow is free
>   Till the day of his death, if a life so divine
> Should not raise him in bliss above mortal degree:
> Mild Mabel-ni-Kelly, bright Coolun of curls,
>   All stately and pure as the swan on the lake;

Her mouth of white teeth is a palace of pearls,
And the youth of the land are love-sick for her sake![3]

Quite apart from the question of how Gaelic Brooke's verse is, much of the importance of *Reliques of Irish Poetry* lay simply in its being published at all. In the book's preface, which was of at least equal importance to the translations themselves, Brooke argued that the discovery of Ireland's Gaelic heritage by those Irishmen ignorant of the language in which it was written—those Irishmen, that is, who on the whole controlled the political, social, and economic life of Ireland—could inspire the divided nation to a new condition of mutual understanding and harmony:

The British muse is not yet informed that she has an elder sister in this isle; let us then introduce them to each other! together let them walk abroad from their bowers, sweet ambassadresses of cordial union between two countries that seem formed by nature to be joined by every bond of interest, and of amity. Let them entreat of Britain to cultivate a nearer acquaintance with her neighboring isle. Let them conciliate for us her esteem, and her affection will follow of course. Let them tell her, that the portion of her blood which flows in our veins is rather ennobled than disgraced by the mingling tides that descended from our heroic ancestors.[4]

This is as close as Brooke gets to a point of view that might be described as nationalist. In truth her position is essentially that which will be identified in the nineteenth century as cultural-unionist, predicated on the assumption, or hope, that the confluence of Ireland's two different cultures will inevitably lead to political harmony among the English, the Irish, and the Anglo-Irish.[5] Brooke's work also is part of an eighteenth-century tradition of interest in Gaelic culture, realized most recklessly in Macpherson, but also to be found in Swift ("The Description of an *Irish Feast*") and other Anglo-Irish writers. Henry Brooke himself had once toyed with the idea of translating the ancient Fianna tales into English. All these efforts were made in the context of a political situation in which the Protestant rule of Ireland, for all Henry Brooke's worries about Jacobitism, seemed relatively secure, and in which the investigation of Gaelic culture could be seen as the work of the colonizer benevolently trying to understand the colonized.

There is, of course, another set of very different political implications to be drawn from the antiquarian ambitions manifest in a work like Brooke's *Reliques of Irish Poetry*. From this position, probably unthinkable to Charlotte Brooke, the revitalization and authentication of Ireland's Gaelic culture leads directly to the marginalization of Brooke's class, and ultimately to a separatist politics and the reversal of the political and cultural hierarchies that governed eighteenth-century Irish life. It may seem a very long way from Charlotte Brooke's optimistic appeal for mutual cultural understanding and the confidently English and neo-classical tone of her translations to the heady, unlicensed romanticism and radically nationalist message of James Clarence Mangan's nineteenth-century translation of a Gaelic poem entitled "Roisín Dubh": "O! the Erne shall run red/With redundance of blood. . ./And gun-peal, and slogan cry,/Wake many a glen serene,/Ere you shall fade, ere you shall die,/My Dark Rosaleen!" [6] Yet Ireland was to traverse this distance in little more than half a century.

PART TWO

THE NINETEENTH CENTURY

INTRODUCTION

Among those in attendance at the Belfast Harp Festival in July of 1792, the event that stands at the beginning of nineteenth-century Ireland's preoccupation with recovering the Gaelic past, was a young Protestant barrister named Theobold Wolfe Tone. Six years later, Tone would lead a seminal, although doomed, insurrection, and he attended the harp festival not for the music, but rather for the opportunity that the event provided for organizing anti-British marches on behalf of the Society of United Irishmen, which he had founded the year before. In fact, Tone seems to have had little use for the antiquarian movement. "July 13," he wrote in his diary; "the harpers again. Strum. Strum and be hanged." [1]

The moment is an instructive one for a consideration of the development of Irish poetry in English from the eighteenth to the nineteenth century. In Tone's day, both the antiquarian movement and Tone's particular brand of militant nationalism, shaped in large part by the French Revolution, were in their infancy, and there seemed to be no necessary connection between them, as Tone's diary entry so bluntly indicates. It was only in the nineteenth century, when the antiquarian movement celebrated at the Belfast Harp Festival had become a dominant feature of Irish culture, and the revolutionary nationalism that Tone espoused had become a powerful force in Ireland's political life, that the view developed that culture and politics were vitally, even urgently, intertwined, both part of an overarching effort to establish, define, and forcefully assert a distinctive national identity. This preoccupation with identity dominated all aspects of Ireland's cultural and political life in the nineteenth century, and most of the poetry written between the days of Tone and those of Charles Stewart Parnell not only reflected it but also played a crucial, and often quite self-conscious, role in its development.

The emergence of national identity as a central issue resulted largely from two events, both of which had to do with English politics and culture. The Union of 1800 made the question of Irish identity altogether more problematic and urgent than it had been in the eighteenth century; after 1800, the considerable and growing power of the British Empire, committed to absorbing Ireland and its culture into its own political hegemony and cultural traditions, threatened to subsume all aspects of Irish life.[2] The effort to establish a viable Irish identity in the face of this pressure was also powerfully affected by English romanticism, which provided both a vocabulary and a visionary philosophy that inspired the idealization of Ireland as a spiritual, transhistorical essence, the particular domain of the romantically defined poet, and, through the imaginative powers of the poet, capable of inspiring men to extraordinary actions, up to and including armed rebellion.

This need to redefine the very idea of Irish nationhood—related to but qualitatively different from the ambiguities of identity experienced by eighteenth-century Anglo-Irish writers such as Swift and Goldsmith—was responsible for a striking paradox in nineteenth-century Irish writing: the coincidence of a marked increase in diversity of voice and subject matter with a singleness of purpose or vision that sought to contain if not eliminate difference. The broad range of nineteenth-century Irish poetry is particularly remarkable in comparison with the poetry written in the eighteenth century. Nineteenth-century poets working in conjunction with translators and scholars unearthed and recreated a wealth of Gaelic literature, including ancient epics, political poems, and folk songs. Moreover, they managed to redefine the boundaries and capabilities of verse in English, incorporating into their work some of the formal qualities of verse written in Irish, an effort designed to resist the literary colonization of Ireland so evident in the neo-Augustan forms of much eighteenth-century Irish poetry in English. At the same time, poets committed to various kinds of social realism, taking their cues from the rise of the realistic novel in nineteenth-century Ireland, exposed the underside of Irish life, especially the plight of the socially and economically disadvantaged Irish peasant. Although much of the writing in this vein was arguably inhibited by a tendency to Anglicize Irish experience, there was a marked effort to write about the social and economic realities of Irish life from the inside, especially in the poetry written about the famine of the 1840s. Political poetry also became greatly diversified in the nineteenth century; the rise of the popular ballad and the establishment of inexpensive periodicals such as *The Nation* essentially democratized both the writing and the reading of poetry. The Anglo-Irish tradition represented by Swift and Goldsmith in the eighteenth century continued to flourish in the nineteenth century, but often in significantly different channels. Samuel Ferguson, an Anglo-Irish Protestant with strong Unionist convictions, devoted most of his literary career to the effort to recover the country's Gaelic past, and Lady Wilde, a woman with solid Anglo-Irish credentials, became the most militant of the nationalist poets writing for *The Nation* in the 1840s. The voice of Catholic Ireland, barely audible in the eighteenth century, was increasingly heard in the nineteenth century, most notably in the work of James Clarence Mangan, who was as much a product of Dublin's Catholic underclass as Ferguson was of the Protestant Ascendancy, and also in the nationalist verse of lesser-known writers such as Mary Kelly and John Keegan Casey. Despite this diversity, the overriding project of creating a distinctive national identity tended to limit the ability of many of these poets to reflect fully the complexities of nineteenth-century Irish life. Driven by a thoroughly romantic concept of Ireland as essentially spiritual, their writing often excluded or repressed that which it could not easily assimilate, and tended to transform all kinds of experience and difference into the terms of its nationalist vision.[3] This inclination no doubt accounts for some of the weaknesses that seem more or less specific to nineteenth-century Irish poetry at its worst: a tendency to rely on abstraction and generalization, a relative lack of individually realized experience and emotional nuance, and an indifference to the relationship between formal elements and thematic concerns.

The nineteenth-century preoccupation with identity is most evident in the political poetry of the period, particularly in the work of a fairly large number of women who wrote nationalist verse for the Young Ireland movement in the 1840s or on behalf of the Fenians in the 1860s. Much of the work of these women is indistinguishable from nationalist poetry written by men; and in that which is not, specific issues of gender, many of which were explored by women writing in the eighteenth century, are displaced by feminine—but not feminist —perspectives on conventional nationalist themes and images. More generally, the periodicals that made poetry accessible to a relatively broad and diversified readership were usually committed to specific political visions that served to limit the nature of what was published and read. *The Nation,* for example, disseminated a quintessentially romantic concept of Irish identity.

The antiquarian enterprise was somewhat less vulnerable to the most restrictive of those pressures, in part because of the sheer weight and diversity of the material that it brought to light, and in part because of the force of scholarly objectivity. Indeed, the specific political ramifications of antiquarianism could differ widely: whereas an Anglo-Irish Protestant such as Ferguson saw himself as working to integrate Gaelic culture with the English tradition and thereby fortify the Union, for other poets working in this vein, such as Edward Walsh and James Clarence Mangan, antiquarianism represented a means of validating the Irish claim to political as well as cultural sovereignty, while marginalizing Anglo-Irish Protestants. Nevertheless, translators and poets on both sides of this line generally shared the underlying assumption that Ireland was essentially a spiritual and transhistorical phenomenon embodied in and best understood through its native literature.[4]

Given the dominance of the issue of national identity in nineteenth-century Irish writing, it is hardly surprising to find marked coincidences throughout the century between periods of great political ferment and times of significant activity on the cultural front. The most notable of these was the 1840s, a decade that witnessed the rise of Young Ireland, the culmination of the drive for repeal of the Union, and the horrors of the famine. *The Nation,* with its romantic, essentialist aesthetics and politics, was founded near the beginning of this decade.[5] One of the three men who started up the paper was Charles Gavan Duffy, not a poet himself, but a man who embodied much of the spirit of his age. Born of poor parents in Co. Monaghan and a journalist by trade, Duffy was an active leader of the Young Ireland movement and a frequent contributor of essays and editorials to *The Nation.* He was arrested and tried for sedition in 1848, and in 1855 emigrated to Australia. In 1845, he published a collection of popular essays and poems by various hands entitled *The Ballad Poetry of Ireland,* which was reprinted over and over throughout the century. (By 1869, it was in its fortieth edition.) If Theobold Wolfe Tone's rejection of the musicians at the Belfast Harp Festival in 1782—"Strum and be hanged"—might be taken to indicate a gap in the eighteenth-century Irish sensibility between the cultural and the political, Duffy's introduction to *The Ballad Poetry of Ireland* expresses the very different view of cultural and political Ireland that developed in the half-century between the harp festival and the publication of the first issue of *The Nation.* For Duffy, the aesthetic worth and political relevance of the ballads that he had collected were one and the same; to his mind the ballads amounted to an expression of a transcendent, timeless Ireland that would have been unrecognizable to the eighteenth-century barrister. The ballads, Duffy says, "are Irish, not in the accident of their birthplace, like some of the great men whom we claim as countrymen on doubtful grounds, but *essentially,* in character and spirit."[6] That statement would have made little or no sense to Irish writers like Swift and Goldsmith, but it goes directly to the heart of the work of their successors.

IRELAND IN TRANSITION:
THOMAS MOORE

It is worth remembering that Thomas Moore (1779–1852) lived his first twenty-one years in the eighteenth century. He was, in fact, born three years before the swearing-in of Grattan's Parliament, ten years before the start of the French Revolution (and the publication of Charlotte Brooke's *Reliques of Irish Poetry*), nearly twenty years before the 1798 rebellion, and just five years after the death of Oliver Goldsmith. Many of the Penal Laws were still being enforced when Moore was growing up in Dublin, and he was able to enter Trinity College in 1795 only because of a change in that institution's centuries-old policy of excluding Catholics. An important influence on the young Moore was the poet Samuel Whyte, who counted Moore among the most famous pupils who attended his Dublin academy. Despite the tendency to see Moore as an Irish romantic,[1] his work is marked by a neo-classical sensibility: it aspires to elegance, polish, and harmony; it is perfectly content working within accepted poetic conventions and diction; it relies on relatively static, inorganic forms and structures (one reason, perhaps, that the first stanza in so many of Moore's poems is the strongest); it tends toward the general and abstract rather than the particular and concrete; it steers clear of unbridled subjectivity or fantasy; and it is designed to appeal to a small, essentially elite (and English) audience. At the same time, Moore's poetry about Ireland, particularly his *Irish Melodies,* published in ten numbers between 1807 and 1834, anticipated some of the central preoccupations of Irish poetry written in English in the nineteenth century. His setting of traditional Irish airs to English lyrics looked ahead to efforts to translate Ireland's Gaelic culture into English; his flirting with nationalist themes, including the definition of Ireland as essentially spiritual, laid some groundwork for the more ardently, overtly nationalist poets that followed in his wake; his blending of music and poetry undoubtedly contributed to the development in the nineteenth century of the popular political ballad; and finally, the ever-present note of muted melancholy that haunts Moore's poetry was echoed, more darkly and more urgently, in the profound pessimism that colored so much Irish writing after the famine of the late 1840s.

In one of several self-reflexive poems in *Irish Melodies,* "Silence is in our festal halls" (a tribute to Sir John Stevenson, who arranged many of the Irish airs for which Moore wrote lyrics), Moore describes the Irish poet as having fallen silent:

> But, where is now the cheerful day,
>   The social night, when, by thy side,
> He, who now weaves this parting lay,
>   His skilless voice with thine allied;
> And sung those songs whose every tone,
>   When bard and minstrel long have past,
> Shall still, in sweetness all their own,
>   Embalm'd by fame, undying last.[2]

This passage is revealing not just because it typifies Moore's preoccupation with things lost to the past but also because it defines Moore's highly aesthetic and passive concept of art. Moore's faith in the aesthetic rather than the social qualities of art is particularly visible in the distinction that he drew between music and poetry. Moore never hesitated to say that his first love was music and that his poetry was subservient to it. "I only know," he once said, "that in a strong and inborn feeling for music lies the source of whatever talent I may have shown for poetical composition, and that it was the effort to translate into language the emotions and passions which music appeared to me to express that first led to my writing any poetry at all deserving the name."[3] In a poem entitled "On Music," Moore describes this difference in even more revealing terms:

> Music, oh how faint, how weak,
>   Language fades before thy spell!
> Why should Feeling ever speak,
>   When thou canst breathe her soul so well?
> Friendship's balmy words may feign,
>   Love's are e'vn more false then they;
> Oh! 'tis only music's strain
>   Can sweetly soothe, and not betray.[4]

The conventional argument that music is a more powerful carrier of emotion than is language is compounded here by the assertion that language is not to be trusted in these matters. Betrayal is a common theme in Moore's work, and the notion that language has the potential to betray feelings—for one's lover, perhaps, but also for one's country—underscores Moore's tendency to embrace if not indulge the aesthetic dimension of art, often at the expense of the rational or social one. This inclination is particularly significant in an Irish poet adapting Irish airs to the English language and representing Ireland to an English audience. William Hazlitt's scathing denunciation of *Irish Melodies* may be overstated—"If a country can hear from its heart's core only these vapid, varnished sentiments, lip-deep, and let its tears of blood evaporate in an empty conceit, let it be governed as it has been"[5]—but it does point to a real limitation in Moore's writing about Ireland, and one that became more pronounced as his English reputation grew. Most critics agree that the best of Moore's poems about Ireland are in the early numbers of *Irish Melodies*.

Nevertheless, it is not for nothing that Moore enjoyed for so long the reputation of Ireland's national poet, and his significance to the tradition of Irish poetry in English, particularly as it develops through the nineteenth century, needs to be acknowledged and accounted for. Indeed, Moore's position embodied almost every major facet of Ireland's complex social and political situation in the nineteenth century, and of its tangled relationship with England: he was a middle-class Irish Catholic educated at Trinity College, where he had befriended the revolutionary Robert Emmet; he wrote, and often performed, for an English Protestant audience; he was transforming airs from the Gaelic tradition into poems written in English and shaped by English neo-classical conventions; and he was, in these poems, often complaining, albeit in muted tones, of England's mistreatment of Ireland, and at least hinting at the need for some kind of change, including the emancipation of Catholics advocated at the time by Daniel O'Connell.

At Trinity College, Moore worked on a translation of Anacreon. His decision to try his hand at setting traditional Irish airs to English lyrics embodied one of the fundamental shifts in Irish writing from the neo-classical tendencies of the eighteenth-century to the more romantic and more broadly nationalist concerns that emerged in the nineteenth century. There has been considerable controversy about the value and reliability of Moore's version of Irish music: the polished, enervating eloquence of *Irish Melodies* often betrays the earthy energy that generally characterizes the originals. Yet, in part because it was so popular and influential, Moore's work represents an important point of contact between Ireland's two cultures. Not only did Moore attempt to recast part of the Gaelic tradition in terms of Anglo-Irish and English culture (the *Irish Melodies* were based loosely on Edward Bunting's written record of the music played at the Belfast Harp Festival in 1792), but also he took the result into the drawing-rooms of the English upper classes. By his own testimony, Moore was well aware of how far he might be straying from scholarly accuracy; he was simply not interested in the kind of authenticity that preoccupied someone like Ferguson later in the century. "Had I not," he once said, "ventured on these very allowable liberties, many of the songs most known and popular would have been still sleeping, with all their authentic dross about them, in Mr. Bunting's first volume."[6] If, as Seamus Deane has argued, Moore "took some of the fruits of antiquarian labour and processed them for general consumption,"[7] he also demonstrated the cultural and political potency of making the Irish tradition accessible to an audience that, not only in England but increasingly in Ireland throughout the nineteenth century, spoke only English.

The evidence for Moore's importance to the enterprise of translation, one of the central preoccupations of nineteenth-century Irish writing, is quite concrete. The long, wavering verse line that characterized much of Ferguson's and Mangan's poetry (and that Yeats adopted in his early efforts to give a distinctly un-iambic and un-English quality to his poetry) appears frequently in Moore's *Irish Melodies*. Although Moore's handling of the long line is often relatively unsophisticated, tending to lapse into a predictable, potentially numbing mix of iambs and anapaests, some of his poems achieve a rhythmic flexibility that quite effectively embodies some of the qualities of verse in Irish. The opening stanza of "At the mid hour of night" is perhaps the best-known example:

> At the mid hour of night, when stars are weeping, I fly
> To the lone vale we lov'd, when life shone warm in thine eye;
> And I think oft, if spirits can steal from the regions of air,
> To revisit past scenes of delight, thou wilt come to me there,
> And tell me our love is remember'd, even in the sky.[8]

It seems unlikely that Moore, who did not know Irish, set out deliberately to incorporate into English verse the rhythms of Irish verse, as Ferguson and others did later; rather, because his lines were shaped to the rhythms of Irish music and not to the iambic norm of English poetry, he on occasion came close to the qualities of Irish verse, which relies relatively little on rhythmic patterns based on differences between stressed and unstressed syllables.

The music of Gaelic Ireland had another, less strictly aesthetic, significance for Moore, and for many Irish poets writing in his wake. "Surely if music ever spoke the misfortunes of a people," Moore once said, "or could ever conciliate forgiveness for their errors, the music of Ireland ought to possess those powers."[9] Although, in the view of more ardently nationalist poets later in the century, seeking "forgiveness for their errors" would seem an intolerably modest ambition for Irish poetry, Moore's poetry about Ireland represents a significant step away from eighteenth-century nationalist verse written largely on behalf of the ruling Anglo-Irish and toward nineteenth-century nationalist verse written on behalf of the Irish nation as a whole, particularly on behalf of the Catholic majority so often ignored in eighteenth-century concepts of Irish independence. Moore popularized what was to become one of the central tenets of nineteenth-century Irish nationalism: the definition of Ireland as a transhistorical, spiritual essence, a sacred cause worthy of, if not demanding, great sacrifice, and opposed, in its very nature, to the more successfully materialistic but spiritually bankrupt culture of England. And Moore's practice of associating, however obliquely, the cause of Ireland with the ideals of perfect love and transcendent religious experience managed to appeal to nationalists of far more ardent convictions than those held by Moore himself.[10] The opening stanza of "Erin, Oh Erin" is characteristic:

> Like the bright lamp, that shone in Kildare's holy fane,
>   And burn'd thro' long ages of darkness and storm,
> Is the heart that sorrows have frown'd on in vain,
>   Whose spirit outlives them, unfading and warm.
> Erin, oh Erin, thus bright thro' the tears
> Of a long night of bondage, thy spirit appears.[11]

This spiritualizing, romanticizing and, at times, sentimentalizing of Ireland usually comes at England's expense. When, for example, Moore presented these lines, from a poem entitled "Sweet Innisfallen," to England's drawing-room society, there could have been little doubt as to where the "paths of care" led or where the "crowded haunts" were to be found:

> Sweet Innisfallen, long shall dwell
>   In memory's dream that sunny smile,
> Which o'er thee on that evening fell,
>   When first I saw thy fairy isle.
>
> 'Twas light, indeed, too blest for one,
>   Who had to turn to paths of care—
> Through crowded haunts again to run,
>   And leave thee bright and silent there.[12]

This note of lament for the lost pastoral ideal of Ireland is specifically that of the exile, and was heard increasingly in nineteenth-century Irish poetry, especially after the devastation of the famine.

A number of the *Irish Melodies* that explore the relationship between England and Ireland also anticipate later, more overtly nationalist writing in their use of Irish history to generate political sentiment, although in Moore's hands the past is rarely a rallying cry for strong, active feeling in the present. Indeed, Moore generally uses the past as a screen rather than a catalyst for nationalist feeling. History is presented as irrevocably past, and rarely does Moore associ-

ate either images of Gaelic Ireland as a culturally rich and politically independent society or views of Ireland as the victim of centuries-old injustice with the
condition of Ireland in the first decades of the nineteenth century or with the
rising tide of nationalist feeling. "Let Erin remember the days of old," Moore
writes, "Ere her faithless sons betray'd her." [13] But for Moore, remembering
leads only to resignation and stasis. "Let Erin remember the days of old"
contains a striking image that reveals much about how Moore sees and uses the
past in his art:

> On Lough Neagh's bank as the fisherman strays,
> When the clear cold eve's declining,
> He sees the round towers of other days
> In the wave beneath him shining;
> Thus shall memory often, in dreams sublime,
> Catch a glimpse of the days that are over;
> Then, sighing, look through the waves of time
> For the long-faded glories they cover. [14]

The story, taken from Giraldus Cambrensis's *Topographia Hiberniae*, of the
fisherman who sees the round tower of ancient Ireland beneath the waters of
Lough Neagh represents the past as existing not in any actual, concrete mode,
but rather as a romanticized version of Ireland, an idealization that can be
experienced only through memory and fantasy. The image also insists on the
distance between past and present, separated as they are by the distancing
"waves of time." Glimpses of this romantic, ideal Ireland that lies always out
of reach are more enervating that animating; they bring about only a sense of
loss, a sighing for a past that is "long-faded" and permanently covered over.
In one of his best-known poems based on an historical event, "Oh! breathe not
his name," Moore recalls the execution of his friend Robert Emmet for his part
in the failed rising of 1803. Moore's poem is focused on Emmet's famous
speech in the dock, in which he asked for no epitaph until "my country take
her place among the nations of the earth," [15] and it eagerly embraces that silence
while embalming Emmet himself in stately, funereal rhythms and tones:

> Oh! breathe not his name, let it sleep in the shade,
> Where cold and unhonour'd his relics are laid:
> Sad, silent, and dark, be the tears that we shed,
> As the night-dew that falls on the grass o'er his head. [16]

Even when the poem, in its final stanza, looks ahead to some kind of liberation
from that sadness, silence, and darkness, and so, presumably, toward Emmet's
hope of Ireland taking its place among the nations of the world, it does so in

imagery and language that muffle whatever nationalist feeling might be generated by considering what Emmet stood for and what happened to him:

> But the night-dew that falls, though in silence it weeps,
> Shall brighten with verdure the grave where he sleeps;
> And the tear that we shed, though in secret it rolls,
> Shall long keep his memory green in our souls.[17]

The poem may carry a submerged threat, especially in that final line, but the promised land of Irish independence is kept far in the distance, and the means of reaching it, which might well include the kind of violent rebellion that Emmet undertook, are passed over in favor of unthreatening, pastoral images of natural regeneration. It is a highly accomplished poem, expertly negotiating the gap between Emmet's execution and Moore's English drawing-room audience, but part of its accomplishment consists in belying the kind of nationalism that it seems to honor.

A distancing historical framework occasionally enables Moore to defend his passively romantic aesthetics. Moore's note to his self-reflexive poem "Oh! blame not the bard" slyly supplies the kind of cover or mask that Moore's poetic sensibility seems always to require. "We may suppose," Moore says, "this apology to have been uttered by one of those wandering bards, whom Spenser so severely, and perhaps, truly, describes in his state of Ireland."[18] (As Moore no doubt knew, this back-handed compliment to Spenser was more likely to please his English readers than his Irish ones.) The justification that Moore provides in the poem for the tendency on the part of the Irish poet to "fly to the bowers,/Where Pleasure lies," and so to abandon the "holier flame" of poetry committed to the cause of Irish independence, is that the poet, whether of Moore's time or of Spenser's, is living in a dark age, in which Ireland's "pride is gone by" and its "spirit is broken."[19] There is some historical truth to this explanation for the aesthetic tendencies of Moore's work, as well as for the note of resignation and melancholy that haunts it; the years following the Union of 1800 ("Oh! blame not the bard" first appeared in the third number of *Irish Melodies,* published in 1810) were lean and inactive ones for the cause of Irish nationalism, in marked contrast to the heady days of Grattan's Parliament and the 1798 insurrection. And as Moore could easily observe from his ambiguous if much-admired position as an Irish poet in English drawing-rooms and from the fate of his friend Robert Emmet, it could be quite dangerous to speak out too boldly on behalf of Irish nationalism. As Moore says in "Oh! blame not the bard": "O'er the ruin her children in secret must sigh,/For 'tis treason to love her, and death to defend."[20]

The Irish poet may be compelled, as Moore says, "to try to forget, what he never can heal,"[21] but he does have one crucial political function, even in the

blackest of times: to keep alive the transcendent spirit of Ireland. This conception of the artist is at least as nationalist as it is romantic, and it leads to
precisely what Moore saw himself as doing in those English drawing-rooms
during early years of the century:

> The stranger shall hear thy lament on his plains;
> > The sigh of thy harp shall be sent o'er the deep,
> Till thy masters themselves, as they rivet thy chains,
> > Shall pause at the song of their captive, and weep![22]

Although for many Irish poets who followed Moore, causing the English to
weep was not nearly a sufficient poetic ambition, Moore's importance for those
poets, and for the development of Irish cultural nationalism in the nineteenth
century in general, is not to be denied.

IRELAND TRANSLATED

On a visit to West Cork in 1723, Jonathan Swift recorded his impressions of the local landscape in verse written in Latin. William Dunkin, the eighteenth-century Irish poet who later translated Swift's "Carberiae Rupes," was given to writing Latin and English versions of the same poem, usually publishing them side by side. Indeed, when an Irish poet of the eighteenth century thought about translation, his mind turned naturally to classical texts, as did that of his counterpart on the other side of the Irish Sea. A century later, Irish poets looking for literary inspiration were finding it not in ancient Greece and Rome but rather in the long and rich tradition of writing in the Irish language. Although the roots of this development lie in the eighteenth century, as indicated by James Macpherson's fraudulent versions of Ossian in the early 1760s and Charlotte Brooke's 1789 volume, *Reliques of Irish Poetry,* it is in the nineteenth century that translation begins to dominate and define Irish writing in English. The movement started in earnest with the publication in 1831 of James Hardiman's *Irish Minstrelsy,* stimulated the establishment of several periodicals committed to reviving Ireland's native literature (*The Dublin Penny Journal* in 1832, *Dublin University Magazine* in 1833), and proceeded steadily through James Clarence Mangan's best work in the 1840s to Samuel Ferguson's ambitious attempts in the 1860s and 1870s to translate into English verse a number of prose epics from pre-Christian Ireland.

On the surface, the purpose of this enterprise was antiquarian, to recover a culture that was, like the language in which it was written, threatened with extinction. This interest in translation developed at the same time that the Irish language suffered its most alarming decline. (It is estimated that between 1788 and 1851, the percentage of Irish-speaking people in Ireland fell from 50 to 25, in part as a result of the enormous influence of Daniel O'Connell's conviction that the Irish language was an impediment to Catholic emancipation and repeal of the Union.[1]) As a response to this culturally devastating problem, translation assumed that the disappearance of the Irish language could not be prevented, and the translation of so much Irish writing into English inevitably contributed to the steady decline of the Irish language throughout the nineteenth century. There were also literary and cultural, as opposed to antiquarian, motives behind the attention paid to translation. An Irish literature written in English but based on the tradition of writing in Irish, and carrying a distinctive imprint from the Irish language, might well be considered more truly national than the Irish writing done in English in Swift's day. At the very least, translations from the Irish could be cultivated by writers in Ireland as a means of differentiating themselves from English writers, and so of resisting the powerful influence of Victorian literature. More distinctively political motives were also at work in the translation movement, and the enterprise had distinctively political ramifications. On the one hand, antiquarianism pointed directly to nationalism and, more specifically, to Catholic liberation. The discovery of the wealth of the native literary tradition lent cultural authority to political movements on behalf of the oppressed Catholic majority and to separatist thinking in general, marginalizing the governing class of Anglo-Irish Protestants by reminding them that they were not really Irish.[2] Attempts to rescue the native literature through translation were inevitably read as nationalist in effect if not in intention; Mangan's translations were eagerly embraced by nationalists of all stripes, including the most militant, to whom the meaning of a poem such as "Dark Rosaleen" was as unambiguous as it was welcome. On the other hand, antiquarianism could also be regarded as a means of strengthening rather than shattering the Union of 1800. From this position, argued most effectively by Ferguson, the recovery of Ireland's native culture could reduce rather than aggravate sectarian and cultural differences both within Ireland and between Ireland and England. The precedent for this line of reasoning was to be found in Charlotte Brooke's argument in *Reliques of Irish Poetry* that the translation of Irish culture into the terms of English culture could not but help further the "cordial union between two countries that seemed formed by nature to be joined by every bond of interest, and of amity."[3] This point of view had special appeal to Anglo-Irish Protestants, who saw their political and cultural authority increasingly endangered by the rising tide of nationalist sentiment in the early decades of the nineteenth century. For Ferguson and others of his station, antiquarianism was very much a matter of class self-interest, and they were eager to see that the enterprise did not fall into the wrong hands. Thus Ferguson, in a series of scathing review articles of Hardiman's *Irish Minstrelsy,* accused Hardiman and his translators not just of making bad translations but also of pandering, in a dangerous way, to Catholic and nationalist interests.[4]

Whatever the motives of individual writers or groups of writers, and whether the past to be recovered was the distant, heroic past to which Ferguson gravitated or the more politically volatile past of Irish verse and song written during the Elizabethan and Cromwellian conquests, which attracted translators like Mangan and Edward Walsh, the development of translation as a primary means of recovering Ireland's "other" culture laid the groundwork for the literary revival at the end of the century. More generally, it helped redefine the concept of Ireland as a political and cultural entity. Both views of translation—that it could eventually lead to political separation from England and, alternatively, that it could be used to further some kind of mutual understanding and tolerance —rested on very different assumptions about the nature of Ireland from those held by writers like Swift and Dunkin. Moreover, translation tended to encourage an idealized view of Ireland, not merely as the victim of conquest or as a collection of contending peoples, but as the embodiment of a centuries-old and culturally rich tradition, a view that stands behind many of the political, social, and cultural transformations that characterize Irish life in the nineteenth century.

The translations of Mary Balfour (1780–1819) made material from the Irish tradition accessible to English-speaking people on both sides of the Irish Sea, but ultimately they were limited by their inability to break free from the essentially alien forms and rhythms of English verse. A schoolteacher who was the daughter of a Church of Ireland rector from Derry, Balfour published only one volume of poems: *Hope: A Poetical Essay* (1810), consisting of the lengthy, discursive, neo-Augustan title poem, some patriotic ballads, and a number of translations from the Irish. She also contributed eight translations to the second edition of Edward Bunting's *A General Collection of the Ancient Music of Ireland* (1809). It is more than coincidental that Thomas Moore's *Irish Melodies* were based on Bunting's versions of traditional Irish airs; the first number of *Irish Melodies* appeared two years before *Hope,* and many of Balfour's translations from the Irish are characterized by the same languid melancholy that marks Moore's early work, without, however, the submerged nationalist currents that animate the best of Moore's writing. Balfour's versions also tend more to fall into the iambic norm of English verse. Nevertheless, they are on the whole no worse than Charlotte Brooke's, or those of several of her contemporaries whose reputations exceeded hers and whose work has survived to the present day. The novelist Gerald Griffin's version of a seventeenth-century Irish love song, "Eibhlín a rún," for example, is commonly considered part of the standard canon of nineteenth-century Irish writing, while Balfour's more accomplished version of the same poem is long forgotten. Both translations can be accused of betraying the spirit of the original, both excise the graphic sexual language and imagery of the Irish song, and both are plagued by conventional poetic diction and predictable iambic rhythms. But Balfour's final image of an ageing lover is more concretely realized than the abstractions with which Griffin concludes his translation. First, Griffin's final stanza:

> Youth must with time decay,
>   Aileen aroon!
> Beauty must fade away,
>   Aileen aroon!
> Castles are sacked in war,
> Chieftains are scattered far,
> Truth is a fixed star,
>   Aileen aroon![5]

Here is Balfour's conclusion:

> Long has this silvered hair,
>   Ellen a Roon,
> Sighed in the wintry air,
>   Ellen a Roon:
> But when your star I view,
> Still beats my heart so true,
> Still thinks of love and you,
>   Ellen a Roon.[6]

Like Charlotte Brooke before her and Samuel Ferguson after her, Balfour wrote from a position of assumed cultural superiority and, like Brooke and Ferguson, she seemed motivated by a desire to bring the Irish tradition not just to the surface but also into some kind of accord with the English tradition. In her narrative poem "Kathleen O'Neil," an Englishman traveling in Ireland encounters a ghost who turns out to be "one of the ladies of the O'Neil family," who had been carried off by the banshees and endowed with immortality.[7] It is later explained that this vision is granted only to the Irish, and the English traveler, because his glimpse of Kathleen O'Neil suggests an inherent sympathy with Irish culture, is taken to an Irish castle where he learns more about the powerful O'Neil clan. The poem concludes with a patriotic lyric entitled "My native Erin." The English traveler asks to be read as a self-image of Balfour and her class in Ireland: always to some degree strangers, but also willing to participate in that other culture separated from them by religion, class, and centuries of discord.

The importance of Thomas Furlong (1794–1827) to the history of translation from the Irish has less to do with the quality of his work—which is, on the whole, not substantially better than that of Mary Balfour—than with the place where most of it first appeared: Hardiman's *Irish Minstrelsy,* a collection of translations by five different hands published in 1831 and the object of a famous, scathing review by the young Samuel Ferguson. At first glance, Furlong might seem an unlikely candidate for such attention. He was the son of a

Co. Wexford farmer, and as a young man was apprenticed to a Dublin grocer. His propensity for writing verse first attracted the notice of John Jameson, better known for distilling whisky than discerning poetic merit, who gave Furlong some of the support that he needed; one result was the publication, in 1819, of a collection gloomily entitled *The Misanthrope*. Although Furlong was during these years an ardent advocate of Catholic emancipation and a friend of Daniel O'Connell, the poems in this volume have little to do with Irish culture. But five years later, in a privately printed edition, Furlong published a satirical poem entitled "The Plagues of Ireland." About this time, Hardiman, searching for translators to help with his project to rescue from oblivion "the literary remains of a people once so distinguished in the annals of learning," [8] invited Furlong to render into English verse some of Hardiman's own literal prose translations of Irish poems and songs. Furlong's immediate response to the opportunity evinces astonishing ignorance of, and consequent prejudice toward, the Irish tradition. As Hardiman tells the story in his "Memoir" of Furlong: "Acquainted only with the English words associated with our native airs, he smiled incredulously at the asserted poetical excellence of the original lyrics, and even questioned their existence. . . . 'If,' said he, 'they possess any merit, I cannot conceive how they could have remained so long unknown'." [9] Whatever its accuracy, this story played nicely into Ferguson's hands. Three years after the publication of *Irish Minstrelsy* (and seven years after Furlong's untimely death from consumption), Ferguson attacked Hardiman's volume for perpetuating cultural fraud. Writing in part out of sectarian and political motives—he read Hardiman as a fanatical Catholic and a committed separatist—and writing for the readership of the unionist *Dublin University Magazine,* Ferguson argued that the translations were counter-productive, "so unlike the originals both in sentiment and style, as to destroy alike the originality and the interest of Irish minstrelsy for those who can only appreciate it through such a medium." [10] Furlong came in for particularly harsh words: "Mr. Furlong is now no more, and as he has left behind him nothing worthy to live, so must his name also so soon pass from the precincts of an obscure fame." [11] Although this obloquy was to some extent unwarranted, there is more than a little truth to Ferguson's charge that Hardiman's translators were in general guilty of "a morbid desire . . . to elevate the tone of the original to a pitch of refined poetic art altogether foreign from the whole genius and *rationale* of its composition." [12] Unfortunately for Furlong and the four other translators who contributed to Hardiman's volume (Henry Grattan Curran, John Dolton, William Hamilton Drummond, and Edward Lawson), Ferguson's four-part review of *Irish Minstrelsy* was enormously influential (and is still regarded today as a central document in the history of nineteenth-century Irish poetry).

From the point of view of cultural nationalism, as opposed to Ferguson's cultural unionism, Furlong's heart eventually came to be in the right place, even if his poetic talent was never quite equal to the task. In 1827, just before he died, he wrote a poem entitled "The Spirit of Irish Song," which invests Irish art with distinctive, superior qualities:

> Lov'd land of the bards and saints! to me
> There's nought so dear as thy minstrelsy;
> Bright is Nature in every dress,
> Rich in unborrowed loveliness;
> Winning in every shape she wears;
> Winning she is in thine own sweet airs;
> What to the spirit more cheering can be
> Than the lay whose ling'ring notes recall
> The thoughts of the holy, the fair, the free,
> Belov'd in life, or deplor'd in their fall!
> Fling, fling, the forms of art aside—
> Dull is the ear that these forms enthrall;
> Let the simple songs of our sires be tried—
> They go to the heart, and the heart is all.[13]

The poem rests on a thoroughly romantic identification of Irish art with all that is natural and an implied identification of non-Irish (that is, English) art with an inhibiting artificiality. Furlong was not, however, able to take his own advice about what Irish art should be, largely because he was unable to fling aside the forms of the art of his friend Thomas Moore. Almost all his translations in *Irish Minstrelsy* are shaped by the iambic/anapaestic rhythms of Moore's verse, as well as by Moore's obsession with harmonious sound effects. Furlong's version of the famous "Roisín Dubh," the sixteenth-century Irish poem that Mangan was to transform into one of the nationalist landmarks of nineteenth-century Irish poetry in English, is hard to distinguish from many of Moore's *Irish Melodies:*

> Long, long with my dearest, thro' strange scenes I've gone,
> O'er mountains and broad valleys I still have toil'd on;
> O'er the Erne I have sail'd as the rough gales blew,
> While the harp pour'd its music for my Roisin Dubh.[14]

And when Furlong turns to translating the songs of Turlough Carolan, thereby carrying on the eighteenth century's fascination with the blind Irish harper, the rhythms are Moore's, not Carolan's, as is evident in these lines from "Peggy Corcoran":

> The nobles of Spain have been seen at her side,
>> They have paus'd in delight on her beauty to gaze—
> But come, fill the wine, be the goblet supplied,
>> And each string that I touch shall ring loud in her praise.[15]

That last anapaestic tetrameter line, which relies for its harmony in part on an internal rhyme between a stressed and a relatively unstressed syllable, testifies to Furlong's considerable skill in picking up the subtleties of Moore's verse.

Ferguson's argument that Hardiman's translators tended to refine out of their versions the concrete details that characterize the originals identified a problem that seemed to plague many early translators, who worked to convert Irish verse and song into the forms and conventions of English poetry. Moore's melodies are frequently guilty of embracing poetic generalizations and abstractions that look back specifically to eighteenth-century English verse rather than to the Irish tradition, and Furlong's translations follow Moore's in this regard. What is at stake here can perhaps best be seen by comparing versions of the same Irish poem by Ferguson and Furlong. In his review of *Irish Minstrelsy,* Ferguson provided a number of "corrective" translations of his own, including his well-known "Cashel of Munster," a poem that is remarkable not only for its flexible rhythms, resisting the English tradition's emphasis on differences between stressed and unstressed syllables, but also for the ways in which it is built around specific details. The oft-quoted first stanza provides an example of both these qualities:

> I'd wed you without herds, without money, or rich array,
> And I'd wed you on a dewy morning at day-dawn grey;
> My bitter woe it is, love, that we are not far away
> In Cashel town, though the bare deal board were our marriage-bed this day![16]

The reference to the "bare deal board" is in the original, "Caiseal Mumhan" —the corresponding line reads, "i gCaiseal Mumhan is gan de leaba fúinn ach clár *bog* déil" [17]—but in Furlong's version it disappears, as Furlong presses the unfamiliar Irish material into the familiar confines of English poetic form and diction:

> I would wed thee my dear girl without herds or land,
> Let me claim as a portion but thy own white hand;
> On each soft dewy morn shall I bless thy charms,
> And clasp thee all fondly in my anxious arms.

> It grieves me, my fairest, still here to stay,
> To the south, to the south love! let us haste away;

There plainly, but fondly, shall thy couch be spread,
And this breast be as a pillow to support thy head.[18]

As the title of his first book of poems, *The Misanthrope,* suggests, there was a dark streak of melancholy in Furlong. According to one account, he lived alone, shunned all human company, including that of servants, religious ministers, and physicians, and rarely left his house.[19] His melacholy is most evident in work that falls outside the boundaries of translation. In this regard, he is an inheritor of Thomas Dermody's romanticism, as opposed to Moore's less dramatic brand, and some of his poetry in this vein does not deserve the oblivion to which it has been consigned. For example, "The Doom of Derenzie," a long narrative poem published in 1829, two years after Furlong's death, is written in a remarkably supple blank verse and shot through with Gothic effects, while managing to remain sensitive to particular human emotion, as is evident in this description of a wizard named Wrue learning that his young, unmarried daughter is with child:

> Who shall tell
> Or think what Wrue experienc'd as he learn'd
> The story of her ruin?—Through his frame
> There ran a sudden chillness—his aged head
> Grew giddy—in their sockets his dim eyes
> Turn'd wildly—and upon his lips appear'd
> A strange foul tinge of blackness. On that evening
> A burning fever seiz'd him, and he lay
> In wild and lonely misery;—so went by
> With him ten long sad days, and on the last,
> When reason came again, and he could bear
> The light that shone around, he turn'd and call'd
> Upon his Margaret—thrice he call'd—she came not—
> Nor from that gloomy morn did his sad eye
> Ever behold the maiden.[20]

Charles Gavan Duffy included one of Furlong's poems in his influential collection, *The Ballad Poetry of Ireland,* and in introducing Furlong to his readers, he made the acute observation that Furlong's achievement came "at a time when he had to create a reading public in the country."[21] This problem confronted writers like Mangan and Ferguson as well—in some ways, it was the central problem for all nineteenth-century Irish poets writing in English— but Furlong was something of a pioneer in this regard, and he helped create the readership for later poets and translators whose work surpassed his own.

It is not surprising that Hardiman failed to invite the Cork-born poet J. J.

Callanan (1795–1829) to contribute to *Irish Minstrelsy;* indeed, it is likely that
he had never heard of him. By the mid-1820s, this reclusive, little-known
young man had appeared in print only once—six of his translations from the
Irish were published in *Blackwood's Magazine* in 1823—and his first collection
of poems was not published until 1830, the year after his death.[22] Moreover,
unlike Furlong, Callanan had no patron like John Jameson, and his restless
wandering through West Cork had brought him in the way of none of the
people at the center of Ireland's literary life in the 1820s. But had Hardiman
seen, and been able to appreciate, Callanan's six translations in *Blackwood's,*
his collection might have had a markedly more authentic cast. Partly because
he knew the language, and partly because he had experienced native Irish
culture with some intimacy, Callanan managed to translate a number of Irish
songs and poems into an English verse that, especially when compared with
the work of someone like Furlong, was remarkably true to many of the distinctive qualities of Irish verse. According to George Sigerson, whose collection,
Bards of the Gael and the Gall, was to carry the antiquarian enterprise of
translation into the literary revival at the end of the century, Callanan was the
first Irish poet "to give adequate versions of Irish Gaelic poems." [23]

The man responsible for this relative breakthrough was a self-made romantic;
like Dermody and Furlong, Callanan lived a life marked chiefly by tortured
perceptions of himself as an outcast and a victim. In Lisbon the year of his
death, he wrote in his journal, "what a dark waste I leave behind." [24] Born in
Cork to an apparently pious Catholic couple, Callanan attended Maynooth for
several years before deciding that the priesthood was not for him. He wandered
the corridors of Trinity College for two years—he was enrolled as a medical
student, but his only academic distinction was two poetry prizes—and then
drifted in and out of Cork, and into the hills and glens of West Cork, in search
of Irish songs and stories. His commitment to this enterprise was, like so much
else in his life, hedged round with self-doubt. He wrote to Thomas Crofton
Croker, who was also collecting Irish folk materials in West Cork at the time,
that he had decided to take up translation as "a serious occupation," because
the field was "a department where I should find few or no antagonists." [25]
When he published one group of translations, he prefaced his work with a
curiously disaffected statement: "The following songs are specimens of the
popular poetry of later days. I have translated them as closely as possible, and
present then to the public more as literary curiosities than on any other account." [26] Less came from all this than even what little Callanan might have
hoped for; his projected volume of translations, *Munster Melodies,* never mate-
rialized, and at the time of his death, he had published only a handful of poems
in a few periodicals.

Still, Callanan's achievement is considerable, and out of proportion to the
limited quantity of his published work. Like Mangan and Ferguson, and other

translators who began working later in the century, Callanan was a cultural archeologist, committed to unearthing and preserving literary and folk artifacts threatened with extinction as the hold of the Irish language on the culture continued to weaken. Callanan's versions of the Irish songs and poems he found in the wilds of West Cork, written in an English verse notably sensitive to the assonantal patterns and flexible rhythms of poetry in Irish, represented a translation of the Irish-language tradition less overtly intended for an English audience than were Moore's *Irish Melodies,* and more willing to put its poetic trust in the provincial as opposed to the cosmopolitan. Moreover, by leaning away from the central forms and conventions of English verse, Callanan's translations insisted on the validity of the Irish tradition, and so resisted the powerful tendency to see Irish-language poetry as a lower form of art that stood only to gain by being made to conform to the allegedly more civilized conventions of the dominant English tradition. Although Callanan was unquestionably influenced by Moore and the English romantics, particularly Byron, his work also resisted the tendency to refine away or gloss over the unfamiliar, somewhat rough-edged aspects of the native Irish experience, including strong anti-English feeling. Indeed, Callanan anticipates Mangan in his ability to fuse his own personal experience of loss and disaffection with a nationalist interpretation of the condition of post-Union Ireland.

Although Callanan's most significant work is his translations, he spells out his aesthetics in several original poems, including the lengthy, semi-meditative "The Recluse of Inchidony," which Yeats unfairly dismissed as "a bad poem in the manner of *Childe Harold.*" [27] Set on the island of Inchidony, just south of Clonakilty, and bearing some resemblance to Wordsworth's *The Prelude* as well as to Byron, "The Recluse of Inchidony" defines Callanan's poetic personality as shaped by loneliness and alienation ("No friend but this wild lyre,— no heritage but song" [28]), and yearns, in true romantic fashion, for a long-lost innocence. But the position of an Irish poet at the beginning of the nineteenth century was not the same as that of an English poet at that time, and the pressures of political reality eventually lead "The Recluse of Inchidony" away from a strictly meditative mode and toward a consideration of the condition of Ireland, identified with Callanan's own sense of alienation and oppression. Callanan's nationalism is not exactly militant, at least by the standards of the later Young Ireland and Fenian movements; at one point, the narrator of "The Recluse of Inchidony" addresses England with these words: "O may the minstrel never live to see/Against thy sons the flag of green unfurl'd." [29] But his nationalism is more directly expressed than is Thomas Moore's, and it is inextricably bound up with both his romanticism and his antiquarianism. The links among romanticism, antiquarianism, and nationalism—the trinity that informs much Irish poetry written in English in the nineteenth century—are explored in Callanan's "Gougane Barra," which takes as its romantic setting a lake in a remote, mountainous region of West Cork associated with St. Finbar, allegedly the founder of Cork City, because of a holy island in the middle. In Callanan's hands, this place of traditional religious significance is transformed into an embodiment not just of the romantic qualities of innocence and natural beauty but also of Ireland's Gaelic civilization, seen as threatened with corruption if not extinction at the hands of the dominant English culture. This double sense of corruption—of innocence by experience, and of the Gaelic tradition by the English—is figured in the River Lee, which originates at Gougane Barra and flows down to and through Cork City. Callanan identifies himself with the Gaelic poets, whom he sees laboring under the shadow of "the Saxon's dark bondage and slaughter,"[30] and defines his own poetic ambitions in terms of cultural recovery:

> High sons of the lyre, oh! how proud was the feeling,
> To think while alone through that solitude stealing,
> Though loftier Minstrels green Erin can number,
> I only awoke your wild harp from its slumber,
> And mingled once more with the voice of those fountains,
> The songs even echo forgot on her mountains,
> And gleaned each grey legend, that darkly was sleeping
> Where the mist and the rain o'er their beauty was creeping.[31]

This antiquarian impulse has both nationalist and romantic implications. On the one hand, the poem expresses the hope that an awareness of the Irish tradition, and so of what is at risk in the colonialization of Ireland, will inspire efforts toward cultural and political independence: "Still, still in those wilds may young liberty rally,/ And send her strong shout over mountains and valley."[32] At the same time, the poet himself, should he succeed in bringing this about, is guaranteed a romantically conceived immortality: "I too shall be gone;—but my name shall be spoken/Where Erin awakes, and her fetters are broken."[33]

Callanan comes closest to realizing these considerable ambitions in the best of his translations. Often focused sympathetically on marginal, subversive figures—a prisoner in "The Convict of Clonmel," an outlaw in "The Outlaw of Loch Lene," an Irish leader with a reputation for trouble-making in "Dirge of O'Sullivan Bear"—these poems not only refuse to sentimentalize or Anglicize native Irish experience, but they also carry implicit messages that specifically invite interpretations along nationalist lines. At the same time, they serve as imaginative versions of Callanan's tortured self-perceptions. "Dirge of O'Sullivan Bear" encourages a nationalist reading in part by relying on an unflinching realism to retell the legendary story of how Morty Oge O'Sullivan of Bearhaven, "long . . . a turbulent character in the wild district he inhabited," as Cal-

lanan says in his notes to the poem,[34] was betrayed by his servant Scully and
shot while defending his castle against an English attack. As the story has it,
O'Sullivan's body was then dragged through the sea from Bearhaven to Cork,
where his head was cut off and placed on a spike near the jail. Callanan's
version of the story focuses graphically on these potentially inflammatory details, while placing O'Sullivan in the tradition of nationalist martyrs:

> Dear head of my darling,
> How gory and pale,
> These aged eyes saw thee
> High spiked on their gaol;
> That cheek in the summer sun
> Ne'er shall grow warm,
> Nor that eye e'er catch light,
> But the flash of the storm.[35]

The note of the traditional Irish lament runs throughout the poem, and the curse
on the betrayer Scully is delivered in terms that have inescapable implications
for an Ireland in the midst of the campaign for Catholic emancipation:

> Long may the curse
> Of his people pursue them;
> SCULLY that sold him,
> And soldier that slew him,
> One glimpse of Heaven's light
> May they see never;
> May the hearth-stove of hell
> Be their best bed for ever![36]

Moreover, these nationalist sentiments are embodied in specifically un-English
rhythms and sound patterns, linking nationalism and antiquarianism. Several
types of sound patterns taken from Irish-language poetry can be seen in this
passage: the muted rhyme between "curse" and "pursue," where the rhyme
shifts from a stressed to an unstressed syllable, as well as the assonantal link
between the terminal "sold him" and the medial "soldier" in the following
line. "The Outlaw of Loch Lene," another of Callanan's translations narrated
by sympathetic but socially marginalized characters serving both as embodi-
ments of Ireland in relation to England and as projections of Callanan's romantic self-image, is especially notable for its longer, even more flexible line,
constructed around various kinds of assonantal links. Indeed, this poem of
frustrated love clearly anticipates the "wavering" long line of Mangan and
Ferguson that Yeats so admired:

O would that a freezing sleet-winged tempest did sweep,
And I and my love were alone far off on the deep!
I'd ask not a ship, or a bark, or a pinnace to save,—
With her hand round my waist, I'd fear not the wind or the wave.

'Tis down by the lake where the wild tree fringes its sides,
The maid of my heart, the fair one of Heaven resides—
I think as at eve she wanders its mazes along,
The birds go to sleep by the sweet wild twist of her song.[37]

When Callanan departs from this distinctively Irish voice, it is usually because of the heavy influence of Byron and the English tradition. "The Recluse of Inchidony," for example, is written in Spenserian stanzas, a form that was not likely to inspire much sympathy among Callanan's Irish readers, especially those living in Cork. Callanan also occasionally falls under the powerful spell of Moore, especially in the Jacobite songs included in his translations from the Irish, poems in which a nationalist position is never far from the surface. The singular music of Moore's liquid blend of iambs and anapaests, and the melancholy passivity that informs his nationalism, can be heard in what is arguably the best of Callanan's Jacobite songs, "O Say My Brown Drimin":

My strong ones have fallen—from the bright eye of day,
All darkly they sleep in their dwelling of clay;
The cold turf is o'er them;—they hear not my cries,
And since Louis no aid gives I cannot arise.[38]

This poem also contains, however, one of those graphic images that tie Callanan so closely to the Irish tradition, and resist the polishing that Moore so often gave his Irish materials:

When the Prince, now an exile, shall come for his own,
The isles of his father, his rights and his throne,
My people in battle the Saxons will meet,
And kick them before, like old shoes from their feet.[39]

At moments such as these, which are quite frequent in Callanan's work, the truth of Charles Gavan Duffy's judgment of Callanan seems self-evident; Callanan's translations, Duffy said—and Duffy included six of Callanan's poems in *The Ballad Poetry of Ireland*—"preserve the idiomatic peculiarities of the language to a wonderful degree, and are among the most racy and characteristic we possess." [40]

In the fragment of autobiography that he wrote near the end of his life, James

Clarence Mangan (1803–1849) remarked that he shared with Moore "the honor, or the disreputability,—as it may be considered,—of having been born the son of a grocer." [41] The parallels between these two dominant figures in nineteenth-century Irish writing begin and end with that coincidence; indeed, Mangan's significance to the development of Irish poetry in English might well be defined in terms of the differences between his art and Moore's. Whereas Moore's aesthetics can be traced back to eighteenth-century, neo-classical English verse, Mangan writes from a decidedly romantic position, and one shaped largely by German rather than English romantic thinking. While Moore played calculatedly and even shamelessly to an English audience, Mangan seemed completely indifferent to English opinion, publishing all his works in Ireland. And whereas the nationalist implications of Moore's art are often muffled by the mesmerizing qualities of his harmonious verse or cloaked in a carefully constructed suggestiveness necessary to his position as an Irish poet writing and performing for English audiences, Mangan's poems about Ireland, responding in part to the intense political realities of the 1840s and driven by a tendency to identify the miseries of his own life with the condition of Ireland, are marked by a passion and urgency not observable before him in Irish poetry, with the possible exception of Swift at his most aggravated. Juxtaposing Mangan's famous translation "Dark Rosaleen" against one of Moore's more effectively nationalist poems, "The Irish Peasant to His Mistress," reveals the extent to which Mangan, writing on the heels of Moore's *Irish Melodies,* carried the art of translation into romantic and overtly nationalist territory. Moore's poem operates at a relatively abstract level, and is constructed around a perfectly balanced dichotomy between Ireland and England, and more specifically between the Irish Catholic church and the English Anglican church, that suggests harmony and restraint rather than disjunction or urgency. The second stanza of the poem plainly demonstrates these qualities:

> Thy rival was honour'd, while thou wert wrong'd and scorn'd,
> Thy crown was of briers, while gold her brows adorn'd;
> She woo'd me to temples, while thou lay'st hid in caves,
> Her friends were all masters, while thine, alas! were slaves;
> Yet cold in the earth, at thy feet, I would rather be,
> Than wed what I lov'd not, or turn one thought from thee.[42]

Mangan's poem, by comparison, just barely manages to keep feeling under control. Constructed around frenzied, litany-like repetitions, informed by a strong sense of the personal, and daringly conflating images of religion, love, and warfare, it works to evoke in a highly charged way the spiritual qualities ascribed to Ireland with relative serenity in Moore's lines:

Over dews, over sands
   Will I fly for your weal;
Your holy delicate white hands
   Shall girdle me with steel.
At home . . . in your emerald bowers,
   From morning's dawn till e'en,
You'll pray for me, my flower of flowers,
   My Dark Rosaleen!
   My fond Rosaleen!
You'll think of me through Daylight's hours,
My virgin flower, my flower of flowers,
   My Dark Rosaleen![43]

Whatever the realities of his life, which are by no means undisputed, Mangan certainly cultivated a romantic image of himself as a man cursed with an incurable melancholy, forced to live in extreme economic deprivation, and inevitably alienated from his fellow-men: an image very much of a pattern with the lives of several romantically inclined Irish poets who preceded him, including Thomas Dermody in the eighteenth century and Furlong and Callanan in the nineteenth. "A ruined soul in a wasted form" is how he described himself in his autobiography,[44] and as if to guarantee the alienation so crucial to this self-image, he courted eccentricity with considerable flair and success. As his friend Charles Gavan Duffy remarked, Mangan, attired in his long blue cloak and tall witch's hat from which his thin gold hair trailed, "looked like the spectre of some German romance rather than a living creature."[45] He was the son of a Catholic grocer in Fishamble Street, Dublin, he reported in his autobiography, and during his adolescence his family's fortunes, like those of many middle-class Irish families in the 1820s, suffered a steady decline, until Mangan was forced to give up his education and go to work as a scrivener. The work was no doubt stifling to one of Mangan's apparently oversensitive nature, and he did put in long hours. It is unlikely, however, that his autobiography, written when Mangan's health and sanity were under severe stress, and in an obvious effort to make his life over in the terms of his own romantic self-image, should be trusted in its claim that he worked from morning to midnight every day, or in its depiction of his fellow-scriveners as "serpents and scorpions and all hideous and monstrous things, which writhed and hissed around me, and discharged their slime and venom over my person."[46] In the early 1830s, Mangan started publishing poems, many of them colored by an unhealthy, morose melancholy ("A Broken-Hearted Lay," "My Mausoleum," "Life Is the Desert and the Solitude"), in *The Comet*, a Dublin literary periodical, and translations from German in *The Dublin Penny Journal*, edited by the musician and antiquarian George Petrie. In 1838, having, through Petrie, come to know the Irish scholars Eugene O'Curry and John O'Donovan, Mangan secured a post in the Dublin office of the Ordnance Survey, an ambitious project to map Ireland and research its local place-names and traditions, and here Mangan probably acquired what knowledge he had of the Irish language. The British government ended the project three years later, and Mangan found work as an assistant cataloguer at Trinity College Library, where he apparently worked, on and off, until 1848. There is some evidence that by the late 1830s Mangan was an alcoholic and possibly addicted to opium as well (not the only basis of comparison to Edgar Allen Poe). He was dismissed from his Trinity College post, and seems to have spent his last months in homeless wandering, extreme poverty, and recurrent illness. He died a victim of starvation or possibly cholera, and, as if to verify his image of himself as the lonely, alienated artist, his funeral was attended by five (some say three) people.[47]

That image is projected in much of Mangan's poetry, sometimes indirectly, as in his translations, at other times quite explictly, as in the many poems of personal complaint that Mangan wrote in the early 1830s and in his last years. As Yeats once observed, Mangan "brought one thing into the world that was not there before, one new thing into letters—his misery."[48] The persistent melancholy that permeates these poems may owe something to at least one unsuccessful love affair; Mangan's "A Broken-Hearted Lay," for example, speaks of both "the dark ingratitude of man" and "the hollower perfidy of woman."[49] But the deep-seated philosophical scepticism observable in a number of these poems seems part of the nineteenth-century crisis of religious doubt. The first stanza of "The One Mystery," for example, is comparable to some of the lyrics of despair that Tennyson wrote during the 1830s and 1840s, and later published as *In Memoriam:*

> 'Tis idle! we exhaust and squander
>   The glittering mine of thought in vain;
> All-baffled reason cannot wander
>   Beyond her chain.
> The flood of life runs dark—dark clouds
>   Make lampless night around its shore:
> The dead, where are they? In their shrouds—
>   Man knows no more.[50]

On the whole, Mangan's poetry in this vein tends to be more effective when cast in dramatic frameworks rather than directly confessional modes. "Twenty Golden Years Ago," for example, is written from the compelling point of view of a man sitting in a German café and looking back over his life, while in "Siberia," Mangan's feelings of desolation are projected through an imagined wasteland landscape, a striking anticipation of one of the central symbols of modernist art:

> In Siberia's wastes
>   Are sands and rocks.
> Nothing blooms of green or soft,
> But the snow-peaks rise aloft
>   And the gaunt ice-blocks.
>
> And the exile there
>   Is one with those;
> They are part, and he is part,
> For the sands are in his heart,
>   And the killing snows.[51]

The landscape of "Siberia" has more than psychological implications or metaphysical significance. The poem was published in the spring of 1846, just months after the first large-scale failure of Ireland's potato crop, at the beginning of the devastating famine that transformed the landscape of rural Ireland into a Siberia of suffering and death. In general, the work upon which Mangan's reputation chiefly rests, his translations from the Irish, invites being read in the context of Ireland's political, social, and economic condition in the 1840s. And Mangan sounds a distinctly anti-English as well as un-English note in his versions of Irish poems. From the point of view of the English tradition, there is, for example, something undeniably subversive, formally as well as thematically, about Mangan's "O'Hussey's Ode to the Maguire." The poem is based on an early seventeenth-century poem about the Irish leader Hugh Maguire, who took part in the long march from Ulster to Munster that culminated in the decisive defeat of the Irish by Elizabeth's forces at the Battle of Kinsale in 1601. Abandoning not just the iambic norm of English verse but also the mellifluous iambic-anapaestic rhythms popularized by Moore, Mangan constructs a long, extremely flexible line built loosely around the kinds of assonantal and consonantal links that characterize poetry in Irish:

> Though he were even a wolf ranging the round green woods,
> Though he were even a pleasant salmon in the unchainable sea,
> Though he were a wild mountain eagle, he could scarce bear, he,
> This sharp, sore sleet, these howling floods.[52]

The poem concludes with a violent, not to say incendiary, image: *"But the memory of the lime-white mansions his right hand hath laid/In ashes warms the hero's heart!"* [53] "O'Hussey's Ode to the Maguire" demonstrates the extent to which Mangan was willing to depart from his sources to rewrite the original in terms of a romantic concept of the victim-hero in accord with his own self-image. It is instructive, in this regard, to read Mangan's version against an unrhymed translation published by Ferguson in his 1834 review of Hardiman's *Irish Minstrelsy,* a translation from which Mangan was probably working. Here, for example, is Ferguson's sixth quatrain:

> In the country of Clan Daire
> It grieves me that his fate should be so severe:
> Perhaps drenched with the cold wet dropping of the thickets,
> Perhaps exposed to the high heaven's floods.[54]

In Mangan's version of this passage, that hedging "perhaps" is nowhere to be found. Moreover, flying in the face of the fact that Maguire was traveling through Ireland with an army, Mangan makes his hero into a lost, lonely figure that bears more resemblance to Mangan's tortured image of himself than it does to the historical Hugh Maguire:

> It is my bitter grief—it cuts me to the heart—
> That in the country of Clan Darry this should be his fate!
> O, woe is me, where is he? Wandering, houseless, desolate,
> Alone, without or guide or chart![55]

Mangan's romantic conception of himself as an alienated artist, and his romantic emphasis in general on individualism, not to say eccentricity, differentiates his art from both the inevitably depersonalized nationalist verse of a writer such as Thomas Davis and the scholarly objectivity of a translator such as Ferguson. What is perhaps most remarkable about Mangan's translations from the Irish, which may account in large part for Yeats's attraction to Mangan, is that at the same time that they advance both nationalism and antiquarianism, they manage, through the romantic nature of the aesthetic that drives all of Mangan's writing, to maintain a certain distance from both enterprises, and so to interrogate, implicitly at least, the basic assumptions of both. By stamping his translations so plainly with the mark of his own romantic individualism, Mangan might be said to call into question the entire enterprise of translation, a literary enterprise that sees language ideally as a transparent medium of cultural exchange.[56] The very quality that gives Mangan's translations so much of their emotional force—the tendency to internalize political and social reality, to see Ireland's victimization at the hands of the English as a macrocosmic version of his own suffering and alienation—maintains a strong personal pressure that resists the self-effacement required of a fully committed nationalist aesthetic. Mangan's translations insist on seeing nationalist priorities in the context of other, often competing, concerns, including religious faith and romantic concepts of the centrality of self.

By most accounts, Mangan was a remarkably apolitical person until very near the end of his life. Duffy, who knew Mangan well from the late 1830s through the 1840s, reports that when he started *The Nation* in 1842, and Mangan began contributing to it, Mangan steered clear of the political associations and commitments around which the magazine was founded:

> I thought the gifted and gallant young men associated in the enterprise, who were afterwards known as "Young Irelanders," would bring him companions for his mind and heart for the first time and that his slumbering nationality would be awakened by their design to raise up their country anew and place a sceptre in her hands. But his habit of isolation had hardened; he shuddered at the idea of social intercourse. He refused to come to our weekly suppers, and I could only make him known to them individually from time to time.[57]

Mangan did not openly embrace nationalism until 1848—the fourth harrowing year of the famine, and the year of the disastrous Young Ireland rising and the resulting arrest, imprisonment, and exile of a number of Young Irelanders whom Mangan knew personally. When he did, he did so with all the passion of his nature and all the zeal of the religious convert, as this passage from a letter that he wrote to John Mitchel in 1848 demonstrates: "I promise, in a special manner . . . that I will begin in earnest to labour for my country henceforward, and that, come weal or woe, life or death, glory or shame, the triumphal chariot or the gallows, I will adhere to the fortunes of my fellow-patriots." [58] This kind of language was bound to please militant nationalists like Mitchel, an extremely influential pioneer in the reading of Mangan's entire life and career through a nationalist lens, and a poem such as "Dark Rosaleen," with its charged fusion of the personal and the public, and its conflation of religious imagery, the language of passionate love, and images of violence, certainly invites a nationalist interpretation. But Mangan's best translations demonstrate an ability to negotiate between the self-effacing demands of nationalism and a romantic aesthetic that privileges the individual, and therefore to embody a complex relationship between nationalism and romanticism. One of these is certainly the "Lament over the Ruins of the Abbey of Teach Molaga," first published in *The Nation* in 1846. A comparison of this poem with a translation that Ferguson made from the same Irish original, usually attributed to the West Cork poet Seán Ó Coileáin (John Collins), reveals the strengths of Mangan's art. The subject of both poems, the Franciscan Abbey at Timoleague, in West Cork (not far from Callanan's Inchidony), was burned by an English force in 1642. Ferguson's version depoliticizes that past by emphasizing and universalizing

the abbey's decay over the years. It also describes the military destruction of
the abbey in relatively abstract terms:

> Oh! the hardship, oh! the hatred,
>   Tyranny, and cruel war,
> Persecution and oppression,
>   That have left you as you are![59]

Mangan's version is more rhetorically dramatic and more specific:

> Oh! woe, that Wrong should triumph thus!
> Woe that the olden right, the rule and the renown
> Of the Pure-souled and Meek should thus go down
>   Before the Tyrannous!
>
> Where wert thou, Justice, in that hour?
> Where was thy smiting sword? What had those good men done,
> That thou shouldst tamely see them trampled on
>   By brutal England's Power?[60]

But no sooner does Mangan sound that note most likely to appeal to the
nationalist sensibility than he shifts ground to a highly personal perspective,
from which the condition of Ireland, in 1642 or 1846, is forced into the background. The next stanza of the poem specifically describes this transformation:

> Alas! I rave! . . . If Change is here,
> Is it not o'er the land? Is it not too in me?
> Yes! I am changed even more than what I see.
>   Now is my last goal near![61]

Once the poem's focus is redirected from the abbey's decay and destruction,
representing the destruction of Ireland at the hands of the English, to the
speaker's feelings of approaching death, the historical realities and their nationalist implications recede, and the subjective romantic sensibility takes over.
This sensibility does not displace the historical or nationalist dimensions of the
poem; rather, they coexist in a dialogue in which each is seen in the context of
the other. This relationship is made clear in the poem's final stanza, for which
there is no corollary in the original poem or in Ferguson's translation, and in
which the speaker's sense of personal loss and decay is placed in a literally and
metaphorically resonating relationship with his country:

> I turned away, as toward my grave,
> And, all my dark way homeward by the Atlantic's verge,

Resounded in mine ears like to a dirge
The roaring of the wave.[62]

In a number of Mangan's translations, the personal as opposed to the communal (or nationalist) takes the form of individual religious faith. The extent and
nature of Mangan's commitment to the Catholicism of his upbringing are hard
to determine—he wrote in his autobiography that he had often been plagued
by doubts not "of the great truths of faith" but of "my own capacity . . . for
salvation"[63]—but in these poems, complaints about the condition of Ireland are
usually followed by the expression of hope for some kind of divine guidance, if
not intervention, rather than human action. In "Kathaleen Ny-Houlihan," a
version of an eighteenth-century Jacobite poem by the Munster poet Liam Ó
hIfearnáin (William Heffernan), Mangan's language is quite explicit and volatile in its characterization of Ireland's victimization by the English:

Sore disgrace it is to see the Arbitress of thrones,
Vassal to a *Saxoneen* of cold and sapless bones!
Bitter anguish wrings our souls—with heavy sighs and groans
We wait the Young Deliverer of Kathaleen Ny-Houlihan![64]

But this is followed by a call for prayer, and so the poem is, in some ways,
deflected from its nationalist implications:

Let us pray to Him who holds Life's issues in His hands—
Him who formed the mighty globe, with all its thousand lands;
Girding them with seas and mountains, rivers deep, and strands,
To cast a look of pity upon Kathaleen Ny-Houlihan![65]

This juxtaposition of nationalist complaint and religious resignation also governs one of Mangan's most highly regarded translations, the lengthy "Lament
for the Princes of Tyrone and Tyrconnell (Buried in Rome)," in which the
pagan *caoine,* associated specifically with the Irish culture whose decline at the
hands of the English is represented by the exiled sixteenth-century Irish leaders
whom the poem mourns, gives way at the poem's conclusion to a conventional
Christian appeal: "Embrace the faithful Crucifix,/And seek the path of pain and
prayer/Thy Savior trod."[66]

Mangan's life and art were wrapped in and inspired by such contradictions.
Behind them all was not just an ability to live with the condition of ambiguity
and uncertainty that has plagued so many Irish writers, caught between two
languages and two cultures, but a gift for constructing a unique body of art out
of that condition. When he was sixteen years old, Mangan wrote an autobiographical poem entitled, presumptuously enough, "Genius." It is not a very

accomplished piece of work, but it concludes with a remarkably prophetic image of "the untiring breast . . . scorning all, and shunned of all," traveling through "years and years of crushed hopes," and committed to one, strikingly Beckettian endeavor: "Searching a desolate Earth for that it findeth not." [67] That may be as close as it is possible to get to this elusive figure, arguably the most important Irish poet of the nineteenth century.

Writing to his publisher, John O'Daly, in 1844, Edward Walsh (1805–1850) described his forthcoming collection of translations from the Irish, *Reliques of Irish Jacobite Poetry,* as the work of a man who was "intimately acquainted with the manners and feelings of the people" and who felt "with all a poet's feeling, the curse and crime of the tyrant." [68] This statement is a fair assessment of what characterizes Walsh's work, and what distinguishes it from that of Mangan: a first-hand knowledge of Irish culture and the Irish language, and an unqualified commitment to the cause of Irish nationalism. Indeed, the fusion of antiquarianism and nationalism can be seen in Walsh's work with a clarity difficult if not impossible to find in the writing of any other nineteenth-century Irish poet. The son of a Cork militiaman, Walsh spent most of his boyhood and adolescence in the remote Co. Cork village of Millstreet, twenty miles east of Killarney. It was here that he learned Irish and, in the manner of Callanan before him, wandered the countryside collecting stories and songs in the native language. Walsh became politically active as a young man, and in the 1830s was imprisoned for participating in the campaign to eliminate the tithes that Catholics were forced to pay to the Church of Ireland. Like Mangan, he contributed to George Petrie's *Dublin Penny Journal* in the 1830s and, when *The Nation* was founded in 1842, he began publishing there as well. (It seems likely that Mangan and Walsh knew each other personally; they were both friends of Charles Gavan Duffy as well as of Petrie.) Walsh's nationalist convictions continued to get him into trouble; in 1842 he lost a post as a schoolteacher in Glaunthane because of a strongly pro-Repeal poem that he had published in *The Nation.* After a brief tenure as a sub-editor for a Dublin periodical, he returned to teaching, in a highly undesirable post at the Spike Island Convict Depot. Here, in 1848, he met the nationalist John Mitchel, who was then leaving Ireland under lock and key, having been sentenced to fourteen years' transportation for treason and felony. Judging by his account of the meeting in his *Jail Journal,* Mitchel was as bewildered as he was impressed with the fervency of Walsh's nationalist sentiments:

A tall gentleman-like person in black but rather over-worn clothes, came up to me and grasped my hands with every demonstration of reverence. . . . Tears stood in his eyes as he told me he had contrived to get an opportunity of seeing and shaking hands with me before I should leave Ireland. . . . He stooped down and kissed my hands. 'Ah!' he said, 'you are now the man in all Ireland most

to be envied.' . . . Perhaps this man does really envy me, and most assuredly I
do not envy him.[69]

The meeting apparently cost Walsh his job at Spike Island, and not long after
he took what was to be his last, and arguably his lowest, teaching post, at the
Cork Union Workhouse. He died in Cork in 1850.

Walsh's nationalism is evident in the poems he published in *The Nation*
during the 1840s. Little in these works distinguishes them from the heavily
didactic popular ballads that made up the core of that journal's published poetry,
but translation provided Walsh a means of projecting his nationalist convictions
onto an historical and dramatic backdrop that significantly enriched his writing.
In *Reliques of Irish Jacobite Poetry,* Walsh was establishing the validity of a
body of eighteen-century writing in Irish that was virtually unknown to Swift
and his circles in Anglo-Irish Dublin, while at the same time writing about
post-Union Ireland, a nation still under English rule and still yearning for a
Young Pretender, now in the form of Young Irelanders like Mitchel and Thomas
Davis, to redeem it. A comparison of Walsh's "Captivity of the Gael," a
translation of an eighteenth-century Jacobite poem by the Irish poet Eoghan
Ruadh Ó Súilleabháin (Owen Roe O'Sullivan), with a version of the same
poem by Mangan reveals the extent to which Walsh's translations are shaped
by his commitment to nationalism. Mangan's version is marked by his usual
romantic obsession with melancholy, and by his religious faith:

> Times have darkened . . . and now our holy
> Altars crumble, . . . and castles fall;
> > Our groans ring through Christendee.
> Still, despond not! He comes, though slowly
> He, the Man, who shall disenthral
> > The Proud Captive of Shane Bwee![70]

Walsh's translation of approximately the same passage has at least as much in
common with the nationalistic verse of *The Nation* as with the Jacobite tradition
from which it is taken:

> And O! the deep gloom of my wild-throbbing breast,
> > That men who should die to avenge her,
> See fair Erin smitten, evicted, oppress'd,
> > In chains of the treacherous stranger!
> And O! that the doom of the tyrant were come,
> > And the salt drops were dried that now fall free,
> And a proud nation's force could procure a divorce
> > From the dull, plodding plunderer, *Shaun Bui!*[71]

Walsh's separatist political views are closely associated with his sense of Ireland's linguistic crisis. In the introduction to his second collection of translations, *Irish Popular Songs* (1847), he describes that crisis as he experienced it in rural Munster:

> The writer of these remarks has been often painfully amused at witnessing the embarrassment of a family circle, where the parents, scarcely understanding a word of English, strove to converse with their children, who, awed by paternal command, and the dread of summary punishment at the hands of the pedagogue, were driven to essay a language of which the parents could scarcely comprehend a single word.[72]

This disjunction and its political consequences inform much of Walsh's poetry. In "A Lament for the Gael," for example, Walsh recasts the eighteenth-century poet William Heffernan's complaint about poets of his day writing songs to the popular air "Shaun Bui" into a nationalist protest against the replacement of Irish by English in the nineteenth century:

> Alas for the records of ages afar,
>   The chiefs of our olden day's glory,
> The shield of the stranger, the valiant in war,
>   The light of the *Seanachui's* story!
>   When billows of song
>   Pour'd their wild tide along,
> And minstrels' gay lays might enthral thee;
>   But our poets to-day
>   Have a new-fangled lay—
> They rhyme to the measure of *Shaun Bui!*[73]

In "Mo Craoibhin Cno," one of Walsh's best-known original lyrics (Mitchel, in his *Jail Journal* account of his meeting with Walsh on Spike Island, remembered Walsh as "author of *Mo Craoibhin Cno* and other sweet songs"[74]), the conventional contrast between the natural beauty of the country girl and the artificial sheen of the made-up city girl ("mo craoibhín cnó" means, figuratively, "my darling with nut-brown hair") is given specific political and linguistic significance:

> I've heard the songs by Liffy's wave
>   That maidens sung—
> They sung their land the Saxon's slave,
>   In Saxon tongue—
> Oh! bring me here that Gaelic dear

Which cursed the Saxon foe,
When thou didst charm my raptured ear,
Mo craoibhin cno!
And none but God's good angels near,
Mo craoibhin cno! [75]

The often blatantly nationalist motives of Walsh's poetry should not be allowed to obscure his genuinely antiquarian intentions or his considerable achievement in this area. Beginning with the view that the Irish language, with its "pleasing stream of liquid sounds," is particularly well-suited to lyric poetry, and that Irish verse is singularly successful at "the beautiful adaptation of the subject of the words to the song measure," Walsh says, in the introduction to *Irish Popular Songs,* that he has worked particularly hard in his translations to avoid "the fault of not suiting the measure of the translation to the exact song-tune of the original," [76] which he says may be observed specifically in the translations of Charlotte Brooke and of the contributors to Hardiman's *Irish Minstrelsy.* Walsh has a particularly good ear for the complex sound patterns around which Irish verse is constructed, as can be seen in the assonantal and alliterative links, and the various kinds of terminal and internal rhyme, employed in the opening stanza of "Captivity of the Gael":

> I wander'd the moorland all weary and worn,
>   Fell sorrow my pathway pursuing;
> Revolving what fetters our chain'd limbs have borne,
>   Sad sighing at Erin's undoing:
> Our princes' sad thrall, and our fair cities' fall,
>   And wide wasted plains did appal me;
> And my tongue cursed that day of the false Saxon's sway,
>   When Erin was shackled by *Shaun Bui!* [77]

Probably the most impressive of Walsh's efforts in this direction is the lyric "Have You Been at Carrick?," a translation of a Munster song in which Walsh uses the long, flexible line employed more commonly by Mangan and Ferguson:

> Have you been at Carrick, and saw you my True-love there?
> And saw you her features, all beautiful, bright, and fair?
> Saw you the most fragrant, flowering, sweet apple tree?—
> O! saw you my lov'd one, and pines she in grief like me? [78]

As the title of *Irish Popular Songs* indicates, Walsh shared with his fellow-Corkman Callanan an interest in Irish folk culture. His "Mairgréad ní Chealleadh" bears comparison to Callanan's "The Outlaw of Loch Lene" and "The Convict of Clonmel" in its emphasis on narrative, its thematic focus on marginalized characters, and its sophisticated handling of the formal conventions of the popular ballad. Based on the story of a famous seventeenth-century Cork outlaw named Daniel O'Keefe, who stabbed his mistress to death after discovering that she had betrayed him to the English, the poem also, in addressing the question of betrayal, manifests the nationalist concerns that permeate Walsh's writing, as is evident in the outlaw's description of his crime:

> The moss couch I brought thee
> To-day from the mountain,
> Has drank the last dregs
> Of thy young heart's red fountain—
> For this good *skian* beside me
> Struck deep and rung hollow
> In thy bosom of treason,
> Young Mairgréad ní Chealleadh.
>
> .   .   .
>
> And while to this lone cave
> My deep grief I'm venting,
> The Saxon's keen bandog
> My footsteps is scenting;
> But true men await me
> Afar in Dunhallow.
> Farewell, cave of slaughter,
> And Mairgréad ní Chealleadh.[79]

Walsh rarely wrote this well. Despite his concern to make his translations fit the measure of the original Irish poems, the rhythms and sound patterns of Walsh's translations tend to be remarkably similar, at times identical, even when he is working from very different Irish poems or poets, and he generally is unable to transcend either the conventions of the popular ballad or the homogenizing demands of a nationalist aesthetic. Still, as Robert Farren has argued, Walsh needs to be remembered "as one who tipped our verse in the way that would lead it to distinction," [80] and his accomplishment rests not just in the formal qualities of his poetry, but with the evocation of the Irish past in ways that are meaningful to the present.

Perhaps more than that of any other Irish poet of the century, the work of Samuel Ferguson (1810–1886) reflects the complex realities and ambiguities of nineteenth-century Ireland. Although he was a Protestant with strong anti-Catholic feelings, Ferguson devoted most of his career to reviving and salvaging a culture identified almost wholly with Catholic Ireland. Also, Ferguson was very much an Ulster poet, but the literary tradition to which he contributed so significantly had little use for Ulster, viewing it as closely allied with the industrial materialism of England (Belfast's shipbuilding industry, for instance), and therefore as alienated from the spiritualism of Celtic Ireland, centered largely in the rural west and southwest of the island and in literary, nonindustrial Dublin. Ferguson's aesthetics and politics, embodied in his cultural unionism, were essentially pragmatic and utilitarian, seeing art and scholarship as means to establishing a healthier and more peaceful society; and yet the result of much of his work directed to those ends was to create an extremely romantic version of Ireland. Finally, although Ferguson was a committed unionist, the Celtic revival movement that he helped create has always been associated with some degree of political separatism.[81]

Ferguson's Belfast family had belonged to the landed gentry; but his father apparently lost most of his property when Ferguson was growing up, and the family experienced severe economic difficulties. After attending the Belfast Academical Institution, which was founded in the year of his birth by the poet William Drennan, Ferguson managed to get to Trinity College. He never finished a degree there, but in the early 1830s he met in Dublin those antiquarians associated with the Irish Ordnance Survey who were so important to Mangan: George Petrie, John O'Donovan, and Eugene O'Curry. In 1834, at the age of twenty-four he made his first significant mark in the world of Dublin letters with an astonishingly self-confident and informed four-part review of Hardiman's *Irish Minstrelsy.* Published in the *Dublin University Magazine,* founded the previous year by a group of Trinity College Tories and committed to conservatism and anti-Catholicism ("The more that Popery steps forth into the light of day ... the more shall we detest the abominations of that accursed superstition, and prove her to be the enemy of the human race in time and in eternity"[82]), Ferguson's essays attacked Hardiman's Catholic bias and what Ferguson saw as the ineptitude of his translators, including Thomas Furlong. At the conclusion of his fourth essay, Ferguson appended his own verse translations of nineteen poems that he thought were badly translated in Hardiman's collection. Although somewhat uneven in quality, these poems included some of Ferguson's most remarkable work as a translator ("Cashel of Munster," "Mild Mabel Kelly," "The Fair Hills of Ireland," for example), and they quickly established him as an important part of the rapidly developing antiquarian movement. Ferguson contributed an impressive number of poems and essays to various periodicals throughout the 1830s. In 1848, the year of his marriage into the wealthy Guinness family, he appeared before the newly formed Protestant Repeal Association and, inspired by the English government's disastrous mishandling of the famine, spoke out against the Union that he had supported all his life. Also in the 1840s, he began work on his verse translations of ancient Irish epics, which were not published until much later

(1865), and on the book-length narrative poem, *Congal* (1872). In 1878, Ferguson was knighted; he was one of the few Irish writers of his century to have been awarded that distinctly English honor.[83]

Ferguson and Mangan are often yoked together as the two chief predecessors of the literary revival, but in truth their politics and aesthetics, as well as their lives, were poles apart. In a poem written in 1847 entitled "To Clarence Mangan," Ferguson differentiates between Mangan's claims to be an Irish poet and his own in terms that reveal some of the attitudes that alienated him from the Catholic readership to which Mangan appealed:

> *I* sometimes doubt if I have Irish blood in me,
>   So often in these mazes do I lose my clue,
> Mixing Danes with Milesians, and the clear-faced Saxon
>   With the hairy-dirty children of Boru.[84]

Ferguson's cultural ambitions for Ireland rested on an unyielding belief in the necessity of maintaining a political and cultural hierarchy that was demonstrably—and sometimes, as in these lines, appallingly—prejudiced against Catholics. This position was significantly hardened by the insecurity felt by Ferguson's class in the early decades of the nineteenth century in the face of O'Connell's successful drive for Catholic emancipation and his later work for repeal. Behind this insecurity lay the same fears that would fuel Protestant opposition to Home Rule later in the century; in an essay published in the *Dublin University Magazine* in 1833, Ferguson said: "if Catholic emancipation produce repeal, so surely will repeal produce ultimate separation; and so sure as we have separation, so surely will there be war levied, estates confiscated, and the Popish church established." [85] These fears explain the hysterical bigotry displayed in some of Ferguson's early writing. In his review of Hardiman's *Irish Minstrelsy,* his remarks on Catholics rival Mangan's deranged ravings about his fellow-scriveners in his Dublin law office:

> We will leave the idiotic brawler, the bankrupt and fraudulent demagogue, the crawling incendiary, the scheming, jesuitical, ambitious priest—that perverse rabble on whom the mire in which they have wallowed for the last quarter of a century, has caked into a crust like the armor of the Egyptian beast, till they are case-hardened invulnerably in the filth of habitual imprudence, ingratitude, hypocrisy, envy, and malice. . . .[86]

One way to ensure the continued cultural if not political dominance of Anglo-Irish Protestants in the face of a rising tide of Catholicism was to secure control of the movement to revive Ireland's Gaelic past, a movement fraught, as Ferguson well knew, with intimations of "ultimate separation." The distinctly political implications of Ferguson's role in the antiquarian movement were not lost on Yeats, whose unstinting praise for Ferguson's work was to some extent motivated by Yeats's identification with Ferguson as a fellow Protestant toiling under siege in the fields of Celtic lore. In any case, for a cultural unionist such as Ferguson, the whole enterprise of translation from Irish into English, with its self-evident implications of a cultural hierarchy, was far less compromising than it was for a committed nationalist (and Catholic) such as Walsh.

Despite Ferguson's political motivations, and despite the limitations of his knowledge of the Irish language (he almost certainly did not know it as well as either Walsh or Callanan did), a number of the translations that he published as "correctives" to those appearing in Hardiman's *Irish Minstrelsy* were as remarkable for their ability to express the spirit if not the letter of the original Irish poems on which they were based as were Mangan's translations for the way in which they transformed translation into a mode of self-expression. Some of Ferguson's success can be accounted for by his decision to construct his translations around the line as the basic unit of measure, as a means of negotiating the significant prosodic differences between Irish and English verse.[87] The most accomplished of Ferguson's translations, "Cashel of Munster," demonstrates the advantages of this strategy. The first stanza of the original poem, "Caiseal Mumhan," reads as follows:

> Phósfainn thú gan bha gan phunt gan áireamh spré,
> agus phógfainn thú maidin drúchta le bánú an lae.
> 'S é mo ghalar dubhach gan mé is tú, a dhianghra mo chléibh,
> i gCaiseal Mumhan is gan de leaba fúinn ach clár *bog* déil.[88]

A more-or-less literal translation, line by line, is:

> I would marry you without cows, without pounds, without a portion of dowry,
> and I would kiss you on a morning of dew with the whitening of the day.
> It is my melancholy sickness that I and you are not, intense love of my bosom,
> In Cashel in Munster and with no bed under us but a bog-deal board.

Ferguson's translation abandons conventional iambic metrics and line-measure, extending each line as far as necessary to contain the substance of each corresponding line of the original:

> I'd wed you without herds, without money, or rich array,
> And I'd wed you on a dewy morning at day-dawn grey;
> My bitter woe it is, love, that we are not far away
> In Cashel town, though the bare deal board were our marriage-bed this day![89]

A comparison of these lines with the opening stanza of Furlong's translation in *Irish Minstrelsy,* which Ferguson was attacking, reveals the extent to which Ferguson was breaking new ground:

> I would wed thee my dear girl without herds or land,
> Let me claim as a portion but thy own white hand;
> On each soft dewy morn shall I bless thy charms,
> And clasp thee all fondly in my anxious arms.[90]

Ferguson criticized Hardiman's translators for betraying the spirit of the original by imposing on it the characteristics of a different sensibility and culture: "All the versifiers seem to have been activated by a marked desire, neither healthy nor honest, to elevate the tone of the original to a pitch of refined poetic art altogether foreign from the whole genius and *rationale* of its composition."[91] Although Ferguson's translations sometimes rely on English metrics and conventional poetic diction, his work at its best demonstrates a genuine imaginative sympathy with the Irish tradition. His versions of several songs by Turlough Carolan, the Irish harpist and composer so favored by a number of eighteenth-century Irish poets writing in English, represent Ferguson at his most sensitive and sympathetic, as evidenced in the comparison made earlier with Charlotte Brooke's versions of these poems.[92]

Like Callanan and Walsh, Ferguson was deeply interested in Ireland's folk culture, and a number of the ballads that he wrote, for the most part in the 1830s, rank among his best writing. But Ferguson's work in this area differs decidedly from that of Walsh and Callanan in its assumption that any understanding of Irish folk culture must include the experience of Ulster. One of Ferguson's earliest ballads, "The Forging of an Anchor," no doubt sounded strange to readers who identified Irish folk culture principally with the songs of Munster. Eschewing most traces of romantic convention and the harmonies of Moore, Ferguson's poem relies on an appropriately rough-edged realism to describe an industrial reality as common to Belfast culture in the nineteenth century as it was unknown outside Ulster:

> The roof-ribs swarth, the candent hearth, the ruddy lurid row
> Of smiths that stand, an ardent band, like men before the foe,
> As, quivering through his fleece of flame, the soiling monster, slow
> Sinks on the anvil:—all about the faces fiery grow;
> "Hurrah!" they shout, "leap out—leap out;" bang, bang the sledges go:
> Hurrah! the jetted lightnings are hissing high and low—
> A hailing fount of fire is struck at every squashing blow.[93]

"Willy Gilliland: An Ulster Ballad" takes as its hero an outlaw figure driven by hatred of the English, but unlike the protagonists of Callanan's "The Outlaw of Loch Lene" or "The Convict of Clonmel," Gilliland cannot readily be assimilated into conventional Celtic ideas of nationalism. He is a Scots Presbyterian who fought the English at Scotland's Bothwell Bridge in 1679, and then fled to Ulster, where he was forced into hiding, and Ferguson's poem calls specific attention to how Gilliland's anti-English feelings are governed by the sectarian divide between Scots Presbyterians and English Anglicans:

> And there, his hand upon the Book, his knee upon the sod,
> He fill'd the lonely valley with the gladsome word of God;
> And for a persecuted kirk, and for her martyrs dear,
> And against a godless church and king he spoke up loud and clear.[94]

Perhaps because it so effectively employs the long, flexible line and complex assonantal patterns that characterize Ferguson's translations from the Irish, his best-known ballad, "The Fairy Thorn," has often been read in the context of the development of the Celtic revival. Yeats, who admired the poem greatly—he found it to be attractively enveloped in "the soft lustre of idyllic thought"[95] —had more than a little to do with this interpretation. The poem's third stanza exemplifies some of the formal qualities that appealed to Yeats, and indeed influenced some of his own early poetry:

> They're glancing through the glimmer of the quiet eve,
>   Away in milky wavings of neck and ankle bare;
> The heavy-sliding stream in its sleepy song they leave,
>   And the crags in the ghostly air.[96]

In recounting how a young girl is carried off by the fairies when she ventures out one night with three friends to dance around a hawthorn tree associated with supernatural creatures, the poem also powerfully evokes the folk superstitions that so fascinated Yeats and the other figures in the literary revival.[97]

The troubled decade of the 1840s was a period of great stress for Ferguson. He suffered a breakdown of some sort in 1845, and spent a year recuperating on the continent. His problems were in part a result of pressures brought to bear by various events, most notably the famine, on his unionist views; in 1848, in an address to the newly formed Protestant Repeal Association, he backed off his lifelong commitment to the Union. "It was perfectly evident," he said, "that if on the first day of January 1847, we had a local Legislature in this country, . . . moneys [would] have been raised adequate for preserving the lives of all her Majesty's subjects who, since that time, owing to the mismanagement of the Imperial Legislature, have lost their lives."[98] Although this statement was relatively radical for someone of Ferguson's persuasion, Ferguson was in fact looking back to relatively conservative and decidedly exclusionist eighteenth-century notions of legislative independence for Ireland. In any case, Ferguson did not hold to this position for long. He also was careful to distinguish his attitudes from those of more separatist groups. "I sympathized with the Young Ireland poets and patriots while their aims were directed to a restoration of Grattan's parliament in which all the estates of the realm should have their old places," Ferguson recalled the year before his death, explaining his opposition to Home Rule. "But I have quite ceased to sympathize with their successors who have converted their high aspirations to a sordid social war of classes carried on by the vilest methods." [99] Most of Ferguson's political poems appeared in the 1840s, and while they expressed strong anti-English sentiments, they resisted embracing an unqualified nationalism. A lengthy satire entitled "Inheritor and Economist" (1849) pointedly describes the effects of the famine and sharply attacks the *laissez-faire* economics that governed England's response to it, but stops considerably short of recommending any action in response, concluding on a note of Christian resignation and hope for divine assistance. "When This Old Cap Was New," included in Charles Gavan Duffy's *The Ballad Poetry of Ireland,* looks back to the days of Grattan's parliament as a model with which to contrast the sordid present:

> Our Parliament did sit
>   Then in our native land,
> What good came of the loss of it
>   I cannot understand.
>
>   .   .   .
>
> What rights we wanted then
>   Were asked for above board,
> By a hundred thousand gentlemen,
>   And rendered at the word.
>
>   .   .   .
>
> But patriots now-a-days,
>   And state reformers, when
> A starving people's cry they raise,
>   Turn out like Trenchermen.[100]

In the most accomplished of his political poems, "Lament for Thomas Davis," published in 1847, two years after Davis's death, Ferguson presents Davis's nationalism as a call not for the overthrow of the present political hierarchy but rather for a return to an earlier, more satisfactory period in Ireland's history. The rhetoric that Ferguson attributes to Davis harks back specifically to eighteenth-century Anglo-Irish notions of patriotism—"So callest thou . . . /For a nation's rights restored" [101]—and the poem celebrates Davis's anti-sectarianism more than it does his separatist tendencies.

Ferguson also began translating some of Ireland's pre-Christian epics in the 1840's, although most of this work was not finished until the 1860s and 1870s. It might be argued that these stories of Ireland's legendary heroes appealed to Ferguson in part because they seemed so remote from the political and cultural pressures of the day, but in fact Ferguson's epic translations are anything but politically and culturally neutral. They make much of the capacity for loyalty on the part of the Irish as portrayed in these legendary tales, and for a unionist such as Ferguson, loyalty was a quality that had a specific bearing on nineteenth-century politics. Also, Ferguson's rejection of violence as a solution to Ireland's problems stands behind even the most military of his epic translations. In "Conary," a poem in which division within a ruling class leads not just to battle but to an attack on Ireland by warriors recruited from England and elsewhere, Ferguson's fear of the consequences of violence for nineteenth-century Ireland lies just below the surface of a speech such as this:

> . . . slay our reverend sages of the law,
> Slay him who puts the law they teach in act;
> Slay our sweet poets, and our sacred bards,
> Who keep the continuity of time
> By fame perpetual of renowned deeds;
> Slay our experienced captains who prepare
> The youth for martial manhood, and the charge
> Of public freedom, as befits a state
> Self-governed, self-sufficing, self-contained;
> Slay all that minister our loftier life,
> Now by this evil chance assembled here,
> You leave us but the carcass of a state,
> A rabble ripe to rot, and yield the land
> To foreign masters and perpetual shame.[102]

More often than not, the cause of tragedy in Ferguson's versions of these tales is the failure to heed the voice of reason and restraint. Ferguson's political and cultural unionism also helps account for the otherwise puzzling exclusion, in his extensive retelling of Ulster's Red Branch Cycle, of the stories of the heroic exploits of the cycle's most famous character, the warrior Cuchullain, an icon of nineteenth-and twentieth-century Irish nationalism. In "The Naming of Cuchullain," Ferguson's only poem concerning this warrior, Cuchullain is an innocent young boy, and when the local bard and seer prophesies the greatness of Cuchullain's future, he does so in terms—"fixed obedience, discipline, and patience" [103]—more amenable to Ferguson's political outlook than to that of the militant nationalists who took Cuchullain as their paragon.

Ferguson's epic translations display a Victorian novelist's sense of narrative pacing and attention to realistic detail. They are, however, frequently marred by Ferguson's efforts to heroicize his material by means of a pseudo-Homeric diction, often resulting in the kind of ludicrousness that Flann O'Brien, in *At Swim-Two-Birds,* delights in parodying: "At end and side wall, thrice a hundred steeds/Groom'd sleek, ear active, eating corn and hay," and "Of high Tir-Conal's herdful hills and fishy-teeming floods;/Of all the warm vales, rich in goods of glebe-manuring men." [104] Nevertheless, these renderings into English verse of the ancient legends of Ireland, more than his lyric translations or folk ballads, made Ferguson an important predecessor to the literary revival, anticipating both Standish O'Grady's two-volume *History of Ireland* (1878, 1880) and Lady Gregory's *Cuchulain of Muirthemne* (1902) and *Gods and Fighting Men*(1904). Ferguson's version of the legendary story of the lovers Deirdre and Naosi was also an important source for plays by Yeats (*Deirdre,* 1907) and Synge (*Deirdre of the Sorrows,* 1910). There are instructive differences between Ferguson's version of this story and those by Yeats and Synge; whereas the two literary-revival plays are intent on incorporating the story of how the two lovers were betrayed by the possessive King Conor into the tradition of nationalism, in which betrayal figures as an important theme, in Ferguson's "Deirdre," the tragedy of the lovers stems less from the betrayal of a hallowed principle of spiritual nationalism, embodied in the love of Deirdre and Naosi, than from a general disregard for what Naosi calls "mutual trust." The speech in which Naosi argues for taking at their word the agents of the king when they come to bring the lovers back to Ireland is a set-piece spelling out the political philosophy behind Ferguson's faith in the British connection and in sectarian cooperation in general:

> Man lives by mutual trust. The commonwealth
> Falls into chaos if man trust not man.
> For then all joint endeavours come to nought,
> And each pursues his separate intent,
> Barked by no other labour than his own.[105]

Lady Wilde, pointing to the death of the hero of *Congal* at the hands of the idiot-son of a provincial chief, found Ferguson's most impressive achievement in epic translation symbolic of "our poor Irish cause: always led by a hero, always slain by a fool." [106] But in fact Ferguson's account of the defeat of the provincial king of Ulster by his tribal enemy, Domnal, follows the pattern observable in his other epic translations of Irish leaders destroyed by failing to listen to the voice of reason and pacifism. Among the departures that Ferguson makes from the original tale on which *Congal* is based is his employment of various supernatural elements to warn Congal against going into battle against

Domnal.[107] Ferguson also introduced into his plot several sympathetic women characters, including a fiancé for Congal, and in her mouth he puts words that, from Ferguson's point of view, were urgently applicable to nineteenth-century Ireland:

> Yet, oh, bethink thee, Congal, ere war kindles, of the ties
> Of nurture, friendship, fosterage; think of the woeful sighs
> Of widows, of poor orphans' cries; of all the pains and griefs
> That plague a people in the path of battle-wagering chiefs.[108]

It is useful to consider Ferguson's nineteenth-century cultural unionism as an extension of Charlotte Brooke's eighteenth-century belief, expressed in the preface to her *Reliques of Irish Poetry,* that the people of Ireland and England, and, inside Ireland, people of Irish and English descent, could live together peacefully and fruitfully if only they were culturally "better acquainted." [109] But it is equally important to recognize the differences between the political and cultural contexts in which these two members of Ireland's Protestant Ascendancy were working to recover and preserve Ireland's Celtic past. Brooke, writing before the 1798 insurrection, before the union, before Catholic emancipation, and before the famine, enjoyed a certain innocence that simply was not available to Ferguson. Ferguson's generation of Protestants was acutely aware of forces that threatened their dominance of Ireland, if not their very existence, forces that would have been all but inconceivable half a century earlier to the daughter of Henry Brooke working from a position of apparently invulnerable security. In some ways, those forces lent additional urgency to Ferguson's appeal for becoming "better acquainted," for working toward "mutual trust." But as it turned out, they also inevitably meant that both Brooke's and Ferguson's visions of a healthy, symbiotic relationship between Ireland's two principal cultures were bound to come to nothing.

CHAPTER SEVEN

IRELAND ANGLICIZED

A reader in search of the most detailed, systematic exploration in verse of Irish history, or of the most socially conscious poetry about the political and economic realities of nineteenth-century Ireland, will find it not in the work of poet-translators such as Mangan and Ferguson, nor in that of the nationalist poets who emerged in the middle decades of the century, but rather in that of two Irish poets, Aubrey de Vere and William Allingham, both of whom were perfectly comfortable with the forms and conventions of English verse, and extremely uncomfortable with arguments for removing the English presence from Ireland. There were, in fact, a number of Irish poets in the nineteenth century who wrote about Ireland, sometimes quite compellingly and authoritatively, with little regard for the tradition of writing in the Irish language or for the political ambitions of nationalism. Although much of this writing could be seen, from certain nationalist points of view, as essentially betraying the Irish experience by Anglicizing it, it also might be argued that poets in this category anticipate the course of twentieth-century Irish writing nearly as much as do Mangan and Ferguson. At the very least, the work of poets such as de Vere and Allingham and, to a lesser extent, George Darley, Thomas Irwin, and John Francis O'Donnell reveals many of the cultural pressures and differences that shaped individual poets and defined the development of Irish poetry in English in the nineteenth century. De Vere, born into a distinguished Anglo-Irish Protestant family—his father, Sir Aubrey de Vere, was a highly regarded poet in his own right—converted to Catholicism, and, although fiercely opposed to nineteenth-century nationalism, devoted a considerable portion of his poetic career to writing for an English audience about the history of Ireland's struggles for independence. Allingham's work was colored by a strong streak of social realism and political commitment; his book-length narrative poem *Laurence*

Bloomfield in Ireland is the only nineteenth-century Irish poem to explore fully the social, political, and economic realities of rural Ireland in the years after the famine. But he was also capable, as an Anglo-Irishman born into a family with Protestant Ascendancy roots, of badly sentimentalizing the Irish rural experience. Although he was praised by the Fenian leader John O'Leary, who published excerpts from *Laurence Bloomfield in Ireland* in the militantly nationalist paper, *The Irish People,* Allingham was himself extremely hostile to the nationalist agenda, and whereas much of his work rests on a faith in the literary value of provincial experience, anticipating the work of Patrick Kavanagh, among others, in this regard, Allingham was himself a relatively cosmopolitan man who lived as much in England as he did in Ireland, and who counted Tennyson among his close friends. Poets such as de Vere and Allingham also help demonstrate important developments in the tradition of Irish poetry in English that occurred between the eighteenth and the mid-nineteenth century. Allingham's interest in the land issue, for example, can be seen as an extension of Goldsmith's and Laurence Whyte's, revealing much about changes in Irish rural life in the nearly one hundred years between the publication of "The Deserted Village" and *Laurence Bloomfield in Ireland.* Darley's uninhibited romanticism looks back to Thomas Dermody's work several decades before him. More generally, the tendency of these Irish poets to turn toward England for their literary predecessors and masters, rather than to the Irish tradition then being unearthed all around them, reveals the same assumptions, conscious or unconscious, about the cultural superiority of the English tradition that eighteenth-century writers such as Swift and Goldsmith embraced as a matter of course.

While Mangan represents one direction that romanticism took in nineteenth-century Irish poetry, a direction strongly marked by national if not nationalist preoccupations, George Darley (1795–1846) represents quite another. Darley probably had little or no contact with Mangan's Ireland; born into a Dublin Anglo-Irish Protestant family, he attended Trinity College between 1820 and 1825, studying mathematics and science, and spent nearly all his adult years living in semi-seclusion in London, publishing works on mathematics as well as poetry. Darley's verse, consisting of two lengthy dramatic poems, three poetic dramas, and a handful of lyrics, bears little imprint of his years in Ireland, and even less evidence of an awareness of all that was happening in Irish literary circles in the early decades of the century, including the translation enterprise. Darley's influences and models were the English romantics (as opposed to Mangan's interest in German romanticism), and the English Jacobean poets. (One of Darley's poems was in fact mistakenly included in an 1861 anthology of seventeenth-century English lyrics.) Moreover, his romantic aesthetics made it possible, if not necessary, for him to resist anchoring his poetry in any specific historical reality, including that of his native Ireland. "Poetry," he wrote in the preface to his first published work, *The Errors of Ecstasie* (1822), "is of such a nature, that if not intrinsically good, no local or otherwise relative circumstances can possibly avail it." [1]

All this is not, however, to say that Darley has no place in the tradition of Irish writing. Indeed, Darley's tendency to exclude Irish material from his work represents one way that a writer in Darley's position might attempt to resolve the many complexities and ambiguities inherent in that position. Darley's interest in English romanticism places him in a line of Irish writers going back back to Samuel Whyte and Thomas Dermody in the eighteenth century, and the frenzied, often breathless intensity of much of Darley's poetry anticipates some of the qualities of Mangan's writing. And Darley seems to have experienced that passionate attachment to Ireland manifest in so many Irish writers, including Dermody, who chose to live in one kind of exile or another. His biographer says that the childhood years that Darley spent with his grandfather in rural Co. Dublin (his parents went to America shortly after he was born) left a lasting impression on him, and that his letters are filled "with the passion of an exile" for "scenes which had assumed for him a beauty almost legendary." [2] Darley himself once said, 'I have been to *La belle France* and *bella Italia,* yet the brightest sun which ever shone upon me broke over Ballybetagh mountains."[3] Although the spiritually charged romantic landscape of most of Darley's poetry tends to be neither Irish nor English, there are specific references to Irish places in Darley's work—the Giant's Causeway in Co. Antrim figures in *Nepenthe,* for example—and he did write a few poems about Ireland's legendary past, including one, "The Fight of the Forlorn," in which some of the ambiguities of his own position are projected onto the figure of an ancient Irish bard: "Bard! to no brave chief belonging,/Hath green Eirin no defenders?" [4]

Nepenthe, a lengthy vision poem that Darley published in 1835, is usually considered his most significant achievement, and it demonstrates the extent to which Darley's work is grounded in romantic notions of transcendence, and not very interested in "local or otherwise relative circumstances." Described by Graham Greene as a "wild medley of Shelley, Milton, and Keats, made a single whole by the feverish personality of Darley himself," [5] the poem recounts a dream-vision in which the narrator is taken out of historical time and into an imaginative experience of the extremes of human emotion and perception. The following passage reveals both some of the strains caused by the poem's relentless striving for poetic intoxication, and Darley's ability to evoke a spiritually charged landscape and experience:

> Feeling my impetuous soul
> Ravish me swifter than Earth's roll
> Tow'rds bright day's Eoan goal;
> Or if West I chose to run

> Would sweep me thither before the sun:
> Raising me on ethereal wing
> Lighter than the lark can spring
> When drunk with dewlight which the Morn
> Pours from her translucent horn
> To steep his sweet throat in the corn.[6]

The poem ends with the narrator's longing for a return to his home, embodying perhaps Darley's yearning for his native Ireland, which is envisioned as offering a pastoral, spiritual alternative to the unfulfilling materialism of England:

> Alas! why leave I not this toil
> Thro' stranger lands, for mine own soil?
> Far from ambition's worthless coil,
> From all this wide world's wearying moil,—
> Why leave I not this busy broil,
> For mine own clime, for mine own soil,
> My calm, dear, humble, native soil!
> There to lay me down at peace
> In my own first nothingness.[7]

If this is meant to refer to Ireland, it is more an image of romantic liberation or primal innocence than it is the Ireland to be found in the work of poets such as de Vere or Allingham.

The status of Aubrey de Vere (1814–1902) as an Irish poet is far less problematic than that of Darley. In his long career, de Vere wrote about the famine of the 1840s, published a lengthy sequence of lyrics chronicling Ireland's history and, in his later years, produced his own version of the Irish epic material translated by Ferguson and Standish O'Grady. On more than one occasion, Yeats included him as part of the company of nineteenth-century Irish poets who laid the foundations for the Irish literary revival.[8] Nonetheless, as Yeats also noticed, de Vere's writing is too heavily and too eagerly indebted to English poetry to occupy quite the same territory as that claimed by Mangan and Ferguson. De Vere's masters were chiefly Wordsworth, Coleridge, and Tennyson, and in even the best of his voluminous writing about Ireland, the disjunction between the materials of his art and the forms in which they are cast is all too evident; as Yeats put it, "the part that is Irish in subject is often alien in form."[9] Also, de Vere's poetry about Ireland may lack the passion of Mangan's and the commitment of Ferguson's because those qualities are products of an intimacy with Irish culture that de Vere seems not to have experienced. He was born into an established and culturally advantaged Anglo-Irish Protestant family; de Vere's father, Sir Aubrey de Vere (1788–1846), wrote a series of sonnets on Irish history and landscape that Wordsworth described as "the most perfect of our age." [10] After attending Trinity College, de Vere set out, quite calculatedly, to establish himself in the world of English letters. He became friends with Wordsworth, Landor, Tennyson, and Newman, among others, and he wrote and published prolifically, in verse and prose. Through it all, however, he never lost touch with what was happening in Ireland, and he developed genuine sympathies for the plight of Irish Catholics; he worked hard to alleviate the suffering of famine victims in the vicinity of his family's Co. Limerick estate, Curragh Chase, and he once recalled that in 1829, at the passing of Catholic emancipation (he was fifteen at the time), he "climbed to the top of a pillar opposite the house, and waved a torch in the gathering darkness." [11] In the middle of his life, he converted to Catholicism, although he was not inclined to embrace the nationalism that was becoming increasingly associated with it during the mid-nineteenth century. Indeed, de Vere's lifelong aversion to nationalist ambitions of a militant stripe was only deepened by his conversion; for de Vere, Catholicism was attractive in part because it rested on the principle of obedience, and therefore required loyalty to the established social and political hierarchy. "Catholicism," he once said, "is so essentially founded on Faith, and therefore on obedience, that I have never been able to understand how anyone can be a real Catholic, understanding and loving his religion, who is not a thorough Loyalist, both as regards his Church and the State." [12]

The ambiguities of de Vere's position as an Irish writer are strikingly evident in his writing about the famine. In a prose tract published in 1848, entitled *English Misrule and Irish Misdeeds,* de Vere advocates emigration as a policy for alleviating Ireland's economic difficulties, but in a relatively lengthy poem entitled "The Year of Sorrow," published the following year, he speaks sympathetically about Irish suffering:

> But thou, O land of many woes!
> What cheer is thine? Again the breath
> Of proved Destruction o'er thee blows,
> And sentenced fields grow black in death.
>
> In horror of a new despair
> His blood-shot eyes the peasant strains
> With hands clenched fast and lifted hair
> Along the daily-darkening plains.! [13]

But even at moments such as these, de Vere maintains an emotional and politically neutralizing distance from his subject matter, felt here in the controlled regularity of the stanzaic and metrical patterns and in the tendency toward abstraction. And at other times he advocates a religious resignation that depoliticizes the famine altogether:

> From ruined huts and holes come forth
> Old men, and look upon the sky!
> The Power Divine is on the earth:
> Give thanks to God before ye die![14]

De Vere's most ambitious undertaking, and his most significant contribution to nineteenth-century Irish poetry in English, is his poetic history, *Inisfail: A Lyrical Chronicle of Ireland,* first published in 1861. The idea of constructing such a history out of a sequence of lyric poems rests on the assumption that Ireland is essentially spiritual, an increasingly popular notion in nineteenth-century Irish aesthetics and politics, especially among far more militantly nationalist writers. "I have endeavoured," de Vere wrote in the preface to *Inisfail,* "to be true to the inner spirit of Irish History." [15] Indeed, it might be argued that Inisfail represents the most extensive historical exploration of the spiritual nature of Ireland in nineteenth-century Irish poetry. In practice, however, *Inisfail* leaves much to be desired, in large part because the sensibility behind the poem too often seems alien to the project of recovering poetically Ireland's past. Reading de Vere's "The March to Kinsale," describing the defeat of the Irish at the hands of Elizabeth's army in 1601, against Mangan's "O'Hussey's Ode to the Maguire," dramatizing the same historical moment, reveals some of the consequences of that alienation. The passionate urgency of Mangan's poem, and its profound and powerfully realized connections to the tradition of poetry in Irish, are nowhere to be found in de Vere's verse, which is generally marked by predictable rhythms and an artificial diction that sounds distinctively English echoes.

Inisfail does succeed in employing a wide range of dramatic voices, in the manner of Browning, to recount selected moments in Ireland's history, including its legendary past. The sequence begins with the Norman invasion of the twelfth century and proceeds, with various flashbacks to the pagan and early Christian periods, through the eighteenth century. In "The Bard Ethell," for example, de Vere projects the culture of twelfth-and thirteenth-century Ireland through the sensibility of a one-hundred year-old blind and deaf Irish bard, who dramatically provides the long perspective convenient to de Vere's religious resignation:

> Man's deeds! man's deeds! they are shades that fleet,
> Or ripples like those that break at my feet.
> The deeds of my Chief and the deeds of my King

> Grow hazy, farseen, like the hills in spring.
> Nothing is great save the death on the Cross![16]

The dramatic voice in "The Wedding of the Clans" is the very different but equally effective one of a young virgin pledged, for political purposes, to marry the chief of another clan:

> He has kill'd ten chiefs, this chief that plights me;
>   His hand is like that of the giant Balor:
> But I fear his kiss; and his beard affrights me,
>   And the great stone dragon above his door.
>
>   .   .   .
>
> Had I buried, like Moirin, three mates already,
>   I might say, "Three husbands! then why not four?"
> But my hand is cold and my foot unsteady
>   Because I never was married before![17]

When de Vere's writing in *Inisfail* seems least indebted to his English masters, he takes on a voice influenced by Moore, as in these lines from "Dirge of Rory O'More," about the Leinstermen who organized the conspiracy that led to the Ulster rising of 1641:

> Up the sea-sadden'd valley at evening's decline
> A heifer walks lowing; "the silk of the kine;"
> From the deep to the mountain she roams, and again
> From the mountains' green urn to the purple-rimmed main.
>
>   .   .   .
>
> Was he thine? Have they slain him? Thou seek'st him, not knowing
> Thyself too art theirs—thy sweet breath and sad lowing!
> Thy gold horn is theirs; thy dark eye, and thy silk!
> And that which torments thee, thy milk, is their milk![18]

De Vere's versions of Ireland's ancient epics are the least successful of his writing about Ireland. The workmanlike quality that dulls most of de Vere's poetry is more or less unrelieved in these narrative poems, collected in *The Foray of Queen Maeve and Other Legends of Ireland's Heroic Age* and published in 1882. The very idea of producing his own versions of the material, much of it recently (and successfully, in de Vere's view[19]) translated by Ferguson and O'Grady, betrays the deliberate, professional side of a poet who probably wrote and published too much. Moreover, precisely because de Vere's source material for these poems was so indigenously Irish (among the tales he retold were the story of Deirdre and Naosi and the epic perhaps most central to the Irish tradition, the *Táin Bó Cúailnge*), the gap between Irish subject matter and English poetics is especially evident and harmful in this work. It is this side of de Vere that no doubt prompted Yeats's analysis of de Vere's "defect of genius": "he seems to me, despite his noble placidity, his manifold and moving exposition of Catholic doctrine and emotion, but seldom master of the inevitable words in the inevitable order, and I find myself constantly distinguishing, when I read him, between that calculable, considered, intelligible and pleasant thing we call the poetical, and that incalculable, instinctive, mysterious, and startling thing we call poetry." [20] This may be somewhat unfair to de Vere, and it reveals at least as much about Yeats's early romanticism as it does about de Vere's writing; but anyone reading through the voluminous corpus of de Vere's Irish poetry would be hard put to dismiss it altogether.

Thomas Caulfield Irwin (1823–1892) has been called the "Irish Keats" [21] and "perhaps, the only Irish Tennysonian." [22] But Irwin was considerably less committed than was de Vere, his only rival to either of those two titles, to writing about Ireland, and relatively little of his poetry has to do with Irish themes. Still, he was highly regarded in the literary circles of his day, including Irish ones; he contributed to both *The Nation* and the *Dublin University Magazine,* and was recruited by the Fenian leader John O'Leary to write for *The Irish People* in the 1860s. One sizable volume of his poems, *Irish Poems and Legends; Historical and Traditionery* (1869), was devoted exclusively to Irish subjects and includes a number of poems that compare with de Vere's efforts in *Inisfail* to construct an accessible Irish past. Irwin's father was a relatively well-off physician in Warrenpoint, Co. Down, and Irwin enjoyed a privileged and exceptional education, including travels on the continent with a private tutor. The family fortune was, however, apparently lost when Irwin was in his mid-twenties, and he took up journalism to supplement his income from poetry. Little is known about Irwin's life, but he was reportedly an eccentric, at least according to this description of him given in a letter to Ferguson from the Irish antiquarian John O'Donovan: "I understand that the mad poet who is my next-door neighbour claims acquaintance with you. He says I am his enemy, and watch him through the thickness of the wall which divides our houses. He threatens in consequence to shoot me. One of us must leave. I have a houseful of books and children; he has an umbrella and a revolver." [23]

Irwin's Keatsian and Tennysonian impulses are most often felt in a lush, descriptive poetry focusing on landscapes very different from the lonely, wasted landscapes in the work of J. J. Callanan or the detailed provincial settings of Allingham's poetry about his native Co. Donegal. Irwin's landscapes are largely generic, carrying few if any traces of the violence, oppression, poverty, and famine that transformed the Irish countryside in the nineteenth century. This passage, from one of a sequence of descriptive sonnets, is characteristic:

> While into cloudy silence ebbs each sound,
> And sifts the moulting sunlight warm and mellow
> O'er sandy beach remote, or slumberous flood,
> Or rooky, red brick mansion by the wood,
>   Mossed gate, or farmyard hay-stacks tanned and yellow.[24]

This tendency to generalize, and to write in such a way as to be, as he puts it in the preface to *Irish Poems and Legends,* "acceptable to *all* classes who read Irish or English verses," [25] does not serve Irwin particularly well when he turns to writing about Ireland. Nonetheless, *Irish Poems and Legends* contains a group of poems that, although less ambitious or systematic than de Vere's *Inisfail,* constitutes a kind of history of Ireland, and several poems speak with historical authenticity and contemporary relevance. "The Wanderings and Lamentations of Queen Gormflaith," Irwin's version of the story of a tenth-century daughter of one Irish king and wife to two others who ended her days in poverty and loneliness, contains several descriptions of the queen wandering an Irish landscape laid waste by the Viking invasion that compellingly evoke the condition of post-famine Ireland:

> Lo! in the windy darkness of the long nights wander I,
> When earth and sea are rolled in the same blackness as the sky,
> Over the desolate land alone, by passes drear where prowl
> The wolves—and now by solitary cities where the owl
> Hoots at the morn; by fields of battle cumbered thick with dead
> Where I see the heavy eagle from his feast of famine red
> Disturbed, a moment rise, and settle heavily again,
> With outstretched claw and bloody beak tearing the flesh of men.[26]

This historical sequence also contains what is probably Irwin's most impressive work, a narrative poem entitled "Swift" that dramatizes the passion behind Swift's relationship with the two women in his life.[27] The description of Swift's famous ride to Vanessa's house outside Dublin, and of the moment in which he supposedly flung Vanessa's letter to Stella on the table and departed without a word, displays an energy, concreteness, and compression of dramatic action not often found in Irwin's writing:

> XVI.
> At length, beneath its woody gloom,
>   Old Marley's cloister ends his way.
>   He lights—he knocks. The pigeon's plaint
>   Swoons fitfully above and faint;
>   And glimmers through the garden's bloom
>   The river's sheet of glassy grey.

XVII.

Lo! from her memoried laurel bower,
　　Where oft she sat alone, to hear
　　　　His coming, she is hastening now,
　　　　To meet him with a joyous brow,
　　Though saddened by th' impending hour,
　　　　And shuddering with an unknown fear.

XVIII.

She enters—springs to meet him. God!
　　Can passion demonize a brow
　　　　Of spirit-splendour! In a breath
　　　　The letter's thrown; and he, like death,
　　Is gone, Hark! Ringing from the road
　　　　His horse's trampling echoes now.[28]

Irwin's poem not only pays homage to Swift's powers as a satirist but also argues for Swift's relevance, despite class and ideological differences, to nineteenth-century nationalism:

XXXIV.

His spirit lives within his page:
　　Dissective subtlety of glance;
　　　　Keen truth, to make the merriest mourn,
　　　　Fierce wit, that brightens but to burn,
　　Are there; and cold, ironic rage,
　　　　Withering a world it views askance.

XXXV.

What, though amid our warrior band,
　　An alien patriot he be,
　　　　Whose combat clang for Ireland's right,
　　　　In reason half, if half in spite,
　　Still shall we hang his mighty brand
　　　　In Freedom's sombre armoury.[29]

Yeats's remark that William Allingham (1824–1889) was "the poet of Ballyshannon, though not of Ireland" only partly accounts for Allingham's marginal status among nineteenth-century Irish writers.[30] After all, Yeats's distinction between a provincial writer such as Allingham and a presumably more national one such as Thomas Davis is not particularly meaningful, as writers like Joyce and Patrick Kavanagh have demonstrated. And Allingham did write a number of poems, including a book-length narrative, *Laurence*

Bloomfield in Ireland, that are of decidedly national import, however much they may be confined to Allingham's native Co. Donegal. In fact, Allingham's tenuous position in nineteenth-century Irish writing probably has less to do with his provincialism then with his aesthetics and politics. As is especially evident in *Laurence Bloomfield in Ireland,* Allingham wrote out of a commitment to social realism and liberal humanism, neither of which sits easily with the romantic aesthetics and often sectarian politics of nineteenth-century nationalism. Allingham's Anglo-Irish background, combined with his overt loyalties to English literature—like Aubrey de Vere, he saw himself as part of the world of English rather than Irish letters—worked to diminish his reputation in certain circles in Ireland. Finally, Allingham's work can be seen, in many ways, as an extension of eighteenth-century Anglo-Irish culture—his views on Irish nationalism, for example, were much closer to those of Henry Grattan than to Davis's—precisely the tradition that nineteenth-century writers of a romantic-nationalist persuasion were seeking to displace.

Allingham's attachment to his native Ballyshannon was as profound as Yeats's to Sligo or Callanan's to West Cork. "The little old Town where I was born," he wrote in a fragment of autobiography, "has a Voice of its own, low, solemn, persistent, humming through the air day and night, summer and winter. Whenever I think of that town I seem to hear the Voice." [31] Nevertheless, Allingham's Anglo-Irish roots—his ancestors settled in Ballyshannon during the reign of Queen Elizabeth, and his father was a prosperous local merchant —generated a typical division in his sensibility: "I came early to the consciousness that I was living in a discontented and disloyal country," he once said.[32] His literary ambitions pulled him decidedly in the direction of England. He started a correspondence with Leigh Hunt when he was nineteen, and before the end of his life had become close to Tennyson as well as to D. G. Rossetti and other pre-Raphaelites. In 1874, he was made editor of the influential *Fraser's Magazine.* He settled permanently in England in 1863, after working for the Customs Office in various parts of Ulster, including Belfast and Ballyshannon. Like Joyce, however, he spent much of his time in exile preoccupied with Ireland. Tennyson reportedly once said to him: "You don't care a pin about the grand Empire of England. You ought to be proud surely to be a part of it. There you are, with an English name, English in every way, but you happened to be born in Ireland, therefore you are for it." [33]

The tendency among some of Allingham's readers, including Yeats, to see him essentially as a lyrical poet—in Yeats's words, "a poet of the accidental and fleeting" [34]—underestimates Allingham's accomplishment, particularly in his most significant Irish work, *Laurence Bloomfield in Ireland* (1864). In its themes and its commitment to social realism, this poem is closer to the nineteenth-century Irish novel than to nineteenth-century Irish poetry. Its plot, embodying many of the tensions behind the agrarian agitation of the nineteenth century, is clearly indebted to such works as Maria Edgeworth's *The Absentee* (1812) and William Carleton's *Valentine McClutchey* (1847). The protagonist, a young, well-intentioned, Cambridge-educated Anglo-Irishman, returns to his family's estate in an area modeled on Allingham's Ballyshannon, and is quickly drawn into an escalating hostility between his land agent, a Mr. Pigot, and the peasants on the estate, the more discontented of whom have formed a secret society (the Ribbonmen) committed to asserting their cause, by violent means if necessary. After Pigot directs the eviction of a group of tenants, Bloomfield dismisses him, but the Ribbonmen's plan to kill him is carried out anyway. This story comes to a rather unconvincing conclusion, with Bloomfield and his tenants enjoying a new, trouble-free era based on compassion and peasant proprietorship. The poem demonstrates both Allingham's unflinching social realism—"nothing can be more graphic than many of the sketches in it," de Vere once said[35]—and his liberal humanistic values, especially in its advocacy of peasant ownership (anticipating the series of land acts passed by parliament between 1870 and 1903), and its rejection of violence as a legitimate means of improving the condition of Irish peasants. It is a testament to the poem's powers of describing and analyzing the injustices of landlord-tenant relations that O'Leary, despite Allingham's unequivocal rejection of the methods and assumptions of militant nationalism, published extracts from the poem in *The Irish People* and praised it generously.[36]

Laurence Bloomfield in Ireland takes on issues more or less ignored by most nineteenth-century Irish poets; the poem has, in fact, more in common with eighteenth-century works such as Goldsmith's "The Deserted Village" and some of Laurence Whyte's poems about the land than it does with the poetry of Mangan or Ferguson. Its depiction of post-famine rural Ireland is remarkably unromanticized, as in this description of the area around Bloomfield's estate:

> The cornstacks seen through rusty sycamores,
> Pigs, tatter'd children, pools at cabin doors,
> Unshelter'd rocky hill-sides, browsed by sheep,
> Summer's last flow'rs that nigh some brooklet creep,
> Black flats of bog, stone-fences loose and rough,
> A thorn-branch in a gap thought gate enough,
> And all the wide and groveless landscape round,
> Moor, stubble, aftermath, or new-plough'd ground,
> Where with the crows white seagulls come to pick.[37]

The poem also exhibits a considerably sophisticated and sympathetic grasp of the political and human realities defining the condition of the tenants:

> To them belongs no sense of commonweal,
> Authority as alien still they feel,
> Ruled, without partnership or wholesome pride,
> By Government that governs from outside.
> Their native Church, where peasant sons might rise,
> The rulers first despoil'd, and now despise.
> Trade, wealth, flow elsewhere, why they cannot guess,
> Save by constraint of ruling selfishness.
> In their own narrow bound, the constant fight
> For land goes on, with little ruth or right,
> So far as they can see; but every man
> Take all advantage that he safely can.[38]

Perhaps its most impressive quality is its identification and analysis of the underlying issues of the nineteenth-century agrarian crisis. For Bloomfield, the social and economic oppression suffered by the peasants at the hands of indifferent landlords was a symptom of a political system built on the principle of enslavement and the abuse of power:

> Mark the evil of a low estate;
> Not Poverty, but Slavery,—one man's fate
> Too much at mercy of another's will.[39]

If the poem can be faulted on dramatic grounds for substituting caricature and stereotype for complex, psychologically convincing characterization, it does, as Seamus Deane has pointed out, get to the center of the land issue "partly because the hostile positions were so calcified that the stereotype was both unavoidable and a true reflection." [40] This argument cannot, however, account for or justify all the poem's lapses into stereotype and caricature; there are occasions when this tendency seriously undermines the poem's authority as a document of social realism. Allingham himself had his own doubts about *Laurence Bloomfield in Ireland,* although on different grounds. In 1860, when he was about a third of the way through composing the poem, he wrote in a letter: "But alas! when all's done, who will like it? Think of the Landlord and Tenant Question in flat decasyllables!" [41] And when he finished the last chapter, or installment—the poem was serialized in twelve issues of *Fraser's Magazine* in 1862 and 1863—he wrote in his diary:

> A story in 5000 lines,
> Where Homer's epic fervour shines,
>   Philosophy like Plato's—
> Also, I sing of Paddies, Priests,

And Pigs, those unromantic beasts,
Policemen and Potatoes![42]

All these reservations aside, and acknowledging that it lacks the insider's authority of a poem such as Patrick Kavanagh's "The Great Hunger," *Laurence Bloomfield in Ireland* stands as a significant part of that tradition in Irish writing, beginning with Goldsmith's "The Deserted Village," committed to exposing, and improving, the political, social, and economic realities of Irish rural life.

This commitment informs a number of Allingham's ballads and lyrics as well. "The Ruined Chapel," for example, describes a landscape emblematic of the emptiness of post-famine rural Ireland:

> By the shore, a plot of ground
> Clips a ruin'd chapel round,
> Buttress'd with a grassy mound;
>   Where Day and Night and Day go by,
> And bring no touch of human sound.
>
>   .   .   .
>
> Or when, as winds and waters keep
> A hush more dead than any sleep,
> Still morns to stiller evenings creep,
>   And Day and Night and Day go by;
> Here the silence is most deep.[43]

A more dramatic lyric about rural Irish life is "The Girl's Lamentation," a ballad spoken by a young country girl who has been seduced and then abandoned. Her story, a staple of nineteenth-century fiction, is rarely found in romantic-nationalist poetry about rural Ireland. Much of the poem's considerable force depends on the authentic simplicity of the voice, and on Allingham's powers of narrative compression:

> With grief and mourning I sit to spin;
> My Love pass'd by, and he didn't come in;
> He passes by me, both day and night,
> And carries off my poor heart's delight.
>
> There is a tavern in yonder town,
> My Love goes there and he spends a crown,
> He takes a strange girl upon his knee,
> And never more gives a thought to me.

Says he, "We'll wed without loss of time,
And sure our love's but a little crime;"—
My apron-string now it's wearing short,
And my Love he seeks other girls to court.

．　．　．

To the river-bank once I thought to go,
And cast myself in the stream below;
I thought 'twould carry us far out to sea,
Where they'd never find my poor babe and me.

Sweet Lord, forgive me that wicked mind!
You know I used to be well-inclined.
Oh, take compassion upon my state,
Because my trouble is so very great!

My head turns round with the spinning-wheel,
And a heavy cloud on my eyes I feel.
But the worst of all is at my heart's core;
For my innocent days will come back no more.[44]

Poems such as these are the exception among Allingham's ballads and lyrics. Even some of his best-known lyrics betray a tendency to sentimentalize that seems to result from his position as an outsider to the native culture. "The Winding Banks of Erne," for example, is characterized by a tone of easy sentiment and stereotyped images of Ballyshannon that are very far from the social realism of *Laurence Bloomfield in Ireland:*

Adieu to Ballyshanny! where I was bred and born;
Go where I may, I'll think of you, as sure as night and morn,
The kindly spot, the friendly town, where everyone is known,
And not a face in all the place but partly seems my own.[45]

Although this lyric is subtitled "Or, the Emigrant's Adieu to Ballyshanny," its shortcomings as a poem about the experience of emigration can readily be seen by comparing it with poems such as James Orr's eighteenth-century "Song: Composed on the Banks of Newfoundland" and Thomas D'Arcy McGee's nineteenth-century poems of exile. If as Yeats said of Allingham more than a hundred years ago, "It is time for us over here to claim him as one of our own, and give him his due place among our sacred poets,"[46] it is also time to make clear the ground of that importance: his commitment to making Irish poetry socially responsible and sensitive to the changed and tragic political and economic realities of nineteenth-century rural Ireland.

John Francis O'Donnell (1837–1874) is of interest to the development of Irish poetry in English in the nineteenth century in part because of the failings of his work. Many of the fundamental divisions that both plagued and inspired so many nineteenth-century Irish poets—between a desire to write about Ireland and an aesthetics relying on English poetics, between a commitment to Irish nationalism and loyalty to the British crown, between an Irish readership and an English one—are present in O'Donnell's work with an unusual, and usually debilitating, sharpness. Indeed, his work was split almost schizophrenically between nationalist poetry published in Ireland (where he was considered by some readers to be John Keegan Casey's only competitor for the unofficial title of "the Fenian poet") and poetry with and without Irish themes published in English periodicals. Born in Limerick, O'Donnell published his first poems in a Kilkenny journal at the age of fourteen, and he became an extremely prolific professional writer and journalist, contributing poetry and prose to a variety of Irish and English magazines and newspapers. In Ireland, he wrote both for Young Ireland's *The Nation* and for the Fenian paper, *The Irish People,* while in England, having won the admiration of Charles Dickens, he published much of his verse in Dickens's *All the Year Round.* O'Donnell served as editor of various publications, including *The Irish People,* in the early 1860s. His poems were not collected for publication in book form until 1891, seventeen years after his early death; a selection from the hundreds of poems that had appeared in periodicals was published by the Southwark Irish Literary Club, a forerunner to Yeats's Irish Literary Society, in 1874.

The strengths of O'Donnell's writing have little to do with Ireland or the Irish tradition. Like Irwin, whom he most resembles, O'Donnell enjoyed considerable powers of description, which he often brought to bear on rural landscapes in a way that connects him with English landscape poetry. The lushness of imagery and sound in the best of his poems probably owes more than a little to Tennyson and Keats, and tends to obscure the tensions in O'Donnell's divided sensibility. These tensions tend to show up when he turns his attention to Ireland. "Reminiscences of a Day," for example, records a Co. Wicklow landscape in some detail, although the description seems more generic than specifically Irish, and its chief function is to evoke romantic impulses of a Wordsworthian character:

> O dim delicious heaven of dreams—
> This land of boyhood's dewy glow—
> Again I hear your torrent streams
> Through purple gorge and valley flow,
> Whilst fresh the mountain breezes blow.
> Above the air smites sharp and clear—
> The silent lucent spring it chills—
> But underneath, moves warm amidst
> The bases of the hills.[47]

In a revealing moment, O'Donnell introduces nationalist sentiments into this meditative lyric, attempting, more or less unsuccessfully, to integrate them with his romantic perception of the landscape:

> Far from the cities, far from streets—
>   Far from the cries of suffering wrongs,
> Away from scenes where Commerce beats
>   Its praises upon iron gongs,
>   How sweet to listen to the songs
> Which tell me, spite of all despairs,
>   The Holy Land that gave me birth
> Shall yet rise up, and reign and rule
>   O'er her own seas and earth.[48]

The awkwardness of this junction discloses the gap between O'Donnell's English sensibility and his Irish one, and between a romantic philosophy rooted in English aesthetics and a political point of view rooted in the principle of separation.

In dividing his work so distinctly between Irish and English audiences, O'Donnell tended to avoid rather than confront the contradictions inherent in his position as a nineteenth-century Irish poet writing in English. This evasion may explain why the ambiguities of that position proved more inhibiting than inspiring for his poetry. A useful point of comparison in this regard is the work of Mangan, which powerfully exploited some of the same tensions between romanticism and nationalism that seem to hinder O'Donnell. Both O'Donnell's "Adare" and Mangan's "Lament over the Ruins of the Abbey of Teach Molaga" center on a solitary walker who comes across the ruins of an abbey, Timoleague in Co. Cork in Mangan's poem, Monasteranenagh Abbey in Co. Limerick in O'Donnell's. Mangan's poem compellingly internalizes the destruction of the abbey and the alienation of the culture that it represents, while keeping in focus the political realities that lay behind what the narrator sees, but O'Donnell's narrator remains a detached observer, cut off by his poetic diction and forms from either a personal or a political understanding of what he is witnessing:

> Three Hundred Years in channelled stones,
>   Hewn in some quarry vast and fair,
> But touched with melancholy grey—
>   That habit of our Irish air—
>   Which slays, but still knows when to spare.
> Chancel, quadrangle, tower are here,
>   Gaunt cloisters, roof and mullions riven,

> With that clear interspace through which
> Souls, tired of flesh, looked out to heaven.[49]

This quality of the literary tourist, as opposed to the cultural integrity evident in the rhythm, diction, and tone, of Mangan's poem, leaves O'Donnell, even in the best of his work, outside both of the traditions, English and Irish, to which he sought to appeal with equal and separate conviction, and which provided the divided and ambiguous ground of much nineteenth-century Irish poetry.

IRELAND POLITICIZED

Irish nationalist poetry of the nineteenth century has existed under a critical shadow at least since Yeats proclaimed it to be propaganda masquerading as art. Although much of the political poetry produced in Ireland from the 1840s on was overly didactic, even jingoistic at its worst, and although it tended to romanticize Irish history and political reality (which Yeats himself would later be accused of doing), it embodied significantly new attitudes toward Irish society as well as Irish poetry. The nature and ambitions of political poetry were radically redefined from what they had been in the eighteenth century. Swift's political satires were written out of neo-Augustan aesthetics and notably un-romantic assumptions about the practical nature of the political as well as the poetical enterprise, and Swift's audience, like his concept of Irish independence, was limited to the governing Anglo-Irish class. The project of nineteenth-century political poetry, on the contrary, was nothing less than the creation of an idealized, essentially spiritual Ireland and the establishment of a new cultural identity based on that ideal. It also argued for a far more radical notion of political independence—up to and including the liberation of Ireland from English rule—than that which had informed most eighteenth-century writing, and it took as its ideal audience the entire nation. Such an ambitious view of poetry's mission could not have existed before romanticism; it is no accident that the anthology of nationalist verse found in nearly every literate household in nineteenth-century Ireland was entitled *The Spirit of the Nation*.

This new nationalist ideology, and the poetry that was its lifeblood, exhibited a powerful capacity to absorb or appropriate diverse experiences. Antiquarianism, which had been an important part of Irish cultural life since the end of the eighteenth century and reached a peak in the first half of the nineteenth century, became, in the embrace of nationalism, chiefly a means of justifying political separatism. This transformation can be seen with striking clarity in an elegy written by the Young Ireland poet Thomas D'Arcy McGee in honor of one of Ireland's most distinguished scholars of the Irish language, John O'Donovan. McGee transforms O'Donovan's scholarship into the discovery of timeless truths about an idealized Ireland and O'Donovan into the kind of nationalist hero with whom O'Donovan himself would have been most uncomfortable:

> He toiled to make our story stand
> As from Time's reverent, runic hand
> It came, undeck'd
> By fancies false, erect, alone,
> The monumental arctic stone
> Of ages wreck'd.
>
>   .   .   .
>
> O'er all low limits still his mind
> Soar'd Catholic and unconfined,
> From malice free.
> On Irish soil he only saw
> One state, one people, and one law,
> One destiny![1]

Religious feeling also was readily adapted to the project of investing Ireland with a spiritual character; political poems drawing on the idea of religious martyrdom were a commonplace of nineteenth-century political poetry. Nationalism also tended to absorb certain tenets of romanticism—the entire political and cultural project of nationalism was romantic in theory—but it also generally suppressed elements of it, most notably individualism, that it could not accommodate. The conflict between romantic individualism and nationalist ideology was manifest most powerfully in Mangan's poetry. It was also evident, but less fruitful, in the work of several women poets of the nineteenth century. These writers' commitment to writing nationalist verse often meant the suppression of an individual point of view and of issues of gender. Nationalist verse written by women sometimes employed gendered imagery, seeing the famine and emigration from the point of view of a mother or an abandoned lover, for example, but it showed little interest in exploring the kind of gender-related questions investigated by eighteenth-century women such as Mary Barber and Laetitia Pilkington. In part because it tended to turn a blind eye to difference and complexity, the visionary nature of nationalist ideology was, in the end, as limiting as it was inspiring. This ideology failed to create the political and economic situation in which its cultural agenda could be realized in part because it defined politics and economics in terms of an essentialist identity that existed outside political and economic realities.

The poetry that sprang from and fueled this ideology tended also to abstract individual and local experience to a national level. It did, however, bring into Irish poetry certain specific experiences and ways of seeing those experiences. Although nationalist political theory proved ill-equipped to respond to the famine,[2] nationalist poetry did not; moreover, nationalist poets tended to interpret the disaster in the context of an entire history of oppression and injustice, and, more optimistically, to see it as a potential catalyst for redemption or revolution, or both. Poems about exile and emigration, part of a tradition going back at least as far as Goldsmith's "The Traveller," took on a heightened intensity in post-famine nationalist verse, and increasingly sounded the note of melancholy that has marked so much Irish writing from the second half of the nineteenth century on. Nationalist poetics also revitalized a number of poetic forms, most notably the elegy and the popular ballad. Adapted to nationalist purposes, the elegy—Davis's for Owen Roe O'Neill, Ferguson's and Mary Kelly's for Davis, Denis Florence McCarthy's for Daniel O'Connell, and McGee's for John O'Donovan, among others—exploited the idea of lost opportunities and the notion of blood sacrifice, suggesting that the death being lamented would ultimately lead to political salvation.[3] The popularity of the ballad demonstrated that there was a place for a popular art form in the nationalist movement, but at the same time, since nationalist poets tended to take the form straight from the English tradition, its success revealed the extent to which the nationalist movement and the Ireland to which it appealed was already profoundly Anglicized.

Young Ireland Poets

"His poetry is but a fragment of the man," John Mitchell said of Thomas Davis (1814–1845),[4] meaning it as the compliment that Davis no doubt would have taken it to be. Davis never set out to be a poet, and his poetry is clearly the work of a man not fully committed to his art; even his close friend and advocate Charles Gavan Duffy conceded that much of it was ephemeral and poorly executed.[5] But Davis's considerable importance to nineteenth-century Irish poetry derives in large part from his not putting poetry first; it was precisely Davis's conviction that Irish poetry ought to be subservient to one specific political purpose, to what Mitchell called "arousing national spirit,"[6] that inspired the best of Davis's work and accounts for much of his extraordinary influence on other Irish poets. Behind this view of poetry lay a belief in the power of culture to function as an agent of political change,[7] the same essentially romantic faith in the ability of poetry to make something happen that fueled the literary revival that later so disparaged Davis's poetry.

Davis's brief adult life was given over almost wholly to his commitment to cultural and political nationalism. Born in Mallow, Co. Cork, to a Protestant family of British extraction (his father, of Welsh descent, had been a surgeon in the Royal Artillery, and his mother's family traced its roots in Ireland back to the Cromwellian settlement of Cork), Davis graduated from Trinity College in 1836, emerging from that unionist institution with a most un-unionist set of political convictions. His work as a journalist brought him into the circle of Duffy and John Blake Dillon, and in 1842 the three men founded *The Nation,* designed, according to its famous motto, "to create and foster public opinion in Ireland, and to make it racy of the soil." [8] Over the next three years, Davis threw his considerable and wide-ranging energies into *The Nation,*contributing poems and essays on everything from sculpture to soil conservation. Like many of the writers for *The Nation,* Davis belonged to O'Connell's Repeal Association, but split with O'Connell over a proposal for nonsectarian education in Ireland. Davis's commitment to recruiting middle-class Protestants to the nationalist cause further alienated him from O'Connell, anticipating the eventual rupture, after Davis's death, between the Young Ireland movement and the Repeal Association. Davis's belief in non-sectarianism also alienated him from more militant nationalists, for whom the barrier between Protestant and Catholic that Davis sought to break down provided the most meaningful way of understanding Ireland's political problems.

Although Davis was closely associated with nationalists of a relatively militant stripe, his own views were anything but revolutionary. Davis's politics were based more on education than on insurrection; in his view, Ireland could not achieve a meaningful independence without educating its populace, especially about history. In an essay titled "The History of Ireland," he wrote: "To make our spirit lasting and wise as it is bold—to make our liberty an inheritance for our children, and a charter for our prosperity—we must study as well as strive, and learn as well as feel." [9] Davis's poetry and poetics were defined by this view. "Whatever he wrote had still the same aim," Duffy said, "to raise up his people by making then better men and better patriots." [10] There is something remarkably utilitarian about this view, especially in a writer so engaged by the romanticized Ireland of nineteenth-century nationalism. With no evident self-consciousness, Davis could publish an essay entitled "Hints for Irish Historical Painting," consisting almost entirely of an extensive list of recommended subjects for Irish painters and sculptors, beginning with "The Landing of the Milesians" and concluding with "The Lifting of the Irish Flag of a National Fleet and Army." The circumstances of Davis's own writing of verse reveal an extraordinarily practical approach; he came to the conclusion that the country needed inspiring patriotic poetry, and so, as Mitchell says, "set to work to manufacture the article wanted." [11]

This is the side of Davis that the young Yeats found so distressing. But there is another side to Davis's aesthetics and politics, one more acceptable to the romantic character of nineteenth-century nationalism and of the literary revival. As Seamus Deane has said, Davis was, especially in his poetry, "inventing the symbolism of a complete 'spiritual' nationhood, finding its chief alternative in British utilitarianism." [12] This romantic faith in an essentialist, spiritual nation, and in the power of art to evoke that nation, makes Davis sound at times remarkably like Yeats in his early years. This passage from Davis's prose writings, for example, is hard to distinguish from the rhetoric of such early essays by Yeats as "Ireland and the Arts" or "The Celtic Element in Literature":

> Nationality . . . is the summary name for many things. It seeks a literature made by Irishmen and coloured by our scenery, manners and characters. It desires to see art applied to express Irish thoughts and belief. . . . It would thus create a race of men full of more intensely Irish character and knowledge, and to that race it would give Ireland. [13]

As Yeats was quick to point out, however, Davis's poetry rarely achieved the transcendent awareness that the romantic side of his aesthetics demanded, rarely was able to call into being the spiritual Ireland that lay behind the nationalist vision. This failing in Davis's verse might be attributed to his penchant for abstraction or his tendency to adopt a tone of relentless exhortation. Or it may simply be that, as Deane says, "Davis had a good heart but a cloth ear." [14] It also has to do with the exclusion of the individual from Davis's poetry. Without the presence of the kind of romantically realized self that makes Mangan's poetry so powerfully resonant and suggestive, Davis's verse, even when it is trying to evoke a transcendent ideal of the nation, tends to lapse into empty abstraction and conventional imagery, as in these familiar lines from "Nationality":

> A nation's voice, a nation's voice—
> It is a solemn thing!
> It bids the bondage-sick rejoice—
> 'Tis stronger than a king.
> 'Tis like the light of many stars,
> The sound of many waves,
> Which brightly look through prison bars,
> And sweetly sound in caves.
> Yet is it noblest, godliest known,
> When righteous triumph swells in tone. [15]

Nevertheless, Davis's political poems at their best exhibit a considerable rhetorical sophistication and effectiveness, manifest largely in an ability to negotiate between conflicting positions and divergent readerships. Davis is particularly good at exploiting history for this purpose; his selective and highly interpretive reading of Irish history is markedly different from more comprehensive and scholarly nineteenth-century poetic histories of Ireland, such as de Vere's *Inisfail*.[16] In a poem entitled "The Geraldines," Davis focuses on the history of the Geraldine family as a way of appealing to nineteenth-century Protestants on behalf of the cause of nationalism without alienating his Catholic readers; the Geraldines first came to Ireland, as Davis says, "in Strongbow's van,"[17] but were gradually Hibernicized and finally became committed to the cause of Irish independence—a pedigreed paradigm for what Davis wanted to see happen to the Irish Protestants of his day. In "The Penal Days," Davis recounts the horrors of the oppression of Irish Catholics—a theme certain to appeal to his Catholic readers—but for the purpose of asserting the need for sectarian unity in the present:

> They're gone, they're gone, those penal days!
> All creeds are equal in our isle;
> Then grant, O Lord, thy plenteous grace,
> Our ancient feuds to reconcile.
> Let all atone
> For blood and groan,
> For dark revenge and open wrong;
> Let all unite
> For Ireland's right,
> And drown our griefs in freedom's song.[18]

By far the most accomplished of Davis's poetry in this vein looks back to the rise of the Irish Volunteers, the establishment of Grattan's parliament, and the insurrection of 1798. For a mid-nineteenth-century Protestant seeking to negotiate between Protestant and Catholic readers, between conservative and militant nationalists, and between the ambiguities inherent in his own background and position, this is a highly usable part of Ireland's past. Davis's hero from this period is Grattan, not Wolfe Tone: "Of the long line of Protestant patriots Grattan is the first in genius. . . . He had immeasurably more imagination than Tone; and though he was far behind the great Founder of the United Irishmen in organizing power, he surpassed him in inspiration."[19] Davis's admiration for Grattan is clearly rooted in his own tendency toward constitutional rather than insurrectionary nationalism. But his poetry about the end of the eighteenth century not only celebrates the significance of Grattan's parliament but also acknowledges the important role of the militant Volunteers in making the parliament possible. The contemporary implications are not hard to find; the parallel suggests that the Repeal Movement, built on O'Connell's rejection

of militant nationalism, probably could not succeed without at least the threat
of violence being sounded in, among other places, the pages of *The Nation*.
But the implied parallel between these two moments in Ireland's history does
not fully commit Davis to either a militant or a constitutional position: rather,
it provides him with a means of negotiating between them. "The Dungannon
Convention" demonstrates how effectively Davis was able to do this. The
convention itself, an assembly in the parish church at Dungannon of 250 representatives of the Irish Volunteers, stood chiefly for Protestant interests and had
a fully constitutional goal, legislative independence; but it also had standing
behind it a clearly insurrectionist threat in the presence of nearly 50,000 armed
man. In his poetic recreation of this scene, Davis makes much of the sectarian
diversity of the Volunteers, playing down the Protestant cast of what the group
presented and wanted:

> A Protestant front-rank and Catholic rear—
> For—forbidden the arms of freemen to bear—
> Yet foemen and friend are full sure, if need be,
> The slave for his country will stand by the free.
> By green flags supported, the Orange flags wave,
> And the soldier half turns to unfetter the slave![20]

The conclusion of the poem articulates a position that would both appeal to
many of *The Nation's* more militant readers and speak to more cautious nationalists, including Irish Protestants who would see themselves as Grattan's political descendants, and whom Davis was always trying to reach:

> The church of Dungannon is empty once more—
> No plumes on the altar, no clash on the floor,
> But the councils of England are fluttered to see,
> In the cause of their country, the Irish agree;
> So they give as a boon what they dare not withhold,
> And Ireland, a nation, leaps up as of old,
> With a name, and a trade, and a flag of her own,
> And an army to fight for the people and throne.
> But woe worth the day if to falsehood or fears
> She surrenders the guns of her brave Volunteers![21]

As his editor put it, Davis "saw that the surest way to induce a nation to
rise to higher things was to imbue them with the idea that they had already
accomplished much."[22]

Davis and the other poets of *The Nation* have been credited with establishing
the popular song and ballad as an effective vehicle for political ideology.

Models for this kind of writing were also part of the usable past of the late eighteenth century, which provided Davis with the songs and ballads of such writers as Mary O'Brien, Edward Lysaght, James Orr, and William Drennan as well as with valuable political paradigms. Davis's ballad, "Song of the Volunteers of 1782," written to the air "Boyne Water," clearly owes a formal debt to late-eighteenth-century popular verse, while also, like "The Dungannon Convention," looking back to 1782 for a way of reconciling conflicting forces in the nationalist movement of the 1840s. On the one hand, it acknowledges, in a relatively inflammatory tone, the significance of militancy in the struggle for Irish independence:

> Remember still, through good and ill,
>   How vain were prayers and tears—
> How vain were words, till flashed the swords
>   Of the Irish Volunteers.
> By arms we've got the rights we sought
>   Through long and wretched years—
> Hurrah! 'tis done, our freedom's won—
>   Hurrah for the Volunteers![23]

But the poem is essentially a eulogy to Grattan and Henry Flood, and it also implies a connection between the poets of *The Nation* and eighteenth-century Protestants such as Swift, William Molyneux, and Charles Lucas:

> And bless the men of patriot pen—
>   Swift, Molyneux, and Lucas;
> Bless sword and gun, which "Free Trade" won—
>   Bless God! who ne'er forsook us!
> And long may last the friendship fast
>   Which binds us all together;
> While we agree, our foes shall flee
>   Like clouds in stormy weather.[24]

Davis's best-known poem, "Lament for the Death of Eoghan Ruadh O'Neill," is set in another crucial moment of Ireland's history, the Confederate rebellion of the 1640s; and this poem, especially in comparison with much of Davis's writing about the late eighteenth century, is unambiguous in its emotional appeal to militant nationalists of the 1840s, who tended to read Irish history as a narrative justifying revenge. The poem's fictional framing as a dialogue between a member of Eoghan Ruadh's camp and a messenger just arrived with the news of Eoghan Ruadh's death enables Davis to avoid the doctrinaire tone that damages so many of his political poems. Although the poem has its awkward moments (it is said to be the first poem Davis ever wrote for *The Nation),* it is marked by an emotionally compelling flexibility of rhythms that became increasingly rare as Davis matured into a more practiced, more conventional writer of verse. As the final stanza of the poem illustrates, much of the power of "Lament for the Death of Eoghan Ruadh O'Neill" comes from Davis's ability to move between the elegiac note of lament and a political rage full of implications and inspiration for Davis's readers:

> Soft as woman's was your voice, O'Neill! bright was your eye,
> Oh! why did you leave us Eoghan? Why did you die?
> Your troubles are all over, you're at rest with God on high,
> But we're slaves, and we're orphans, Eoghan!—why didst thou die?[25]

That final modulation from "you" to "thou" reinforces the poem's recreation of O'Neill as a Christ-like martyr and a permanent part of the idealized, spiritual Ireland that Davis's poetry sought to forge out of the materials of Irish history. It is a tribute to Davis's powers as a poet that "Lament for the Death of Eoghan Ruadh O'Neill" has itself become, in true romantic fashion, one of the icons of that ideal Ireland.

In his speech at the Davis Centenary in 1914, Yeats told the story of how Lady Wilde, when a young girl in Dublin, came one day upon a great, impenetrable crowd of people in the street. When she asked a shopkeeper what was the cause of the crowd, she was told it was the funeral of Thomas Davis. And when she asked, "Who was Thomas Davis, I have never heard of him," the shopkeeper responded, "He was a poet." [26] From certain points of view, this notion that Davis was above all a poet seems dubious. But as Yeats recognized, Davis could at times write with great force and conviction precisely because he was relatively innocent of poetic self-consciousness. In praising Davis's "Lament for the Death of Eoghan Ruadh O'Neill," Yeats said:

> When I compare it with 'O'Hussey's Ode to the Macguire', or with any good
> poem of Allingham's . . . I see at once that Mangan could have given it a more
> personal rhythm, and that Allingham would not have used those words of
> newspaper rhetoric 'living death', but that neither could have been so poi-
> gnant. Davis is mourning, not as poet, but as man.[27]

Of the numerous poets associated with the Young Ireland movement of the 1840s, the most significant, apart from Davis, were Denis Florence MacCarthy (1817–1882) and Thomas D'Arcy McGee (1825–1868). The work of both these poets demonstrates the tendency of nationalist poetry to appropriate romanticism and antiquarianism for its own ends; MacCarthy especially draws on the Irish past to express an idealized concept of Ireland as a spiritual entity that transcends the accidents of history. Both poets, but particularly McGee, attempt to interpret in nationalist terms the famine of the late 1840s and the massive emigration that followed it, both of which occurred after Davis's untimely death.

Certainly in comparison with Davis, MacCarthy fits much more closely the model of the nineteenth-century man of letters. Born in Dublin in 1817, and once intending to be a priest (he studied at Maynooth), MacCarthy was publishing in Dublin periodicals before he was twenty. In the 1840s, in addition to contributing poetry and prose to a variety of publications, especially *The Nation,*he edited two anthologies, one of Irish ballads and one of Irish writers of the seventeenth and eighteenth centuries. His first book of poems, entitled *Ballads, Poems and Lyrics, Original and Translated,* was published in Dublin in 1850. He was well-read in English literature, especially English romanticism —he published a life of Shelley in 1872—and was also highly regarded as a translator of Spanish verse and drama. At one point in his career, MacCarthy was considered to be the successor to Thomas Moore, and the influence of Moore's poetic practice and his romanticism is unmistakable. Moore's work was a crucial part of the tradition that nationalism absorbed and revised, and in an ode that MacCarthy wrote on the centenary of Moore's birth in 1879, he presents a thoroughly romantic and nationalist view of Moore as part of a timeless Irish tradition still capable of inspiring contemporary poets and shaping Ireland's future:

> And round that throne whose light to-day
> O'er all the world is cast,
> In words though weak, in hues though faint,
> Congenial fancy rise and paint
> The spirits of the past
> Who here their homage pay—
> Those who his youthful muse inspired,
> Those who his early genius fired
> To emulate their lay:
> And as in some phantasmal glass
> Let the immortal spirits pass,
> Let each renew the inspiring strain,
> And fire the poet's soul again.[28]

The anapaestic rhythms and harmonious sound patterns of Moore's lyricism can be found in MacCarthy's "Kate of Kenmare," one of his more romantic poems, in which the romantic view of love as a state of transcendent purity independent of material circumstances is employed to evoke the idea of Ireland as a spiritual and timeless entity; the bereft lover is the exiled nationalist whose

memory and imagination provide a spiritual nation to replace the material one
that he has lost:

> To him who far travels how sad is the feeling,
>   How the light of his mind is o'ershadowed and dim,
> When the scenes he most loves, like the river's soft stealing,
>   All fade as a vision, and vanish from him!
> Yet he bears from each far land a flower for that garland
>   That memory weaves of the bright and the fair;
> While this sigh I am breathing my garland is wreathing,
>   And the rose of that garland is Kate of Kenmare.[29]

Like Davis, MacCarthy was essentially a cultural nationalist. In the introduction to his anthology of seventeenth-and eighteenth-century Irish writers, he
defines Ireland's colonization chiefly in cultural terms:

> The fate of Ireland has certainly been most singular, and in her case spoilation
> has been carried to an extent unparalleled in the annals of any other nation.
> Not content with the plunder of the material riches of the country, the insatia-
> ble and avaricious hand of robbery has wished to snatch from her the unsub-
> stantial, yet consoling splendours of her traditions.[30]

For MacCarthy, the idea of Irish independence was very much associated with
the recovery of these unsubstantial yet consoling splendors, and a significant
part of his work has this nationalist-antiquarian purpose. His *Poems,* published
the year of his death, contains several lengthy narrative poems based on the
Irish epic tradition, including a rather scholarly version of an episode from the
Táin Bó Cuailnge and a narrative ballad, "The Foray of Con O'Donnell,"
recounting an episode from John O'Donovan's *Annals of the Four Masters.*
Also, many of MacCarthy's original lyrics employ internal rhyme schemes that
are meant to suggest the assonantal patterns that govern poetry in Irish.

In much of MacCarthy's more blatantly nationalist verse, however, Irish
history is cast in relatively ahistorical terms, providing the poet with a means
of defining the spiritual quality of nationhood that many nineteenth-century
nationalists associated with Ireland. In "The Pillar Towers of Ireland," for
example, written in 1846, MacCarthy presents the round towers of early Christian Ireland less as monuments of a specific period in Irish history than as
symbols evoking an essentially mystical Ireland that transcends particular historical moments:

> The pillar towers of Ireland, how wondrously they stand
> By the lakes and rushing rivers through the valleys of our land;

In mystic file, through the isle, they lift their heads sublime,
These gray old pillar temples, these conquerors of time![31]

"The Clan of Mac Caura," one of MacCarthy's most accomplished historical poems, argues for the comparative antiquity of Irish civilization. "When her glory [Venice's] was all to come on like the morrow,/ There were chieftains and kings of the clan of Mac Caura"[32]—an argument carrying the same nationalist implications that lay behind the translations of Mangan and Ferguson. MacCarthy also tends to idealize the Irish past and the Irish landscape in ways calculated to reach a relatively wide audience and to evoke an Ireland that is more than the sum of its historical moments or its specific places:

> What a moment of glory to cherish and dream on,
> When far o'er the sea came the ships of Heremon,
> With Heber, and Ir, and the Spanish patricians,
> To free Inis-Fail from the spells of magicians.
>
> . . .
>
> From that hour a Mac Caura had reigned in his pride
> O'er Desmond's green valleys and rivers so wide,
> From thy waters, Lismore, to the torrents and rills
> That are leaping forever down Brandon's brown hills;
> The billows of Bantry, the meadows of Bear,
> The wilds of Evaugh, and the groves of Glancare—
> From the Shannon's soft shores to the banks of the Barrow—
> All owned the proud sway of the princely Mac Caura![33]

McGee is the Young Ireland poet most concerned with the famine, but the best of his poems have more to do with one of the famine's chief consequences, emigration, than with the famine itself. Although McGee is less accomplished and less varied a poet than MacCarthy, his work effectively portrays the experience of emigration, while revealing how emigration tended to produce romanticized perceptions of Ireland and, accordingly, militant nationalist politics. MacGee had first-hand experience of emigration. He was born in Carlingford, Co. Louth, in 1825, but at the age of seventeen went to Boston to live with an aunt. He was back in Ireland in the mid-1840s, and became a leading figure in the Young Ireland movement, working for and frequently contributing to *The Nation*. In the aftermath of the 1848 insurrection, he escaped to the U.S., and ten years later moved to Canada, where he became a prominent political figure. It was about this time that his views on Ireland underwent a radical change, and in a speech he made while visiting Ireland in 1865, he bitterly attacked the Fenians, calling them "Punch-and-Judy Jacobins, whose sole scheme of action seems to be to get their heads broken."[34] Three years later, he was assassinated, presumably by a member of a revolutionary organization.

Like James Orr's poems about emigration, written in the wake of Orr's forced exile following the 1798 insurrection, McGee's poems politicize the experience of exile. "The Woeful Winter: Suggested by Accounts of Ireland, in December, 1848," for example, sees emigration as sapping Ireland's political and cultural energies:

> Alas! alas! for Ireland, so many tears were shed,
> That the Celtic blood runs palely, that once was winy red!
> They are flying, flying from her, the holy and the old,
> Oh, the land has alter'd little, but the men are cowed and cold.[35]

McGee's poems also demonstrate how the experience of exile, because it places the emigrant in a position from which the homeland can be realized only through imagination and memory, tends to encourage idealized views of Ireland, thereby reinforcing romantic-nationalist perceptions.[36] This quality in McGee's work can be seen in a poem entitled "To Duffy in Prison," presumably written just after McGee left Ireland in 1848 and Charles Gavan Duffy, along with other Young Ireland leaders, was arrested and imprisoned. The narrator of the poem, writing from somewhere in North America, conjures up an ideal Ireland, in an imaginative act that is the province of both the poet and his readers:

> I dreamt I reach'd the Irish shore, and felt my heart rebound
> From wall to wall within my breast, as I trod that holy ground;
> I sat down by my own hearth-stone, beside my love again—
> I met my friends, and Him, the first of friends, and first of Irish men.[37]

The poem then reads Duffy's character in equally romantic terms, and concludes with a burst of intensity worthy of Mangan, expressing a romantic faith in redemption through suffering:

> They will bring you in their manacles beneath their bloody rag—
> They will chain you like the Conqueror to some sea-moated crag—
> To their fiends it will be given your great spirit to annoy—
> To fling falsehood in your cup, and to break your martyr-joy;
> But you will bear it nobly, as Regulus of eld—
> The oak will be the oak, and honour'd e'en when fell'd:
> Change is brooding over earth, it will find you 'mid the main,
> And, throned between its wings, you'll reach your native land again.[38]

That kind of romanticization of Ireland usually implies the romanticization of the Irish poet as well. In a poem titled "The Celts," McGee celebrates the legendary Irish poet Ossian as "the primal poet," identified with the spiritual essence of Ireland. But McGee also wonders, somewhat despairingly, whether that spirit can be found in his world:

> Oh, inspired giant! Shall we e'er behold
> In our own time
> One fit to speak your spirit on the wold,
> Or seize your rhyme?[39]

It seems fair to say that, at least in the work of nationalist poets like MacCarthy and McGee, the answer to that question is no.

The Fenian Movement

Nationalist poetry in nineteenth-century Ireland was, by definition, popular poetry. Operating out of strong political convictions and relatively utilitarian notions about the function of art, writers such as Davis, MacCarthy, and McGee rejected the ultimately elitist aesthetics that stood behind much eighteenth-century poetry and sought to make their work available to as wide a readership as possible.[40] John Keegan Casey (1846–1870), born the year after Davis died, belongs to the second generation of poets in this category, and his work carried the democratic impulse behind the poetry of Young Ireland to its logical conclusion, a full-scale commitment to using the popular ballad and narrative verse as vehicles for nationalist sentiment. Casey's work also reinterpreted the major themes and motifs of the nationalist poetry of the 1840s and 1850s in the light of the more militant Fenian brand of nationalism to which he subscribed. The son of a Catholic schoolteacher in Co. Westmeath, Casey published his first poem, under the pseudonym "Leo," in *The Nation* when he was just sixteen, and his first volume of poems, *A Wreath of Shamrocks: Ballads, Songs and Legends,* appeared when he was only twenty. His poetry was extremely popular in Ireland—a number of his ballads were circulated widely as broadsheets before being published in periodicals or books—and at the same time well regarded in London literary circles;[41] the *London Review* described Casey's poems as "treason . . . put in a fascinating, tolerant, and intelligent shape," adding that "no Saxon could feel overvexed at being railed at so eloquently in his own language."[42] Casey taught school for two years, and worked as an agent for a flour mill. He was associated with the Fenian movement, and in 1867, the year of the Fenian insurrection, was arrested and held in Mountjoy Prison for eight months. Released on the condition that he leave Ireland, he disguised himself as a Quaker and lived under a false name near Dublin Castle, continuing to publish nationalist poems under his pseudonym and to make political speeches. However, his health, never very strong, had apparently been affected by his imprisonment, and he died in 1870, at the age of twenty-three. According to some reports, his funeral was attended by as many fifty thousand people.

Casey's political views were considerably more militant than those of Davis, MacCarthy, and McGee. He was staunchly opposed to any form of constitutional nationalism, and eager to represent his brand of nationalism as an improvement on that of an earlier time:

> There is no excuse for an Irishman who attaches himself to what is called the constitutional body in Ireland. . . . The mere subservience to English authority is a libel on patriotism and nationality, for it is impossible to serve God and the Devil at the same time. Agitation on the moral force ground was tried in O'Connell's time to the fullest extent. Millions were joined in it; yet, after all it was weak and powerless. When the famine was over, and O'Connell dead, we might as well never have gathered on Tara's hill.[43]

His comments on aesthetics reveal the influence of romanticism, but for Casey, art was primarily defined by its relationship to political convictions. Poetry may be, as he said once, "the electric wire that bears the Promethean flame of heaven down to earth," but that flame clearly burns brightest when illuminating the cause of Irish independence conceived in spiritual, transcendent terms:

> Everything gross and material, everything sensual and depraved is untouched by its [poetry's] charm, for tyrant's song never bare the haloed splendour of the poet's touch. But as the life of a nation is its freedom, in the poetry that has kept up that spirit and intensified the natural yearning against oppression we find the music truest, bravest, and tenderest.[44]

The discrepancy between Casey's relatively exalted aesthetic and his practice as a popular poet is common to many nineteenth-century Irish nationalist poets. For those writers, the poet is much more likely to produce haloed splendor when he is writing directly to ordinary people, and this means relatively simple diction and conventional stanzaic and metric forms. It also means poetry that relies heavily on plot and character and on dialogue, including attempts to reproduce the English spoken by Irish peasants. Most of those qualities can be found in Casey's best-known ballad, "The Rising of the Moon," set, like many of Casey's political poems, during the insurrection of 1798.[45] (One measure of the distance between Casey's nationalism and that of Davis is Casey's preoccupation with the 1798 rising, versus Davis's interest in the establishment of Grattan's parliament.) The poem is constructed around an exchange between two Irishmen just before the insurrection begins, and concludes with something like a moral lesson, an affirmation of the relevance of the 1798 rising to the political realities of Ireland in the turbulent 1860s:

> Well they fought for poor old Ireland
>   And full bitter was their fate
> (Oh! what glorious pride and sorrow
>   Fills the name of Ninety-Eight.)
> Yet, thank God, e'en still are beating
>   Hearts in manhood's burning noon,
> Who would follow in their footsteps
>   At the risin' of the moon![46]

Most of Casey's political ballads are governed by a less optimistic reading of Irish history. "Carroll Bawn" re-views the '98 rising from the perspective of a young woman whose lover has died on the gallows for his part in the insurrection, and the poem ends on a note not of redemption through martyrdom, but rather of a longing for death:

> The meadow path is lonely,
>   The hearth is cold and dim,
> And the silent churchyard blossom
>   Blooms softly over him;
> And my heart is ever yearning
>   For the calm rest coming on,
> When its weary pulse lies sleeping
>   Beside my Carroll Bawn.[47]

Casey's birthplace is not far from where Oliver Goldsmith grew up in Co. Westmeath roughly a century earlier, and Goldsmith was an important figure for Casey. Casey's interest in Goldsmith says much about how nineteenth-century nationalists absorbed and rewrote the literary traditions that they inherited. Casey wrote a tribute that presents Goldsmith as an exile, yearning "for other scenes away/In my own land across the sea."[48] The poem concludes with Casey, a "Celtic minstrel," paying his respects to his fellow Irish poet:

> Here, in the spot thy feet oft pressed,
>   A Celtic minstrel tribute pays
>   To all thy strange and generous ways,
> Thy faults, thy virtues, and the rest.
>
> Peace to the clay! Let other men
>   Chant forth thy fame in golden song;
>   I stand and ask, among the throng,
> Where will thy like be found again?[49]

This eulogy is perfectly content to blink at the substantial political, social, and aesthetic differences between the worldly eighteenth-century Anglo-Irish man of letters and the provincial nineteenth-century Fenian balladeer, and that final question, echoing the question that McGee asks about the legendary Irish poet Ossian at the end of "The Celts," clearly implies that Goldsmith is to be counted part of a tradition of Irish poetry that leads quite naturally to the kind of popular nationalist verse that Casey writes.

Women and Politics

The project of nationalism in nineteenth-century Ireland demanded the subjection of the individual to the national, the sacrifice of personal identity to political commitment,[50] and that phenomenon was nowhere more evident than in the writings of the many women who wrote nationalist poetry. Issues of gender, like many questions of difference that were obscured by nationalist ideology because they could not be readily assimilated to its political and cultural agenda, were rarely explored in the verse of these women poets; rather, they tended to settle for a slight feminizing of the rhetoric of nationalism, or for the provision of a female (as opposed to feminist) perspective on historical and contemporary events assigned symbolic value by nationalist ideology.

For some of the women committed to writing political poetry in the middle decades of the nineteenth century, class was at least as important as gender in shaping their relationship to their subject matter. Class was certainly important to the work of Lady Dufferin (1807–1867), born Helen Selina Sheridan and part of a distinguished Anglo-Irish family that included the eighteenth-century dramatist Richard Brinsley Sheridan, Lady Dufferin's grandfather. At the age of eighteen, Helen Selina Sheridan married the heir to the Marquess of Dufferin and Ava, and thereafter she lived mainly in England and Italy, visiting Clandeboye, the Dufferin family's estate in Co. Down, in the summers. She did write occasionally about Ireland, specifically about the famine and emigration. It is doubtful that Lady Dufferin had much personal experience of the famine, but her son, the fifth Lord Dufferin, visited Skibbereen in West Cork in 1846, and reported what he saw in graphic detail.[51] The handful of poems that Lady Dufferin wrote on these issues at times betrays her position as an outsider, but her attempts to portray the famine and its effects from a point of view inside the disaster marks a significant departure from much eighteenth-century Anglo-Irish verse. Also, Lady Dufferin aspired to be a popular poet, and she relied on the same ballad and song forms used by the Young Ireland poets. Her poems about the famine and emigration are distinguished, however, from much of the poetry written by men in response to those events by the extent to which they focus on the destructive impact of the famine on love and the family. Her best-known poem, "The Irish Emigrant," falls into this category, and also exemplifies her efforts to appeal to a wide audience. Narrated by an Irish peasant on the brink of departure from the place where his wife and child recently died of starvation, the poem is simple and direct, and its voice is at least as authentic as that of most of the poetry about the famine written by poets who were much less socially distant from it:

> I'm sitting on the stile, Mary,
>   Where we sat, side by side,
> That bright May morning long ago
>   When first you were my bride.
> The corn was springing fresh and green,
>   The lark sang loud and high,
> The red was on your lip, Mary,
>   The love-light in your eye.
>
>   . . .
>
> 'Tis but a step down yonder lane,
>   The little Church stands near—
> The Church where we were wed, Mary—
>   I see the spire from here;
> But the graveyard lies between, Mary—
>   My step might break your rest,—
> Where you, my darling, lie asleep
>   With your baby on your breast.[52]

This tendency to interpret political events in terms of the individuals affected by them can also be seen in Lady Dufferin's "The Emigrant Ship," another poem narrated by a male survivor of the famine in which concrete references to the life that has been lost are used to generate emotion:

> But the poor turf-fire is out at last, and our hearths are black and chill;
> There is no life; there is no sound; the old man sits no more
> Within the shadow of the thatch, beside the cottage door;
> The child has ceased its playing in the shallow brook close by;
> No kindly smoke is climbing up the grey and empty sky.[53]

The ambiguity of Lady Dufferin's position as a member of the Protestant Ascendancy trying to write with authority about Irish peasants—her social distance from the world that she is describing is revealed in that "kindly smoke"—is particularly evident in her use of dialect, which teeters on the brink of stage-Irishry. "Terence's Farewell to Kathleen," another of the Irish poems for which Lady Dufferin is remembered, invites being read, in the manner of much of the love poetry of Thomas Moore, in nationalist terms. The narrator is a man addressing his lover as she sets out for England, but the lame attempts at rendering colloquial speech undermine the poem's nationalist ambitions: "them English" are "decaivers by nature," the narrator warns his lover, adding, "Ya'll be spakin' sich beautiful English,/ Sure I won't know my Kathleen agen." [54]

The work of Cecil Francis Alexander (1818–1895), the wife of a Protestant rector with few if any of the aristocratic connections enjoyed by Lady Dufferin, represents the unionist point of view as unqualifiedly as Lady Dufferin's work expresses the nationalist position. Born Cecil Francis Humphreys, she was the daughter of a Norfolk soldier who became a landholder in Co. Wicklow and Co. Tyrone. Her husband, William Alexander, whom she married in 1849, eventually became the Bishop of Derry and Raphoe, and the couple was deeply committed to the church. Cecil Francis Alexander first made her reputation as the author of sacred songs and hymns, some of which reportedly went through forty to fifty editions. Like many poets on the nationalist side, Alexander employed popular verse forms in her political poetry, and wrote mainly in narrative and dramatic modes. She also drew on Irish history for dramatic moments that could be interpreted as politically relevant and inspiring to the present. Her long narrative poem "The Siege of Derry" retells the story of the holding of Derry City against James II's forces in 1689, as important a symbol for unionist ideology as the 1798 rebellion was for nationalism. Alexander's poem is set on the day that the English broke the siege, and is structured around a dialogue between a widower and his daughter inside the city walls. The implications for nineteenth-century unionism are never far beneath the surface, as is evident in the widower's account of how the siege began:

> 'Twas the Lord who gave the word when His people drew the sword
> For the freedom of the present, for the future that awaits.
> O Child! thou must remember that bleak day in December
> When the 'Prentice-Boys of Derry rose up and shut the Gates. [55]

Alexander's poetry is also of interest for its commitment to portraying Scots-Ulster culture. Alexander's chief predecessor in this project is James Orr, and like Orr, Alexander relies on the Scots-Irish dialect spoken in Ulster to authenticate her regionalism and her representations of indigenous folk culture. "The Legend of Stumpie's Brae," which Alexander said was written in "the peculiar semi-Scottish dialect spoken in the north of Ireland," [56] tells the story of a rural couple who murder a peddler and then cut off his legs at the knees to fit the corpse into the peddler's peck. The murdered man's ghost, which makes a particularly gruesome sound, haunts the couple:

And through the door, like a sough of air,
    And stump, stump, round the twa,
Wi' his bloody head, and his knee banes bare—
    They'd maist ha'e died of awe.[57]

Although the poem carries no overt political implications, it does represent an
effort to authenticate a specific cultural tradition that, from a unionist point of
view, was every bit as threatened by nineteenth-century political realities as
were, from a nationalist point of view, the legends and stories of Gaelic Ireland.

Of the work of Lady Wilde (1821–1896), who wrote under the pen name
"Speranza," the Fenian poet John Casey said, "Speranza's poetry is like the
whirl of a cataract—indignation, resolve, firmness, and spirit, all roll out." [58] It
is a reasonably accurate assessment. As a young woman in the late 1840s,
before she married William Wilde, a prominent Protestant physician, and before
she became the mother of her famous son, Jane Francesca Elgee wrote political
poetry that was more fiercely, more passionately, more militantly nationalist
than anything written by Thomas Davis or most other contributors to *The
Nation* during those politically charged years. The unrestrained quality of Lady
Wilde's political verse reflected both a romantic temperament and the zeal of a
convert.[59] Her background was thoroughly Anglo-Irish Protestant: her father
was an attorney, and his father a rector and archdeacon in the Church of Ireland;
her mother was the daughter of another cleric, and her maternal great-
grandfather a well-known physician in Georgian Dublin and a friend of Swift.
Jane Elgee's decision in her early twenties to go against her family and devote
herself to the cause of Irish independence was, according to at least one account, characteristically sudden, based on an inspiring and altogether accidental
encounter with the poetry of Richard D'Alton Williams, a particularly incendiary Young Ireland poet. (According to another story about the young Jane
Elgee, she had not even heard of Thomas Davis as late as 1845, the year of his
death.[60]) In any case, she began contributing nationalist verses to *The Nation,*
and in 1848, when the editor, Charles Gavan Duffy, was arrested on a charge
of sedition, she wrote two editorials for *The Nation* that threw all caution to the
wind. "One bold, one decisive move," she wrote in one of them, "Jacta Alea
Est" ("The Die is Cast"). "One instant to take breath, and then a rising; a
rush, a charge from north, south, east and west upon the English garrison, and
the land is ours." [61] After her marriage to William Wilde, who generally shared
her political convictions, Lady Wilde continued to write essays and verse of a
nationalist character, but she and her husband dissociated themselves from the
Fenian movement of the 1860s, in part because of the failure of the Young
Ireland rising of 1848.[62]

Lady Wilde's aesthetics were as strongly colored by romanticism as they
were shaped by her nationalist convictions. In a poem entitled "A Remon-

strance: Addressed to D. Florence MacCarthy," she defines the poet in these
terms:

> The Poet soars with eagles, breathes pure ether,
> Basks in the light that suns the mountain peak,
> And sings, from spirit altitudes, such strains,
> That all the toilers in life's rugged furrows
> Are forced, for once, to lift the bow'd-down head,
> And look on Heaven.[63]

Like many of her fellow nationalists, she also saw Ireland in romantic terms,
as a spiritual being worthy of complete devotion and any sacrifice, and the poet
as a priest with extraordinary powers of inspiration. "Oh! that my words could
burn like molten metal through your veins," she wrote in the essay "Jacta Alea
Est," [64] and her self-reflexive poem "To Ireland" is permeated with romantic
diction and ambition:

> My country, wounded to the heart,
>   Could I but flash along thy soul
> Electric power to rive apart
>   The thunder-clouds that round thee roll,
> And, by my burning words, uplift
> Thy life from out Death's icy drift,
> Till the full splendours of our age
> Shone round thee for thy heritage.[65]

In the famine of the late 1840s, Lady Wilde found an occasion in the real
world commensurate to this romantic conception of Ireland as "wounded to
the heart," and she wrote about the disaster with considerable sympathy, even
intimacy. In one of her best-known poems, "The Famine Years," first published
in *The Nation* in 1847, she describes the sufferings of the famine victims from
the inside point of view of "a gaunt crowd on the highway":

> . . . the blood is dead within our veins—we care not now for life;
> Let us die hid in the ditches, far from children and from wife;
> We cannot stay and listen to their raving, famished cries—
> Bread! Bread! Bread! and none to still their agonies.
> We left our infants playing with their dead mother's hand:
> We left our maidens maddened by the fever's scorching brand.[66]

Lady Wilde's famine poems also place this suffering in its political context,
seeing the famine as part of a centuries-old narrative of English neglect and

oppression and as the proverbial last straw capable of inspiring the Irish to rebellion and freedom. And she does not hesitate to justify, in Christian terms, armed rebellion. Few if any of the Young Ireland poets were as insistent in defining the cause of Irish independence in religious terms, or as radical in portraying England as the embodiment of sin and godless materialism, the elimination of whose presence in Ireland is seen as a sacred cause. In a poem entitled "The Enigma," the Irish are presented as victims not just of political oppression but also of an unholy tyranny, and an unambiguous call for action is sounded in full confidence that Ireland's cause is God's cause:

> Pale victims, where is your Fatherland?
> Where oppression is law from age to age,
> Where the death-plague, and hunger, and misery rage,
> And tyrants a godless warfare wage
>   'Gainst the holiest rights of an ancient land.
>   . . .
> Oh! had ye faith in your Fatherland,
>   In God, your Cause, and your own Right hand,
> Ye would go forth as saints to the holy fight,
> Go in the strength of Eternal right,
> Go in the conquering Godhead's might—
> And save or AVENGE your Fatherland![67]

There is an apocalyptic quality to Lady Wilde's writing that has little tolerance for anything not on the grand scale. "You and other poets," she once said to a friend, "are content to express your own little soul in your poetry. I express the soul of a great nation. Nothing less would satisfy me, who am the acknowledged voice in poetry of all the people of Ireland."[68] It is a preposterously romantic claim, and much is missing from the poetry that comes out of such a view. But this "young lady of fashion," as she was described by one Young Ireland writer,[69] did manage to make herself over into her image of what a nationalist poet should be. As one of her contemporary admirers said:

Miss Jane Francesca Elgee . . . could scarcely have been taught to regard with sympathy the native poor people whom she saw suffering around her, or the men who had embraced their cause. But, in the end, no voice that was raised in the cause of the poor and the oppressed; none that denounced political wrongdoing in Ireland was more eagerly listened to than that of the graceful and accomplished woman known in literature as Speranza, and in society as Lady Wilde.[70]

Mary Kelly (c. 1825–1910) belonged very much to "the native poor people" and "the men who had embraced their cause." Born in Headford, Co. Galway, Kelly was contributing poems to *The Nation*, under the pseudonym "Eva," as early as 1845. Through her association with *The Nation*, she met Kevin Izod O'Doherty, a medical student who was also writing for the paper, and who, after he and Kelly had become engaged, was arrested and transported to Australia. As A. M. Sullivan, the editor of *The Nation* for more than twenty years, described it, O'Doherty "was writing unmistakably seditious prose, while 'Eva' was assailing the constituted authorities in rebel verse." [71] The bulk of Kelly's poems, although somewhat less aggressive than most of Lady Wilde's work, are decidedly of this nature. (Her *Poems*, published in 1877, was dedicated "To the Memory of John Mitchell and John Martin, 'Felons' of '48.'") Most of them were written when Kelly was in her early to mid-twenties, and they often betray an unmediated influence from the English romantics. Her most interesting work treated the conventional themes and motifs of nationalist art and rhetoric from a woman's perspective, although it fell short of seriously interrogating the ways in which nationalist ideology tended to absorb issues of gender. In Kelly's poetry, women are usually presented as enablers, assigned the subsidiary function of inspiring men to political action, and any potential conflict between private, individual feeling and the requirements of a commitment to the nationalist project is minimized, if not eliminated altogether. In a poem entitled "The Patriot Mother," for example, the mother of a young man offered the chance of saving his life by turning informer passionately urges her son to give his life for his country. In her willingness to give up her son, the mother is endorsing the principal of blood-sacrifice, and her appeal presents the cause of Irish independence as a timeless, transcendent truth that readily outweighs the desires or life of any one person:

> I have no one but you in the whole world wide,
> Yet, false to your pledge, you'd ne'er stand at my side;
> If a traitor you lived, you'd be farther away
> From my heart, than if true, you were wrapped in the clay.
>
> Oh, deeper and darker the mourning would be
> For your falsehood so base, than your death, proud and free—
> Dearer, far dearer than ever to me,
> My darling, you'll be on the brave gallows tree.[72]

"The Patriot Mother" is set during the 1798 rebellion and, like many nineteenth-century nationalist poems, it presents the insurrection as having great symbolic significance for the present. In a poem entitled "The Fallen Queen," Kelly considers another symbol of nationalist ideology, that of Ireland as a queen. Kelly is less interested in exploring any feminist implications of this kind of icon than in establishing its symbolic authority. Kelly's queen, although fallen, is an emblem of Ireland's ideal nationhood, and she is presented specifically as the embodiment of spiritual truth in the midst of materialist tyranny:

> For traitor Might may trample down
>   Whate'er is pure and true;
> But Right still wears her golden crown,
>   And claims her glorious due.
> So ev'n amid their cruel power
>   I still can stand serene,
> And hold undimmed the sacred dower
>   Of one, a true-born queen.
>
> For God hath given to me a place,
>   And set on me a sign
> That mortal hand can ne'er deface,
>   Nor I can ne'er resign.
> And though above the land and wave
>   The spoiler strong is seen,
> He's not the less a robber knave,
>   Nor I the less a queen.[73]

At times, however, Kelly's tendency to feminize nationalist rhetoric points away from conventional nationalist attitudes that would suppress individualism. Her "Lament for Thomas Davis," for example, especially when read in comparison with Ferguson's elegy for Davis, resists seeing Davis's death as part of, or justified by, the movement for Irish independence. Rather, the poem registers the emotional effect of his death in the language of a woman who has lost her lover:

> I mourn thee, Thomas Davis, dark, dark and wearily;
> Oh, shut the light from out mine eyes, for I cannot bear to see;
> I cannot look upon the earth and you no longer there:
> 'Tis now, and evermore will be, as my heart is, cold and bare.
> Thomas Davis! Thomas Davis! *acushla sthore machree!*
> My heart, my heart is pouring out black, bitter tears for thee.[74]

Turlough Carolan, the Irish harpist and composer so important to eighteenth-century Irish poets writing in English, wrote a love song addressed to a girl named Bridget Cruise. (The poem was translated by Thomas Furlong for James Hardiman's *Irish Minstrelsy.*) The speaker is smitten by Bridget's beauty, but unable to secure her love. Mary Kelly, in a poem entitled "Bridget Cruise to

Carolan," re-views the situation of Carolan's poem. Kelly's Bridget praises
Carolan's powers of inspiration in decidedly romantic terms:

> I listen to the floods that pour
>   From that sweet fount of song,
> And bathe my spirit o'er and o'er,
>   And thus they roll along.
> I look upon the drooping lid
>   That veils those darkened eyes,
> And think how Heaven is from us hid
>   By your enshrouding skies![75]

That Kelly's Bridget is obsessed not with the lover in Carolan's poem but with
the poet himself, conceived in a thoroughly romantic manner—and a poet who
had by the time of this writing become an icon of nationalist poetics—says
much about Kelly's writing and about the domination of romantic nationalist
concepts of Ireland in nineteen-century Irish poetry.

The name of Ellen Mary Patrick Downing (1828–1869) is usually paired
with that of Mary Kelly. (In his essay "The Influence of National Poetry," John
Casey referred to them as Lady Wilde's "queenly sisters in song." [76]) Like
Kelly, Downing wrote nationalist verse for *The Nation* in the late 1840s, using
the pen-name "Mary." She also fell in love with a Young Ireland writer who
became a political fugitive about the same time that Kevin O'Doherty was
transported to Australia. When she lost her lover, Downing fell back on her
Catholic faith, and a year later entered a convent, where she spent the remainder
of her life. The linking of Kelly and Downing does Kelly something of a
disservice. Downing's poetry is on the whole considerably less mature than is
Kelly's (she was just twenty, at the time of the Young Ireland rising, and
twenty-one when she went into the convent). Her work is of interest chiefly
because of its attempt to conflate Irish Catholicism and nationalism, to spiritual-
ize Irish nationhood by defining it specifically in terms of Catholic doctrines
and symbols. This position went against the grain of much nationalist thinking
during the nineteenth century, particularly Davis's anti-sectarian principles. In
a poem entitled "The Old Church at Lismore," for example, said to have been
the last poem that she wrote before taking the veil, Downing identifies the
redeemed Ireland of the future with the survival of specific practices and icons
of the Catholic Church:

> So shall the land for us be still the Sainted Isle of old,
> Where hymn and incense rise to heaven, and holy beads are told;
> And e'en the ground they tore from God in years of crime and woe,
> Instinctive with His truth and love, shall breathe of long ago![77]

Ellen O'Leary (1831–1889) was at least as close to the Fenian movement as Mary Kelly and Ellen Mary Patrick Downing were to Young Ireland. Born in 1831 in Tipperary, she was the sister of John O'Leary, the Fenian leader and editor of its major newspaper, *The Irish People*. Ellen O'Leary's life was, as the editor of her one volume of verse said, "part of the secret history of her own country." [78] Especially after her brother was sentenced, in 1865, to twenty years of penal servitude, she took an active part in the Fenian movement, at one point helping to engineer the escape from prison of the founder of the Fenians, James Stephens. Yeats, who knew O'Leary when she was living with her brother in Dublin after his return to Ireland in 1885, remembered her as being without rancor or bitterness. "No fanaticism could thrive amid such gentleness," he said. "She . . . needed upon her difficult road no spur of hate." [79] This attitude was not altogether a good thing as far as her poetry went. Even her early poetry, much of it published in *The Irish People* during the rebellious 1860s, lacked the passion and anger of Lady Wilde's writing. Also, O'Leary's nationalist verse, like much of the Fenian poetry of the 1860s, tended to recycle the themes and motifs of Young Ireland verse. The one distinctive feature of her work was its attempt to represent with sympathy and accuracy the rhythms and idioms of colloquial speech. Charles Gavan Duffy's judgment that O'Leary wrote "not in conventional stage Irish, but in the authentic tongue of a peasant born and bred in the shade of Slievenamon" [80] may need some qualification, especially for modern readers, but O'Leary's use of colloquial speech patterns does at times enhance her efforts to portray realistically the situation of Irish peasants in the decades following the famine. Her poems are certainly more authentic in this regard than is the work of Lady Dufferin, as can be seen in "A Ballad," spoken in the voice of a widow left with three children and scant means of supporting them:

> The gale day last November, 'twas to me the bitter day;
> The rent was due, and my last cow the bailiffs drove away.
>
> . . .
>
> I am a poor lone woman now, three children by my side,
> And how, or where, God only knows, I'm for them to provide.
> Year after year, and bit by bit, the land they took away;
> A few small acres and the house are all I hold to-day.
> 'Twas not wet summers or *the blight* that ever brought me down:
> We had no lease, nor could we thrive under the landlord's frown.[81]

Unfortunately, by the time that O'Leary was writing, nationalist poetry had settled into the comfortable but deadening ruts of convention and cliché, one of which was the woman's point of view. Not until nearly the end of the century, with the beginnings of the literary revival, would Irish poetry inspired by cultural and political nationalism, as well as poetry written by Irish women, begin seriously to question those shopworn attitudes and practices in the search for new ways of expressing an Irish experience undergoing constant and rapid change.

PART THREE

THE LITERARY REVIVAL

INTRODUCTION

The Irish literary revival was less a product of contemporary political or literary factors—the death of Parnell in 1891, as Yeats once argued, or the publication in 1878 and 1880 of Standish O'Grady's two-volume *History of Ireland,* with its purple-prose versions of ancient Irish legends—than of various cultural forces that had been developing throughout the nineteenth century.[1] The emergence of translation as a significant mode of poetic discourse in the 1830s and 1840s provided both practical precedent and theoretical justification for one of the revival's most basic assumptions: that the reconstruction of Ireland's cultural past, and the attempt to establish a cultural identity around that reconstruction, would be carried out not in the language of that past, but rather in that of the cultural and political forces responsible, in large part, for its demise. The tradition of translation had always rested, somewhat uneasily, on the assumption that the Irish language was no longer a viable cultural medium for the majority of Irish people, and the division between leaders of the literary revival, such as Yeats and Lady Gregory, and supporters of the Gaelic League's ambitions to restore Irish as the dominant language of the island, such as Douglas Hyde, grew naturally out of the ambiguities surrounding translation in the nineteenth century, when the language suffered its most dramatic decline. Moreover, this split between the revival and organized efforts to save the language had significant implications for the revival's precarious relationship with the native Irish population, symbolizing if not embodying apparently unbridgeable cultural differences between the essentially Anglo-Irish Protestant leadership of the revival and the Gaelic, Catholic majority of Irish people in whose name the revival was, in theory at least, undertaken.[2]

While the translators of the nineteenth century helped legitimate the revival's commitment to English rather than Irish, the general tendency toward the Anglicization of Irish writing in the nineteenth century provided a precedent for the assumption that the revival's principal architects would be—and, from some points of view, should be—Anglo-Irish. Indeed, as the social status of the Ascendancy continued to decline, and as relatively militant nationalist forces began to gain strength in the wake of the death of Parnell, the dominant class became particularly anxious to retain control of the nation's cultural life, which had been in their hands since the eighteenth century. The Anglo-Irish effort to maintain a cultural aristocracy to offset their increasingly uncertain political and social position worked itself out in a number of ways in the writing that came out of the revival. The tendency of revival writers, for example, to look past Ireland's great Christian period from the fifth through the eighth centuries to its pre-Christian heroic period had the effect of minimizing the Catholic dimension of the Irish consciousness.[3] Also, by defining the culture depicted in the literature of Ireland's pagan past as essentially aristocratic, revival writers from Anglo-Irish backgrounds were able to advance and justify their own social and cultural position at the expense of more democratic representations of Irish society.[4] "The Celt was essentially aristocratic," the Irish Literary Society of London was told in 1899 by the coeditor of the influential *A Treasury of Irish Poetry* (1900); "there is no trace of any democratic feeling such as grew up in the English towns."[5] The cultural authority of the Anglo-Irish who directed the revival was also established by attacking and excluding the Irish Catholic middle-class on the ground that middle-class materialism, associated with English culture, could not be reconciled with an understanding of the true nature of Irish identity, defined as spiritual and aesthetic.[6] In effect, this position appropriated the nineteenth-century nationalist distinction between spiritual Ireland and material England and converted it into both a justification for a highly aestheticized, even mystical vision of Ireland and a means of affirming the status of the Anglo-Irish cultural aristocracy at the expense of the Catholic middle class. All this lies behind the revival's specifically self-reflexive interest in legendary heroes such as Cuchulain and the representation, especially in the early poetry of Yeats and of revival writers such as John Todhunter and T. W. Rolleston, of Ireland as the land of a "Celtic Twilight" romanticism, *"a Druid land, a Druid tune,"* as Yeats once put it.[7]

The attempt by many revival writers to distance their work from political issues, a position encouraged if not required by the relatively precarious status of the Anglo-Irish ruling class at the end of the century, also grew in part out of nineteenth-century Irish writing, especially the rise of popular nationalist verse from the 1840s on. Precedents from the earlier part of the century were used by the revival as negative rather than positive models; Yeats's aesthetic critique of the poetry produced by the Young Ireland movement was simply the most overt manifestation of an aesthetic and political attitude that ran deep in revival thinking and colored much of the poetry associated with it. "There is not a patriotic poem in the book," A. E. boasted upon the publication in 1904 of his anthology *New Songs*.[8] By associating the romanticism that lay behind the nineteenth century's idealization of Ireland with *fin-de-siècle* aestheticism and various forms of mysticism, Yeats and his followers were working to sunder the linkage between romanticism and nationalism that the Young Ireland poets and their successors had built up. This aesthetic position inevitably generated a disjunction between the revival's vision of Ireland and the social, political, and economic reality of the nation's life at the turn of the century, a disjunction that added fuel to the argument advanced by the revival's enemies that the movement was betraying rather than representing the Irish experience. One place where such a disjunction was most visible, and most vulnerable, was the revival's depiction of rural Ireland. The revival's tendency to romanticize the Irish peasantry as a culturally privileged aristocracy not only blinked at the appalling living conditions of many Irish peasants at the time (and at the rise of organized opposition to the landlords, many of them Anglo-Irish, who were held to be responsible for those conditions), but also failed to register the cultural as well as economic significance of various land-reform acts passed late in the century, culminating in Wyndham's Land Act of 1903, which in effect made it possible for Irish peasants to become that most unromantic of classes, bourgeois proprietors.

In part because it was alienated from the population as a whole, the revival was, from the beginning, almost certain not to achieve all its ambitions, particularly those aimed at creating a cultural identity for what Yeats called the "whole people" of Ireland.[9] Moreover, the revival planted the seeds of its own destruction by pointing the way to a rise in Gaelic consciousness that would inevitably, despite all the movement's doctrines of aesthetic purity, be wedded to the various forces working at the time for a political independence guaranteed to disempower the Anglo-Irish. Moreover, the revival depended romantically not just on an image of Ireland as a conquered nation but also on an image of its own leadership as heroically alienated from a majority defined as essentially Philistine. In other words, the revival could not afford success: neither the political success of the nationalist movement, nor even the success of its own agenda of cultural unity and identity. "The Tragic Generation" is what Yeats, reflecting back on his work and his colleagues in the 1880s and 1890s, termed it all, and A. E., in a rare moment of Yeatsian bitterness, looked around at the ruin of what Yeats had called "the dream of my early manhood, that a modern nation can return to Unity of Culture" [10] and pronounced it all a "grim mechanic state." [11]

Nevertheless, the significance of the revival for the development of Irish poetry in English is difficult to overestimate. Especially when considered against the backdrop of nineteenth-century poetry in Ireland, with its need to establish a counter-hegemonic voice governed by nationalist ambitions that effectively minimized rather than encouraged variety and difference, the poetry of the literary revival can be seen as having extended significantly the range of poetic discourse in Ireland, as well as broadening the very idea of what Irishness was and could be.[12] In an effort to define and establish an identity specific to Ireland that might be used to resist the advent of modernization, the revival in fact brought into Irish writing a host of aesthetic and cultural ideas that tended to place Ireland in the context of a European, if not international, cultural environment. The *fin-de-siècle* aesthetics of the London literary world, the *symboliste* theories of French writers, Eastern occultism—all these were found relevant to Irish culture, and Irish culture was found relevant to all of them. At the same time, the translation enterprise was carried forward in ways that extended its boundaries, broadening and enriching the concept of the Irish tradition. George Sigerson's *Bards of the Gael and Gall* (1897) insisted on the pluralistic nature of that tradition, as opposed to the almost exclusively Gaelic emphasis of translators working earlier in the century, while Douglas Hyde's versions of Connacht folk songs brought to the attention of readers who did not know Irish the rich tradition of folk literature in the native language. Another useful barometer of the kind of change that the revival brought about is the substantial body of poetry written by women during this period. The emergence of women as significant contributors to nationalist poetry in the nineteenth century helped pave the way for women poets in the revival, but whereas issues of gender were often obscured in the poetry of women writing earlier in the century, the work of the women poets associated with the revival assumed the freedom not only to address such questions but also to use gender difference as a means of interrogating a wide range of cultural and political assumptions. The revival also produced a number of writers who challenged some of the movement's most fundamental assumptions from within. The attempt in the work of Joseph Campbell and Padraic Colum to represent with some degree of realism and from the inside Ireland's folk culture and the rural life that sustained it is one example of this, as is the fusion of nationalism and Catholicism in the poetry of several poets who participated in the Easter Rising. Moreover, the work in translation of two of the Rising poets, Thomas MacDonagh and Patrick Pearse, can be seen as an effort to replace the early revival's idea of the Celt with a more culturally authentic representation of the Gael. Finally, Seamus O'Sullivan and James Stephens attempted to represent in a relatively realistic mode the Irish urban experience, anticipating the urban realism of much twentieth-century Irish fiction while implicitly holding up to question the revival's contention that the Irish identity was essentially rural. Indeed, Yeats's lament in 1907—the year of the riots over Synge's *The Playboy of the Western World* at the Abbey Theatre in January and of the death of the Fenian leader John O'Leary in March—that the revival's dream of cultural unity in Ireland was past, and that Irish poets had become "protesting individual voices," [13] might well be read as an affirmation of how the revival, in its failings as well as its successes, moved Irish poetry out of the nineteenth century and into the twentieth.

CHAPTER NINE

TRANSLATION:
GAEL, GALL, AND PEASANT

At the same time that translation firmly connected the revival to its roots in the earlier decades of the nineteenth century—George Sigerson's first book was a second series of *Poets and Poetry of Munster,* the first series of which was published in 1849, and included a number of Mangan's translations—it also contributed to the revival's diversification of poetic discourse. Sigerson's *Bards of the Gael and Gall* (1897), for example, reconstructed the Irish tradition in relatively pluralistic terms, rejecting the conventional nationalist view and its tendency to glorify the native Gaelic tradition at the expense of any other. Sigerson's book of translations functioned in fact like a kind of literary history, representing not just the heroic, legendary past—the territory of Ferguson's verse epics in the 1860s—but also poems and songs from the Norse and Norman strands of the Irish tradition. One effect of this broadening of the concept of Irishness was to discourage the association, encouraged in much nineteenth-century translation, between antiquarianism and political separatism. At the same time, Douglas Hyde's transcriptions and translations of the love and religious songs of Connacht established the authority of Ireland's rich and largely oral folk tradition. Some translators working earlier in the century, such as J. J. Callanan and Edward Walsh, had made inroads into this area, but Hyde's work, in part because of Hyde's position in the literary revival and language movement, generated a currency and respectability for this material, indigenous to the remote districts of the island, not always accorded earlier efforts to preserve it. In part because they were working out of a commitment to scholarly accuracy, the translations of Sigerson and Hyde also tended to counter the *fin-de-siècle* aestheticism that characterized much of the poetry associated with the so-called Celtic Twilight phase of the literary revival. Hyde's work in particular can be seen to anticipate the anti-aesthetic tendencies in the work of Synge and the emphasis on colloquial speech that marked the development of a distinctively modern writing in Ireland.

Nonetheless, the work of both Sigerson and Hyde, like much of the poetry of the early years of the revival, appears escapist when read against the background of the pressing political, economic, and social issues of the closing decades of the nineteenth century. Hyde's translations of the songs of Connacht, however much they managed to resist the more blatant romanticization of the peasant life that became a staple of much revival writing, interpreted rural Ireland in the ahistorical terms of folk culture, thereby overlooking the realities of the land war and of the gradual, constitutional drive for peasant proprietorship, a movement that was to transform the Irish peasantry into a bourgeois class that bore little resemblance to the values and images embodied in Hyde's work. Sigerson's researches into Ireland's past, broad-minded as they were, could be viewed, especially in the face of the rapidly developing pressures for some kind of Irish independence, as somewhat futile exercises in the arcane, or, worse, as part of an attempt by the threatened Anglo-Irish to maintain a foothold in Irish culture. Finally, the whole enterprise of translation and language revival was permeated by the atmosphere of a lost cause. This was particularly true of Hyde's argument for de-Anglicizing Irish culture and his attempt, through the Gaelic League, to revive the language. In fact, the language had declined precipitously even from its threatened position during the 1830s and 1840s, when Mangan and Ferguson were at their height, and, ironically, had passed beyond the point where it could be rescued at the very moment that the most organized and concerted effort to save it was launched.

Sigerson (1836–1925), an Anglo-Irishman born in Ulster (Strabane) and educated in Paris and Cork, seems to have had little interest in restoring Irish to its previous stature as the nation's chief language, and he certainly was opposed to the separatist and exclusionist implications of the language movement. His *Bards of the Gael and Gall* was dedicated both to the Young Irelander Charles Gavan Duffy, described as "a representative of the Gael," and to Hyde, "a descendant of the Gall" [1]—a concise expression of Sigerson's view of Irish culture as consisting of a blend of interdependent traditions, rather than of an irreconcilable difference between two principal traditions or, as nationalist history would have it, the oppression of one tradition by another. Sigerson spelled out his view of the Gael and Gall in a lecture delivered to the opening of the National Literary Society in Dublin in 1892, a few months before Hyde's more famous, and very different, lecture, "The Necessity for De-Anglicising Ireland." In his address, carrying the less didactic, more scholarly title of "Irish Literature: Its Origin, Environment, and Influences," Sigerson specifically associated a certain kind of militant patriotism with a narrow, exclusionist reading of the Irish tradition, and argued that such a position betrayed the actual diversity and richness of that tradition:

let me say that I am taken with dismay when I find some of my patriotic young friends deciding what is and what is not the Irish style in prose and the Irish note in poetry. . . . it is scarcely too much to say that you may search through all the Gaelic literature of the nation, and find many styles, but not this. If it ever existed, it existed outside our classic literature, in a rustic or plebeian dialect. It must be counted, but to make it exclusive would be to impose fatal fetters on our literary expression. As in other countries, there were not one but many styles, differing with the subject, the writer, and the age.[2]

And in the preface to *Bards of the Gael and Gall,* Sigerson reminded his readers: "It is not the Gael only who mourns. Many bards bear foreign names. Their fathers had crossed with the Normans, or with later settlers, yet they claimed the country's heritage as their history, and they make appeal to all its ancient traditions. . . . A Norman Nugent feels the pang of exile as keenly as an O'Neill." [3]

Sigerson could trace part of his ancestry back to the Norse presence in Ireland in the ninth and tenth centuries, and in *Bards of the Gael and Gall,* he argues with particular forcefulness for reevaluating the Norse contribution to Irish culture. Rejecting the conventional nationalist view of the Norse as marauders who destroyed much of Gaelic civilization, Sigerson attempts to document the ways in which the Norse were integrated into Gaelic culture, enriching it and extending its horizons. Among the book's translations is a substantial group of poems, under the heading of "Gael and Norse," that interrogate conventional notions of the Norse as just another wave of invaders and colonizers. The "Lay of Norse-Irish Sea-Kings," for example, attributed by Sigerson to "Artur Mac Gureaich, the blind," describes the arrival of the Vikings in Ireland from the point of view of the Vikings rather than that of the "conquered" Gael. The poem also insists on both the prowess of the Vikings and their value to Ireland:

> Ne'er did Finn or Fianna know
> Gallant chiefs of deeds more grand,
> Nor could Erinn braver show
> Than this fair-haired battle band.[4]

The poem concludes with a statement of the blind Irish poet's obligation to record the achievements of the Norse leaders—"Be it now the blind bard's care/Him to sing, strong, sage, and fair" [5]—and it is not difficult to see Sigerson himself, an Anglo-Irish poet and translator of Norse extraction working in the increasingly nationalist atmosphere of the late nineteenth century and in the wake of the exclusionist discourse of nineteenth-century nationalism, behind that mask.

If the substance of Sigerson's translations insisted on seeing Irish culture as a
blend of differing traditions, in contradistinction to both nationalist and Celticist
versions of the Irish past, the form of many of the translations in *Bards of the
Gael and Gall* challenged another notion about the Irish tradition that was
thriving in the early years of the revival. Sigerson's critique of "Celtic Twilight" aestheticism is advanced in the preface. "Those who want to associate
Irish poetry with effusiveness of thought and luxuriance of language," he says,
"will be surprised to find that bardic poetry was characterized by classic reserve
in thought, form, and expression." [6] Sigerson's translations, especially of pre-
Christian Irish verse, work hard to embody this "higher grace of classic firmness," [7] a quality absĕnt from much of the writing associated with the early
years of the revival and from much of the work done in translation before
Sigerson. "The First Elegy," attributed by Sigerson to the period of the "Milesian Invaders," and based on a story about a woman who died of shame upon
seeing her husband bathing naked and thinking him a stranger, sounds a note
quite alien to the poetic conventions that dominated Irish writing in the 1890s:

> Sate we sole, in cliff-bower—
> Chill winds shower—
> I tremble yet—shock of dread
> Sped death's power.
> The tale I tell: fate has felled
> Fáil most fine.
> She a man, bare, beheld,
> In sun shine,
> Shock of death, death's dread power,
> Lowered fell fate,
> Bare I came, hence her shame,
> Stilled she sate. [8]

In "The Cold Night of Innisfail," from the legendary Fenian cycle of Irish
writing, this quality of spareness and compression is enhanced by Sigerson's
attempts at working into English verse some of the complex patterns of rhyme
and assonance that characterize poetry in Irish:

> Cold, cold,
> Chill, this night, is Lurc's wide wold;
> Foodless now the gaunt deer goes,
> High o'er hills the snows are rolled.
>
> Cold to death
> Sweeps the broad'ning tempest's breath;

Round the fords the whirlpools roar,
Rills through ridges pour in wrath[9]

In a moment of presumably understated irony, Hyde once said that Sigerson rarely "allowed himself to be seduced from the severe path of scholarship."[10] And there is something plodding and stilted about many of Sigerson's translations, especially when read against the work of earlier translators such as Ferguson and Mangan. No doubt this accounts in part for his limited influence on revival writers. On the dedication page of *Bards of the Gael and Gall,* Sigerson describes himself as "one of the Gall-Gael" and as president of the National Literary Society of Ireland, an organizational pillar of the revival; but in fact this attempt to associate his pluralism with the revival was not nearly as effective as was Hyde's call for de-Anglicizing Irish culture.[11] Not until a reaction to the revival set in, in the work, for example, of Austin Clarke and F. R. Higgins, did Sigerson's attempt to replace the romantic idealization of the Celt with an understanding of the complex, pluralistic nature of the Gaelic tradition begin to take hold.

Although Sigerson and Hyde (1860–1949) represent two different stances toward the issue of the Irish language, and therefore toward the purposes of translation, and although Hyde's focus is, by comparison with Sigerson's, decidedly provincial (the folk songs of one rural district), Hyde shared with Sigerson the assumption that the translator must be committed to scholarly accuracy. In the preface to *Love Songs of Connacht* (1893), addressed to Sigerson, Hyde claims that his translations of folk songs are to be distinguished from the work of previous translators, including Mangan and Ferguson, because they attempt "to reproduce the vowel-rhymes as well as the exact metres of the original poems."[12] Whether or not Hyde's translations are in fact more authentic than the work of Mangan and Ferguson, not to mention that of Callanan and Walsh, Hyde's versions of Connacht folk songs are remarkably successful in conveying the note of melancholy that pervaded the remote, vulnerable world of Irish-speaking Ireland at the end of the nineteenth century. The dark past of that world and its apparently bleak future are both refracted powerfully though songs having to do with failed love or departed lovers: "My Grief on the Sea" ("Abandoned, forsaken,/To grief and to care,/Will the sea ever waken/Relief from despair?"), "Ringleted Youth of My Love" ("Like a bush in a gap in a wall/I am now left lonely without thee,/And this house I grow dead of, is all/ That I see around or about me"), and "The Brow of Nefin" ("But so it is not in this world/For myself and my thousand-times fair,/For away, far apart from each other,/Each day rises barren and bare"[13]). At times that sense of a damaged past and a threatened future suggests Hyde's own problematic position as a poet and scholar working at the end of the nineteenth century to prevent the extinction of a language and its culture. "I Am Raftery," based on a poem by

Antoine Ó Reachtabhra (Anthony Raftery), supposedly one of the last Irish-language folk-poets in Co. Mayo, is a well-known example, but at least equally effective is Hyde's version of a song of lament attributed to the legendary Fenian-cycle poet Ossian, the model for a very different representation of the Irish poet in Yeats's *The Wanderings of Oisin:*

> I make no music, I find no feast,
>   I slay no beast from a bounding steed,
> I give no gold, I am poor and old,
>   I am sick and cold without wine or mead.[14]

As is evident in these lines, Hyde's translations, like some of Sigerson's, are marked by a spareness and directness not often found in the work of their predecessors or in the relatively romantic poetry of the early stages of the revival. Hyde's work also specifically embodies the idioms and colloquialisms of the speech of peasants whose English has been colored by the forms and structures of Irish, thereby resisting the conventional poetic diction of much nineteenth-century Irish poetry in English and anticipating one of the central qualities of twentieth-century Irish writing. A number of Hyde's versions of the songs of Connacht also refer to sexuality with an explicitness that is rarely found in the love poetry of the revival but that is very much part of the Gaelic tradition. The erotic specificity in this description of a woman, from a translation entitled "Little Child, I Call Thee," is notably absent, for example, from the early love poetry of Yeats:

> Pure white hand and shapely finger,
>   Limbs that linger like a song;
> Music speaks in every motion
>   Of my sea-mew warm and young.
>
> Rounded breasts and lime-white bosom,
>   Like a blossom, touched of none,
> Stately form and slender waist,
>   Far more graceful than the swan.[15]

Finally, Hyde's translations often unblinkingly describe the streak of brutality and violence in rural Irish life, recorded as far back as Swift's "The Description of an *Irish-Feast*" (1720), but for the most part elided from the literary revival's recreation of Gaelic Ireland. Hyde's lengthy translation of a curse poem, "Bruadar and Smith and Glinn," anticipates some of Synge's work:

> Glinn in a shaking ague,
>   Cancer on Bruadar's tongue,

Amen, O King of the Heavens! and Smith
   For ever striken dumb.
        Amen!
       .   .   .

Smith without child or heir,
   And Bruadar bare of store,
Amen, O Jesus! hear my voice,
   Let Smith be bent in chains.
        Amen!
       .   .   .

Blight skull and ear, and skin,
   And hearing, and voice, and sight,
Amen! before the year be out,
   Blight, Son of the Virgin, blight.
        Amen![16]

There are other ways in which Hyde stood apart from the aesthetics and politics of the literary revival. His advocacy of the Irish language as the only authentic medium for Irish writing—embodied most effectively in the Gaelic League, which he founded in 1893, the year he published *Love Songs of Connacht*—separated him from most of the revival's central figures, most notably Yeats, and from Sigerson's pluralistic vision of the Irish tradition as well. Also, although it is possible that Hyde was not fully aware of the separatist implications of the language movement and the Gaelic League,[17] he certainly began his career with unqualified, even militant convictions about nationalism. Some of his earliest poems, published in one of the most important publications of the early phase of the revival, *Poems and Ballads of Young Ireland* (1888), are very much in the vein of the Young Ireland and Fenian political balladry that Yeats found so useless. And Hyde's famous call for de-Anglicizing Ireland was couched in terms that deliberately echoed the tone and fervor of nineteenth-century nationalist writing:

In a word, we must strive to cultivate everything that is most racial, most smacking of the soil, most Gaelic, most Irish, because in spite of the admixture of Saxon blood in the north-east corner, this island *is* and will *ever* remain Celtic at the core.[18]

Looking back over the language movement and the literary revival from the vantage point of 1923 and the foundation of the Free State, Hyde said that the Gaelic League was "the spiritual father of Sinn Fein"[19]—not the kind of ancestry that Yeats, for one, would be likely to embrace.

Nonetheless, there are qualities in Hyde's work that made him a welcome figure in the literary revival. His representation of the Irish peasantry was constructed in the ahistorical terms of folk art, and thus tended to ignore the kind of political pressures—especially the drive for peasant proprietorship—that many revival writers saw, often wishfully, as irrelevant to the enterprise of establishing a significant Irish literature in English. Read as expressions of universal melancholy, Hyde's love songs of Connacht suggest a retreat from the kind of poetic engagement with rural issues represented most effectively in Irish poetry in English by Goldsmith in the eighteenth century and William Allingham in the nineteenth.[20] Also, Hyde could be seen as someone who was working to salvage certain cultural values of the past in the face of the distressing rise of materialism in the present.[21] Certainly Yeats was eager to read Hyde in this nostalgic way; in the preface to a limited edition of *Love Songs of Connacht,* published by Yeats's Dun Emer Press, Yeats said of Hyde's subject-matter:

> These poor peasants lived in a beautiful but somewhat inhospitable world, where little has changed since Adam delved and Eve spun. Everything was so old that it was steeped in the heart, and every powerful emotion found at once noble types and symbols for its expression. But we live in a world of whirling change where nothing becomes old and sacred, and our powerful emotions unless we be highly trained artists express themselves in vulgar types and symbols.[22]

The extent to which Hyde himself can be held to account for this romanticization of his work, or the extent to which he can be seen, as Ferguson was seen before him, as attempting to shore up the increasingly threatened position of the Anglo-Irish by dominating and controlling the antiquarian enterprise, is difficult to determine. What is certain is that the relatively slim body of verse translations that Hyde left behind him—Yeats once complained about Hyde's increasing involvement in political and cultural organizations, lamenting "the great poet who died in his youth"[23]—has a significance to the development not just of translation but of Irish poetry in English that far exceeds Hyde's own understanding of what he was doing: "throwing some of these songs," as he put it in the preface to *Love Songs of Connacht,* "into English verse—such as it is."[24]

CELTICISM AND ROMANTICISM

Yeats's theory that the death of Parnell in 1891 opened the way for the Irish literary revival rests on an assumption about the necessary separation of literature from its political and social context that governed much of the writing that the revival produced.[1] Indeed, many of the writers associated with the revival, especially in its early years, quite calculatedly drove a wedge, fashioned in large part out of the Pateresque aesthetics of *fin-de-siècle* England, between Irish art and Irish politics or, more specifically, between Irish romanticism and Irish nationalism, the very connection upon which was built so much nationalist writing earlier in the century. From some points of view—certainly from many nationalist ones—this enterprise threatened to betray the urgent political needs and future of a nation presumably on the brink of some kind of dramatic change, while maintaining the cultural domination of the many by the few for which earlier Anglo-Irishmen such as Samuel Ferguson had labored in the face of equally strong pressures for political change. Many of the leading figures of the revival had credentials that looked suspicious to a committed nationalist, and for some of them at least, Irish culture appeared to be merely a stop on the line, an exotic, romantic territory to be explored but then left behind.[2]

Without setting aside this view completely, it is also possible to see the revival less as an attempt to falsify or gloss over the realities of Irish experience than as an effort to broaden a poetic discourse that had become increasingly narrowed by a nationalist ideology committed to constructing a relatively monolithic counter-hegemonic response to the colonization of Ireland in the years following the Union of 1800. Some of the romantic qualities usually associated with the poetry of the early revival can be found in earlier nineteenth-century Irish writing: its heavy reliance on symbolism, its preference for the fleeting impressionism of the lyric, its view of art as a means to spiritual transcendence, its interpretation of Ireland as an essentialized, spiritual being, its corresponding identification of materialism with English culture, and its tendency to look back rather than forward. But the importation into Irish writing of French theories of symbolism, of a *fin-de-siècle* world-weariness from the English decadent movement, of the late-Victorian aesthetics of English writers such as Swinburne, Morris, and Rossetti, and of various strains of mysticism and occultism appropriated from Eastern thought substantially redefined the concept of Irish culture, and not always in ways that betrayed the Irish experience. "We need not fear," Lionel Johnson told a meeting of the National Literary Society in Dublin in 1894, "lest an Irish poet should cease to be Irish, if he study and borrow and adopt the best achievements of foreign art to the service of the Irish Muses." [3]

The tendency of writers working in the early years of the revival to romanticize the Irish experience and then abandon it is manifest in the work of John Todhunter (1839–1916). Born of Quaker ancestry before the advent of Young Ireland, Todhunter belonged to the generation of Yeats's father, but it was Yeats who brought him, relatively late in his career, to an interest in writing about Ireland. Todhunter had moved to London in 1874, settling at Bedford Park, where he was a friend of the Yeats family. In the late 1880s, Todhunter and Yeats worked together closely, Todhunter reading his poems to Yeats and helping Yeats correct proofs of *The Wanderings of Oisin*. [4] Todhunter was present at the meeting at Yeats's house in 1891 at which the Southwark Club was changed into the Irish Literary Society. Todhunter's collection of Irish poems, *The Banshee,* was published in 1888 (the year of the publication of the revival anthology *Poems and Ballads of Young Ireland,* which included four of Todhunter's poems), making it, next to Katharine Tynan's *Shamrocks* (1887), the earliest collection of poems identifiable as belonging to the literary revival. Nevertheless, although he published a life of Patrick Sarsfield in 1894 and some versions of ancient Irish legends *(Three Bardic Tales)* in 1896, Todhunter never fully committed himself to the revival, as Yeats had urged him to do, and he went on to write plays for the English stage, a study of Shelley, and poems very much in the English tradition.

"A noble chant over the sorrows of Ireland . . . something between Walt Whitman and the Scotch Ossian," Yeats described the title poem of *The Banshee;* the comment gets to the central qualities of Todhunter's poetry and his romanticization of Ireland. [5] *The Banshee* is permeated by a note of romantic melancholy that, while it looks back to the laments of Moore and Mangan, also ascribes to the Irish condition a universality and passivity that depoliticize that condition. The opening of "The Banshee" is a case in point:

> Green, in the wizard arms
> Of the foam-bearded Atlantic,

> An isle of old enchantment,
> A melancholy isle,
> Enchanted and dreaming lies;
> And there, by Shannon's flowing,
> In the moonlight, spectre-thin,
> The spectre Erin sits.
>
> An aged desolation,
> She sits by old Shannon's flowing,
> A mother of many children,
> Of children exiled and dead,
> In her home, with bent head, homeless,
> Clasping her knees she sits,
> Keening, keening![6]

However misty their vision of Ireland, these lines indicate the extent to which Todhunter was looking for ways to challenge the conventional verse forms and regular rhythms that dominated Irish poetry in English in the nineteenth century.

Todhunter is best known for his political ballad "Aghadoe," a poem that delivers its conventional theme of betrayal through the unconventional voice of a young girl whose republican lover has been betrayed to the British by her brother. The poem opens with a description worthy of Moore:

> There's a glade in Aghadoe, Aghadoe, Aghadoe,
> There's a green and silent glade in Aghadoe,
> Where we met, my love and I, love's fair planet in the sky,
> O'er that sweet and silent glade in Aghadoe.[7]

But when it shifts to expressing the girl's suffering, the complex of emotions that the girl is experiencing is reflected in more flexible rhythms and in a voice capable of a considerable range of feeling:

> Oh! my curse on one black heart in Aghadoe, Aghadoe,
> On Shaun Dhuv, my mother's son, in Aghadoe!
> When your throat fries in hell's drougth, salt the flame be in your mouth,
> For the treachery you did in Aghadoe!
>   . . .
> I walked to Mallow town from Aghadoe, Aghadoe,
> Brought his head from the gaol's gate to Aghadoe,
> Then I covered him with fern, and I piled on him the cairn,
> Like an Irish king he sleeps in Aghadoe.[8]

Even more striking is Todhunter's "Under the White-Boy Acts, 1800. An Old Rector's Story," the lead poem in *Poems and Ballads of Young Ireland*. In this poem, which narrates the experience of a former yeoman who watched in horror as the captain of his troop cut down a blind fiddler standing by the roadside during the time of the violent "Whiteboy" movement in rural Munster, a distinctly Browningesque quality of voice carries the traditional political ballad of nineteenth-century nationalist writing into the territory of psychological realism. The description of the killing is remarkable not only for its unflinching vividness but also for its astute measuring of the psychological and political significance of the incident:

> You'd never think a man's last agony
> Could look so like a joker's antics, played
> To raise a laugh. Yet no one laughed, I think.
> We had pushed across the stream. I saw them lift
> His head, with long grey hair dabbled with blood.
> The sword had caught him under the right ear,
> And through the gash his poor, scared, struggling heart
> Simply pumped out his life. . . .
>
> . . .
>
> An ugly business that. I never knew
> How my Lord felt about that sad mistake;
> Such things *will* happen under martial law,
> And ill-judged acts, done through excess of zeal,
> The king's commision covers in such times.
> We heard no more of it. But all that night
> I felt myself next-door a murderer,
> And rode with a sick chill about my heart.
> No more pride in my uniform; no more
> Delight under the ghastly glaring moon
> That showed me Tom's dead face![9]

The sure hand behind this voice is not, unfortunately, always to be found in Todhunter's poetry about Ireland. In fact, when he attempts to write dramatic verse from the point of view of the native Irish, he falls into a stereotyping that betrays his position as a cultural outsider or as someone on his way to another destination, as indeed he was.

William Larminie (1849–1900) appears to be much more seriously committed than Todhunter to the aims of the revival, especially its antiquarian dimension. A Mayo man, he collected local folk-tales, publishing a volume entitled *West Irish Folk-Tales and Romances* in 1898. (Yeats was far readier to praise his work as a folklorist than as a poet.) His most important collection of poems

on Irish themes, *Fand,* published in 1892, contained lengthy versions of two
stories taken from Ireland's ancient heroic literature, that of the conflict between
Fand and Emer over Cuchulain (later adapted by Yeats for the stage as *The
Only Jealousy of Emer),* and that of the battle of Moytura (the basis of Ferguson's epic verse translation, *Congal,* published in 1872). He also developed a
detailed theory on the use of assonance that Austin Clarke, among others, was
to find important to his efforts to construct a poetry in English sensitive to the
formal structures of poetry in Irish.[10] Larminie was also something of a mystic,
and his poetry on Irish subjects often seems less interested in those subjects
than in using them as vehicles for exploring aspects of spiritual experience. In
this he anticipates the work of A. E., who in fact admired Larminie. "He is a
mystic," A. E. said, "but his mysticism is never incoherent and is always
profoundly philosophical." [11] This philosophical quality is particularly evident
in Larminie's long poem "Fand," based on the story of the attempt by the wife
of the Irish god of the sea to lure Cuchulain away from his wife, Emer. For
Larminie the story is chiefly an occasion for a consideration of the relationship
between spiritual and physical reality, with Cuchulain functioning as a dramatic
embodiment of philosophical ambiguity. Much of the poem is written in a blank
verse that seems closer to Milton than to anything in the Irish tradition, but the
poem does contain moments of considerable dramatic force (and moments
when Larminie experiments with flexible verse forms), such as this speech by
Emer arguing for the physical over the spiritual:

> Man is the shadow of a changing world;
> As the image of a tree,
> By the breeze swayed to and fro,
> On the grass, so changeth he;
> Night and day are in his breast;
> Winter and summer, all the change
> Of light and darkness and the season's marching;—
> Flowers that bud and fade,
> Tides that rise and fall.
> Even with the waxing and the waning moon
> His being beats in tune;
> The air that is his life
> Inhales he with alternate heaving breath;
> Joyous to him is effort, sweet is rest;
> Life he hath and death.[12]

In the "Epilogue" to "Fand," Larminie employs Irish legend and landscape to
insist on the presence of the spiritual in the physical in a verse form governed
principally by assonance, "a style of versification," as Larminie says in a note

to the volume, "which, in the hands of Irish Gaelic bards, both ancient and modern, has shown itself to be in no way inferior to rhyme": [13]

> Is there one désires to hear
>   If, within the shores of Eirë,
> Eyes may still behold the scene
>   Fair from Fand's enticements?
>
> Let him seek the southern hills,
>   And those lakes of loveliest water,
> Where the richest bloom of spring's
>   Burns to reddest autumn:
> And the clearest echo sings
>   Notes a goddess taught her.
>
>   .   .   .
>
> And though many an isle be fair,
>   Fairer still is Inisfallen,
> Since the hour Cuhoolin lay,
>   In the bower enchanted:
> See! the ash, that waves to-day,
>   Fand its grandsire planted.
>
> When from wave to mountain top
>   All delight thy sense bewilders,
> Thou shalt own the wonder wrought
>   Once by her skill'd fingers,
> Still, though many an age be gone,
>   Round Killarney linger. [14]

Larminie stood somewhat apart from the literary revival's various organizations and publications. None of his poems, for example, was included in *Poems and Ballads of Young Ireland*. T. W. Rolleston (1857–1920), on the other hand, was at the center of the movement in its formative stages, and his poetry represents much more clearly than does the work of either Todhunter or Larminie the revival's romanticization of Irish experience. A graduate of Trinity College, and a student of German as well as of classical Irish literature (he translated Whitman's *Leaves of Grass* into German), Rolleston founded the *Dublin University Review* in 1885, and as editor published the work of Yeats, Hyde, and Katharine Tynan. Along with Yeats, Tynan, and John O'Leary, he was responsible for the publication of *Poems and Ballads of Young Ireland* in 1888, and in 1891 he became the first secretary of the Irish Literary Society in London. With his father-in-law, Stopford A. Brooke, he published in 1900 arguably the most influential of all anthologies, *A Treasury of Irish Poetry*, that not only gathered in one place the work of a wide variety of writers associated with the revival but also made plain the connections between the revival and Irish poetry in English written earlier in the nineteenth century.

Rolleston wrote the preface poem for *Poems and Ballads of Young Ireland,* and it is a work that clearly discloses the romantic assumptions of both his work and the literary revival. Like the title of the volume, the poem pays tribute to the Young Ireland movement of the 1840s, yet it also makes clear the extent to which the poets represented in this book see themselves as constituting a new Young Ireland, determined not to emulate or revive the earlier movement but to rewrite the tradition represented by Thomas Davis and the *Nation* poets in terms of a more strictly romantic vision of Ireland. The poem is entitled "To John O'Leary":

> Because you suffered for the cause;
> > Because you strove with voice and pen
> To serve the Law above the laws
> > That purifies the hearts of men;
>
> Because you failed, and grew not slack,
> > Not sullen, not disconsolate;
> Nor stooped to seek a lower track,
> > But showed your soul a match for Fate;
>
> Because you hated all things base,
> > And held your country's honour high;
> Because you wrought in Time and Space
> > Not heedless of Eternity;
>
> Because you loved the nobler part
> > Of Erin; so we bring you here
> Words such as once the nation's heart
> > On patriot lips rejoiced to hear.[15]

By depicting O'Leary less as a political hero than as a romantic figure working "in Time and Space/Not heedless of Eternity," the poem establishes the ground on which the revival was to build, a romanticism that in effect looked back beyond Young Ireland's fusion of romanticism and nationalism to early Irish romantics such as Thomas Dermody and Samuel Whyte and, of course, to the English romantic movement.

This kind of romanticism permeates Rolleston's poetry. The landscapes in his work are more generically romantic than specifically Irish. The title poem of *Sea Spray: Verses and Translations* (1909), for example, purports to celebrate the natural beauty of the Co. Wicklow seacoast, but in fact uses the landscape as a vehicle for a Wordsworthian meditation on nature and memory:

O bays of Wicklow, and gorse-crown'd headlands
　　Whose scent blows far on the seaward breeze,
How oft have I yearned in the tranquil midlands
　　For one brave shock of your lifting seas!
How oft it may be in days hereafter
　　Shall rise the thought of you, phantom-fair,
Shall steal the sound of the sea-waves' laughter
　　On ears grown dull with time and care!
Waves, wash my spirit, and lonely places,
　　If well I loved you, and aught you knew,
Mark deep my heart with immortal traces
　　Of shining days when I dwelt with you![16]

Rolleston also tended to romanticize the Irish peasant, as in this description, from a poem entitled "Cois na Teinadh" ("Beside the Fire"), of the hearth in a peasant's cottage:

There Honour shines through passions dire,
　　There beauty blends with mirth—
Wild hearts, ye never did aspire
　　Wholly for things of earth!

　　　　.　.　.

And still around the fires of peat
　　Live on the ancient days;
There still do living lips repeat
　　The old and deathless lays.

And when the wavering wreaths ascend,
　　Blue in the evening air,
The soul of Ireland seems to bend
　　Above her children there.[17]

This view of the peasant as the repository of the Irish tradition and as wholly divorced from materialism is common to much revival writing, and forms the basis of Yeat's celebration of the peasant.

Like Todhunter and Larminie, Rolleston did a fair amount of work in translation. In 1900, he published a study entitled *Imagination and Art in Gaelic Literature,* and in 1909 a volume of versions from the Irish entitled *The High Deeds of Finn and Other Bardic Romances of Ancient Ireland.* A number of the poems in *Sea Spray* are represented as translations of Irish poems or as being based on Irish originals. Rolleston's romantic tendencies are quite plainly evident in these poems. "Midir the Proud Invites Queen Etain to Fairyland," for example, might be compared to Yeats's early lyric "The Stolen Child":

> Come with me, Etain, O come away,
>   To that Oversea Land of mine!
> Where music haunts the happy day,
>   And rivers run with wine.
> Careless we live, and young and gay,
>   And none saith 'mine' or 'thine'.[18]

The romantic spirit of Rolleston's poems based on the Irish-language tradition ignores the essentially classical qualities that Sigerson identified as central to the Irish tradition, and their formal structures are dominated by English rhythms and poetic conventions. One notable exception to this is Rolleston's best-known poem, "The Dead at Clonmacnoise," a translation from an Irish poem attributed to Angus O'Gillan. This poem resists the romanticization of Irish culture so evident in "Midir the Proud Invites Queen Etain to Fairyland," and is constructed around relatively flexible rhythms:

> In a quiet-water'd land, a land of roses,
>   Stands Saint Kieran's city fair,
> And the warriors of Erinn in their famous generations
>   Slumber there.
>
> There beneath the dewy hillside sleep the noblest
>   Of the Clan of Conn,
> Each below his stone: his name in branching Ogham
>   And the sacred knot thereon.
>
>   .   .   .
>
> Many and many a son of Conn the Hundred-Fighter
>   In the red earth lies at rest;
> Many a blue eye of Clan Colman the turf covers,
>   Many a swan-white breast.[19]

What is most striking about this poem, especially in the context of the literary revival's construction of an Irish past, is the way in which it reads this landscape generally associated with Ireland's Christian past—Clonmacnoise was once one of the centers of European Christianity—in almost exclusively pagan terms, nearly displacing the monastic community founded by St. Kiernan in the sixth century with the pagan culture that lies buried beneath it. "The Dead of Clonmacnoise" exemplifies the general tendency of the revival to celebrate Ireland's pagan past at the expense of its Christian one, a strategy of obvious political advantage to a movement directed for the most part by a class alienated from contemporary Irish Catholicism.

The classical restraint of "The Dead at Clonmacnoise," so uncharacteristic of both Rolleston and literary revival poets in general, is more characteristic of the work of Lionel Johnson (1867–1902). Johnson played an important part in the development of revival aesthetics by challenging what he saw as an unfortunate provincialism in the work of earlier Irish writers. Johnson's background fitted him for this role. Born in Kent and the son of an Irish army officer, he was educated in the classics at Oxford and became a prominent member of the Rhymers' Club in London at the end of the century. He came to the revival through his association with Yeats. In 1894 he delivered an address, entitled "Poetry and Patriotism," to the National Literary Society in Dublin in which he encouraged Irish writers to stop taking Young Ireland as their starting point and not to shy away from finding their literary models outside Ireland. "Our race is not lost by spreading itself over the world," he said, "and our literature would not lose its Irish accent by expeditions into all lands and times." [20] This rationale justified a number of controversial interests embraced by some revival figures, most notably Yeats, including the French *symboliste* movement and the aesthetics of the *fin-de-siècle* movement in England. It also stands at the head of an important strain in twentieth-century Irish writing, represented by poets such as Denis Devlin and John Montague, that seeks to place the Irish experience and Irish writing in a European, if not international, context. In his remarks to the National Literary Society, Johnson also thought it necessary to remind his audience that there was nothing inherently British or decadent about a healthy interest in matters of style.[21]

In practice, Johnson brought to bear on Irish poetry in English two qualities not usually associated with the revival: classicism and Catholicism. Johnson's classicism is advanced most effectively in a poem celebrating an English king, "By the Statue of King Charles at Charing Cross," which both describes Johnson's aesthetics in its admiration of the statue that is its subject and embodies them in its own formal qualities:

> Although his whole heart yearn
> In passionate tragedy:
> Never was face so stern
> With sweet austerity.[22]

Johnson converted to Catholicism in 1891, about the same time that he became interested in the Irish literary revival, and his religious poetry is strongly colored by nationalist thinking, particularly in its representations of the principle of political martyrdom. In "Ireland's Dead," for example, the conventional icon of mother Ireland is conflated with that of the Blessed Virgin, and although

the classical spareness and compression of the poem mark it clearly as Johnson's, the sentiments it expresses echo nationalist writing of the 1840s or 1860s
and anticipate some of the nationalist poetry of Patrick Pearse and Joseph Mary
Plunkett:

> Mother, dear and fair to us,
> Ever thus to be adored!
> Is thy sword grown timorous,
> Mother of misericord?
>
> For thy dead is grief on thee?
> Can it be, thou does repent,
> That they went, thy chivalry,
> Those sad ways magnificent?
>
> What, and if their heart's blood flow?
> Gladly so, with love divine,
> Since not thine the overthrow,
> They thy fields incarnadine.[23]

Johnson's highly aestheticized Catholicism was very different from the prag-
matic, day-to-day faith practiced by most Irish Catholics at the end of the
nineteenth century.[24] As Yeats pointed out in *The Trembling of the Veil*, it was
"Historic Catholicism, with all its counsels and its dogmas" that inspired
Johnson, and its effect on him was often more romantic than religious; in
Yeats's words, it "stirred his passion like the beauty of a mistress." [25] The effect
on Johnson's Irish poetry can be seen most plainly in a relatively long poem,
"Ireland," written in 1894 and used as the title poem for Johnson's second
collection of poems, published in 1897. Johnson's most extensive and significant Irish poem, "Ireland" offers a history of the nation's suffering that pointedly depoliticizes the Irish past by transforming it into an emblem—and quite
a romantic one—of melancholy:

> Thy sorrow, and the sorrow of the sea,
> Are sisters; the sad winds are of thy race:
> The heart of melancholy beats in thee,
> And the lamenting spirit haunts thy face,
> Mournful and mighty Mother! who art kin
>   To the ancient earth's first woe,
> When holy Angels wept, beholding sin.[26]

The entire poem can be read as a prayer in response to this melancholy, its
ultimate aim being not redress of the grievances so romantically described but

the evocation of a state of religious ecstasy. For all Johnson's classicism, "Ireland" contains one of the most romantic, spiritualized versions of Ireland in all of nineteenth-century Irish poetry in English:

> And yet great spirits ride thy winds: thy ways
> Are haunted and enchaunted evermore.
> Thy children hear the voices of old days
> In music of the sea upon thy shore,
> In falling of the waters from thine hills,
>   In whispers of thy trees:
> A glory from the things eternal fills
> Their eyes, and at high noon thy people sees
> Visions, and wonderful is all the air.
>   So upon earth they share
> Eternity: they learn it at thy knees.[27]

The poem ends with a call to the Blessed Virgin, who has displaced the icon of mother Ireland, to intercede for Ireland with her son; thus, the image of the sacrificial Christ, employed by nationalist writers earlier in the century as a symbol of and justification for political martyrdom, is transformed into a relatively remote and static figure, and any suggestion of political revolution is replaced by religious faith and resignation. This pattern of moving from essentialized depictions of Ireland's sufferings to images of an idealized Ireland and finally to some form of religious resignation can be found in Irish poetry written earlier in the century, but Johnson's poetry, because of its unqualified commitment to making poetry the vehicle of religious experience and ecstasy, carries it to an extreme that elides the nationalist ambitions present in earlier writing in this vein.

"In my library I have all the knowledge of the world I need," Johnson once reportedly told Yeats.[28] The artificiality and bookishness of Johnson's poetry is more than a matter of classical aesthetics; Yeats's line about Johnson—that he "loved his learning better than mankind" [29]—might well be taken as a critique of Johnson's work. Still, Johnson's attempt to filter Irish life through the double lens of classicism and "Historic Catholicism" provided new ways of seeing and writing about the Irish experience.

With the exception of Yeats, no writer associated with the revival left as strong and distinctive a mark on other writers as did George Russell (1867–1935), known as A. E. Indeed, it might be said that this Ulster-born poet, painter, dramatist, journalist, mystic, and socialist made a greater contribution to the development of Irish literature through encouraging and championing other writers than by his own writing. The list of writers indebted to A. E. constitutes an impressive syllabus of modern Irish literature, including Padraic

Colum, Eva Gore-Booth, Alice Milligan, Susan Mitchell, Seamus O'Sullivan (all of whom appeared in A. E.'s anthology, *New Songs,* published in 1904), Oliver St. John Gogarty, James Joyce, Austin Clarke, F. R. Higgins, Patrick Kavanagh, and Frank O'Connor. Also, A. E. advanced his unconventional views on mysticism, aesthetics, nationalism, and socialist politics in an astonishing variety of forums. In addition to his painting and poetry, his work as a dramatist was important to the development of theatre early in the revival; his *Deirdre* (1902) was one of the first plays staged by the Irish Literary Society, the forerunner of the Abbey Theatre. His numerous essays and editorial work —he edited the *Irish Homestead* (in which some of Joyce's early stories were first published) between 1905 and 1923, and the equally influential *Irish Statesman* from 1923 to 1930—contributed significantly to the discourse that helped shape modern Irish writing and politics. Finally, although his life rested on a deep-seated faith in spiritual reality and he often seemed to exist in a twilight world of mysticism and visions, A. E. worked tirelessly on behalf of the rural cooperative movement in Ireland.

A. E.'s importance as a poet is easily lost sight of amid his other activities. Yet, in part because of its unswerving commitment to an essentially romantic aesthetic defining the poet's function as providing access to spiritual experience, his poetry represents more effectively than that of any other writer associated with the revival the movement's interest in what Yeats called "the Unseen Life." [30] At the same time, A. E.'s work also reveals the limits of that interest, or at least the ways in which it can be seen as in conflict with the interests of cultural nationalism. The split that developed between Yeats and A. E. centered on this issue, and A. E. was himself very much aware of the difference between an aesthetic committed to establishing a cultural identity, however romantically defined, and one committed to making the invisible world visible. He once said that "birth in Ireland gave me a bias toward Irish nationalism, while the spirit that inhabits my body told me that the politics of eternity ought to be my only concern." [31] In the end, cultural nationalism simply was not sufficient. "If I held your views," he wrote to Yeats in 1900, "I could never write another line." [32]

A. E.'s faith in the spiritual, including mysticism and the occult, colored everything that he wrote as well the aesthetics in which his art was grounded. In an essay entitled "Literary Ideals in Ireland," part of a controversy in 1899 between Yeats and A. E. over the question of cultural nationalism versus spiritualism, A. E. argued that the poet and the mystic were necessarily one:

To regain the spiritual consciousness with its untrammeled ecstasy, is the hope of every mystic. That ecstasy is the poetic passion; it is not of nature, though it may breathe within it, and use it, and transform its images by a magical power. To liberate art from life is simply to absolve it from the duty laid upon it by academic critics of representing only what is seen, what is heard, what is felt, what is thought by man in his normal—that is, his less exalted, less spiritual moments, when he is least truly himself.[33]

From this point of view, the conventional association of Ireland with spiritual fulfillment and England with material prosperity, and the idealization of Ireland that lay behind much nationalist thinking earlier in the century, served more as a powerful vehicle for expressing "spiritual consciousness with its untrammeled ecstasy" than as a vehicle for exploring political, social, or even broad cultural issues. A. E.'s preface to *New Songs,* his collection of new poets, took a notably less tolerant position regarding Young Ireland than that advanced by Rolleston in his preface poem to *Poems and Ballads of Young Ireland* sixteen years earlier. "There is no sign," A. E. said, "that the tradition created by the poets of *The Nation* which had inspired so many young poets in Ireland has influenced the writers represented here."[34] And in an essay entitled "Nationality and Imperialism," written a few years earlier, A. E. defined the concept of nationality in terms that made previous idealizations of Ireland seem positively mundane:

> The idea of the national being emerged at no recognisable point in our history. It is older than any name we know. It is not earth born, but the synthesis of many heroic and beautiful moments, and these, it must be remembered, are divine in their origin. Every heroic deed is an act of the spirit, and every perception of beauty is vision with the divine eye, and not with the mortal sense. The spirit was subtly intermingled with the shining of old romance, and it was no mere phantasy which shows Ireland at its dawn in a misty light thronged with divine figures, and beneath and nearer to us, demigods and heroes fading into recognisable men.[35]

As Yeats once put it, A. E. "has written an ecstatic pantheistic poetry which reveals in all things a kind of scented flame consuming them from within."[36] A. E.'s poem "The Great Breath" exemplifies the misty, twilit imagery, abstract diction, and generically romantic landscapes that characterize much of his poetry, while expressing his view that spiritual reality can be realized only in the absence or destruction of the physical (including, by implication, the political, social and cultural):

> Its edges foamed with amethyst and rose,
> Withers once more the old blue flower of day:
> There where the ether like a diamond glows
>   Its petals fade away.

> A shadowy tumult stirs the dusky air;
> Sparkle the delicate dews, the distant snows;
> The great deep thrills, for through it everywhere
> The breath of Beauty blows.

> I saw how all the trembling ages past,
> Moulded to her by deep and deeper breath,
> Neared to the hour when Beauty breathes her last
> And knows herself in death.[37]

There is a *fin-de-siècle* world-weariness in all this, and a fierce distrust of materialism, which A. E. shared with the early Yeats. There is also a faith in the reforming power of the human spirit that looks back to the English romantics and to their followers in the Irish tradition.

In part because it attempts to transcend the physical, rather than engage in the kind of dramatic dialogue between physical and spiritual that characterizes many of Yeats's poems in this vein, A. E.'s poems often seem static or vapidly abstract. They have also frequently been accused of being obscure, and of exhibiting little or no interest in matters of technique and style.[38] Moreover, his poetry demonstrates little interest in the efforts made through the nineteenth century to import into English verse the formal qualities of poetry written in Irish. Still, at his best, and particularly in those poems having to do with Irish subject matter, A. E. not only achieves a considerable lyricism but also, because of the nature and intensity of his spiritual vision, opens up Irish poetry to a new range of ambitions and interests. "Carrowmore," one of A. E.'s best-known Irish lyrics, is an example of this dimension of his work. The poem employs a long line rich in assonance that comes close at times to the flexible, "wavering" line that Yeats so admired, and that the revival took from Mangan and Ferguson:

> It's a lonely road through bogland to the lake at Carrowmore,
> And a sleeper there lies dreaming where the water laps the shore;
> Though the moth-wings of the twilight in their purples are unfurled,
> Yet his sleep is filled with music by the masters of the world.[39]

In what is perhaps his most accomplished poem based on the Irish tradition, "Children of Lir," A. E. converts the well-known Irish legend about the transformation of the children of the god Lir into swans into a powerful, complex allegory for the presence of the divine in the human:

We wake from our sleep in the bosom where cradled together we lay:
The love of the dark hidden Father went with us upon our way.

And gay was the breath in our being, and never a sorrow or fear
Was on us as, singing together, we flew from the infinite Lir.

Through nights lit with diamond and sapphire we raced with the children of dawn,
A chain that was silver and golden linked spirit to spirit, my swan,
Till day in the heavens passed over, and still grew the beat of our wings,
And the breath of the darkness enfolded to teach us unspeakable things.

.   .   .

Still gay is the breath in our being, we wait for the bell branch to ring
To call us away to the Father, and then we will rise on the wing,
And fly through the twilights of time till the home lights of heaven appear,
Our spirits through love and through longing made one in the infinite Lir.[40]

A. E. eventually went sour on Ireland, disappointed, as was Yeats, by the
failure of his vision to be realized in the Ireland that emerged in the first
decades of the twentieth century. In 1932, three years before his death, he said:
"I would like to fly from Dublin, even from Ireland, so much do I dislike the
bigoted Catholics and political louts who are dominant. . . . Ireland as a nation
I have no further interest in."[41] And although in 1916 he saw the Easter Rising
as a glimmer of hope on an otherwise bleak horizon—his poem "Salutation"
spiritualized the rising at least as much as Yeats aestheticized it in "Easter
1916"—he eventually revised this view and in a later, bitter lyric, "Waste,"
formally indebted to Lionel Johnson and echoing with the voice of the late
Yeats, he portrayed the rising and all that was associated with it as a failure in
the only terms that mattered to him, those of the spirit:

> All that heroic mood,
> The will to suffer pain,
> Were it on beauty spent,
> An intellectual gain:
> Had a fierce piety breathed
> O'er wrong or fallen life,
> Though strife had been unwise
> We were not shamed by strife:
>
> Had they but died for some
> High image in the mind,
> Not spilt the sacrifice
> For words hollow as wind!
>
> Darkened the precious fire:
> The will we honour most
> Spent in the waste! What sin
> Against the Holy Ghost![42]

A. E. nonetheless devoted much of his energies in the last years of his life, particularly in the pages of the *Irish Statesman,* to finding ways of reconciling Ireland's two main traditions.[43] In some ways, he was still pursing the ambition of his youth to create what he called the "national ideal" or, as he put it in the early, palmier days of the revival, "to let that spirit incarnate fully which began among the ancient peoples, which has haunted the hearts and whispered a dim revelation of itself through the lips of the bards and peasant story-tellers." [44] Even in the heady, romantic atmosphere of those early days, only A. E. could have made such a statement with such complete confidence and sincerity.

CHAPTER ELEVEN

CELTICISM AND FEMINISM

"My work has got more masculine," Yeats told Lady Gregory early in the century. "It has more salt in it." [1] Yeats was, at the time, in the process of remaking his poetic self by casting off the Celtic Twilight style that had characterized his earliest poetry and the work of other Irish poets associated with the literary revival in the 1880s and 1890s. And many of the aesthetic qualities associated with the poetry of the early revival—its interest in symbolism, its fascination with the occult and mysticism, its development of the "long wavering line" and a generally languorous tone ("the trumpet has given way to the viol and the flute," as Yeats once put it [2]), and its distrust of poetry dominated by specifically political or social ambitions—might be considered as more feminine than masculine, at least as Yeats constructed those categories. In any case women played an extraordinary role in the development of the early revival's aesthetics and cultural attitudes. Women were crucial to all areas of the revival—Katharine Tynan's correspondence with Yeats in the 1880s and early 1890s contributed significantly to the development of Yeats's early aesthetics and sense of cultural nationalism, for example, and Lady Gregory played a key role in the establishment of the Abbey Theatre—but women's voices were most clearly and consistently heard in poetry. *Poems and Ballads of Young Ireland* (1888), the first important collection associated with the revival, included the work of four women, which accounted for more than one-fourth of the poems in the volume, and the book was edited by Ellen O'Leary and Katharine Tynan, along with Yeats and John O'Leary. More than half the poems in A. E.'s *New Songs* (1904), representing a second generation of revival poets, were written by women.

The emergence of women's voices is one manifestation of the broadening of poetic discourse that characterized the revival. Moreover, in the context of the tradition of women poets in Ireland, beginning with Mary Barber, Constantia

194

Grierson, and Laetitia Pilkington in the early decades of the eighteenth century, the work of women associated with the revival was particularly successful in employing a feminine, at times feminist, perspective to interrogate conventional, male-dominated aesthetics and political and cultural assumptions. Some of these writers examine with authority and scepticism traditional cultural icons, particularly nationalist symbols portraying Ireland as feminine. Rose Kavanagh, in a monologue attributed to the legendary Dervorgilla, forces a reconsideration of one of the most powerful symbols of betrayal in nationalist ideology, and Emily Lawless, in "After Aughrim," takes on the voice of Mother Ireland to question the conventional nationalist representation of Ireland as an ideal, goddess-like figure of love and beneficence. Finally, perhaps because most of these women regarded themselves as seriously marginalized in a culture and a literary movement dominated by men, there is a maverick quality to some their work, a restlessness that resists formal as well as thematic conventions—a quality that was of considerable consequence to the development of Irish poetry written by men as well as by women in the twentieth century.

Rose Kavanagh (1859–1891) is one of the earliest poets associated with the revival. She was born six years before Yeats, and died of consumption the year that the Irish Literary Society was founded in London. Born in Co. Tyrone and educated at a convent in Omagh, she went to Dublin in 1879 to study at the Metropolitan School of Art, preceding Yeats there by a few years. She became a close friend of George Sigerson and his daughter Dora, and began publishing poems in Dublin periodicals in the 1880s. Although her poetry had not been published in book form at the time of her death, three of her poems were included in *Poems and Ballads of Young Ireland,* and Yeats published one, "Lough Bray," in his *A Book of Irish Verse* in 1895. Much of her work exhibits the romantic tendencies evident generally in early revival poetry, romanticizing both Irish landscape and Irish history. "Lough Bray" views the Irish landscape through a Wordsworthian lens of memory and transcendence, albeit in relatively simplistic diction and conventional rhythms:

> A little lonely moorland lake
> > Its waters brown and cool and deep—
> The cliff, the hills behind it, make
> > A picture for my heart to keep.
>
> For rock and heather, wave and strand,
> > Wore tints I never saw them wear;
> The June sunshine was o'er the land—
> > Before, 'twas never half so fair!
>
> .   .   .
>
> And over all the summer sky;
> > Shut out the town we left behind;

> "Twas joy to stand in silence by,
> One bright chain linking mind to mind.[3]

"The Northern Blackwater," demonstrating what Katharine Tynan described as "an exquisite delicacy of expression"[4] in Kavanagh's writing, and carrying rhythmic echoes of Thomas Moore, internalizes the Irish landscape in a specifically romantic manner:

> Oh, the broom banks of the river are fair,
> Now the wild briar is blossoming there—
> Now when the green banks so calmly repose,
> Lulled by the river's strange chant as it goes,
> Laughing beneath the gold eyes of the broom,
> Flashing so free when the heather's in bloom,
> Blushing all o'er at the kiss of the sun,
> Tranquil again as the gaze of a nun.
>
>   .   .   .
>
> Once in the Maytime your carol so sweet
> Found out my heart in the midst of the street.
> Ah! how I listened, and you murmured low
> Hope, wide as earth and as white as the snow;
> Hope that, alas! like the foam on your breast,
> Broke and was drifted away from its rest.[5]

The connection between Kavanagh and Moore—and Moore's formal influence on the poets of the early revival is difficult to overestimate—is also very much in evidence in "St. Michan's Churchyard," Kavanagh's poem about Moore's friend Robert Emmet, about whom Moore wrote one of his best-known poems, "Oh! breathe not his name." Like Moore, Kavanagh effectively depoliticizes Emmet's revolutionary views, placing Emmet in the context of a romantic pastoralism ("One spot I know set well apart/From life's hard highway, life's loud mart"), and describing the narrator's visit to this green space within the city in remarkably Wordsworthian terms:

> The slender elm above that stone
> Its summer wreath of leaves had thrown
> Around the heart so quiet grown.
>
> A robin, the bare boughs among,
> Let loose his little soul in song—
> Quick liquid gushes, fresh and strong.

And quiet heart and bird and tree
Seemed linked in some strange sympathy
Too fine for mortal eye to see—

But full of balm and soothing sweet
For those who sought that calm retreat,
For aching breast and weary feet.[6]

At times, however, Kavanagh views the Irish tradition from a distinctly feminine perspective that provides a way of questioning some of its cultural and political assumptions. The most striking instance is her "Dearvorgill," a monologue written in the voice of Dervorgilla, who is usually portrayed in nationalist histories as a symbol of the betrayal of Ireland for personal gain. Kavanagh writes from inside this controversial figure whose love for the Gaelic chieftain, Dermot MacMurrough, is said to have led to warfare between two Gaelic clans and thus to MacMurrough's invitation to the Normans, and Kavanogh's sympathetic portrait has political implications. Living out her years at Mellifont Abbey, Dervorgilla, although repentant, is unable to escape her guilty past, in part because she lives in a culture that can find no place for Christian forgiveness. The poem ends with Dervorgilla identifying herself with Mary Magdalene, a daring association that calls into question the morality of nationalist ideology:

. . . Give me penance and pain,
Give me time and more tears to wipe out the red stain
Of my own guilty guilt; and, O Lord, let me cling
To the foot of Thy cross, whence the pure healing spring
Of redemption may flow over me, as it flowed
O'er the woman who bore to Thy blest feet the load
Of her woe and transgressions; Thy pardon was laid
On her fair burning brows. I will pray as she prayed,
I will weep as she wept; and my vigils I'll keep
By Thy cold, wounded feet, while the holy ones sleep.[7]

The work of two other women writing poetry in the 1880s and 1890s, Katharine Tynan and Nora Hopper, can be identified with the characteristics of the Celtic Twilight phase of the literary revival. Tynan (Mrs. H. A. Hinkson) (1861–1931) is by far the better known of the two, in part because of her long and close association with Yeats. When her first book of poems on Irish themes, *Shamrocks,* appeared in 1887—it was the first single collection of poems associated with the revival, appearing a year before *Poems and Ballads of Young Ireland*—Tynan was hailed as "the queen of Irish song."[8] Her second book of Irish poems, *Ballads and Lyrics* (1891), was described by Yeats as "a thoroughly Irish book, springing straight from the Celtic mind and pouring itself out in soft Celtic music."[9] The daughter of a prosperous Clondalkin farmer, Tynan was a devout Catholic, which may account for at least part of her attraction for Yeats as he set about to create a literary movement reflective of a culture from which he was alienated by his religion.

Tynan's first book of poems, *Louise de Valliéres,* published in 1885, was suffused with pre-Raphaelite aesthetics. It was Yeats, who once referred to Tynan as "an Irish Christina Rossetti,"[10] who steered her work into Irish channels. But she never quite left behind the Pateresque aestheticism of her earliest writing, and although she was a strong supporter of the land reform movement—as a young woman she had joined the Ladies' Land League—and an ardent supporter of Parnell after the division caused by the O'Shea divorce case, her poetry bears few traces of the political and social world in which she lived. Even her poems with religious themes are generally statements of abstract feelings of piety, rather than expressions of Irish Catholicism. When she turned to the Irish past for inspiration and material, she tended, as did many revival writers, to ignore Ireland's Christian past in favor of the legendary pre-Christian literature of its earlier periods, and to romanticize this material. Her "Children of Lir," for example, converts the well-known story from Ireland's pagan past of the transformation of Lir's children into swans into a poem of romantic longing for a golden age that can never be recovered:

> Gone is all the glory of the race of Lir;
> Gone and long forgotten like a dream of fever:
> But the swans remember all the days that were.[11]

In "The Dark Rose," Tynan rewrites one of Ireland's most politically vital symbols into a romantic love poem addressed to Ireland that is quite overt about what it excludes:

> Let others tell your history, memories,
> Counting your heroes. Not for these or those
> I love you; only for yourself, Dark Rose.[12]

Tynan was at her best when working out of the tradition of folk songs and popular ballads, for which the simplicity of her diction and rhythms were more appropriate. "The Wild Geese," her version of a Jacobite lament, a form that few revival writers seemed able to resist, is a case in point:

> I have heard the curlew crying
> On a lonely moor and mere;

And the sea-gull's shriek in the gloaming
   Is a lonely sound in the ear:
And I've heard the brown thrush mourning
   For her children stolen away;—
But it's O for the homeless Wild Geese
   That sailed ere the dawn of day!

For the curlew out on the moorland
   Hath five fine eggs in the nest;
And the thrush will get her a new love
   And sing her song with the best.
As the swallow flies to the Summer
   Will the gull return to the sea:
But never the wings of the Wild Geese
   Will flash over seas to me.

And 'tis ill to be roaming, roaming
   With the homesick heart in the breast!
And how long I've looked for your coming,
   And my heart is the empty nest!
O sore in the land of the stranger
   They'll pine for the land far away!
But Day of Aughrim, my sorrow,
   It was you was the bitter day![13]

One sign of the extent to which Tynan's work in these years was absorbed by the revival and her association with Yeats is that few of her poems exhibit the interest in specifically feminine perspectives visible in the work of Kavanagh and other women poets of the period. Tynan's role in the revival effectively ended just about the time the movement was being officially organized. Two years after the publication of *Ballads and Lyrics,* which appeared the same year that the Irish Literary Society was founded in London, and four years after Yeats met Maud Gonne (the exact nature of the relationship between Tynan and Yeats is not known, but she was apparently jealous of Yeats's infatuation with Gonne), she married the writer Henry Hickson, and, as Todhunter and Johnson would do a few years later, left the revival behind her.

Like Tynan, Nora Hopper (1871–1906) was energetically championed by Yeats, but for different reasons. Whereas Tynan brought to the budding revival movement Catholic credentials and pre-Raphaelite aesthetics, in Hopper Yeats saw an imagination inspired by a kind of spiritualism that he regarded as central to the revival's attempts to construct a new Irish identity. In an essay published in 1895, the year after Hopper's *Ballads in Prose* had been published to considerable acclaim, Yeats called Hopper "the one absolute dreamer of Irish literature"—undoubtedly a compliment from Yeats's point of view in the 1890s—

and added, "Miss Hopper is only interested in so much of life as you can see
in a wizard's glass." [14] Although Yeats's support did much to advance Hopper
in Dublin literary circles, she suffered from her close association with Yeats.
Her work is very much in the shadow of his, and on more than one occasion
she has been charged with plagiarizing Yeats's writings. [15] *Ballads in Prose,* her
first book, consisted of a number of prose stories and legends taken from Irish
folklore, with each account prefaced by a poem. The poems clearly show the
aesthetic influence of Yeats and the philosophical influence of A. E. In her
"dark rose" poem, "Ros Gheal Dhu," the symbol of Irish nationalism that
Tynan transforms into an emblem vaguely symbolic of love of country, is
presented as embodying a spiritual ideal that transcends any specifically Irish
quality. The poem is very much in keeping with Yeats's early theories about
symbolism as a form of discourse that must have "the perfections that escape
analysis" [16]:

> A greeting, Dark Rose, where thou sittest a-spinning,
> A thread without ending, and without beginning:
> A thread of all colours, gold, purple, and blue:
> Dark Rose, 'neath thy thorn-tree, how wears the day through?
>
> 'My day it wears onward 'twixt spinning and weaving,
> The noise of men's laughter, the cry of their grieving
> Drifts slow by my thorn-tree like drifting of snow,
> And on the old branches the new blossoms blow.
>
> 'I heed not the sorrow, nor mock at the laughter,
> I weave the white sark and the yellow veil after:
> I have trodden the grapes, I have pressed out the wine,
> And all men shall drink of this vintage of mine.
>
> 'One snatches the laurel I twined for his brother,
> One kisses my feet: I heed one nor another:
> Am I Death, O my children, or Life! Can ye tell—?
> Or the ghost of maid Truth that was drowned in her well?' [17]

Although most of the poems in *Ballads in Prose* rewrite the folk tradition in
such terms, in "A Connaught Lament" Hopper resists the spiritual symbolism
that dominates most of her work, writing in a voice that speaks with the kind
of authenticity that characterizes Hyde's translations of Irish folk songs:

> My heart in my bosom is black as a sloe!
> I heed not cuckoo, nor wren, nor swallow:
> Like a flying leaf in the sky's blue hollow
> The heart in my breast is that beats so low.

Because of the words your lips have spoken,
(O dear black head I must not follow)
My heart is a grave that is stripped and hollow,
As ice on the water my heart is broken.[18]

Two years after *Ballads in Prose* appeared, Hopper published a collection of poems, *Under Quicken Boughs,* that turned out to be her last contribution to the poetry of the literary revival. (*Songs of the Morning,* published in 1900, has little to do with Ireland, and Hopper died six years later at the age of thirty-five.) Most of the poems in this volume use the Irish experience as a vehicle for spiritualism, and their unsophisticated style and voice rarely achieve the authenticity of "A Connaught Lament." "I agree with what you say about Nora," Yeats wrote Katharine Tynan just after Hopper died in 1906, "and the way our Irish fairyland came to spoil her work." [19] The remark, although a bit presumptuous and a bit unfair (after all, it was Yeats who urged Hopper to write about "our Irish fairyland"), gets close to Hopper's greatest weakness, which she shared with other early-revival writers: an inability to integrate effectively her romantic faith in spiritual reality with her understanding of the Irish experience.

The work of other women poets associated with the revival, most notably Emily Lawless, Dora Sigerson, Ethna Carbery, Alice Milligan, and Moira O'Neill, more successfully and more authentically explored Ireland's folk tradition, drawing on the genre of popular poetry and song that the Young Ireland poets had done so much to energize and politicize in the middle decades of the nineteenth century. At times, these poets provide a specifically feminine perspective on this kind of writing, domesticating and humanizing a form of poetry that in the hands of earlier nationalist writers had functioned at the relatively abstract level of the nation as a whole. The most important of these writers, Emily Lawless (1845–1913), was something of a maverick figure. She was born into a distinguished Anglo-Irish family—her father was the third baron of Cloncurry—that had a history of nationalist commitment; the second baron had been active in the United Ireland movement and in the drive for Catholic Emancipation, and her father is said to have sent a cheque for £100 to John Mitchel's wife when Mitchel was transported.[20] Lawless herself, however, remained a loyalist all her life, although she supported the land-reform movement of the late nineteenth century, as is evident in her well-known novel *Hurrish* (1886). She was deeply interested in Irish history, as well as in the landscape and people of the rural west, and her most accomplished poems take historical events or people as their subject matter. In "Afterward," she defines the poet's role as bringing to life the voices of the past:

Out of the dusk of slow-accomplished Time,
Out of the shadows, out of the long past,

Lifting that past up on thy haughty rhyme,
Wakening those silenced voices, heard at last;
Fierce with the tumults of eight hundred years,
Loud with their cries of echoing strife and scorn;
Soft with their woes; child of their hopes and fears,
Poet we look for, come; awake! Be born![21]

When Lawless is at her best, she not only affirms the value of the past but also interrogates it, rewriting the essentially monolithic tradition of popular nationalist poetry and forcing a reconsideration of some of the assumptions about Irish identity that lay behind it. This position is advanced most effectively in the poems that Lawless wrote about the Wild Geese, a subject that dominated her imagination.[22] Lawless's poems about the Gaelic chieftains and soldiers who fled to the continent after the Battle of Aughrin in 1691 and spent years in the service of the French army fighting Germany and England often hold up to question conventional nationalist representations of them as unqualifiedly heroic and of Ireland as the inspiration for their heroism. In "After Aughrim," from *With the Wild Geese* (1902), Lawless counters the idealized view of Mother Ireland as the nurturer of heroism with one in which she is essentially indifferent to, and unworthy of, her exiled leaders. Lawless does this in part by positioning the poem's narrative voice inside the icon of Mother Ireland:

She said, "They gave me of their best,
They lived, they gave their lives for me;
I tossed them to the howling waste,
And flung them to the foaming sea."

She said, "I never gave them aught,
Not mine the power, if mine the will;
I let them starve, I let them bleed,—
They bled and starved, and loved me still."

.   .   .

She said, "I stayed alone at home,
A dreary woman, grey and cold;
I never asked them how they fared,
Yet still they loved me as of old."[23]

"Clare Coast" recounts the story of how a band of the Wild Geese returned to Ireland around 1720 looking for recruits. Writing from the point of view of one of the men, Lawless goes beyond the traditional lament of the exile to portray the men as disillusioned and unheroic:

Why do we linger here?
Why do we stand and gaze,
Fools, whom fools despise,
Fools untaught by the years,
Fools renounced by the wise?
Heartsick, a moment more,
Heartsick, sorry, fierce,
Lingering, lingering on,
Dreaming the dreams of yore;
Dreaming the dreams of our youth,
Dreaming the days when we stood
Joyous, expectant, serene,
Glad, exultant of mood,
Singing with hearts afire,
Singing with joyous strain,
Singing aloud in our pride,
"We shall redeem her again!"
Ah, not tonight that strain,—
Silent to-night we stand,
A scanty, toil-worn crew,
Strangers, foes in the land!

. . .

War-battered dogs are we,
Fighters in every clime,
Fillers of trench and of grave,
Mockers, bemocked by time.
War-dogs, hungry and grey,
Gnawing a naked bone,
Fighters in every clime,
Every cause but our own.[24]

Lawless also refuses to romanticize the Irish landscape; indeed, her poems about the west tend to describe it in terms of harshness and sterility, rather than in the conventional, nationalist terms that depict Ireland as either a nurturing garden of Eden or a place fostering a wild, romantic imagination.

Lawless's distance from the tradition that she is drawing on can be measured by comparing her Wild Geese poems with those of Thomas Davis. Davis's treatment of the Wild Geese, focusing on their military exploits on the continent after they left Ireland, is wholly celebratory and in keeping with nationalist ideology; the Wild Geese are presented as consummately heroic, and seen from a distance that is intended to elevate them above human stature. As these lines from Davis's "Fontenoy. 1745" demonstrate, Davis wrote about the Wild Geese in thumping, militaristic rhythms appropriate to his vision:

> How fierce the look these exiles wear, who're wont to be so gay,
> The treasured wrongs of fifty years are in their hearts to-day—
> The treaty broken, ere the ink wherewith 'twas writ could dry,
> Their plundered homes, their ruined shrines, their women's parting cry,
> Their priesthood hunted down like wolves, their country overthrown—
> Each looks as if revenge for all were staked on him alone.[25]

In Lawless's "Fontenoy. 1745," apparently a response to Davis's poem, the point of view is much more intimate, and the theme is not military victory or redemption but rather loss and lament. In effect, Lawless rewrites Davis's blatantly nationalist poem into a romantic poem about exile and loss:

> Oh little Corca Bascinn, the wild, the bleak, the fair!
> Oh little stony pastures, whose flowers are sweet, if rare!
> Oh rough and rude Atlantic, the thunderous, the wide,
> Whose kiss is like a soldier's kiss which will not be denied!
> The whole night long we dream of you, and waking think we're there,—
> Vain dream, and foolish waking, we never shall see Clare.[26]

If, as Yeats often said, the literary revival was founded in part on a rejection of the patriotic verse written by Young Ireland poets, then Lawless's poetry about the Wild Geese puts that theory into specific and often quite compelling practice.

The work of Dora Sigerson (1866–1918), the daughter of George Sigerson, is rooted in Ireland's folk tradition, especially the narrative ballad. It is also of particular importance for its integration of Gothic conventions and Irish material. Gothicism can be found in earlier Irish poetry influenced by romanticism, most notably in the work of Thomas Dermody, and it was a staple of much nineteenth-century Irish fiction (the work of Joseph Sheridan Le Fanu, for example); but among poets associated with the literary revival, only Sigerson consistently relied on Gothic conventions and attitudes, rejecting the more ethereal spirituality of a writer like Katharine Tynan. The Gothic streak in Sigerson's writing was related to a profound melancholy that colored most of her work. Her best work, *The Fairy Changeling* (1898) and *Ballads and Poems* (1899), articulates this melancholy through the conventions of the folk tradition. "A Fairy Thorn Tree," Sigerson's version of the legendary folk stories about young girls being carried off by the fairies—the basis of Ferguson's well-known "The Fairy Thorn"—employs a macabre narrative in which a young girl barters her soul to the devil in exchange for that of her drowned lover. The poem is full of Gothic spectacle, most notably in a scene in which the girl digs a grave for herself by the sea and waits for her lover's body to be washed into it:

She dug a grave within the surf and shingle,
    A dark, cold bed, made very deep and wide,
She laid her down all stiff and stretched for burial,
    Right in the pathway of the rising tide.

First tossed into her waiting arms the restless
    Loud waves, a woman very grey and cold,
Within her bed she stood upright so quickly,
    And loosed her fingers from the dead hands' hold.

The second who upon her heart had rested
    From out the storm, a baby chill and stark,
With one long sob she drew it on her bosom,
    Then thrust it out again into the dark.

The last who came so slow was her own lover;
    She kissed his icy face on cheek and chin,
"O cold shall be your house to-night, belovèd,
    O cold the bed that we must sleep within.

"And heavy, heavy, on our lips so faithful
    And on our hearts, shall lie our own roof-tree."
And as she spoke the bitter tears were falling
    On his still face, all salter than the sea.

"And oh," she said, "if for a little moment
    You knew, my cold, dead love, that I was by,
That my soul goes into the utter darkness
    When yours comes forth—and mine goes in to die."

And as she wept she kissed his frozen forehead,
    Laid her warm lips upon his mouth so chill,
With no response—and then the waters flowing
    Into their grave, grew heavy, deep, and still.[27]

Sigerson also renders political themes in Gothic terms. Her version of a Jacobite lyric, "The Flight of the Wild Geese," focuses on the moment of departure from Ireland of the Gaelic leaders:

Wrapt in the darkness of the night,
Gathering in silence on the shore,
Wild geese flown from hiding on the hills,
(Hark! the wolf-hound; thrice he howled before),
Wild geese with forest leaves tangled in their hair.
Is that blood on the heaving breasts of some,
Or dull red clay from fox-deserted lair?[28]

This Gothic romanticization neutralizes the political force of the Jacobite lyric as surely as does Lawless's focus on the Wild Geese as exiles lamenting their lost homeland.

Ernest Boyd complained that Sigerson was guilty of "incredible offenses against all known laws of metrics, style, and even grammar,"[29] and much of her work is technically uneven, not to say awkward. Still, the best of it has a genuine gift for narrative and a streak of dark romanticism that, arguably at least, transcends Boyd's laws. Sigerson also was capable of a distinctly feminist note rarely heard with such clarity in the work of other women poets associated with the revival. "A Vagrant Heart," rails, in exceedingly romantic terms, against women's confinement to domestic concerns:

> Ochone! to be a woman, only sighing on the shore—
> With a soul that finds a passion for each long breaker's roar,
> With a heart that beats as restless as all the winds that blow—
> Thrust a cloth between her fingers, and tell her she must sew;
> Must join in empty chatter, and calculate with straws—
> For the weighing of our neighbor—for the sake of social laws.[30]

The work of Ethna Carbery (Anna Johnston MacManus) (1866–1902) and Alice Milligan (1866–1953), two Ulsterwomen driven by decidedly nationalist politics, often seems closer to the political poetry written by women such as Lady Wilde and Ellen O'Leary in the middle decades of the nineteenth century than it does to that written by other women during the revival, and it demonstrates the extent to which the desire to construct Irish identity around the issue of political and cultural separatism was still very much a force in Irish writing at the end of the nineteenth century. Carbery published much of her poetry in the pages of *The Nation* and *United Ireland,* as well as in the Belfast journal *The Shan Van Vocht,* which she and Milligan edited together from 1896 to 1899. In the year of her death, 1902, her poems were collected and published as *The Four Winds of Eirinn.* In a preface to that volume, Carbery's husband, Seamus MacManus, a playwright and short-story writer, praised Carbery's work in the language of Irish nationalism at it most romantic: "From childhood till the closing hour, every fibre of her frame vibrated with love of Ireland. Before the tabernacle of poor Ireland's hopes she burned in her bosom a perpetual flame of faith."[31] The attitudes that lie behind this kind of rhetoric define much of Carbery's poetry, which was immensely popular in its day. Carbery was familiar with the epic and folk materials that supplied much of the inspiration for the revival's attempt to construct a distinctly cultural as opposed to political nationalism; for example, she made her own prose versions of a number of the tales from Ireland's legendary past.[32] Yet in her hands these materials were almost always translated into the terms of nineteenth-century nationalist discourse. Her poem "Mo Craoibhín Cno," whose title recalls Edward Walsh's pastoral love lyric constructed around verbal echoes of poetry written in Irish, converts the symbol of the nut-tree branch into a reductive icon of Irish separatism, and does so in a voice that bears no trace of Irish-language poetics:

> A Sword of Light hath pierced the dark, our eyes have seen the star.
> O Mother, leave the ways of sleep now days of promise are:
> The rusty spears upon your walls are stirring to and fro,
> In dreams they front uplifted shields—Then wake, Mo Chraoibhin Cno![33]

Like much of the poetry of Young Ireland, this kind of writing has little tolerance for issues of difference or for regionalism; questions of gender are not significant in Carbery's writing, nor is there much trace in her work of the distinctive culture of her native Ulster.

Milligan was much more active in the revival than was Carbery, who died two years before the Abbey Theatre opened its doors. She worked for the Gaelic League, traveling around the country giving lectures on the language revival, and wrote for the Irish theatre in its early days; her play *The Last Feast of the Fianna* was produced by the Irish Literary Theatre in its second season, in 1900. She was, however, as strongly committed to nationalist ideology and aesthetics as was Carbery. Milligan was brought up in a Methodist family in Co. Tyrone, in an atmosphere of hostility toward nationalism. By the time she came to know Carbery in Belfast in the 1890s, however, Milligan had become fully committed to the cause of Irish political independence, and most of her writing is in the service of that cause. Her poetry often conflates the heroism celebrated in Ireland's epic literature with nationalist ideology. Her first book of poems was entitled *Hero Lays* (it was published in 1906 and dedicated to George Sigerson), and was structured around this parallel. In "The Return of Lugh Lamh-Fada," for example, Milligan merges the story of the son of the Irish god of the sea, Mananaan mac Lir, with the tradition of the Jacobite lament. The poem's opening describes Lugh Lamh-Fada in terms that echo the heroic style of Standish O'Grady's *History of Ireland,* which influenced Milligan significantly:

> Lugh Lamh-Fada, mighty and immortal,
> Lordliest of the fosterlings of Mananaan mac Lir,
> Far out of Erin, behind a fairy portal,
> Tarried in bliss till his boyhood's ending year.
>> The whole world held no gladder place to dream in,
>> With honey of the heather fed and milk of magic cows,
>> Where flowers round the towers of apple-blossomed Eman
>> Were mingled with the burdens of heavy-fruited boughs.[34]

Informed of Ireland's sufferings, Lugh Lamh-Fada takes on the Jacobite role of Ireland's redeemer, leaving behind his perfect world of immortality to lead the struggle for Ireland's freedom. In the final poem of *Hero Lays,* "The Man on the Wheel," Milligan introduces a contemporary hero seen as the extension of the mythic heroes celebrated in the rest of the volume—a teacher who travels through the country, much as Milligan herself did on behalf of the Gaelic League, preaching cultural revival and political independence:

> And the fire he has brought to-night through the winter rain and storm
> Is the rallying hope that our race shall live and shall yet prevail;
> See the eyes of the young men glisten, and the aged lean to listen
> To the glorious glowing speech of the yet unconquered Gael.[35]

As the structure of *Hero Lays* suggests, Milligan was a more ambitious and more diverse poet than Carbery. Also, her work exhibits a much stronger capacity for specific, concrete description and imagery than that of most of the nineteenth-century nationalist poets with whom she and Carbery are often associated. "There Were Trees in Tir-Conal," for example, politicizes the Irish landscape, but also vividly recreates a specific historical landscape and a contrasting contemporary one:

> There were trees in Tir-Conal of the territories
> In Erin's youthful, yet remembered days,
> Where now to clothe the leagues of bogland lonely
> Is only heather brown or gorse ablaze;
> Where rivers go from source to sea unshaded,
> Where shine in desolate moors the scattered lakes,
> And sedges only are where once were willows
> And curlews, where were deer in woodland brakes.
>
> The spades of peasants oft the peat uplifting
> Strike bog-black roots of oak or red of fir,
> And then 'tis known, here the primeval forest
> Was murmurous to all winds with leaves astir,
> Where to the sky's blue rim the heath unending
> Lies bare before the honey-searching bees;
> O'er camping hosts once spread the giant branches
> Of oaks in autumn sounding like the seas.[36]

At times Milligan brings to bear on the tradition of nationalist writing a specifically feminine perspective. In "Lament of the Dark Daughter," for example, the story of the captivity of Red Hugh O'Donnell at the beginning of the seventeenth century is told from the point of view of his mother, and maternal feeling works to underscore the nationalist concept of sacrifice:

> MacDonnell, lord of the Isles, though he is my father,
> O'Donnell of Tir-Conal, my husband, too,
> With all his brood of brethren, I would gather
> To be hostage-held, my Prince, as the price of you;
> Yea, I would lie in my dungeon and die there rather
> Than leave you to live there unransomed, my peerless Hugh.[37]

Although Milligan, like many writers associated with the early phase of the revival, often romanticizes the Irish peasant,[38] a poem entitled "A Country Girl" employs the point of view of a rural Irish girl working as a servant in a grand Dublin house—the material of nineteenth-century Irish fiction more than of poetry—to critique the values and manners of Ascendancy society, and to expose the source of an arguably more damaging peasant stereotype than that which informs much of the revival's writing about rural Ireland:

> Ah, not in praying can this night be passed,
> But she, for thoughtless revellers met to dine,
> She whose own lips are used to fast,
> Must hand the silver dish and pour the wine
> 'Mid babble of idle gossip, followed after
> By shallow tinkling laughter.
>
> .   .   .
>
> And yonder at table's end
> Where sits the dull but learned professor,
> The talk to serious lines will tend,
> Of Plunkett's going, his successor,
> And what his chances are at present
> With aid of recent legislation
> To civilize the Irish peasant
> And raise him from his brutish station.[39]

This kind of satire, with its roots in Swift and the eighteenth century, is relatively rare in revival poetry (only the work of another woman poet, Susan Mitchell, falls into this category), and it demonstrates the extent to which Milligan could transcend the relatively rigid conventions and confines of nationalist discourse.

The poetry of Moira O'Neill (pseudonym for Agnes Shakespeare Skine, neé Higginson) (c. 1879–1955), another Ulsterwoman, rejects the nationalist ambition and national focus of Carbery and Milligan in favor of a largely depoliticized and decidedly provincial expression of Ireland's folk tradition. O'Neill's extraordinarily popular *Songs of the Glens of Antrim* (1901), the one book on which her reputation rests, was written, O'Neill says in a brief preface, "by a Glenswoman in the dialect of the Glens, and chiefly for the pleasure of other Glens-people." [40] This local focus ran counter to the revival's attempt to create a national sense of Irish identity and to its tendency to locate the center of that identity in Munster or Connacht. O'Neill did not, however, always make good the intention expressed in her preface. Her dialogue often seems closer to the stage-Irish dialect of nineteenth-century fiction than to the kind of specifically Ulster speech that James Orr, also from O'Neill's native Antrim, effectively employed in his poetry a century earlier. And O'Neill's vision of "Ulster pastoral," as one critic has called it,[41] often shows evidence of class-based condescension. (O'Neill was the mother of the contemporary Anglo-Irish novelist Molly Keane, whose fiction is rooted in the Big-House tradition). Nonetheless, O'Neill was able to articulate certain aspects of the folk tradition effectively, and to great popular acclaim. "Denny's Daughter," for example, expresses the same sense of lost or hopeless love, and is marked by the same specificity of imagery and feeling, that characterize many of the Connacht folk songs translated by Hyde:

> Denny's daughter stood a minute in the field I be to pass,
>   All as quiet as her shadow lyin' by her on the grass;
> In her hand a switch o' hazel from the nut tree's crooked root,
>   Well I mind the crown o' clover crumpled undher one bare foot.
>   For the look of her,
>   The look of her
>   Comes back to me to-day,—
>   Wi' the eyes of her,
>   The eyes of her
>   That took me on the way.
> Though I seen poor Denny's daughter white an' stiff upon her bed,
>   Yet I be to think there's sunlight fallin' somewhere on her head:
> She'll be singin' *Ave Mary* where the flowers never wilt,
>   She, the girl my own hands covered wi' the narrow daisy-quilt. . . .
>   For the love of her,
>   The love of her
>   That would not be my wife:
>   An' the loss of her,
>   The loss of her
>   Has left me lone for life.[42]

O'Neill's most-anthologized poem, "Corrymeela," renders the theme of exile and the nationalist distinction between spiritual Ireland and material England in particularly colloquial terms:

> Over here in England I'm helpin' wi' the hay,
>   An' I wisht I was in Ireland the livelong day;
> Weary on the English hay, an' sorra take the wheat!
>   *Och! Corrymeela an' the blue sky over it.*
>
>   .   .   .
>
> Here's hands so full o' money an' hearts so full o' care,
>   By the luck o' love! I'd still go light for all I did go bare.
> "God save ye, *colleen dhas,*" I said: the girl she thought me wild.
>   *Far Corrymeela, an' the low south wind.*
>
> D'ye mind me now, the song at night is mortial hard to raise,
>   The girls are heavy goin' here, the boys are ill to plase;
> When one'st I'm out this workin' hive, 'tis I'll be back again—
>   *Ay, Corrymeela, in the same soft rain.*[43]

Narrated by strong, independent women, several of O'Neill's poems take up feminist issues, including social conventions regarding women's role in marriage and the relationship between men and women. In a poem entitled "Marriage," a young woman rejects the advice of "an' ould *caillach*" to marry:

> "As sure as ye're young an' fair," says she, "one day ye'll be ugly an' ould.
> If ye haven't a husband, who'll care," says she, "to call ye in out o' the could?
>   Left to yerself,
>   Laid on the shelf,—
>   Now is yer time to marry.
>
>   .   .   .
>
> "I may be dead ere I'm ould," says I, "for nobody knows their day.
> I never fear'd o' the could," says I, "but I'm fear'd to give up me way.
>   Good or bad,
>   Sorry or glad,
>   "Tis mine no more when I marry." [44]

Other of O'Neill's female narrators rail at men's presumption that women are bound to obey them. The poems are never sophisticated, and they often suffer from uneven or unconvincing dialogue, but because of O'Neill's popularity, they brought to the attention of a considerable audience gender issues that often were neglected in the revival's effort to construct a new Irish identity.

When A. E. published his anthology *New Songs* in 1904, he was, he said, trying to represent a second generation of revival figures, writers who stood at some distance from the poets included in *Poems and Ballads of Young Ireland,* published sixteen years earlier, and at an even greater distance from the political poetry of Young Ireland. Four of the eight writers represented in *New Songs* were women. One was Alice Milligan, whose work was, in fact, very much in keeping with the tradition created by *The Nation;* but the work of Ella Young, Susan Mitchell, and Eva Gore-Booth was dominated by what A. E. referred to as "a new mood in Irish verse," [45] which generally meant that it was concerned with the spiritual and mystical impulses that informed A. E.'s own writing. Central to the work of all three of these women writers is the idea that spiritual perception and experience, taken to be the purpose of art, can be achieved only by the repression or even annihilation of the physical world, including the world of social and political reality. As it does in much of the work of A. E., this aesthetic position in effect extends and justifies the general suspicion of specifically political writing that characterized the revival.

The work of Ella Young (1865–1951) provides a particularly instructive instance of this aesthetic view and its effects on poetry. Reared as a Presbyterian in Co. Antrim, Young was fiercely nationalist; her commitment to the literary revival and to the Gaelic League was anything but depoliticized. "It is true that we have no hope of an armed thrust at the might of England," she once said, "but we can tear to pieces the calumnies with which she strives to hide her exploitation. We can revive our ancient culture and our language." [46] Having been in Dublin during the Easter Rising, she later described it, very much in the language of nineteenth-century romantic nationalism, as "the splendour of a Vision that triumphed, and triumphs, over suffering and loss, transmuting failure into a spiritual heritage, a great rose of saintship and warrior-deed; a chalice with the wine of immortality." [47] Few traces of these attitudes, however, appear in her poetry, collected in *Poems* (1906). Informed by a visionary spiritualism, Young's poetry longs for complete transcendence. At its most insistent, this rejection of the physical world flirts with the suicidal, as in "The Virgin Mother":

> I have no longing now, no dreams of bliss.
> But drowsed in peace through the soft gloom I wait
> Until the stars be kindled by God's breath;
> For then you'll bend above me with the kiss
> Earth's children long for when the hour grows late,
> Mother of Consolation, Sovereign Death. [48]

As happens in some of A. E.'s work, Young's spiritualism often eclipses nationalist sentiment and converts the Irish tradition into its own terms. Her portrait of the legendary Irish figure Niamh, for example, transforms Ossian's lover

into a vehicle for an other-worldly, extremely romantic experience, and carries
marked echoes of A. E.'s poetry:

> O pale you are, and sweet, and in your eyes
> The shadow of a dream that daylight kills,
> Woven while you lingered by the crystal rills
> Between the apple-trees of Paradise.
> You gather as you pass with quiet hands
> The dawn-white blossoms, ere their beauty cease:
> The frail, pale blossoms that we see unclose
> One moment, when our hearts have drawn the peace
> Of twilight round them and the enchanted lands
> Glimmer before us, amethyst and rose.[49]

As Ernest Boyd remarked, Young was one of the few revival poets who "could
not have written as they do, had there been no Theosophical Movement." [50]

Another was Susan Mitchell (1866–1926), a considerably more accomplished and sophisticated poet. Although very much an Anglo-Irish Protestant
—she once said in a letter to Seamus O'Sullivan, "The Mitchells have been
Protestants since Luther and probably long before" [51]—she held strong nationalist convictions, and at one point in her life belonged to Sinn Fein.[52] More
important for her poetry was her long and close association with A. E., with
whom she worked as an assistant editor on both the *Irish Homestead* and the
Irish Statesman. But however much her work was influenced thematically by
A. E.'s spiritualism, her poetry rarely depends on the Celtic Twilight voice and
imagery that characterize much of A. E.'s writing, and Ella Young's as well.
Even at its most spiritual, Mitchell's work is marked by a concreteness and
directness that looks back more to seventeenth-century English religious poetry
than to any specific sources in the Irish tradition. "The Heart's Low Door," for
example, from Mitchell's collection *The Living Chalice* (1908), has at its center
the same idea of the spiritual eclipsing the physical that informs much of
Young's writing, but the idea is expressed in a vigorous voice and imagery
strikingly different from that of Young's poetry or of A. E.'s:

> O Earth, I will have none of thee.
>   Alien to me the lonely plain,
> And the rough passion of the sea
>   Storms my unheeding heart in vain.
>
> The petulance of rain and wind,
>   The haughty mountains' superb scorn,
> Are but slight things I've flung behind,
>   Old garments that I have out-worn.

> Bare of the grudging grass, and bare
> Of the tall forest's careless shade,
> Deserter from thee, Earth, I dare
> See all thy phantom brightness fade.[53]

The Living Chalice also contains a number of poems expressing religious doubt and uncertainty, another quality of Mitchell's writing that distinguishes her from A. E. and other revival writers associated with him.

In writing specifically about Ireland, Mitchell is often much closer to those writers, tending to idealize Ireland in a way that neutralizes the specifically political dimension of nationalism. In a poem entitled "Ireland," the traditional nationalist distinction between spiritual Ireland and material England is evoked, but the condition to which the poem aspires is a transcendence that has no need of the material or the political:

> None knows my state, since I uncrownèd go,
> Nor how in dreams Love makes me blossoming trees,
> Through my dumb throat makes sweetest songs outflow,
> And gives me store of kingly gems alsó,
> The amber beads and carved carnelian,
> I keep my state though I uncrownèd go,
>
> I see the regal train, the queen sweeps by,
> After her jewels the proud sunshine flies,
> We are left, oh heart, but you and I
> Need not crave that curious pageantry,
> For here within the fire invisible
> Warms all our house and Love is standing by.[54]

Mitchell found a poetic outlet for her nationalist convictions in satire, a mode that few revival writers, who were working to construct a positive sense of Irish identity, had much use for, at least in the early days of the movement. Mitchell's work in this vein, published in a collection entitled *Aids to the Immortality of Certain Persons in Ireland* (1908), clearly looks back to Swift and eighteenth-century Irish poetry in English. "The Irish Council Bill, 1907," adapts the eighteenth-century nationalist song "The Shan Van Vocht," revived by the Young Ireland movement in the 1840s, not to argue for political revolution or separatism but to attack the Devolution Bill, which amounted to a badly watered-down version of Home Rule:

> Is it this you call Home Rule?
> Says the Shan Van Vocht.

Do you take me for a fool?
    Says the Shan Van Vocht.
To be sending round the hat
Five-and-twenty years for that
Isn't good enough for Pat,
    Says the Shan Van Vocht.

And the Lord Lieutenant too,
    Says the Shan Van Vocht,
Is he still to be on view?
    Says the Shan Van Vocht.
And all them big police,
Monumentally obese,
Must I go on feeding these?
    Says the Shan Van Vocht.[55]

Parody is very much a part of Mitchell's satire. In "Ode to the British Empire," she echoes Kipling's famous "Recessional" to attack her own class:

God of the Irish Protestant,
    Lord of our proud Ascendancy,
Soon there'll be none of us extant,
    We want a few plain words with thee.
        Thou know'st our hearts are always set
        On what we get, on what we get.[56]

Mitchell did not hesitate to question the literary revival and its central figures. Her lengthy "George Moore—A Ballad History" portrays Moore's commitment to the revival as inauthentic, and is particularly merciless in satirizing his conversion to Protestantism by means of parody, this time of Christopher Marlowe's "The Passionate Shepherd to His Love":

No more to pagan carelessness I skip down Ely Place,
Softly I glide through Dublin with the convert's timid grace.
The lamp of Protestant reform lights up my bashful face.

Ye pretty little Papist maids, whatever your degree,
Come hither fearlessly and sit on my converted knee,
Bid me to live and I will live your Protestant to be.[57]

Mitchell was not afraid to take on Yeats, calling attention to the gap between the revival's effort to construct a meaningful identity for all of Ireland and Yeats's exclusionist politics and aesthetics. In "The Voice of One," a poetic dialogue among three figures representing Yeats, Edward Martyn, and Moore,

Mitchell parodies Yeats's style as a means of criticizing what she sees as the increasingly elitist tendencies of Yeats's work:

> The Drama of to-morrow drawth nigh,
> I its inventor, its creator I.
> No theatre, no scenery, no stage,
> No clothes the roving fancy to engage,
> No actors either, for their gestures rude
> Break in upon the spirit's solitude.
> And neither shall my plays have any lines—
> The straitened word the wingéd thought confines.
> No, I will cause that a new thing shall be,
> Plays shall be played in wordless wizardry.
> For I shall sit in any room apart,
> Just sit, and sit, and gaze in my own heart.
> And when I toss the dim locks of my hair,
> Dramas are born in men's minds everywhere.
> And when I wave my slender-pearl-pale hand
> Tragedy glides dream-heavy through the land.
> All the world o'er the uncommercial few,
> Gathering in companies of one and two,
> Sit humbly while the miracle is wrought
> By the unresting ravens of my thought,
> While the mob theatre's expensive cloth
> Makes ever still more fat the murderous moth;
> And dew-pale ladies gather lilies tall
> To weave o'er my white brow Fame's coronal![58]

If Mitchell's work is sharply divided between the spiritual poetry of *The Living Chalice* and the satirical parodies of *Aids to the Immortality of Certain Persons in Ireland,* the work of Eva Gore-Booth (1870–1926) connects the kind of spiritualism evident in Mitchell's writing with specifically feminist concerns. One of the two Gore-Booth sisters of Lissadell in Co. Sligo, who were famously celebrated in Yeats's poem "In Memory of Eva Gore-Booth and Con Markiewicz," Gore-Booth found her initial footing as a poet in A. E.'s circle. Her first collection, entitled *Poems,* was published in 1898, and by the time her second book, *Unseen Kings,* appeared in 1904, she had been fully absorbed into the *New Songs* school. A. E. included five of Gore-Booth's lyrics in *New Songs,* including the often-anthologized "The Little Waves of Breffny," which Katharine Tynan described as "a small masterpiece."[59] After reading *Unseen Kings,* A. E. wrote to Gore-Booth, with characteristic fervor: "I feel you belong to the spiritual class of new Irish people, some of whom write and more do not, but all know that Tirnanogue is no dream and that inwardly we are inhabitants of it and breathe a common air." [60] A number of Gore-Booth's early poems justify this view. "The Little Waves of Breffny" evokes the same twilit atmosphere that characterizes many of A. E.'s poems, albeit in a voice closer to folk tradition:

> A great storm from the ocean goes shouting o'er the hill,
> And there is glory in it and terror on the wind,
> But the haunted air of twilight is very strange and still,
> And the little winds of twilight are dearer to my mind. [61]

Some of Gore-Booth's work also displays the nearly suicidal longing for release from the physical world seen in several of the writers in A. E.'s circle: "My weary soul cries out for peace,/Peace and the quietness of death." [62] It also evinces the same tendency to rewrite the conventional nationalist distinction between spiritual Ireland and material England in specifically spiritualist terms, as in "The Thoughtless Dreamer":

> Thus Ireland many blame and many praise,
>> And she the while, radiant in meadows green,
> And following silently her ancient ways,
>> Is served by hosts of delicate hands unseen.
>
> You whom the bitter hour makest wise,
>> In vain you urge on her your prosperous goal,
> She has visions in her own eyes,
>> She has her destinies in her own soul. [63]

Even before her first book of poems was published, Gore-Booth left Ireland, moving to Manchester in 1897 with her lifelong companion, Esther Roper. From then until the start of World War I, she dedicated herself to women's rights, especially in the area of labor. She also continued to write about Ireland, however, and her Irish poems, including those so admired by A. E. in *Unseen Kings,* fuse the spiritualism observable in such poems as "The Thoughtless Dreamer" with a commitment to feminist issues. Gore-Booth's versions of stories from Ireland's pre-Christian epic tradition often have a specifically feminist edge, contrasting the passionate, heroic women of ancient Irish legend with the lifeless, imprisoned women of her own day, thereby refocusing the revival's heroicizing of Ireland's distant past, as in these lines, from "Lament of the Daughters of Ireland":

> Now is the day of the daughters of Eirinn passed and gone,
>> Forgotten are their great deeds, and their fame has faded away;

Alas, for one glorious hour, one ray of the sun that shone
    On the gold cathbarr of Maeve, and the might of her battle array.
As we sit forlorn at the spindle the hours drag slowly on,
    Hour after hour for ever and ever, cold and discoloured and gray.

                        .   .   .

We are the daughters of crownèd Queens, the children of the sword,
    Our mothers went forth to the battle strong-armed and eager to dare,
Their souls were fierce with freedom, they loved, and they called no man
        lord,
    Freely the winds of Eirinn could tangle their loose-flowing hair.
We who sit by the fireside spinning, gain peace for our soul's reward,
    And the sword slips out of the grasp of hands grown white and feeble
        and fair.[64]

Queen Maeve was a particularly important figure for Gore-Booth, who grew
up within sight of Knocknarae in Co. Sligo, the legendary site of Maeve's
burial. In "A Hermit's Lament for Maeve," Gore-Booth identifies her heroine
with a spiritualism that is set against a specifically male materialism:

Now is the High-Queen vanquished, she has cast her sword aside,
And the stones are gray on Knocknarea,
That build up the cairn of her pride,
And Maeve lies cold in her lonely grave on the haunted mountain side.

Stately of earth-encrusted gold the High-King's dún is built.
Yet fairer by far is the gold of a star,
Or a song with a golden lilt,
Or the dream-gold of the dead Queen's hair and her dagger's carven hilt.[65]

   This distinction between spiritual-feminine and material-masculine has implications for Irish nationalism, as reflected in the conventional use of female
icons to represent nationalist idealizations of Ireland. But it also has important
implications for culture and aesthetics, the areas of chief concern to the literary
revival. Revival writers can in fact be seen as attempting to define and create
an Irish identity that is essentially spiritual-feminine, while identifying English
culture and art in terms that are essentially material-masculine. In part at least,
this may account for the particularly high profile that women had in the revival,
especially in poetry. All this is suggested in Gore-Booth's poem "A Woman's
Rights," which might be read as a kind of manifesto for women poets of the
revival:

Oh, whatever men may say
Ours is the wide and open way.

Oh, whatever men may dream
We have the blue air and the stream.

Men have got their towers and walls,
We have cliffs and waterfalls.

Oh, whatever men may do
Ours is the gold air and the blue.

Men have got their pomp and pride—
All the green world is on our side.[66]

EARLY YEATS

In his introduction to *A Book of Irish Verse,* Yeats divides his nineteenth-century predecessors into those whom he associates with the nationalist poetry of the Young Ireland movement (including James Clarence Mangan) and those whom he sees as significantly influenced by writers and movements outside Ireland. Thus, Samuel Ferguson (associated with Homer), Aubrey de Vere (Wordsworth), and William Allingham ("the lyric poetry of many lands"[1]) are held up as counter forces to a particular Irish tradition defined as essentially and inevitably provincial. Poets such as Ferguson, de Vere, and Allingham, Yeats says, not only worked "apart from politics" but also "were wiser than Young Ireland in their choice of models, for, while drawing not less from purely Irish sources, they turned to the great poets of the world."[2] Like so many of Yeats's critical judgments, this eccentric reading of nineteenth-century Irish poetry in English is more revealing of Yeats's own work than that of the writers he is considering. Yeats's early poetry is most notable for its attempt to fuse an aesthetics drawn chiefly from outside the Irish tradition—English romanticism (especially Blake and Shelley), Pateresque theories of art that were central to the *fin-de-siècle* movement in London, the French *symboliste* movement, and various forms of Eastern occultism and mysticism—with a belief in the poetic and cultural validity of an indigenous Irish tradition and experience. Although Yeats's early writing, as opposed to most of the poetry that he wrote in the wake of the literary revival, often elevates the aesthetic over the realistic (or, as Yeats would put it later in *A Vision,* the antithetical over the primary), for Yeats the relationship between the aesthetics that he constructed largely from models outside the Irish tradition and the interest that he had in reconstructing that tradition was a richly complex, symbiotic one in which the romantic, often escapist tendencies of his aesthetics are contained and concretely realized by his commitment to revitalizing Irish culture, and in which that commitment is made symbolically resonant by his aesthetic vision.[3]

Yeats was not, of course, the first Irish poet to write out of the tension between an aesthetics drawn largely from outside the Irish tradition and a subject matter thoroughly grounded in Irish material. Thomas Moore's *Irish Melodies,* for example, represented one kind of intersection between English poetics and Irish consciousness, and the entire tradition of translation in the nineteenth century was, by its nature, bound up in it. But Yeats's early poetry —that which precedes the publication of his eight-volume *Collected Works* in 1908, the year after the riots at the Abbey Theatre over Synge's *The Playboy of the Western World*—exploits this relationship with a self-consciousness and thoroughness that sets Yeats apart from his predecessors and contemporaries alike. This preoccupation with negotiating between the poles of aestheticism and nationalism defines the real basis and significance of Yeats's quarrel with Young Ireland, and it enabled Yeats, more than any other figure of the revival, to broaden the base of poetic discourse in Ireland without abandoning its distinctive national qualities. Considerably more was at issue here than moving Irish poetry from political to more broadly cultural contexts; Yeats in effect was extending the idea of Irish culture itself to include traditions and forces lying outside the Irish experience.[4]

It was perhaps inevitable that this poetically enabling relationship would manifest itself in unresolvable conflict between the Ireland of Yeats's imaginings and everyday social, political, economic, and religious reality.[5] "The poetry that comes out of the old wisdom must turn always to religion and to the law of the hidden world," he said in an essay written in 1899, "while the poetry of the new wisdom must not forget politics and the law of the visible world; and between these poetries there cannot be any lasting peace."[6] It was probably also inevitable, accordingly, that Yeats's early ambitions to recreate Irish culture according to his imagination and aesthetics—it was hardly a modest goal; Yeats once said that he was working to make the Irish "a chosen race, one of the pillars that uphold the world"[7]—were doomed to failure. But however much this conflict between the real and the imagined Ireland eventually disabled the literary revival, in the early years of his career Yeats made his most memorable Irish poetry out of it.

In much of his earlier poetry, and in the various theories about Irish culture that he advanced in the course of establishing the revival, Yeats clearly gave precedence to the poetry "of the old wisdom," that which, in effect, privileged the aesthetic over the national. Indeed, the entire revival can be seen as a broad-based attempt to aestheticize the romantic nationalism that Young Ireland had done so much to build as the base of a separatist politics in the nineteenth century. The romantic idealization of Ireland had for Yeats very little if anything to do with political revolution, an idea that he was never comfortable with, and everything to do with the celebration of the transforming powers of the poetic imagination.[8] In "To Ireland in the Coming Times," Yeats clearly stakes his claim as an Irish poet on this ground, using it to distinguish himself from the Irish poets who came before him:

> *Nor may I less be counted one*
> *With Davis, Mangan, Ferguson,*
> *Because to him who ponders well*
> *My rhymes more than their rhyming tell*
> *Of the dim wisdoms old and deep,*
> *That God gives unto man in sleep.*[9]

This displacement of a romantic politics by a romantic aesthetics also made it possible for Yeats to use Ireland as a vehicle for expressing his distrust of modern materialism.[10] Thus for Yeats the English-Irish conflict transcended strictly nationalist issues. He wrote to Lady Gregory around the turn of the century: "To transmute the anti-English passion into a passion of hatred against the vulgarity and materialism whereon England has founded her worst life and the whole life that she sends us, has always been a dream of mine." [11] Yeats also perceived Ireland's status as a colonized culture in these broader terms. In a postscript to his essay "The Literary Movement in Ireland," written in 1899, Yeats warned of the insidiously corrupting power of English culture in Ireland: "they fold and unfold their nets before us that may make us like themselves." [12] But, as he went on to reveal in his most uninhibited description of the Arnoldian contrast between English materialism and Irish spiritualism, the danger was more aesthetic than political: "There has been no notorious self-seeker these twenty years, no seller of causes for money down, but he has arisen amongst them; and there has been no man who has lived poorly that he may think well, no master of lofty speech, no imaginative mind, but he has arisen among us." [13]

For the purposes of affirming that "lofty speech," that "imaginative mind," Yeats readily appropriated the Irish literary tradition, especially the legends and epics of pre-Christian Ireland as translated by Ferguson and Standish O'Grady. For Yeats, these texts were less emblems of a lost culture needing to be brought back into circulation, as they were for Ferguson, than avenues to a state of imaginatively enhanced perception. The ancient Irish tradition was, for Yeats, more relevant to various contemporary forms of European romanticism and symbolism than to Irish nationalism, cultural or political. As Yeats argued, in his essay "The Celtic Element in Literature" (1897):

> a new fountain of legends, and, as I think, a more abundant fountain than any in Europe, is being opened, the fountain of Gaelic legends. . . . 'The Celtic movement,' as I understand it, is principally the opening of this fountain, and

none can measure of how great importance it may be to coming times, for every new fountain of legends is a new intoxication for the imagination of the world. It comes at a time when the imagination of the world is as ready as it was at the coming of the tales of Arthur and of the Grail for a new intoxication. The reaction against the rationalism of the eighteenth century has mingled with a reaction against the materialism of the nineteenth century, and the symbolical movement, which has come to perfection in Germany in Wagner, in England in the Pre-Raphaelites, in France in Villiers de l'Isle-Adam, and Mallarmé, and in Belgium in Maeterlinck, and has stirred the imagination of Ibsen and D'Annunzio, is certainly the only movement that is saying new things.[14]

Yeats's long narrative poem, *The Wanderings of Oisin* (1889), which near the end of his life Yeats would remember as an assemblage of "allegorical dreams,"[15] aestheticized one part of the Fenian cycle of ancient Irish epics while adding a touch of *fin-de-siècle* world-weariness:

> She bade them bring us to the hall
> Where Aengus dreams, from sun to sun,
> A Druid dream of the end of days
> When the stars are to wane and the world be done.[16]

Yeats's preoccupation with aesthetics also enabled him to transform the legend of Fergus Mac Roigh, a Red Branch warrior-king tricked out of his throne, into a self-reflexive tale about a deliberate choice of the poetic over the political:

> *Druid.* What would you, Fergus?
> *Fergus.*   Be no more a king,
> But learn the dreaming wisdom that is yours.[17]

Yeats also tended to romanticize the Irish folk tradition and Irish rural life, working against an established tradition of relatively realistic Irish poetry about the land that included two poets high on Yeats's list of admirable Irish writers, Goldsmith and Allingham. As opposed to Goldsmith's analysis of the destruction of Irish rural culture in the eighteenth century at the hands of the forces and philosophy of capitalism, and to Allingham's liberal critique of landlordism in the nineteenth century, Yeats's view of the aesthetically and spiritually empowered peasant is clearly rooted in aesthetics rather than the Irish experience. This view ignored contemporary social realities such as land-reform legislation in the late nineteenth century leading up to the Wyndham Land Act of 1903 that, in theory at least, converted the Irish peasantry into bourgeois proprietors, the one class that Yeats found most inimical to cultural life as he defined it. But

Yeats's ideas about the Irish peasantry are crucial to his aesthetic theories in general, and to the special place assigned to Ireland within those theories. As he wrote in his essay "The Literary Movement in Ireland":

> Irish literature may prolong its first inspiration without renouncing the complexity of ideas and emotions which is the inheritance of cultivated men, for it will have learned from the discoveries of modern learning that the common people, wherever civilization has not driven its plough too deep, keep a watch over the roots of all religion and all romance. Their poetry trembles upon the verge of incoherence with a passion all but unknown among modern poets.[18]

This kind of thinking lies behind such early poems as "The Lake Isle of Innisfree," which owes more to Wordsworthian notions of nature than to any Irish tradition of writing about landscape, and which indeed works hard to obscure the actual place for which it is named by bringing to bear on it the calculated vagueness of Yeats's symbolism:

> And I shall have some peace there, for peace comes dropping slow,
> Dropping from the veils of morning to where the cricket sings;
> There midnight's all a glimmer, and noon a purple glow,
> And evening full of the linnet's wings.[19]

This emphasis on a romantic aesthetic, often combined with Yeats's interest in the occult, occasionally produced poems that, like much of the work of A. E., Katharine Tynan, and other writers associated with the early phase of the revival, are characterized by an ethereal spirituality and by a tendency to identify Ireland with the transcendent. But most of Yeats's early poetry is considerably more adept at negotiating between the poles of aestheticism and human experience than is the work of A. E. and his followers. It is also considerably more self-conscious about the poet's need to effect that negotiation than is the work of most Irish poets writing before or during the revival. Yeats's view of art as providing an intersection between the aesthetic and the real is spelled out specifically in "To the Rose upon the Rood of Time," the preface to a group of poems published in his collection *Poems* (1895) under the heading "The Rose":

> *Red Rose, proud Rose, sad Rose of all my days,*
> *Come near me while I sing the ancient ways —*
> *Cuchullin battling with the bitter tide;*
> *The druid, grey, wood nurtured, quiet eyed,*
> *Who cast round Fergus dreams and ruin untold;*
> *And thine own sadness, whereof stars grown old*

In dancing silver sandaled on the sea,
Sing in their high and lonely melody.
Come near, that no more blinded by man's fate,
I find under the boughs of love and hate,
In all poor foolish things that live a day,
Eternal Beauty wandering on her way.

Come near, come near, come near—Ah, leave me still
A little space for the rose-breath to fill,
Lest I no more hear common things that crave,
The weak worm hiding down in its small cave—
The field mouse running by me in the grass,
And heavy mortal hopes that toil and pass,
But seek alone to hear the strange things said
By God alone to the bright hearts of those long dead,
And learn to chant a tongue men do not know.
Come near—I would before my time to go,
Sing of old Eri and the ancient ways,
Red Rose, proud Rose, sad Rose of all my days.[20]

Yeats's early interest in symbolism, specifically the theories of the French *symboliste* movement, is evident in the deliberately ambiguous symbol of the Rose. Indeed, Yeats's essay "The Symbolism of Poetry" provides a gloss on this important poem. Yeats argues that symbolism should carry literature beyond the scope of rational analysis; symbolism, he says, resists one-to-one relationships, as it "is too subtle for the intellect." [21] Moreover, the presence or absence of this kind of symbolism provides a way of distinguishing between high and low art: "The form of sincere poetry, unlike the form of 'popular poetry,' may indeed be sometimes obscure or ungrammatical as in some of the best of the *Songs of Innocence and Experience,* but it must have the perfections that escape analysis, the subtleties that have a new meaning every day." [22] Not only is the Rose in "To the Rose upon the Rood of Time" a multivalent emblem of the aesthetic power of symbolism, but also it has definite Irish resonances—hardly surprising given the overtly national character of much of the material of the "The Rose" poems. The symbol insists that Ireland itself embodies the poetic and the imaginative as well as the cultural and the political, and the specific Irish figures listed in the poem, the subject of other poems in the group, have meaning only in the context of the transforming imagination, working through a romantic aesthetic vision. At the same time, the poem also argues that that visionary imagination has validity only in the context of ordinary human reality; poetry must be anchored in the specifics of human experience (the world of the real rose-breath as opposed to that of the symbolical Rose), or else the singer will "chant a tongue men do not know," something that a poet attempting a cultural revolution could hardly afford to do. Finally, it is the poem itself that provides the only meaningful intersection of these two realities, and for Yeats, true Irish nationalism, like true art (and unlike the "false" nationalism and art of the Young Ireland movement), must partake of both.

One of Yeats's earliest poems based on Ireland's pre-Christian epic material, "The Madness of King Goll," which was written in 1884 and included, under the title "King Goll," in *Poems and Ballads of Young Ireland* (1888), illustrates one way in which Yeats's early work transforms that material into a self-conscious and culturally conscious negotiation of the dichotomy between the symbolical and the realistic, the Rose and the rose-breath. In Yeats's version of this story, taken from the Fenian cycle, King Goll is both warrior and artist, Irish patriot and romantic poet, embodying the intersection of action and con-templation that, for Yeats, art and nationalism should aspire to. His credentials in the world of action are celebrated with all the political charge of a more blatantly patriotic poem in the Young Ireland tradition:

> From rolling valley and rivery glen,
>   With horsemen hurrying near and far,
> I drew at evening my mailed men,
>   And under the blink o' the morning star,
> Fell on the robbers by the deep,
>   And they inherit the great sleep.[23]

But at the very moment of triumph in the world of action, the king experiences a romantic impulse that drives him into a Sweeney-like solitude and madness:

> But slowly as I shouting slew
>   And trampled in the bubbling mire,
> In my most secret spirit grew
>   A fever and a whirling fire.
> I paused—the stars above me shone
>   And shone around the eyes of men;
> I paused—and far away rushed on
>   Over the heath and spungy fen
> And crumpled in my hands the staff
>   Of my long spear, with scream and laugh
>   And song that down the valley rolled— [24]

In its narrative, its characterization of King Goll, and its style and tone, the poem enacts the rewriting of nineteenth-century political nationalism into the broader terms of romantic aesthetics that was one of the principal aims of the revival, and it stands apart both from earlier nationalist appropriations of Ireland's cultural history and from scholarly antiquarian versions of the past, such as Ferguson's verse translations of similar material.[25]

This negotiation between romanticism and realism is also evident in Yeats's early excursions into Irish folklore. "The Stolen Child," which draws on folk legends about fairies stealing human beings (the inspiration for Ferguson's "The Fairy Thorn"), provides almost a manifesto of Yeats's aesthetic theories. The call of the fairies to the "human child" resonates with the possibility of transcendence and escape through an aesthetic experience, and with a specifically *fin-de-siècle* quality:

> Come away, O human child!
> To the woods and waters wild
> With a fairy, hand in hand,
> For the world's more full of weeping than you can understand.[26]

Like "To the Rose upon the Rood of Time," the poem also insists on the value of the ordinary pleasures of rural life, recognizing that the act of transcendence can deprive as well as elevate:

> He'll hear no more the lowing
> Of the calves on the warm hill-side,
> Or the kettle on the hob
> Sing peace into his breast,
> Or see the brown mice bob
> Round and round the oatmeal chest.[27]

Taking up a folk legend with powerful political implications in "The Valley of The Black Pig," Yeats fuses specifically nationalist sentiment with a broader, mythological vision that embodies the qualities of his romantic aestheticism. In a note to this poem, Yeats acknowledged the political relevance of the myth behind it: "The Irish peasantry have for generations comforted themselves, in their misfortunes, with visions of a great battle, to be fought in a mysterious valley called 'The Valley of the Black Pig,' and to break at last the power of their enemies."[28] In the poem, Yeats emphasizes the romantic qualities of this vision by presenting it as seen through "dream-awakened eyes," but without abandoning the ground of political nationalism that is inherent in the myth:

> The dews drop slowly and dreams gather: unknown spears
> Suddenly hurtle before my dream-awakened eyes,
> And then the clash of fallen horsemen and the cries
> Of unknown perishing armies beat about my ears.

We who still labour by the cromlec, on the shore,
The grey cairn on the hill, when day sinks drowned in dew,
Being weary of the world's empires, bow down to you
Master of the still stars and of the flaming door.[29]

Yeats's use of a long, flexible line here, and in many of his early poems,
embodies on the formal level his view that the poem should provide a point of
intersection between the symbolic and the real, including the national. Yeats
argued in "The Symbolism of Poetry" that the poet working in the tradition of
symbolism will "seek out those wavering, meditative, organic rhythms, which
are the embodiment of the imagination, that neither desires nor hates, because
it has done with time." [30] At the same time, as Yeats was well aware, the long
wavering line has its roots in the attempts of nineteenth-century translators
such as Mangan and Ferguson to reflect in English verse the very un-English
rhythms of poetry written in Irish.

Despite its tendency to make Ireland into a "druid land" and Irish art into a
"druid tune," Yeats's early poetry often reflects quite concretely a wide range
of contemporary and historical Irish experiences. For example, Yeats's early
attempts at the popular ballad—"The Ballad of Father O'Hart," "The Ballad
of Moll Magee," and "The Ballad of the Foxhunter"—demonstrate a commitment to writing for a broad, chiefly Irish Catholic audience, and writing out of
the folk tradition that belongs more or less to that audience. And some early
Yeats poems resist his characteristic tendency to privilege the symbolical. "The
Heart of the Woman," for example, although it has ultimately to do with the
transforming power of love, is written in the direct, unadorned voice that
governs Hyde's translations of Connacht love songs (echoing in particular "My
Grief on the Sea"):

> O what to me the little room
> That was brimmed up with prayer and rest;
> He bade me out into the gloom,
> And my breast lies upon his breast.
>
> O what to me my mother's care,
> The house where I was safe and warm;
> The shadowy blossom of my hair
> Will hide us from the bitter storm.
>
> O hiding hair and dewy eyes,
> I am no more with life and death,
> My heart upon his warm heart lies,
> My breath is mixed unto his breath.[31]

Yeats was also capable on occasion of writing about the rural Irish in decidedly
unromantic terms, as in "The Song of the Old Mother":

I rise in the dawn, and I kneel and blow
Till the seed of the fire flicker and glow;
And then I must scrub and bake and sweep
Till stars are beginning to blink and peep;
And the young lie long and dream in their bed
Of the matching of ribbons for bosom and head,
And their day goes over in idleness,
And they sigh if the wind but lift a tress;
While I must work because I am old,
And the seed of the fire gets feeble and cold.[32]

Finally, despite all Yeats's scepticism about Irish Catholicism, his early poems include at least two attempts—"The Ballad of Father O'Hart" and "The Ballad of Father Gilligan"—to write from inside the Catholic experience. Although these poems are certainly not among the most accomplished of Yeats's early verse, they do show Yeats working against the literary revival's strategy of sidestepping Catholicism by focusing on Ireland's pre-Christian epics and on folk legends from which conventional Christian belief was more or less absent. In "The Ballad of Father O'Hart," Yeats describes a priest robbed of his lands by a conniving "shoneen who had free lands" during the days of the penal laws. The poem's sympathies are not just nationalist but also specifically Catholic:

Good Father John O'Hart
In penal days rode out
To a shoneen who had free lands
And his own snipe and trout.

In trust he took John's lands—
Sleiveens were all his race—
And he gave them as dowers to his daughters,
And they married beyond their place.

But Father John went up,
And Father John went down;
And he wore small holes in his shoes,
And he wore large holes in his gown.[33]

While Yeats's early poems themselves rarely seem conscious of the difficulties inherent in the revival's ambition to recreate Irish culture by fusing romantic aestheticism with cultural nationalism, Yeats himself certainly was conscious of it; indeed, Yeats's sense of the precariousness of the revival, and of his own position as an Irish poet, set in very early. Writing to Alice Milligan in 1894, just three years after the establishment of the Irish Literary Society in Dublin and five years before the publication of *The Wind Among the Reeds,*

Yeats was ready to concede that his plans to revive Irish culture from the
bottom of the social ladder up had to be abandoned:

> My experience of Ireland during the last three years has changed my views
> very greatly, & now I feel that the work of an Irish man of letters must be not
> so much to awaken or quicken or preserve the national ideal among the mass
> of the people but to convert the educated classes to it on the one hand to the
> best of his ability, & on the other—& this is the more important—to fight for
> moderation, dignity, and the right of the intellect among his fellow nationalists.
> Ireland is greatly demoralised in all things—in her scholarship, in her criti-
> cism, in her politics, in her social life. She will never be greatly better until
> she governs herself but she will be greatly worse unless there arise protesting
> spirits.[34]

Seven years later, still well before Synge made his controversial entrance into
the drama of the revival, Yeats found himself nearly at the end of his tether as
one of those protesting spirits. "The arts have failed," he said, in his essay
"Ireland and the Arts" (1901); "fewer people are interested in them every
generation. . . . We who care deeply about the arts find ourselves the priesthood
of an almost forgotten faith." [35] If for Yeats Ireland as it was continually resisted
his vision of Ireland as it could be or ought to be, it is important to remember
that that vision was heavily influenced by a romantic aesthetics that, in its
origins and its ambitions, often had little to do with the historical, social, or
political realities to which it was addressed. Yet the tension between this aesthetics and the various theories of cultural nationalism advanced by Yeats in
these years was anything but paralyzing; indeed, it can be seen as a principal
driving force of his work. Moreover, Yeats saw himself at this time as a writer
who would never abandon his commitment to Ireland. A few years after the
Abbey opened, the theatre's benefactress, Alice Horniman, started a repertory
theatre in Manchester, and approached Yeats about moving the Irish theatre,
which was often playing to nearly empty houses in Dublin. Yeats responded:

> I am not young enough to change my nationality—it would really amount to
> that. I understand my own race and in all my work, lyric or dramatic, I have
> thought of it. If the theatre fails I may or may not write plays—but I shall
> write for my own people—whether in love or hate of them matters little.[36]

Yeats could be said to have written about Ireland more out of hate than out
of love, especially in the years following the collapse of his ambitions for
reconstructing Irish culture. Nevertheless, his commitment to "write for my
own people," under the influence of an aesthetics working with and against it,
enabled him to transform utterly what it meant to do so.

OTHER VISIONS AND REVISIONS

Although the literary revival did much to broaden poetic discourse in Ireland, especially compared to the relatively narrow range of nationalist verse written in the earlier decades of the nineteenth century, the poetry that came out of the movement was characterized by certain distinctive and relatively consistent qualities. This was no doubt due in large part to the extraordinary influence exerted by Yeats on revival aesthetics in general and on numerous poets in particular. Also, the revival was constructed around specific notions about what Irish writing ought to be, in terms both of its relationship to the literary tradition and of the place and function of writers in the contemporary culture. Finally, most of the poetry associated with the revival was based on an essentially romantic aesthetics inherited in part from English romanticism and in part from the forms that romanticism took in nineteenth-century Irish writing. The striking correspondences between the work of Katharine Tynan and Yeats, for example, or between that of A. E. and Susan Mitchell, can be seen as manifestations of a widely accepted aesthetics and view of Irish culture.

There were, however, a number of Irish poets writing at the time of the revival, including some who were quite close to the center of the movement, whose work departed quite markedly and deliberately from the mainstream of revival attitudes and styles. In general, these departures were based on a rejection of the *fin-de-siècle* quality of revival poetry and of the romantic aesthetics that lay behind it. This attitude is nowhere more plainly spelled out than in John M. Synge's "The Passing of the Shee," a poem that critiques both the romantic aesthetics of early Yeats and the mysticism of A. E. while suggesting an alternative subject matter for Irish poetry and an alternative aesthetics through which to express it:

Adieu, sweet Angus, Maeve, and Fand,
Ye plumed yet skinny Shee,
That poets played with hand in hand
To learn their ecstasy.

We'll stretch in Red Dan Sally's ditch,
And drink in Tubber fair,
Or poach with Red Dan Philly's bitch
The badger and the hare.[1]

As this poem indicates, part of Synge's refusal to romanticize or aestheticize
the Irish rural experience was grounded in his interest in Irish folk culture,
which was shared by many of the Irish poets who stood on the margins of the
revival. This realistic approach to writing about rural life is especially true of
Joseph Campbell and Padraic Colum, both of whom extended Douglas Hyde's
representations of folk culture, and, anticipating later critiques of the revival's
characterization of Irish rural life, aspired to represent Irish rural experience
from the inside, rather than from the distanced, often romanticizing, position of
a writer such as Yeats or Todhunter. The relatively realistic aesthetics governing
the work of Synge, Campbell, and Colum also inspired the development of a
distinctly urban poetry in this period, representing aspects of Irish life more or
less ignored in Irish poetry since the time of Swift and generally neglected in
the revival's attempt to construct an Irish identity grounded in rural Ireland.
The urban poetry of Seamus O'Sullivan and James Stephens not only explored
aspects of Irish life conspicuously missing from the poetry of the revival—and,
until the appearance of Sean O'Casey's plays in the 1920s, from the drama
as well—but also, in its reliance on colloquial speech and idiom, implicitly
interrogated the romantic aesthetics that inspired much of the writing of the
revival. The tendency of many revival poets to focus on Ireland's pagan past,
and thereby circumvent or at least downplay the Catholic dimension of Irish
culture, was countered in the work of several poets on the edge of the movement. It is no accident that the poets in this category whose work most specifically embraced Catholicism, Thomas MacDonagh, Patrick Pearse, and Joseph
Mary Plunkett, were active in the Republican movement (all three were executed for their part in the Easter Rising of 1916). Their work rested on an
assumed relationship between Catholicism and political separatism—the work
of Plunkett, in particular, defined political martyrdom in the terms of Christ's
crucifixion—and often overtly spoke for a political agenda in a way very much
at odds with the apolitical aesthetics of the early revival. MacDonagh and
Pearse also sought, in translations from the Irish or in poems based loosely on
Irish originals, to replace the revival's image of the pagan Celt, based in part
on Arnold's ideas about Celticism, with the image of the Catholic Gael; in this
sense, MacDonagh's argument for an "Irish mode" of writing in English can

be read as a critique, in religious as well as cultural terms, of the revival's interpretations of the Irish tradition.

For all the obvious differences between them, Yeats and Synge (1871–1909) had much in common, in part because of their position as Anglo-Irish Protestants committed to reconstructing a culture from which they were inevitably alienated. Synge shared Yeats's distrust of the Catholic middle class. After the riots over *The Playboy of the Western World* at the Abbey Theatre in 1907, even Yeats's caustic attacks on the middle class could not match the viciousness of Synge's remarks in a letter to Stephen MacKenna:

> I sometimes wish I had never left my garret in the rue d'Assas . . . . the scurrility and ignorance and treachery of some of the attacks upon me have rather disgusted me with the middle-class Irish Catholic. As you know I have the wildest admiration for the Irish Peasants, and for Irish men of known or unknown genius . . . but between the two there's an ungodly ruck of fat-faced, sweaty-headed swine.[2]

Also, Synge's plays, for all their efforts to represent Irish peasants from the inside, describe rural communities as unable to accommodate heroic artist figures cut in the mold of Yeats.[3] It is difficult not to see this gap between Synge and his audience as defined by sectarian and class differences, nor to see the hostile reaction to his plays as embodying an apparently insurmountable obstacle to Synge's ambition to give an authentic voice to a community that lay significantly outside his own experience.[4] This ambition is also hindered in his poetry by the influence of English romanticism, particularly Wordsworth. In Synge's "Prelude," for example, the Irish landscape is converted into a generically romantic one, in the manner of nineteenth-century Irish poets such as Aubrey de Vere and Thomas Caulfield Irwin:

> Still south I went and west and south again,
> Through Wicklow from the morning till the night,
> And far from cities, and the sites of men,
> Lived with the sunshine, and the moon's delight.
>
> I knew the stars, the flowers, and the birds,
> The grey and wintry sides of many glens,
> And did but half remember human words,
> In converse with the mountains, moors, and fens.[5]

Nevertheless, Synge's poetry as a whole quite self-consciously interrogates the Celtic-Twilight aesthetics of the revival, while grounding itself in the Irish folk tradition. In the preface to his volume *Poems and Translations,* published in 1909, Synge clearly defines his poetic ambitions as differing from those of Yeats and his revival colleagues:

> In these days poetry is usually a flower of evil or good, but it is the timber of poetry that wears most surely, and there is no timber that has not strong roots among the clay & worms. Even if we grant that exalted poetry can be kept successful by itself, the strong things of life are needed in poetry also, to show that what is most exalted, or tender, is not made by feeble blood. It may almost be said that before verse can be human again it must learn to be brutal.[6]

Yeats saw what Synge was up to; in his own preface to *Poems and Translations,* he said:" the strength that made him delight in setting the hard virtues by the soft, the bitter by the sweet, salt by mercury, the stone by the elixir, gave him a hunger for harsh facts, for ugly surprising things, for all that defies our hope."[7] That hunger for harsh facts and ugly surprising things permeates Synge's poetry. In Synge's hands, the note of regret and loss that characterizes Hyde's translations from the folk tradition and the narrative poems of revival writers such as Moira O'Neill, Dora Sigerson, and Emily Lawless is transformed into a vision of Irish rural experience strongly marked by violence and cruelty. For example, Synge's "Danny" dramatizes graphically what is only threatened or suggested in Hyde's version of an Irish curse poem, "Bruadar and Smith and Glinn":

> It wasn't long till Danny came,
> From Bangor making way,
> And he was damning moon and stars
> And whistling grand and gay.
>
> Till in a gap of hazel glen—
> And not a hare in sight—
> Out lepped the nine-and-twenty lads
> Along his left and right.
>
> Then Danny smashed the nose on Byrne,
> He split the lips on three,
> And bit across the right hand thumb
> Of one Red Shawn Magee.
>
> But seven tripped him up behind,
> And seven kicked before,
> And seven squeezed around his throat
> Till Danny kicked no more.
>
> Then some destroyed him with their heels,
> Some tramped him in the mud,

> Some stole his purse and timber pipe,
> And some washed off his blood.[8]

Not since Swift's "The Description of an Irish-Feast," written nearly two hundred years earlier, had this kind of violence found its way into Irish poetry. But "Danny" represents more than a rare poetic depiction of a cultural fondness for cruelty; read in the context of Synge's portrayal of rural Irish communities as intolerant of those considered subversive, Danny, who is described earlier in the poem as "playing hell on decent girls" and "beating man and boy," and as having "left two pairs of female twins" and "struck the parish priest,"[9] might be read as another, albeit less appealing, version of Christy Mahon. Finally, a poem like "Danny" can be interpreted as critiquing the romantic purposes to which the traditional ballad form had been put by many revival writers.[10]

The extent to which Synge was able to represent the Irish folk tradition in more authentic terms than were poets such as O'Neill, Dora Sigerson, and Lawless (not to mention Yeats) depended significantly on his considerable understanding of and commitment to the Irish language and its literary tradition. The language of Synge's plays can be read as an attempt to fuse Irish and English speech patterns, thereby working against the cultural and political implications of much translation work in the nineteenth century, which in effect conceded that the two traditions were essentially separate.[11] In Synge's poetry, however, there are few traces of the formal qualities of verse in Irish that distinguished the work of earlier translators such as Ferguson, Edward Walsh, and J. J. Callanan. Nevertheless, Synge's poetry draws heavily on folk culture, and can also be associated with the tradition of satirical verse in Irish. "The Passing of the Shee" certainly belongs to this tradition, and "The Curse," presumably directed at the sister of the Abbey actress Molly Allgood, who had expressed her dislike of *The Playboy,* is even more brutal, while specifically echoing Hyde's "Bruadar and Smith and Glinn":

> Lord, confound this surly sister,
> Blight her brow with blotch and blister,
> Cramp her larynx, lung, and liver,
> In her guts a galling give her.
>
> Let her live to earn her dinners
> In Mountjoy with seedy sinners:
> Lord, this judgment quickly bring,
> And I'm your servant, J. M. Synge.[12]

Synge died of Hodgkins disease at the age of thirty-eight, and there is a streak of melancholy and preoccupation with death running through his poetry

that looks back to Mangan and that other dark romantic Irish poet, Thomas
Dermody. At times, Synge seems remarkably close to Mangan's perception of
a symbiotic relationship between personal despair and the condition of Ireland.
For Synge, this relationship was specifically embodied in the culture of the
Aran Islands,[13] which is reflected most pointedly in his plays, but his poetry is
colored by a Mangan-like obsession with mortality often bound up with the
landscape of Ireland in general. "To the Oaks of Glencree," for example,
moves from a Wordsworthian celebration of the landscape to an overpowering
awareness of the speaker's own death and final integration into that landscape:

> My arms are round you, and I lean
> Against you, while the lark
> Sings over us, and golden lights, and green
> Shadows are on your bark.
>
> There'll come a season when you'll stretch
> Black boards to cover me:
> Then in Mount Jerome I will lie, poor wretch,
> With worms eternally.[14]

Yeats's remark that Synge was not capable of a political thought may be
more interesting as a characterization of Yeats's thinking than of Synge's, but
there is some truth in it.[15] Synge's celebration of the alienated individual, in his
poetry as well as in his plays, does suggest a distrust of political as well as
social community. Synge's writing certainly appears distinctly apolitical when
compared with that of Thomas MacDonagh, Patrick Pearse, and Joseph May
Plunkett, all of whom were writing at about the same time. Although all three
of these poets worked out of a romantic notion of the poet not significantly
different, in theory at least, from that which inspired the literary revival,[16] in
their work individual meaning and fulfillment requires some intersection between the private and the public, between individual psychology and communal
politics.[17] The relatively subjective obsession with his own death in Synge's
poetry is transformed in the writing of Pearse and Plunkett especially into a
concern with political martyrdom. These poets also differ markedly from
Synge, and from most of the poets associated with the revival, in the specifically
Catholic focus of their work. Thus, these poets of the Rising challenged two
central assumptions of the revival: that cultural but not political nationalism
was the business of the Irish writer, and that the key to Ireland's cultural
identity lay in its pagan rather than its Christian (or, more to the point, Catholic)
past. These poets also significantly modified the nationalism of Young Ireland
by discarding the nonsectarian dimension of that movement. Finally, these
poets, especially MacDonagh and Pearse, were more knowledgeable about the

tradition of writing in Irish than were many of the writers associated with the revival, including Yeats, and were committed to replacing the revival's romanticized icon of the Celt with a more authentic conception of the Gael, an effort that was indebted in part at least to the thinking of George Sigerson. Indeed, despite the tendency to read these poets chiefly in the light of their participation in the Easter Rising, or of their effort to fuse Catholic mysticism with Irish nationalism, it might be argued that the most significant contribution that these poets made to the development of Irish poetry in English lay in their attempt to write in what MacDonagh called "the Irish mode."

This is especially true of MacDonagh (1878–1916), whose critical study *Literature in Ireland* (1916) stands as a manifesto of the effort to discredit the stereotypes engendered by Celtic Twilight aesthetics. In the preface to this work, MacDonagh argued that an "Irish mode" of writing in English could "come only when English had become the language of the Irish people, mainly of Gaelic stock, and when the literature was from, by, of, to and for the Irish people." [18] MacDonagh also made it perfectly clear that the Irish mode was meant to replace the "Celtic note," which he specifically associated with the *fin-de-siècle* aesthetics of the revival: "I have never been able to discover what exactly people mean by that term, so often used, the Celtic note. I think that in general it is supposed to be something mysterious and vague, something expressing an indefinite sorrow or an unbodied joy, something reminiscent of Maeterlinck's more shadowy plays." [19] MacDonagh's contribution to this effort to unseat the Celt of the revival was, perhaps, made more effectively in his theoretical writings than in his practice as a poet. But MacDonagh's relatively limited work in verse translation contains several striking instances of an ability to make poetry written in English take the impress of verse in Irish, in terms of formal technique and voice. Most notable among these is "The Yellow Bittern":

> The yellow bittern that never broke out
>   In a drinking bout, might as well have drunk;
> His bones are thrown on a naked stone
>   Where he lived alone like a hermit monk.
> O yellow bittern! I pity your lot,
>   Though they say that a sot like myself is curst—
> I was sober a while, but I'll drink and be wise
> For I fear I should die in the end of thirst.
>
>   .   .   .
>
> My darling told me to drink no more
>   Or my life would be o'er in a little short while;
> But I told her 'tis drink gives me health and strength
>   And will lengthen my road by many a mile.

> You see how the bird of the long smooth neck
>   Could get his death from the thirst at last—
> Come, son of my soul, and drain your cup,
>   You'll get no sup when your life is past.[20]

The diction here might be compared to that in some of Synge's poems, but what makes "The Yellow Bittern" distinctively representative of MacDonagh's Irish mode is its employment of terminal, internal, and terminal-medial rhyme and assonance, echoing the heavily patterned music of the original, "An Bonnán Buí."[21] MacDonagh's ability to absorb into his English verse the flexible rhythms of poetry in Irish owes something to the translations of Ferguson and Mangan (the small anthology of poems that MacDonagh appended to *Literature in Ireland* as examples of "the Irish mode" includes seven poems by Ferguson and five by Mangan). This quality is particularly evident in his version of an anonymous poem in Irish, "Druimfhionn Donn Dilis":

> Land, homestead, wines, music:
> I am reft of them all!
> Chief and bard that once wooed me
> Are gone from my call!
> And cold water to sooth me
> I sup with my tears,
> While the foe that pursues me
> Has drinking that cheers.
>
> —Through the mist of the glensides
> And hills I return:
> Like a brogue beyond mending
> The Sasanach I'll spurn:
> If in battle's contention
> I have sight of the crown,
> I'll befriend thee and defend thee,
> My young Druimfhionn Donn![22]

The Druimfhionn Donn Dilis (dear brown white-backed cow) is a traditional nationalist symbol for Ireland, and this poem certainly can be read as embodying the politics that led MacDonagh from the Gaelic League, which he joined in 1902, to the General Post Office on Easter Monday, 1916. There is, however, some danger in the tendency to read back into MacDonagh's poetry his participation in the Rising. On the whole, MacDonagh's poetry is not overtly political. His early work, most of which he kept out of his collection *Lyrical Poems*, published in 1913, was heavily influenced by Yeats's early poetry and by

Wordsworth.[23] In a lecture that he once gave on Irish poetry, MacDonagh laid out an aesthetics that seems strikingly similar to some of Yeats's arguments for privileging the individual over the communal. "The collective is enemy to true sincerity," MacDonagh said. "Propaganda has never produced a poem. A great hymn, whether of religion or patriotism, is rarely other than the cry of a poet, calling to his god or to his country as if he first and alone felt it." [24] And one Mangan poem conspicuously absent from MacDonagh's anthology of the Irish mode is the incendiary "Dark Rosaleen." MacDonagh's poetry is also relatively uncomfortable with the relationship between Catholicism and nationalism established in the work of Pearse and Plunkett. Indeed, MacDonagh's poems on the subject are troubled by a perception of a moral conflict between Catholic teaching and militant nationalism.[25] In "Wishes for My Son," MacDonagh hopes that his son will experience "glorious deed" and "Wild and perilous holy things/Flaming with a martyr's blood," but he also concedes that he himself, because of his religious faith, could not accept the assumptions of a virulently anti-English nationalism:

> But I found no enemy
> No man in a world of wrong,
> That Christ's word of charity
> Did not render clean and strong—
> Who was I to judge my kind,
> Blindest groper of the blind? [26]

Had MacDonagh lived to write more, it is possible that the derivative romanticism of much of his work might have matured into an art more convincingly grounded in the realities of Irish culture, past and present, and more convincingly representative of his own idea of an Irish mode of writing in English. The potential is evident in a translation such as "The Yellow Bittern" or in his narrative poem written out of the folk tradition, "John-John," a poem considerably more authentic in voice than the narrative ballads written by Yeats early in his career. As it is, however, Yeats's description of MacDonagh in "Easter, 1916" as a poet "coming into his force" [27] must suffice.

This is even more true of Pearse (1879–1916), most of whose poetry was written in the last few years of his life. Pearse may be a less accomplished poet than MacDonagh at his best—many of Pearse's poems, especially the largely autobiographical verse that he wrote just before his execution, are marked by a sentimentality and naivete relatively rare in MacDonagh's work—but his poetry more clearly attempts to fuse nationalism with Irish Catholicism.[28] Moreover, Pearse's position in the Irish Volunteers was complemented by the extremely active part that he played in the Gaelic language movement, founding St. Enda's School in 1908 and serving as editor of the Gaelic League's weekly publication, *An Claidheamh Soluis,* from 1903 to 1909. His speeches, stories, and plays as well as his poetry depart sharply from mainstream revival aesthetics in insisting on a necessary connection between cultural revival and separatist politics.

The primary vehicle in Pearse's writing for the fusion of nationalism and Catholicism is an identification between the political martyr and Christ. Perhaps nowhere in his work is this identification more explicitly made than in the conclusion of his nationalist play, *The Singer,* written in 1915. "One man can free a people as one Man redeemed the world," the play's protagonist says. "I will take no pike, I will go into the battle with bare hands. I will stand up before the Gall as Christ hung naked before men on the tree!" [29] This association is the driving force behind the poems that Pearse wrote while in detention just before his execution on May 3, 1916. "A Mother Speaks" implicitly identifies Pearse's martyrdom with Christ's:

> Dear Mary, that didst see thy first-born Son
> Go forth to die amid the scorn of men
> For whom He died,
> Receive my first-born son into thy arms,
> Who also hath gone out to die for men,
> And keep him by thee till I come to him.
> Dear Mary, I have shared thy sorrow,
> And soon shall share thy joy. [30]

In "The Rebel," written in the fall of 1915 when he was also working on *The Singer,* Pearse employs a more oratorical voice, akin to that of his political speeches, which draws on Old Testament rhythms to underscore the connection between revolutionary politics and religious faith:

And now I speak, being full of vision;
I speak to my people, and I speak in my people's name to the masters of my
    people.
I say to my people that they are holy, that they are august, despite their
    chains,
That they are greater than those that hold them, and stronger and purer,
That they have but need of courage, and to call on the name of their God,
God the unforgetting, the dear God that loves the peoples
For whom He died naked, suffering shame.
And I say to my people's masters: Beware,
Beware of the thing that is coming, beware of the risen people,
Who shall take what ye would not give. [31]

The echoes in these lines of Whitman, whose work Pearse came to know through T. W. Rolleston, also implies a communal idea of the poet as a man speaking to an audience, as opposed to the notion of the subjective if not alienated poet governing much of the work of revival writers.[32]

Like MacDonagh, Pearse was at his best when working in translation, whether from his own poems in Irish or those of others. "A Woman of the Mountain Keens Her Son," a translation of one of Pearse's poems in Irish published in his collection *Suantraidhe agus Goltraidhe (Songs of Sleep and Sorrow)* in 1914, expresses a theme similar to that which informs most of his poems in English about his mother. Pearse's tendency in his poems written in English to lapse into sentimentality and abstraction gives way in this poem, under pressure from the Irish original, to concrete imagery and colloquial diction that convey the speaker's sense of loss with a vividness rarely seen in Pearse's writing. At the same time, the poem is sensitive to many of the formal qualities that characterize poetry in Irish:

> Grief on the death, it has blackened my heart:
> It has snatched my love and left me desolate,
> Without friend or companion under the roof of my house
> But this sorrow in the midst of me, and I keening.
>
> . . .
>
> O green-sodded grave in which my child is,
> Little narrow grave, since you are his bed,
> My blessing on you, and thousands of blessings
> On the green sods that are over my treasure.
>
> Grief on the death, it cannot be denied,
> It lays low, green and withered together,—
> And O gentle little son, what tortures me is
> That your fair body should be making clay![33]

One of Pearse's most effective nationalist poems, "Renunciation," a translation of one of his own poems in Irish, powerfully dramatizes the connection between religious asceticism and nationalist martyrdom:

> Naked I saw thee,
> O beauty of beauty,
> And I blinded my eyes
> For fear I should fail.
>
> I heard thy music,
> O melody of melody,

And I closed my ears
For fear I should falter.

I tasted thy mouth,
O sweetness of sweetness,
And I hardened my heart
For fear of my slaying.

I blinded my eyes,
And I closed my ears,
I hardened my heart
And I smothered my desire.

I turned my back
On the vision I had shaped,
And to this road before me
I turned my face.

I have turned my face
To this road before me,
To the deed that I see
And the death I shall die.[34]

Pearse also translated a number of poems from the work of the seventeenth-century Irish poet Seathrún Céitinn (Geoffrey Keating). Pearse found Céitinn's laments over the destruction of the Gaelic aristocracy in the wake of the flight of the earls at the beginning of the seventeenth century and, later, the Cromwellian conquest particularly relevant to his own position as a militantly nationalist poet writing in the second decade of the twentieth century. For Pearse, the project of translation, like that of any writing, was significant only in so far as it had some bearing on the cause of political separatism. His translation of Céitinn's "Óm Sceol ar Ardmhagh Fáill" ("From My Grief on Fál's Proud Plain," in Pearse's version) not only eschews the romanticizing lyricism of a writer like Mangan but also expresses, often quite overtly, the urgency of Pearse's own nationalist convictions:

From my grief on Fál's proud plain I sleep no night,
And till doom the plight of her native folk hath crushed me:
Tho' long they stand a fence against a rabble of foes,
At last there hath grown full much of the wild tare through them.
            .   .   .
If the high chief lived of Aine and Druim Daoile
And the strong lions of Maigue who granted gifts,
There surely were no places for this rabble where Bride meets Blackwater,
But shouts and outcries on high announcing their ruin and rout.[35]

Myriad connections link MacDonagh, Pearse, and Joseph Mary Plunkett (1887–1916); according to Plunkett's sister, he and MacDonagh criticized each other's work, Plunkett helped to publish MacDonagh's *Lyrical Poems* in 1913 and Pearse's *Suantraidhe agus Goltraidhe* in 1914, and MacDonagh made the selection for Plunkett's first book of poems, *The Circle and the Sword,* published in 1913.[36] Yet Plunkett's poetry differs substantially from MacDonagh's and Pearse's. It manifests little interest in negotiating between the traditions of poetry in Irish and of poetry in English, and it operates against a cosmic backdrop that contrasts markedly with the more provincial linkages between Irish Catholicism and Irish nationalism that govern much of Pearse's work.

Plunkett seems to have been obsessed with the crucifixion, and his earliest poems, collected in *The Circle and the Sword,* evoke a sense of religion heavily marked by violence and blood sacrifice, as well as by mysticism.[37] At times, Plunkett's religious sensibility takes on markedly Gothic qualities, as in the opening of an early poem, "I Saw the Sun at Midnight":

> I saw the Sun at midnight, rising red,
> Deep-hued yet glowing, heavy with the stain
> Of blood-compassion, and I saw It gain
> Swiftly in size and growing till It spread
> Over the stars; the heavens bowed their head
> As from Its heart slow dripped a crimson rain,
> Then a great tremor shook It, as of pain—
> The night fell, moaning, as It hung there dead.[38]

Plunkett's obsession with the crucifixion eventually found its way into his writing on the more specific theme of nationalist blood sacrifice. Indeed, nowhere in the poetry of this period is the fusion of religious mysticism and militant nationalism more powerfully evoked than in Plunkett's most politically incendiary poem, "The Little Black Rose Shall Be Red at Last," which was based on Plunkett's marriage to Grace Gifford in his cell on the eve of his execution. In this poem, addressed to "Caitílín ni hUllacháin," Plunkett's lover is an emblem of both his personal redemption and the redemption of Ireland, and sexual consummation is linked to political revolution and violence:

> Because we share our sorrows and our joys
> And all your dear and intimate thoughts are mine
> We shall not fear the trumpets and the noise
> Of battle, for we know our dreams divine,
> And when my heart is pillowed on your heart
> And ebb and flowing of their passionate flood

> Shall beat in concord love through every part
> Of brain and body—when at last the blood
> Oerleaps the final barrier to find
> Only one source wherein to spend its strength
> And we two lovers, long but one in mind
> And soul, are made one only flesh at length;
> Praise God if this my blood fulfils the doom
> When you, dark rose, shall redden into bloom.[39]

There is, of course, a fair amount of romanticism behind this apocalyptic mix of religious martyrdom, political blood sacrifice, and sexual passion, and Plunkett's aesthetics as a whole owe something to the same kind of romantic notions about the artist that governed the work of many revival poets. In an essay entitled "Poetry and Obscurity," published in the *Irish Review* in 1914, Plunkett defined the poet in terms that echo quite specifically the aesthetics spelled out in some of Yeats's early essays on this topic. "An artist is one who has the power of unveiling Nature," Plunkett wrote, "only to substitute the veils of Art. Indeed it is by imposing the veils of Art that he is enabled to show the real qualities and relations of things." [40] Plunkett's faith in the power of his art to transcend his own death, like his faith in the power of the sacrifice of his life for the cause of Irish independence, was as unshakeable as it was romantic. A poem from *The Circle and the Sword* titled "When All the Stars Become a Memory" stands as testimony both to that faith and to the apocalyptic nature of the imagination that conceived it:

> When all the stars become a memory
> Hid in the heart of heaven; when the sun
> At last is resting from his weary run
> Sinking to glorious silence in the sea
> Of God's own glory: when the immensity
> Of Nature's universe its fate has won
> And its reward: when death to death is done
> And deathless Being's all that is to be—
>
> Your praise shall 'scape the grinding of the mills:
> My songs shall live to drive their blinding cars
> Through fiery apocalypse to Heaven's bars!
> When God's loosed might the prophet's words fulfils,
> My songs shall see the ruin of the hills,
> My songs shall sing the dirges of the stars.[41]

Seamus O'Sullivan (1879–1958) was closer to the literary revival, in his life and in his writing, than were any of the Rising poets, and his work bears few if any traces of the nationalist urgency that characterizes a poem such as Plunkett's "The Little Black Rose Shall Be Red at Last." Born James Sullivan Starkey into a Dublin family with a Wesleyan background, O'Sullivan attended University College, Dublin, a few years ahead of Joyce, and became friends with A. E., Yeats, Oliver St. John Gogarty, and Arthur Griffith. On opening night of the Abbey Theatre's first production, December 27, 1904, O'Sullivan played the Blind Man in Yeats's *On Baile's Strand.* The same year, five of his lyrics were published in A. E.'s *New Songs.* Later, he founded the influential *Dublin Magazine,* which he edited for thirty-five years, and to which nearly every important Irish writer of the first half of the century contributed at one time or another. A. E. once referred to O'Sullivan's poetry as "delicate snatchings at a beauty which is ever fleeting," [42] and in the preface poem to his collection *Poems* (1912), O'Sullivan himself said that he was striving to evoke "A wisdom winnowed from light words." [43]

Nevertheless, O'Sullivan's work needs to be distinguished from mainstream revival poetry. O'Sullivan rarely if ever aestheticized or mythologized the rural Irish experience in the manner of Yeats's "Lake Isle of Innisfree" or A. E.'s "The Great Breath." His poetry about rural Ireland is marked by an attention to concrete detail and a tone of restraint more readily associated with Padraic Colum's relatively realistic depictions of rural Ireland, and it uses landscape as a vehicle primarily for personal emotion, usually of loss and grief, rather than for the expression of a mythic or transcendent vision. "The Sheep," from O'Sullivan's first collection of poems, *The Twilight People* (1905), exemplifies these qualities:

> Slowly they pass
> In the grey of the evening
> Over the wet road,
> A flock of sheep.
> Slowly they wend
> In the grey of the gloaming,
> Over the wet road
> That winds through the town.
> Slowly they pass,
> And gleaming whitely
> Vanish away
> In the grey of the evening.
> Ah, what memories
> Loom for a moment,
> Gleam for a moment,
> And vanish away,
> Of the white days

> When we two together
> Went in the evening,
> Where the sheep lay:
> We two together,
> Went with slow feet
> In the grey of the evening
> Where the sheep lay.[44]

Austin Clarke, an admirer of O'Sullivan's work, argued that O'Sullivan's poetry in this vein also carried a political charge, expressing a "melancholy solitude of depopulated places, hinting at the long centuries of opposition, exile and despair." [45] O'Sullivan's negotiation between the political and the personal can be seen in one of his best-known poems, "The Twilight People," originally published in A. E.'s *New Songs:*

> Twilight people, why will you still be crying,
> Crying and calling to me out of the trees?
> For under the quiet grass the wise are lying,
> And all the strong ones are gone over the seas.
>
> And I am old, and in my heart at your calling
> Only the old dead dreams a-fluttering go,
> As the wind, the forest wind, in its falling
> Sets the withered leaves fluttering to and fro.[46]

O'Sullivan also departed sharply from the conventions and assumptions of the revival in his writing about urban Ireland, a facet of Irish experience generally passed over in the revival's attempt to locate cultural identity in an idealized rural Ireland. Although O'Sullivan's poems about Dublin are less accomplished and less iconoclastic than are the Dublin poems of James Stephens, their attention to the underside of Dublin life anticipates the fiction of Joyce rather than harks back to the early poetry of Yeats. The opening of "In Cuffe Street" describes an urban landscape not unlike that represented in the early stories of *Dubliners,* some of which were written about the same time that O'Sullivan was writing his poems about Dublin:

> The senses stifle in this narrow lane,
> Where the fierce merciless summer sun beats down
> On rows of stinking fish, and vegetables
> Half rotten, and tortured flowers with stems of wire
> Enforced to live beyond their fragrant hour
> A horrid death-in-life. . . .[47]

Some of O'Sullivan's Dublin poems implicitly question the revival's romantic preoccupation with rural Ireland by placing a traditional emblem of romanticism, such as the flowers in these lines, in an urban setting where its survival and relevance are highly problematic. In "Lark's Song," one of three poems gathered under the heading of "In Mercer Street," and published first in *Earth-Lover* (1909), one of the most common images associated with romantic transcendence is presented in a significantly unromantic environment that overwhelms a moment of imaginative possibility:

> No more the cage can do him wrong,
> All is forgotten save his song:
> He has forgot the ways of men,
> Wide heaven is over him again,
> And round him the wide fields of dew
> That his first infant mornings knew,
> E'er yet the dolorous years had brought
> The hours of captive anguish, fraught
> With the vile clamour of the street,
> The insult of passing feet,
> The torture of the daily round,
> The organ's blasphemy of sound.
> Sudden some old swift memory brings
> The knowledge of forgotten wings,
> He springs elate and panting falls
> At the rude touch of prison walls.
> Silence. Again the street is grey:
> Shut down the windows—Work-a-day.[48]

It was Colum, rather than A. E. or Yeats, who recognized the ways in which this kind of writing departed from the romanticism of the revival. In a poetic tribute to O'Sullivan after his death in 1958, Colum recalled an incident that he said summarized O'Sullivan's sensibility:

> Montaigne—the last words I heard you speak
> Were that old man's, and I was made elate
> To know that one I left upon the street
> Was still attuned to that astringent mode.[49]

For all its realistic attention to the details of Irish rural life, O'Sullivan's poetry exhibits little interest in the Irish folk tradition. For an attempt to represent that tradition in original verse in English, as opposed to Hyde's translations, one must turn to another of the young writers frequenting the Dublin literary circles that O'Sullivan moved in and out of at the beginning of the century. Joseph Campbell (1879–1944), a Belfastman who signed his early work in Irish, initially was known as much for the lyrics that he had written for a collection of Ulster folk songs, *Songs of Uladh* (1904), as for the poetry that he was beginning to publish. Campbell was the same age as O'Sullivan, but he went to Dublin as a young man with a very different experience of Ireland behind him and very different ideas about what Irish poetry should be. Campbell's writing was thoroughly grounded in the rural life of Ulster and in the folk culture of that region; as a boy he spent his summers on his grandfather's farm in an Irish-speaking region of Co. Antrim. Campbell's work is closer to the tradition of regional poetry represented by earlier Ulster poets such as James Orr than it is to the national cultural agenda set forth by Yeats and his followers. As an Ulsterman who had spent much of his childhood among Irish speakers and who knew the language well (he translated into English the Irish stories of Patrick Pearse), Campbell drew on a complex linguistic mix consisting of Irish, the Scots-inflected English of Ulster, and the standard English that he learned at school.[50]

Campbell was at one time quite close to the revival; he served for several years as secretary of the Irish Literary Society in London, and as a young man in Belfast he knew Ethna Carbery (who was a cousin) and Alice Milligan. Although his commitment to folklore and the Irish language might be seen as generally coincident with the cultural ambitions of the revival, Campbell specifically dissociated himself from the aesthetic assumptions of the movement. In an essay published in *The Nationalist* in 1905, Campbell attacked the revival in no uncertain terms. "There is too much 'poetic moonshine' just now," he said. "Continued musings on the dead unhappy past by contemporary writers can help the nation not at all. . . . Our younger men must shake themselves free of this foisted, anaemic, unnational tradition." [51] Campbell's critique of the revival identified him with the effort of writers such as MacDonagh and Pearse to replace the revival's Celt with a more culturally authentic notion of the Gael.[52] Campbell also was indebted, especially in his collection of poetic portraits, *Irishry* (1913), to Synge's attempts to deromanticize the Irish peasant. Synge's presence can be felt, for example, in the roughedged diction and unblinking realism of "The Pig-Killer":

> The gelded brawn may kick and squeal,
> The bonham wriggle, dumb and blind,
> But Packey spits and pulls a wisp,
> And wipes his hands, and does not mind.
>
> They say that murder ever cries
> For vengeance on the slayer's head;
> But Morrigu, I fear, must wait
> For Packey Byrne till he is dead.[53]

At about the same time that he was questioning the "poetic moonshine" of the revival, Campbell published "I Am the Mountainy Singer," which defined his own aesthetics as rooted in rural realism and the folk tradition:

> I am the mountainy singer—
> The voice of the peasant's dream,
> The cry of the wind on the wooded hill,
> The leap of the fish in the stream.
>
> Quiet and love I sing—
> The cairn on the mountain crest,
> The cailin in her lover's arms,
> The child at its mother's breast.
>
> .   .   .
>
> No other life I sing,
> For I am sprung of the stock
> That broke the hilly land for bread,
> And built the nest in the rock![54]

Apart from Hyde, who was working in translation, no poet writing during the period of the revival was as thoroughly grounded in the folk tradition as was Campbell, and no poet more effectively employed the *genre* of the popular ballad.[55] He wrote a considerable number of poems in which his strong nationalist convictions—he was in on the founding of the Irish Volunteers in 1912, was friends with MacDonagh, Pearse, and Plunkett, and, during the Civil War, was arrested as a sympathizer with the republican cause and spent nearly two years in an internment camp[56]—were refracted through the lens of the folk tradition. "I Gather Three Ears of Corn," from Campbell's early collection *The Rushlight* (1906), is one of these:

> I gather three ears of corn,
> And the Black Earl from over the sea
> Sails across in his silver ships,
> And takes two out of the three.
>
> I might build a house on the hill
> And a barn of the speckly stone,
> And tell my little stocking of gold,
> If the Earl would let me alone.
>
> But he has no thought for me—
> Only the thought of his share,
> And the softness of the linsey shifts
> His lazy daughters wear.

The day will come, maybe,
When we can have our own,
And the Black Earl will come to us
Begging the bacach's bone![57]

Campbell was very much a religious poet, but as opposed to the aestheti-cized Catholicism of Katharine Tynan or the ascetic, intellectual Catholicism of Lionel Johnson, Campbell's Catholicism fused folklore and religion, much in the manner of Hyde's *Religious Songs of Connacht*. At times this mix was wedded to nationalist sentiment, as in Campbell's well-known lyric, "I Am the Gilly of Christ," which draws on an Irish folk legend about Christ wandering through the west of Ireland accompanied by a local peasant who served as his guide. In Campbell's reworking of this story, the gilly (from the Irish "giolla," meaning scout or page) takes on the qualities of a Synge-like tramp figure while also suggesting the "mountainy singer," or the poet himself. The poem also specifically exploits the traditional nationalist distinction between spiritual Ireland and materialist England to convey political emotion:

I am the gilly of Christ,
The mate of Mary's Son;
I run the roads at seeding-time,
And when the harvest's done.

. . .

All know me only the Stranger,
Who sits on the Saxons' Height:
He burned the bachach's little house
On last St. Brigid's Night.

He sups off silver dishes,
And drinks in a golden horn,
But he will wake a wiser man
Upon the Judgment Morn![58]

Some of Campbell's most accomplished poems have neither overt political or religious significance. His love poetry, which owes as much to Hyde's *Love Songs of Connacht* as his religious poetry does to the *Religious Songs of Connacht,* relies on a simplicity and directness, rooted in the folk tradition, that differentiates it from much of the early love poetry of Yeats. "Sile of the Lovespot," from *The Rushlight,* not only draws on the kind of concrete imagery common to much poetry written in Irish—and often displaced by the vague, mystical imagery that characterizes much of the poetry of the early revival—

but also speaks in a colloquial, unassuming voice that, characteristically, resists any aestheticizing or mythologizing:

> He praised my breasts so round and white,
> My amber hair, my eyes of light,
> My singlet without stain or speck,
> The little love-spot on my neck.
>
> He gave me cordwain shoes to wear,
> And ribbands for my neck and hair;
> And then he took his will of me,
> And went away beyond the sea.
>
> He told me he would come again
> With silver and a sword of Spain;
> But now it is the pride o' the year,
> And Art Ó Lúinigh is not here.[59]

Campbell's poetry on Irish themes was not, however, altogether free of the romanticizing tendencies of mainstream revival writing. His first collection of poems, *The Garden of the Bees* (1905), was heavily influenced by Yeats and Keats,[60] and late in his life, Campbell described his poetic sensibility in terms remarkably close to the language and thinking of A. E. "From earliest childhood on," Campbell said in a radio broadcast in 1943, "I have been aware of the misty line that divides reality from unreality. I feel that all things tangible are dream. Rocks and trees can dissolve before one's eyes and become metamorphosed into their viewless essences." [61] In a number of Campbell's poems about ordinary Irish people, this metamorphosis amounts to seeing these characters as part of an idealized history of Irish civilization;[62] the poet's function is to reveal the connection between the present and the ennobling past. This visionary, idealizing tendency, which was somewhat at odds with Campbell's efforts to resist the "poetic moonshine" of the revival, can be seen plainly in "The Man-Child," from *Irishry:*

> Eber's battle-shout
> Is strong
> In you; Amergin's primal song
> Folds you round about;
> The lost mysteries
> Brood in your young eyes;
> And in that little hand
> Of yours the wine of Ireland—
> The dark and fragrant wine

Of nationhood divine—
Is held as in a cup
For unborn mouths to sup.[63]

Despite its theme, this poem decidedly departs from the formal qualities of
much early revival poetry. The poem is more indebted to imagism than to any
specifically Irish movement or tradition, and Campbell was one of the few
poets writing in Ireland during these years whose work clearly reflected modernist poetics. Campbell met T. E. Hulme and Ezra Pound at a meeting of the
Irish Literary Society in London in 1906; three years later he became a member
of the Imagist Group in Soho and began experimenting with imagism in his
own work. This attempt to integrate traditional Irish subject matter with modernism can be seen as another broadening of the base of poetic discourse in
Ireland. "The Old Woman," from *Irishry,* for example, stands distinctly apart
in this regard from most of the poetry being written in Ireland during this
period:

As a white candle
In a holy place,
So is the beauty
Of an agéd face.

As the spent radiance
Of the winter sun,
So is a woman
With her travail done.

Her brood gone from her,
And her thoughts as still
As the waters
Under a ruined mill.[64]

There is considerably less evidence of modernism in the work of Padraic
Colum (1881–1972), the poet most often compared to Campbell as writing out
of an insider's knowledge of Ireland's rural folk culture. "You might say,"
Colum once wrote, "that I had the advantage of the disadvantages that Yeats
and others didn't have." [65] The oldest of eight children, Colum was born in a
Co. Longford workhouse, where his father was master. When he was six, he
went to live with his grandmother and her family in Co. Cavan; he often
accompanied his uncle, who traveled around the country buying fowl for ex-
port, and who entertained his nephew from an apparently inexhaustible store of
local ballads and legends. When, as a young man, Colum went to Dublin, he
took this intimacy with rural Ireland and Irish folklore with him, and it exerted

a powerful influence on his writing. In Dublin, Colum quickly found himself
in the literary circles associated with the revival; in 1904, he published four of
his poems in A. E.'s *New Songs,* and four of his plays about rural Irish life
were put on by the Irish National Theatre Society and at the Abbey Theatre
between 1903 and 1910. In 1907, he published his first collection of poems,
Wild Earth (dedicated to "A. E., who fostered me"), which staked Colum's
claim to represent the rural Irish experience in authentic, realistic terms and
challenged the romanticized and aestheticized versions of that experience embodied in much of the revival poetry that preceded his. Unlike Campbell,
Colum did share the revival's general distrust of political poetry—the poet, he
once said, should be "liberated . . . from the despotism of political fact"—but
for Colum, liberation led not to mythology or aestheticism but to an art committed to representing "the emotional life of the people." [66] One method Colum
used effectively to this end was the dramatic poem or portrait poem, and his
portraits of ordinary rural people—"The Plougher," "A Drover," "The Young
Girl," "An Old Woman of the Roads," "The Suilier"—resisted the tendency
observable in some of the poems in Campbell's *Irishry* to use these characters
as vehicles for exploring broad political, religious, or philosophical themes.

If the "mountainy singer" might be taken to represent the position from
which Campbell wrote about rural Ulster, for Colum the corresponding figure
was the wandering minstrel, the folk poet who made his rounds through the
countryside, much as Colum's uncle once did with the young Colum in tow,
taking his art from what he saw there and testing or proving it by giving it back
to the people from whom it sprang. Relatively late in his life, Colum put
together a collection of his poems, many taken from his earlier books, entitled
The Poet's Circuits. The volume is organized around a wandering minstrel,
who is depicted, in a poem entitled "Fore-piece," in terms that describe Colum's own poetics:

> Out of glimpses
> Of days and nights of women and of men,
> And often with words they spoke to me,
> Of verses they delivered, I made poems. [67]

Although some romanticizing may be unavoidable in this kind of reconstruction
of the past, Colum's poetry, especially that written early in his career, represents
an attempt to speak about, for, and to rural Ireland in a voice and style free
from the romantic aesthetics of the revival. One touchstone for Colum in this
regard was Hyde's translations; as Thomas MacDonagh observed, Colum's
poems "read like other Love-Songs of Connacht omitted from Hyde's book by
some extraordinary mishap." [68] "She Moved Through the Fair," first published

in the expanded edition of *Wild Earth* in 1916, is based on a traditional Irish song, only a few lines of which have survived:

> My young love said to me, "My brothers won't mind,
> And my parents won't slight you for your lack of kind."
> Then she stepped away from me, and this she did say,
> "It will not be long, love, till our wedding day."
>
> She stepped away from me and she moved through the fair,
> And fondly I watched her go here and go there,
> Then she went her way homeward with one star awake,
> As the swan in the evening moves over the lake.
>
> The people were saying no two were e'er wed
> But one had a sorrow that never was said,
> And I smiled as she passed with her goods and her gear,
> And that was the last that I saw of my dear.
>
> I dreamt it last night that my young love came in,
> So softly she entered, her feet made no din;
> She came close beside me, and this she did say,
> "It will not be long, love, till our wedding day." [69]

As is evident here, there is also a melancholy and bleakness in Colum's writing that distinguish it from that of Campbell and of Yeats and his followers. Colum's work is rooted in a post-famine rural consciousness in which redemption by means of the religious faith of Campbell, the mysticism of A. E., or the romantic aesthetics of Yeats is seen as a remote possibility at best. This attitude is reflected in much of Colum's love poetry: "Though I weary with delving,/ With driving the plough,/I lie on a bed/Sleep has gone from now" ("A Man Bereaved") [70]; "Oh, if you ask not for me,/But leave me here instead,/The narrow, narrow coffin/Will shortly be my bed" ("The Young Girl"). [71] His pessimism is expressed more directly in the considerable amount of poetry that Colum wrote about the land and the people who work it. The figure of the ploughman is, for Colum, the markedly unromantic one of a man whose potential has been crippled by his allegiance to a hostile land. The extent to which Colum's attitude in this regard anticipates Patrick Kavanagh's "The Great Hunger" in its effort to strip away romantic characterizations of Irish rural life common to much revival writing is evident in the first poem of *Wild Earth,* entitled "The Plougher" (one of the four poems by Colum included in A. E.'s *New Songs*):

> Sunset and silence! A man: around him earth savage, earth broken;
> Beside him two horses—a plough!
> Earth savage, earth broken, the brutes, the dawnman there in the sunset. [72]

Whatever romantic potential his rural characters may possess, Colum almost always presents their world as one in which the weight of circumstances stifles or eliminates possibility. In this way, Colum's poems about the land not only counter the romanticizing tendencies of much revival writing about rural Ireland but also carry forward the tradition of realistic poetic accounts of the social and economic realities of Irish rural experience, the tradition embodied in Goldsmith's writing in the eighteenth century and William Allingham's in the nineteenth. Colum's well-known "A Drover," although it celebrates the freedom of the drover from many social conventions and pressures, insists, especially in its remarkable closing image, on the impossibility of escaping a past of suffering and insufficiency, the past of famine and post-famine rural Ireland:

> To Meath of the pastures,
> From wet hills by the sea,
> Through Leitrim and Longford
> Go my cattle and me.
>
> I hear in the darkness
> Their slipping and breathing.
> I name them the bye-ways
> They're to pass without heeding.
>
> Then the wet, winding roads,
> Brown bogs with black water;
> And my thoughts on white ships
> And the King o' Spain's daughter.
>
> O! farmer, strong farmer!
> You can spend at the fair
> But your face you must turn
> To your crops and your care.
>
> .   .   .
>
> O! the smell of the beasts,
> The wet wind in the morn;
> And the proud and hard earth
> Never broken for corn;
>
> And the crowds at the fair,
> The herds loosened and blind,
> Loud words and dark faces
> And the wild blood behind.
>
> .   .   .
>
> I will bring you, my kine,
> Where there's grass to the knee;

But you'll think of scant croppings
Harsh with salt of the sea.[73]

That final image of the western seaboard as a place of "scant croppings" also specifically counters more romantic, symbolic representations of the west of Ireland in much revival writing.

As a young man, in the years leading up to the Easter Rising, Colum was quite active in militantly nationalist enterprises. He joined the Irish Volunteers, and took part in the gun-running episode at Howth in 1914. The same year, Colum left Ireland for the United States, chiefly for economic reasons, and he never lived in Ireland after that. Although Colum's reputation grew considerably in the years that he spent lecturing and writing in the United States, his poetry on Irish themes suffered a decided falling-off.[74] The integrity and honesty of perception, the commitment to grounding his poetry about rural Ireland in a realistic aesthetic, and the awareness in his work of Ireland's folk culture and its Gaelic dimension—all these became somewhat dissipated the longer that Colum wrote, and his later poetry about Ireland either recycles earlier work, not always to its advantage, or lapses into the very sentimentalism that *Wild Earth* set out to discredit.

The first collection of poems by James Stephens (1882–1950), published in 1909, was entitled *Insurrections*. It was an appropriate title for a book of verse that energetically and unambiguously called into question the condition of Irish society, conventional religious beliefs and assumptions, conventional attitudes toward women, and the state of Irish poetry and aesthetics in the face of all these circumstances.[75] As it turned out, *Insurrections* marked the beginning of an insurrectionary career. It was also a career thoroughly grounded in a strong suspicion of romanticism in any form.[76] Stephens's anti-romanticism shared more than a little with Synge's writing (Synge's *Poems and Translations* was published the same year that *Insurrections* appeared), and with that of Colum and Campbell, who also distrusted revival romanticism. Yet his work was distinguished from theirs by its urban orientation and focus, as well as its relatively experimental forms.

Stephens was born in Dublin's northside slums, the terrain that O'Casey would later represent on the Abbey stage, and that Stephens himself depicted in his novel, *The Charwoman's Daughter* (1912). "The Dublin I was born to was poor and Protestant and athletic," Stephens once remarked,[77] and *Insurrections* presented that world with an unflinching realism, and, unlike O'Sullivan's portraits of urban Ireland, through the lens of a socialism that not only drew attention to the human dimension of Dublin's appalling poverty but also sought to locate the moral responsibility for it. In "The Street Behind Yours," for example, Stephens describes in unblinking detail a blighted urban landscape, an aspect of Ireland conspicuously absent from earlier Irish poetry:

> Those rigid houses: black and sour.
> Each dark, thin building stretching high.
> > Rank after rank
> > Of windows blank
> Stare from a sullen eye,
> With doleful aspect scowl and glower
> At the timid passer-by.
>
> And down between those spectre files,
> The narrow roadway, thick with mud,
> > Doth crouch and hide,
> > While close beside
> The gutter churns a flood
> Of noisome water through the piles
> Of garbage thick as blood.[78]

Stephens also addresses the reader directly, calling attention to the alienation of most of society from this underworld of poverty and suffering:

> And tho' 'tis silent, tho' no sound
> Crawls from the blackness thickly spread,
> > Yet darkness brings
> > Grim, noiseless things
> That walk as they were dead.
> They glide, and peer, and steal around,
> With stealthy, silent tread.
>
> You dare not walk; that awful crew
> Might speak or laugh as you pass by,
> > Might touch and paw
> > With a formless claw,
> Or leer from a sodden eye,
> Might whisper awful things they knew,
> Or wring their hands and cry.[79]

Behind this portrait of urban despair stands not just Stephen's socialism but also a broadly subversive attitude toward conventional religious views; the world of suffering individuals and an uncaring society that Stephens's novels and short stories as well as his poetry describes is governed by an indifferent, Hardyesque God.[80] In "The Whisperer," from *Insurrections,* a man walking along enjoying a moonlit night and thinking contentedly that "God was everywhere" suddenly hears a voice that tells him that "God has no choice/In this sad maze," and then quotes God as having said, "I care not how ye go,/Or struggle, win or lose, nor do/I want to know."[81] This kind of religious scepticism was most prevalent in Stephen's early verse. Under the influence of Blake and A. E. (to whom *Insurrections,* like Colum's *Wild Earth,* was dedicated), Stephens's poetry about spiritual matters came increasingly to echo the mysticism associated with the revival.

Stephens's early work was also insurrectionary in its treatment of gender, which was not a central concern of much revival poetry, including that of some women associated with the movement. Indeed, no male poet in Ireland before Stephens—and not many female ones—so effectively interrogated conventional male attitudes toward women, particularly perceptions of women as objects to be possessed and controlled by men. As in his early poems on social and religious themes, the more radical the vision in Stephens's poems about women, the more unconventional the form and voice in which that vision is expressed. The first poem in *Insurrections,* "The Dancer," subverts conventional poetic forms and diction as well as accepted views of women by taking as its narrator a music-hall dancer whose lover has just died, and who rejects the role that she is expected to play for her male audience:

> I will not dance:
> I say I will not dance.
> Your audience, pah, let them go home again,
> Sleek, ugly pigs. Am I to hop and prance
>   As long as they will pay,
>   And posture for their eyes, and lay
> My womanhood before them? Let them drain
> Their porter pots and snuffle—I'll not stay.
>
> For he is dead:
> I tell you he is dead.
> My God, did you not hear me say it
> Twice already? I held his groaning head
>   In these remembering arms,
>   And cursed the charms
> That could not stop his going. Must I bay it
> Like a dog to you? Quit your alarms!
>
> They shout and stamp?
> Then, let them shout and stamp.
> Those booted hogs and lechers—I'm away
> To sit beside my dead. O God, you tramp
>   Upon me too, and twine
>   More sorrows round me than are mine
> With unholy concern. . . Don't bar my way,
> I'm going to my dead . . . Ah-h-h, stamping swine![82]

The echo of Browning here sets Stephens distinctly apart from the revival with its connection to English romanticism, while the poem calculatedly demythologizes an icon frequently associated with romantic transcendence (as in Yeats's famous conclusion to "Among Schoolchildren"). At the same time, the poem displaces the portrait of the rural Irishman or Irishwoman central to the Irish folk tradition with an urban figure who, although endowed with genuine passion and feeling, embodies anything but pastoral tranquility. In "The Red-Haired Man's Wife," Stephens transforms a poem taken from the Irish folk tradition into a powerful critique of conventional views of marriage. As in "The Dancer," Stephens writes from inside the woman's point of view and in a voice of aggressive defiance:

> I have taken that vow—
>   And you were my friend
> But yesterday—now
>   All that's at an end,
> And you are my husband, and claim me, and I must depend.
>
> Yesterday I was free,
>   Now you, as I stand,
> Walk over to me
>   And take hold of my hand.
> You look at my lips, yours eyes are too bold, your smile is too bland.
>
> My old name is lost,
>   My distinction of race:
> Now the line has been crossed,
>   Must I step to your pace?
> Must I walk as you list, and obey, and smile up in your face?
>
>   .   .   .
>
> I am separate still,
>   I am I and not you:
> And my mind and my will,
>   As in secret they grew,
> Still are secret, unreached and untouched and not subject to you.[83]

Stephens's loyalty to the concrete and local and his careful attention to the rhythms and idioms of the speaking voice characterize his translations and renderings of poems from the Irish, which may be seen as the culmination of his poetry on Irish themes. These qualities also sharply differentiate Stephens's work in this vein from that engendered by the literary revival's attempts to translate the tradition of writing in Irish into the terms of its own romantic aesthetics and cultural politics. At their best, Stephens's versions from the Irish negotiate with remarkable success between the culture of Gaelic Ireland and that which had replaced it by the time he was writing, recontextualizing the older tradition in terms of the Ireland of his own day.[84] Almost all these poems were published in *Reincarnations* (1918). As the title suggests, Stephens's versions of earlier poems in Irish cannot be considered translations. Stephens makes this quite clear in a note appended to the volume: "This book ought to be called Loot or Plunder or Pieces of Eight or Treasure-Trove, or some name which would indicate and get away from its source, for although everything in it can be referred to the Irish of from one hundred to three hundred years ago the word translation would be a misdescription."[85] Nine of the poems in *Reincarnations* are "after" Dáibhí Ó Bruadair, the seventeenth-century Irish poet whose prolific work, as Thomas Kinsella has put it, "blended the rich colloquial language of his time with the older literary diction."[86] For Stephens, the colloquial side of Ó Bruadair was of most interest, especially those poems expressing rage and unhappiness at the poet's lot. Ó Bruadair's complaint poem, "Seirbhíseach Seirgthe Íogair Srónach Seasc" (translated by Kinsella as "A Shrewish, Barren, Bony, Nosey Servant"), becomes the occasion for Stephens's "Righteous Anger" (often reprinted as "A Glass of Beer"), a curse poem in the vein of Synge in which Ó' Bruadair's rage against being ill-treated is used to voice Stephens's sense of his own perceived alienation:

> The lanky hank of a she in the inn over there
> Nearly killed me for asking the loan of a glass of beer:
> May the devil grip the whey-faced slut by the hair,
> And beat bad manners out of her skin for a year.
>
> That parboiled imp, with the hardest jaw you will see
> On virtue's path, and a voice that would rasp the dead,
> Came roaring and raging the minute she looked at me,
> And threw me out of the house on the back of my head!
>
> If I asked her master he'd give me a cask a day;
> But she, with the beer at hand, not a gill would arrange!
> May she marry a ghost and bear him a kitten, and may
> The High King of Glory permit her to get the mange.[87]

Although Stephens's work in this vein helped define with relative authenticity a tradition romanticized and aestheticized, sometimes beyond recognition, by more mainstream revival writers, it also provided an effective vehicle for his own idiosyncratic poetic voice. Indeed, Stephens's work with the poetry of Ó Bruadair—and with that of Antoine Ó Reachtabhra (Anthony Raftery), the early-nineteenth-century Co. Mayo poet whose work strongly influenced Hyde, and the early-eighteenth-century Co. Kerry poet Aodhagán Ó Rathaille (Egan O'Rahilly) as well—saved him from the lapse into sentimentality that unfortunately affected much of his later verse not based on Irish originals. In any case, Stephens's poetry at its best could well be described by the words of praise in which Stephens once, in a letter written the year before *Reincarnations* was published, paid tribute to Ó Bruadair, that distant but kindred poetic spirit. "I have never met," Stephens said, "such an avalanche of eloquence, poetry and rage under the one skin." [88]

One reason often given for the deterioration in Stephens's poetry after *Insurrections* is that he came too much under the influence of Georgian poetry and poetics.[89] Francis Ledwidge (1887–1917), born five years after Stephens, is the other Irish poet of this time whose work was strongly colored by the Georgian movement, and his writing also cannot be said to have profited from the influence. But Ledwidge's commitment to being a specifically Irish poet was never as unambiguous as was Stephens's in the early years of his career. Writing to his patron and supporter Lord Dunsany at the time of the Easter Rising in 1916, he said: "Coming from Southampton in the train, looking on England's beautiful villages all white with spring, I thought indeed its freedom was worth all the blood I have seen flow. No wonder England has so many ardent patriots. I would be one of them myself did I not presume to be an Irish patriot." [90] By the time that he wrote this, Ledwidge was a British soldier, having chosen the opposite path from that taken by MacDonagh, Pearse, and Plunkett when the Irish Volunteers, of which he was a member and organizer, split over the issue of recruitment for the British army; and whereas MacDonagh, Pearse, and Plunkett were executed for their part in the Easter Rising, Ledwidge, a member of the Royal Inniskilling Fusiliers, died on the battlefield at Ypres, fighting for England.

Much of Ledwidge's work shows signs of strain from attempting to graft one culture or sensibility on to another: Georgian English poetics onto the Co. Meath of Ledwidge's youth, and the voice of an assumed gentility onto a working-class background (Ledwidge had little formal education, and worked on roads as a laborer). "June," from Ledwidge's first collection, *Songs of the Fields* (1916), is enmeshed in the idioms and imagery of Georgian nature poetry:

> Broom out the floor now, lay the fender by,
> And plant this bee-sucked bough of woodbine there,
> And let the window down. The butterfly
> Floats in upon the sunbeam, and the fair
> Tanned face of June, the nomad gipsy, laughs
> Above her widespread wares, the while she tells
> The farmers' fortunes in the fields, and quaffs
> The water from the spider-peopled wells.[91]

In a poem entitled "Ireland," Ledwidge concedes that there is a gap between
his own sense of poetic mission and the cultural ambitions of the literary
revival:

> And then you called to us from far and near
> To bring your crown from out the deeps of time,
> It is my grief your voice I couldn't hear
> In such a distant clime.[92]

One measure of this gap is Ledwidge's problematic attempts to draw on the
legends and traditions that inspired much of the writing of the revival. He wrote
a number of poems based on the pre-Christian Irish sagas, but was as unable in
this genre to escape the dominant influence of Yeats's voice as he was unable
in his landscape poetry to escape the influence of the Georgian poets. Ledwidge
did write one compelling poem on an Irish theme, an elegy for Thomas Mac-
Donagh. Staking a claim in the long tradition of such elegies, including Thomas
Davis's elegy for Owen Roe O'Neill and Samuel Ferguson's for Davis, Ledwidge's poem takes as its starting point MacDonagh's well-known lyric translated from the Irish, "The Yellow Bittern," and it incorporates some of the
sound patterns taken from Irish verse that characterized MacDonagh's writing:

> He shall not hear the bittern cry
> In the wild sky, where he is lain,
> Nor voices of the sweeter birds
> Above the wailing of the rain.
>
> Nor shall he know when loud March blows
> Thro' slanting snows her fanfare shrill,
> Blowing to flame the golden cup
> Of many an upset daffodil.
>
> And when the Dark Cow leaves the moor,
> And pastures poor with greedy weeds,
> Perhaps he'll hear her low at morn
> Lifting her horn in pleasant meads.[93]

That note of regret over lost possibility was, as things turned out, a highly
appropriate one, especially coming from a man whose own life would be lost
a year later in a catastrophe that darkened the face of western civilization,
irredeemably. It is a long way from the unclouded optimism voiced by Yeats at
the beginning of the literary revival in the 1880s to the Great War in which
Ledwidge died, and an equally long way from those early hopes of cultural
renewal to the Easter Rising of 1916, the event that took Thomas MacDonagh's

life. It was even a long way from 1910, when James Stephens first met Mac-
Donagh, to April 1916, when MacDonagh went before a firing squad. As
Stephens was to say of that meeting, in the immediate aftermath of Mac-
Donagh's death: "It is strange to look back to the time when I first knew
Thomas MacDonagh. What with the present war in Europe, and our own small
war in Ireland, that time has so faded and retreated that one recalls it with
difficulty and regards it with something of astonishment." [94] In those few years,
the future of modern Ireland, and indeed of western civilization, had been,
as Yeats seems to have understood intuitively, transformed almost beyond
recognition.

PART FOUR

POETRY IN MODERN IRELAND

INTRODUCTION

If, as Yeats once wondered, that play of his did "send out/Certain men the English shot,"[1] the Ireland that emerged from the Easter Rising and its violent aftermath bore few if any traces of the romantic assumptions about the heroic nature of art and life embedded in Yeats's musings. Although the satirical observation of one Irish writer that "the birth of a terrible beauty in 1916 ended only in the establishment of a grocer's republic"[2] may have overstated matters somewhat, Irish writers working in the wake of that birth found themselves in a cultural and political environment that actively discouraged aesthetic or political, Yeatsian or militantly nationalist, ideas of heroism. Once the revolution was over and the Free State government, headed by the cautious William Cosgrave, was in place, the Irish, in the words of the historian F. S. L. Lyons, "presented to the twentieth century world the strange and paradoxical spectacle of a people who, having pursued with immense tenacity and a great measure of success the goal of independence, were content to rear upon the foundations of that independence one of the most conservative states in Europe."[3] At the center of that conservatism was the need, perceived to be even more urgent in the wake of political independence than it had been before, to establish a distinctive Irish cultural identity, particularly one distinct from English influence. This view encouraged a denial of the pluralistic nature of Irish society in favor of one defined as exclusively Gaelic, and a consequent suspicion of the tradition of Irish writing in English, especially the work of the Anglo-Irish.[4] This new conservative state also empowered the Catholic Church to an extent undreamt of (except perhaps by militant unionists in the North) just a few years earlier. Indeed, the attempt to define Irish culture as essentially Gaelic and Catholic usually meant, in practice, to define it as Catholic, since the Gaelic tradition and the Irish language had become even more marginalized by the time of independence than they had been during the rapid decline of the language in the nineteenth century. The provision in de Valera's Constitution of 1937 recognizing the special place that Catholicism held in Irish society was one benchmark of the cultural and political power of the church in modern Ireland. The Censorship Act of 1929—"the fiercest literary censorship this side of the Iron Curtain," in the words of one Irish poet[5]—was another and, at least from the point of view of most Irish writers, a considerably more pernicious one.

Irish writers working in such a context tended to become what Yeats, as far back as 1907, had predicted they would become: "protesting individual voices."[6] But the image of a strictly adversarial relationship between writer and society oversimplifies the situation, masking the many ironies and ambiguities that governed the condition of the Irish writer in the decades following independence. The Irish-Ireland effort to construct Irish identity around a morally restrictive Catholicism, a narrow and equally restrictive version of the Gaelic tradition, and an idealized notion of rural life not only drove many Irish writers into hostile positions but also generated a whole set of paradoxes and tensions that both inspired and constrained them. The attempt, for example, to see Irish rural life as embodying the uncontaminated essence of the Irish character, itself a reworking of the literary revival's romanticized peasant, was clearly at odds with the economic, social, and psychological realities of the Irish farmer in post-independence Ireland and ignored the sharp decline of an increasingly dissatisfied rural population.[7] It is precisely this gap between cultural image and experience that Patrick Kavanagh's "The Great Hunger" so devastatingly exposed. More generally, the Irish-Ireland campaign for an essentially monolithic culture generated a tension between the needs of the nation and individual fulfillment, a tension represented most forcefully in Yeats's images of the Irish artist as heroically alienated from an imaginatively regressive and repressive Irish society. The conservatism of the new state also existed in uneasy and paradoxical relationships both with the generally liberal and humanist elements of the revolution that had empowered it—a breach between promise and practice relentlessly probed by Austin Clarke—and with the tradition of militant nationalism that it now found itself in need of controlling (it was de Valera's government that, in 1936, declared the Irish Republican Army an illegal organization). Moreover, by associating Irish culture with the past, and by striving for economic as well as cultural self-sufficiency, the Irish-Ireland movement projected an image of Ireland as deliberately cut off from the various modes of modernization, including literary modernism, sweeping through the rest of Europe at the time; indeed, the association in Ireland of modernization with anglicization dominated Irish thinking until the economic policies of Sean Lemass's government in the 1960s demonstrated that political and cultural independence depended on prosperity for success, and so on establishing links with England and the rest of Europe. Finally, the very idea of what constituted the nation of Ireland was, in Irish-Ireland formulations, shrouded in paradox and instability because of partition. Despite the lip service paid to the Easter-Rising republic contained in Articles 2 and 3 of the 1937 Constitution, the attempt to define the Irish identity as essentially Gaelic and Catholic had the predictable effect of excluding the north, and so of affirming the reality if not the necessity of the border.

The poetry that came out of this environment was shaped both by these ironies and ambiguities and by the related need to replace many of the aesthetic values and cultural ambitions of the literary revival, whose romantic, mythic, and heroic vision of Ireland was now seen as sadly but definitely irrelevant. Much of this writing was fiercely anti-establishment; Clarke's critique of Jansenist Catholicism in the 1920s and 1930s and his sustained satirical attacks on Irish political and social life in the 1950s and 1960s belong to that category, as do Kavanagh's savagely deromanticized portrayals of the Irish peasant. Yeats's celebration in the 1920 and 1930s of the Anglo-Irish Protestant tradition can be read, in part at least, as a response to the social and aesthetic realities of post-independence Ireland. And if Yeats's position often seemed to be of little specific value to Irish Catholic writers working in a culture in which the Ascendancy was in fact little more than a relic—John Montague once described the "Sing the peasantry" section of Yeats's "Under Ben Bulben" as "a catalogue of subjects that could only be legitimately treated in parody"[8]—Yeats's view of the artist as struggling to maintain individual and aesthetic integrity in the wake of cultural disaster provided a significant model for Irish poets who saw themselves as living in an indifferent if not hostile society.

In contrast to the mythic and visionary tendencies evident in much of the poetry associated with the revival, Irish poetry in the less heroic era after independence tended to favor relatively realistic modes, as in Kavanagh's representations of rural Monaghan and Clarke's of urban Dublin, a shift of emphasis that accompanied the development of realistic fiction in the 1930s and 1940s. This rise of realism in Irish poetry also called into question the idea of the romanticized west as Ireland's cultural omphalos. "The romantic illusion, fostered by the Celtic Twilight, that the West of Ireland, with its red petticoats and bawneens, is for some reason more Irish than Guinness' Brewery or Dwyers' Sunbeam-Wolsey factory, has no longer any basis whatever," Sean O'Faolain wrote in the influential magazine, *The Bell,* in 1943.[9] The revival had tended to appeal primarily to Ireland's pre-Christian sagas and legends, often as a means for the movement's Anglo-Irish architects to turn a blind eye to the Catholic nature of Irish society, but writers in its wake frequently took Catholicism as a central theme; Clarke showed a special interest in medieval Christian Ireland, while Denis Devlin explored Irish Catholicism in the broad context of religious faith in the twentieth century. Devlin's work, along with that of Thomas Mac-

Greevy, also represented an effort to write about Ireland in the context of European modernism, thereby resisting the provincialism that such writers as Clarke and Kavanagh, even in their most virulent critiques of Irish-Ireland values and assumptions, were inevitably caught in. "We must look outward again or die, if only of boredom," Anthony Cronin wrote in *The Bell* in 1953.[10]

That advice was particularly difficult to take for writers from the north; indeed, the cultural anxiety and ambiguity that partition generated among northern writers inspired a more regional perspective than anything advanced by earlier Ulster poets such as James Orr and Joseph Campbell. John Hewitt's call for a regional politics and aesthetics represented one facet of the impact of partition on northern writers, while Louis MacNeice's tortured sense of a multiply-divided sensibility—torn not just between England and Ireland but also between Ireland and Northern Ireland—constituted another.

Finally, the empowerment of conservative political and cultural forces in postindependence Ireland had predictable and unhappy effects on the work of Irish women poets, producing a relative silence all the more lamentable for its coming on the heels of so much accomplished work by women in the years of the revival. The decades from the 1920s through the 1960s were not, in general, a good time for women's rights in Ireland—as late as the 1960s, there was still a ban on the employment of married women in public service, and very few women gained access to the professions or graduated to third-level education[11] —and women poets, working outside the context of specific political or literary movements such as Young Ireland or the revival, had an increasingly difficult time finding encouragement or even publishing outlets for their work. Indeed, between the closing of Maunsel and Roberts in 1926 and the establishment of the Dolmen Press in 1951, there were no significant indigenous publishers of poetry—written by women or men—in Ireland. Nevertheless, the work of writers such as Blanaid Salkeld, Rhoda Coghill, and Eithne Strong, precisely because it was not part of a male-dominated movement, helped pave the way for the emergence in the 1970s and 1980s of independent, specifically female voices in Irish poetry.

The appearance in the late 1950s and 1960s of a new generation of Irish poets, all born after the establishment of independence, more or less corresponded to the development of the "new Ireland," which, inspired in part by Lemass's economic progressivism, began to reject Irish-Ireland values and attitudes. But these writers—Richard Murphy, Thomas Kinsella, and John Montague—also still had to confront the problem that had so preoccupied earlier Irish writers and so distorted earlier versions of Irish culture: how to construct a meaningful cultural identity in a colonial or post-colonial society. These writers were suspicious both of the icons and stereotypes of Irish Ireland and of the revival's idea of interpreting the past in the interests of an envisioned cultural unity for the future. For these writers, the salient fact about the Irish past was that it was broken or gapped, rendering the modern Irish writer both alienated from the past and without the means with which to construct a redeemed future. Discontinuity became the central condition and theme of their work.[12] From the exalted position conceived by Yeats at the beginning of the century, in which plays and poems might actually cause revolutions, the modern Irish poet had, by the last quarter of the century, become principally the self-conscious voice of instability and doubt, and poetry had become a search for a cultural and personal identity almost certainly not to be found.

CHAPTER FOURTEEN

YEATS

The Irish literary revival lived on into a tenacious old age. Indeed, freeing the Irish imagination from the aesthetic theories and cultural assumptions that had fueled the movement seemed to take considerably longer than it had taken to establish them. Strong traces of the revival were to be found as late as the 1930s, in the work of F. R. Higgins, for example, while poets who had been associated with the movement more or less from the beginning, such as George Russell and Padraic Colum, carried revival attitudes well beyond the *Playboy* riots in 1907 or the Easter Rising in 1916, the two events most frequently taken as marking the end of the literary revival *per se*. But for Yeats, the process of shedding the revival's aesthetics and cultural politics proved much easier than it did for both his followers and many of his successors. To some extent, this change had to do with Yeats's growing allegiance to his Anglo-Irish Protestant background as the remnants of Ireland's Ascendancy came under increasing, and finally fatal, pressure in the years leading up to and beyond the establishment of political independence in the twenty-six counties. But, as always, Yeats's politics were driven largely by his aesthetics, in this instance by the conviction that the rise of middle-class materialism, associated in Yeats's mind with the newly empowered Irish Catholics, constituted a serious and urgent threat to the survival of art. The earlier dream of a cultural revolution and cultural unity was replaced by a faith in the individual, anti-establishment heroic figure, often embodied as the artist under siege, and by a belief that only a cultural if not political aristocracy could provide a safe harbor for the artist in a world bent on philistinism and materialism.

The seeds of Yeats's disillusionment with the ambitions of the revival are to be found in the early stages of his career. His essay "Ireland and the Arts" (1901), which concludes with a ringing declaration that the Irish could become

"a chosen race, one of the pillars that uphold the world," [1] opens in the vein of
cultural elitism and fear for the survival of the arts that came to dominate
Yeats's writing from the second decade of the century on:

> The arts have failed; fewer people are interested in them every generation.
> The mere business of living, of making money, of amusing oneself, occupies
> people more and more, and makes them less and less capable of the difficult
> art of appreciation. . . . We who care deeply about the arts find ourselves the
> priesthood of an almost forgotten faith.[2]

Two years earlier, in the preface to a revised edition of *A Book of Irish Verse,*
Yeats defined the literary revival as "endeavors to create a reading class among
the more leisured classes which will preoccupy itself with Ireland and the needs
of Ireland." [3] But as Ireland approached and then achieved a portion of political
independence, a new urgency, and a new note of resignation and despair, began
to appear in Yeats's writing about Ireland. Yeats's vague commitment early in
his life to the cause of political nationalism, inspired largely through his friendship with John O'Leary, depended in part at least on the assumption that
complete independence was not probable; indeed, it seems likely that much of
the romantic attraction for Yeats of this brand of nationalism was that it appeared to be a lost cause.[4] The need to distance himself from nationalist politics
once it became clear that a successful political revolution could take place
—and once it did take place, in 1916—was strengthened by the inevitable
marginalization of the Anglo-Irish that an independent Ireland entailed and by
a growing conviction that the gap between the aims and values of those empowered by the revolution and his own ambitions for Ireland, a gap that opened up
for all to see in the *Playboy* riots in 1907 and the controversy over the Hugh
Lane pictures six years later, could not be bridged.

Once that gap had, in Yeats's eyes, become an unbridgeable chasm, Yeats
turned with increasing vigor to one of the central assumptions behind the
revival: that art should never be subservient to politics. This aesthetic position,
pushed now to new limits, was spelled out in an essay on Synge, published
three years after the *Playboy* riots and one year after Synge's death.[5] The
argument begins by establishing a division between politics, conceived as the
inorganic," abstract thoughts" of human beings, and the organic, natural world:

> After a while, in a land that has given itself to agitation overmuch, abstract
> thoughts are raised up between men's minds and Nature, who never does the
> same thing twice, or makes one man like another, till minds, whose patriotism
> is perhaps great enough to carry them to the scaffold, cry down natural impulse
> with the morbid insistence of minds unsettled by some fixed idea.[6]

From this assumption, which contains the seed of the well-known lines "Too long a sacrifice/Can make a stone of the heart" in "Easter 1916," [7] Yeats argues for a necessary disjunction between art, aligned with the organic and the individual world of Nature, and politics: "All art is the disengaging of the soul from place and history, its suspension in a beautiful or terrible light to await the Judgment." [8] It is an extreme position, and one that Yeats, with characteristic ambivalence and intellectual acuity, interrogated off and on for the remainder of his life, but it is also a statement that reveals forcefully the extent of Yeats's alienation from Ireland during these years. This alienation underlies his disengagement from the cultural and political ambitions of the revival as well as his attacks on the Irish Catholic middle class as committed to the kind of abstract thoughts that prohibit both "the difficult art of appreciation" and an understanding of the true nature of Irish nationalism, conceived always in spiritual rather than practical terms.

Yeats's abandonment of the lush, Celtic Twilight style of his early lyrics for the more direct, even colloquial voice that emerges in *The Green Helmet* (1910) and *Responsibilities* (1914) was a rejection of style only, not of the faith in the autonomy and superiority of the spiritual and aesthetic. That faith is in fact the driving force of Yeats's relationship with the Ireland that emerged out of all the violence and upheaval of the 1910s, and it is evident even in poems that address specifically political situations. "September 1913," for example, an occasional poem that was first published in *The Irish Times* under the title "Romance in Ireland: On reading much of the correspondence against the Art Gallery," argues that politics, to avoid the pitfalls of "abstract thoughts," must be inspired by the same kind of transcendent, essentially spiritual ambitions that should govern the artist. On this ground, the poem attempts to discredit the nationalist credentials of the materialist middle classes. The problem is, as Yeats fully recognizes, that romantic Ireland may be so intangible as to exist only in the poet's memory and imagination—"Yet could we turn the years again,/And call those exiles as they were" [9]—or, in other words, in the poem itself. This in turn may mean that the poet, and the values that he represents, are more or less irrelevant to the modern world. Thus the poem moves from satirical invective—"What need you, being come to sense,/But fumble in a greasy till/And add the halfpence to the pence"—to elegy—"But let them be, they're dead and gone,/They're with O'Leary in the grave." [10]

The tendency to aestheticize experience, observable in an early lyric such as "The Lake Isle of Innisfree," is still present in Yeats's later writing, if in more complex and sophisticated ways. The most famous instance of this tendency is "Easter 1916," in which Yeats transforms what was arguably the most crucial event in the history of the political separatist movement into an aesthetic triumph, a "terrible beauty" (where "terrible" carries a suggestion of Aristotle's notion of terror, and so of dramatic tragedy). The poem interprets the Rising specifically in theatrical terms—not altogether unreasonably, given the dramatic, not to say melodramatic, nature of the event—seeing Ireland as having been converted by the revolutionaries from a land of O'Connellite comedy ("Being certain that they and I/But lived where motley was worn" [11]) to one of Parnellite tragedy, a transformation, in Yeats's view, devoutly to be wished; in an essay published six years before the Rising, Yeats argued that "tragedy must always be a drowning and breaking of the dykes that separate man from man, and . . . it is upon these dykes comedy keeps house." [12] The specific political consequences of the Rising are absorbed into this "larger" vision, which rewrites the dichotomy between the spiritual and the material (the antithetical and the primary, in the language of *A Vision)* into one between the tragic and the comic. In any case, Yeats is unwilling to concede any necessary political significance to the Rising ("Was it needless death after all?"), and he is equally unwilling to concede that the republic proclaimed on the steps of the General Post Office on Easter Monday was necessarily a good thing; the idea that "England may keep faith/For all that is done and said" [13] most likely refers to some form of Home Rule, with which Yeats was reasonably comfortable, not to republican independence, with which he was not. Moreover, the political revolutionaries who led the Rising, as Yeats recreates them, are more than political martyrs; in their revelation of the terrible beauty lying beneath the surface of the ordinary, material world, they have functioned as poets (and, as Yeats points out, a number of the Rising's leaders were in fact poets). In this sense, and this sense only, the poet is a revolutionary, making personal sacrifices for a spiritual cause and having a heart "with one purpose alone." [14]

"Easter 1916" is an instructive moment in Yeats's writing partly because it represents so clearly Yeats's tendency to transform experience into the terms of his own spiritual and aesthetic values. This stance was, in part at least, a product of his increasingly marginalized position in an Ireland that was changing at what could only seem to him an alarming rate. By the time of the Anglo-Irish War and the Civil War, the alienation that he saw as an inevitable part of the Irish poet's life in "September 1913" had become nearly overwhelming and somewhat less a matter of choice. Yeats spent these summers in his isolated tower at Ballylee while scores of Anglo-Irish houses were being burned to the ground, and it is at this time that isolation, embodied in a voice of self-doubt and despair, becomes a powerful theme in his work. In "Meditations in Time of Civil War," a sequence written in 1922 and published in *The Tower* in 1928, Yeats identifies the artist and the man of violence, specifically himself and the Norman invader who built Thor Ballylee, both of whom are presented, as were the poet and the revolutionaries in "Easter 1916," as alienated from the mainstream of society and as dedicated to transcending their own histories:

Two men had founded here. A man-at-arms
Gathered a score of horse and spent his days
In this tumultuous spot,
Where through long wars and sudden night alarms
His dwindling score and he seemed cast-a-ways
Forgetting and forgot;
And I, that after me
My bodily heirs may find,
To exalt a lonely mind,
Befitting emblems of adversity.[15]

As in "Easter 1916," the specific political concerns at issue are absorbed
into Yeats's concern with aesthetics. The "affable Irregular" and the "brown
Lieutenant and his men,/Half dressed in national uniform" are welded into a
single image of action, invoking Yeats's envy and so his doubts about the value
of his own work: "I turn away and shut the door, and on the stair/Wonder how
many times I could have proved my worth/In something that all others understand or share."[16] In this poem Yeats is far more conscious than he was in
"Easter 1916" of his distance from the events going on outside his tower, and
often beyond his control:

We are closed in, and the key is turned
On our uncertainty; somewhere
A man is killed, or a house burned,
Yet no clear fact to be discerned.[17]

This consciousness of involuntary isolation informs the poem's central theme,
Yeats's doubts about the efficacy or potency of art. These doubts haunted
Yeats's celebration all through the 1920s and 1930s of the romantically alien-
ated artist seeking to restore meaning to a world lost to materialism.

Yeats's rewriting of the Anglo-Irish Ascendancy into an idealized cultural
aristocracy to replace the culturally renewed and unified Ireland that was envisioned in the early days of the revival may be seen as an attempt to shore
himself up against the ruin that seemed always to threaten his romantic idealism.[18] The Anglo-Irish provided the perfect model for Yeats in part because
they were, by the time the Civil War was over, marginalized nearly to the point
of extinction, and so could embody the mythology of the alienated, romantic
individual pitted against a destructively indifferent society. One of the corner-
stones of Yeats's version of the Ascendancy was Lady Gregory and Coole Park.
In the 1890s, Lady Gregory had been important to Yeats chiefly in his attempts
to understand and write about Irish folk culture; also, her translations into
"Kiltartan dialect" of some of the ancient Irish legends and epics (*Gods and*

Fighting Men and *Cuchulain of Muirthemne*) were useful to Yeats in his efforts to recover Ireland's past. But from the time of the *Playboy* riots on, Yeats increasingly praised Lady Gregory as representing the values associated with the Ascendancy, and Coole Park as a symbolic center of a rich and vital cultural life rooted in tradition, and therefore as an oasis for art and civilization in a desert of middle-class philistinism and indifference.[19] Coole Park first appears in this role in "Upon a House Shaken by the Land Agitation," published in *The Green Helmet* (1910). Not only does this poem interpret Coole Park in the eulogistic light that was to dominate Yeats's writing about the Anglo-Irish until the end of his career—it is a place "Where passion and precision have been one/Time out of mind"[20]—but also it uses the Big House as a vehicle for attacking materialism, embodied in the efforts of Irish peasants to dislodge landlords such as the Gregorys and become proprietors. In fact, thanks to the Wyndham Land Act of 1903 and various land reform bills that preceded it, this process had been going on for some time by the time Yeats wrote the poem, and so the poem's anger, bitterness, and fears for the future are grounded in a very real threat.[21] In Yeats's view, this change in Ireland's landlord system threatened to transform the noble peasant of the early revival into a bourgeois class, and so into the enemy of art and civilization—an unhappy testimony to the corrupting power of materialism:

> . . . Although
> Mean roof-trees were the sturdier for its fall,
> How should their luck run high enough to reach
> The gifts that govern men, and after these
> To gradual Time's last gift, a written speech
> Wrought of high laughter, loveliness and ease.[22]

The aggressive arrogance in "Upon a House Shaken by the Land Agitation" was soon replaced by a note of resignation and loss, as Yeats's idealization of the Anglo-Irish continually confronted the realities of that class and of the position of the artist in modern Ireland. The death of Lady Gregory's only son Robert, a fighter pilot shot down over Italy in 1918, provided Yeats with an emblem both of the individualist hero fired by a romantic, poetic recklessness and of a precariously positioned aristocracy threatened with cultural extinction. "An Irish Airman Foresees His Death" presents Gregory as Yeatsian hero, a modern-day Cuchulain motivated to risk his life by "A lonely impulse of delight," seeking and finding, only at the moment of his death, an experience of romantic vitality and transcendence in light of which ordinary life pales to insignificance:

> I balanced all, brought all to mind,
> The years to come seemed waste of breath,

A waste of breath the years behind
In balance with this life, this death.[23]

Yeats goes to some lengths to make the point that Gregory's romantic freedom is rooted in his ambiguous status an an Anglo-Irishman fighting on behalf of the English:

Those that I fight I do not hate
Those that I guard I do not love;
My country is Kiltartan Cross,
My countrymen Kiltartan's poor.[24]

The effect is to heroicize not only Gregory but also his class, whose members, as Yeats said later, were to be celebrated because they "gave, though free to refuse." [25] In his elegy "In Memory of Major Robert Gregory," Yeats places Gregory in a community that is both specifically Anglo-Irish and artistic; Gregory is associated with the Big House—"What other could so well have counselled us/In all lovely intricacies of a house"—and with the arts—"We dreamed that a great painter had been born/To cold Clare rock and Galway rock and thorn." [26] Gregory's death is transformed into an emblem of the threatened end of cultural aristocracy, and so of art itself, and the identification of Gregory with the poet represents less the exuberance of transcendence than the silence of extinction—of the Anglo-Irish and of the romantic imagination:

I had thought, seeing how bitter is that wind
That shakes the shutter, to have brought to mind
All those that manhood tried, or childhood loved
Or boyish intellect approved,
With some appropriate commentary on each;
Until imagination brought
A fitter welcome; but a thought
Of that late death took all my heart for speech.[27]

Yeats writes against this threatened demise of the imagination from this point on in his career. That deathly silence particularly haunts his writing about Ireland and the Anglo-Irish; it is there in "In Memory of Eva Gore-Booth and Con Markiewicz"—"But a raving autumn shears/Blossom from the summer's wreath" [28]—and in his prophetic poems about the destruction of Coole Park— "Here, traveller, scholar, poet, take your stand/When all these rooms and passages are gone." [29] In "Coole Park and Ballylee, 1931," it is extended to mark the end not just of the Anglo-Irish but of the entire history of western civilization:

> We were the last romantics—chose for theme
> Traditional sanctity and loveliness;
> Whatever's written in what poets name
> The book of the people; whatever most can bless
> The mind of man or elevate a rhyme;
> But all is changed, that high horse riderless,
> Though mounted in that saddle Homer rode
> Where the swan drifts upon a darkening flood.[30]

The other cornerstone of Yeats's cultural aristocracy was eighteenth-century Anglo-Ireland, and Yeats characteristically recreated this moment in Ireland's history in terms of his dichotomy between aesthetic and philistine, spiritual and material, with the principal *dramatis personae*—Swift, Goldsmith, Burke, and Berkeley—linked to each other, and to Yeats, in a manner that has meaning only in the context of Yeats's aesthetics and politics.[31] In an essay on Berkeley, written in 1931, Yeats can be seen rewriting each of these four figures into that context:

> Berkeley with his belief in perception, that abstract ideas are mere words, Swift with his love of perfect nature, of the Houyhnhnms, his disbelief in Newton's system and every sort of machine, Goldsmith and his delight in the particulars of common life that shocked his contemporaries, Burke with his conviction that all States not grown slowly like a forest tree are tyrannies. . . .[32]

In his poem "Blood and Moon," Yeats can be observed quite self-consciously creating his romanticized eighteenth century by the sheer force of the poetic imagination and will:

> I declare this tower is my symbol; I declare
> This winding, gyring, spiring treadmill of a stair is my ancestral stair;
> That Goldsmith and the Dean, Berkeley and Burke have travelled there.[33]

To some extent, the emphasis in Yeats's writing on the individual artist-hero and of the idealized community of the Anglo-Irish, past and present, embodied a spirited defense of a besieged artistic integrity that might be said to have offered much to inspire Irish poets working in the wake of the revival. Nonetheless, especially in the increasingly fierce loyalty to his own class that dominated his writing in these years, Yeats effectively wrote himself out of the mainstream of Irish poetry that his earlier work had done so much to enrich and broaden. For many of the poets who came after him, Yeats's often aggressively exclusivist celebration of Anglo-Ireland as the only available environment for the preservation of art was a cultural deadend, and Yeats's position of cultural isolation meant, finally, that his work had little to say about life in postindependence Ireland. The experience of Irish Catholicism, for example, that so preoccupied Austin Clarke's work was almost unimaginable to Yeats, and Patrick Kavanagh's rural Co. Monaghan represented a world that simply could not be seen from the high windows of Thor Ballylee or Coole Park.

An important exception to Yeats's relatively marginalized position within the Irish poetic community was provided by his continuing interest in the traditional ballad, which anchored his work in the native Irish tradition and Irish folk art even after he had abandoned the relatively egalitarian cultural ambitions of his early period.[34] Yeats often used the form, however, especially in the last decade of his life, when he took it up with renewed vigor and new sophistication, to challenge mainstream cultural assumptions, including the patriotic sentiments that had been associated with the ballad since the middle of the nineteenth century and the rise of Young Ireland. In "Come Gather Round Me, Parnellites," Yeats employs the traditional political ballad to heroicize Parnell in specifically Yeatsian terms that call into question conventional nationalist readings of Parnell as part of a tradition of political martyrdom:

> Come gather round me Parnellites
> And praise our chosen man,
> Stand upright on your legs awhile;
> Stand upright while you can,
> For soon we lie where he is laid
> And he is underground;
> Come fill up all those glasses
> And pass the bottle round.
>
> And here's a cogent reason
> And I have many more,
> He fought the might of England
> And saved the Irish poor,
> Whatever good a farmer's got
> He brought it all to pass;
> And here's another reason,
> That Parnell loved a lass.
>
> And here's a final reason,
> He was of such a kind
> Every man that sings a song
> Keeps Parnell in his mind
> For Parnell was a proud man
> No prouder trod the ground,
> And a proud man's a lovely man,
> So pass the bottle round.[35]

Even more subversively, in his Crazy Jane poems, Yeats adopts the traditional ballad and a character drawn from folk culture to give voice to sexual attitudes that were anything but conventional in the Ireland of the 1930s. For example, the abstractly realized conflict between body and soul in "A Dialogue of Self and Soul" is transformed in "Crazy Jane Talks with the Bishop" into the quite graphic terms of the conflict between sexuality and conventional religious teaching, a concern close to Clarke's poetry of the 1920s and 1930s.

Writing in 1966, the fiftieth anniversary of the Easter Rising, Thomas Kinsella argued that Yeats represented the conclusion of a tradition in Irish writing rather than a point of departure for his successors; in the end, Kinsella said, Yeats's obsession with eighteenth-century Anglo-Ireland amounted to "an Anglo-Irish annex to the history of Ireland."[36] And, as Kinsella also pointed out, Yeats himself, writing near the end of his life, argued that his work was, for all its Irishness, vitally inspired by English poetry and the English language:

> I remind myself that though mine is the first English marriage I know of in the direct line, all my family names are English, and that I owe my soul to Shakespeare, to Spenser and to Blake, perhaps to William Morris, and to the English language in which I think, speak, and write, that everything I love has come to me through English; my hatred tortures me with love, my love with hate.[37]

It is a remarkable passage not because it suggests that Yeats was, as one literary historian has argued, "the supreme representative figure of the 'colonialist mentality,' "[38] but because it reveals the agony of the isolation in which Yeats worked and which he made into the substance of his art. That agonized and at times stubbornly heroic isolation was also, it might be argued, the most important legacy that Yeats left to the Irish writers coming after him.

EXITS FROM THE REVIVAL

The establishment of the Irish Free State in 1922 brought to an end a period in Irish history when the possibilities for radical change, both cultural and political, had seemed boundless. As the new state settled into the difficult but not particularly heroic business of governing itself and of constructing a cultural identity that would clearly mark it off from England, many of the ambitions and attitudes that had inspired the literary revival in the 1880s and 1890s began to seem irrelevant, if not a little absurd. Although it did not always prove easy to escape those ambitions and attitudes, in the 1920s and 1930s a number of Irish writers began to find ways out of the revival, some of which were to exert considerable force on Irish writing later in the century. The first part of Austin Clarke's long career exemplifies this process. Clarke began writing in the late teens by mining the same historical material that had been so central to the revival's version of the Irish tradition, the pre-Christian legends of the Ulster cycle and the Fenian cycle. Although in several long versions of these ancient stories—*The Vengeance of Fionn* (1917) and *Thé Sword of the West* (1921)—Clarke attempted to replace the romanticized, Celtic Twilight style in which many revival writers had rendered this material with a voice more authentically representative of the concrete, graphic quality of the originals, he was not breaking substantially new ground, and in the mid-1920s he abandoned this mode altogether, turning instead to the early Christian period of Irish history as a means of writing about his own experience as an Irish Catholic. This was precisely the area of Irish experience that the revival's focus on Ireland's pagan past had more or less calculatedly circumvented but it was becoming of paramount importance as the political and cultural power of the Catholic Church significantly expanded. Oliver St. John Gogarty shared Clarke's humanistic critique of the puritanical strain in Irish Catholicism. Although his work fell more consistently under the shadow of the revival's romanticism than did Clarke's writing, Gogarty's poetry was characterized by an urbanity and a classical restraint that pointed away from the idealized ruralism of the revival. About the same time, Thomas MacGreevy, a much less well-known poet than either Clarke or Gogarty, was quietly opening up Irish poetry to the influence of modernist experimentation; under the influence of T. S. Eliot, MacGreevy employed elliptical syntax, prosodic irregularity, and structuring by symbol and allusion to create a vision of Ireland as a modern wasteland with a fragmented past. This attempt to read Irish culture through the lens of international modernism, which inspired a number of later Irish writers, implicitly rejected the relatively provincial focus of a writer such as Clarke as well as of the revival itself. Another path out of the revival led inward, to a new attempt to represent the Gaelic tradition with formal and substantive authenticity, in contrast to what was now seen as its misrepresentation by Celtic Twilight romanticism and by nineteenth-century translators. The work of F. R. Higgins and Robert Farren in the 1920s and 1930s, along with that of Clarke, specifically rejected the revival's tendency to absorb Ireland's Gaelic tradition into the aesthetics and cultural ambitions of the movement, and focused instead, in often quite technically proficient ways, on remaking Irish poetry in English by working into English verse some of the formal qualities inherent in poetry written in Irish. Higgins and Farren were more limited than liberated by this ambition, and some of their work could be seen as reinforcing Irish-Ireland efforts to define Irish culture in Gaelic terms; the best of Clarke's work in this vein, on the other hand, effectively subverted the narrow, conservative reading of the Gaelic tradition on which those efforts depended.

George Russell once described Oliver St. John Gogarty (1878–1957) as a writer "whose art is to project defined and shapely images," as opposed to the effort in Russell's own work to "melt all form into bodiless spirit." [1] Years earlier, Gogarty, in an effort to distance himself from Russell and his followers, had been less generous; reviewing Russell's anthology of young poets, *New Songs* (1904), Gogarty said that it exhibited "a want of fullness of matter," and embodied "a perfection which belongs to the conservatory." [2] The difference here is a significant one; Gogarty's poetry is marked by a spare, formally disciplined concreteness usually associated with his training in the classics,[3] and he promoted this kind of poetry as more appropriate to the Irish experience than the romantic afflatus that dominated Irish poetry in the nineteenth and early twentieth centuries. In "The Crab Tree," Gogarty takes the crabapple tree as a fitting symbol for Ireland and its history of suffering. Planted in "the thin soil" of Ireland's fragmented cultural history, and bearing a "twisted root" that "grapples/For sap with the rock," the tree also represents the power of artistic form to press ordered meaning out of chaos and suffering, an essentially classical theory of aesthetics that is embodied as well as argued for in the tightly controlled stanzas and short lines of the poem:

> It takes from the West Wind
> The thrust of the main;
> It makes from the tension
> Of sky and of plain,
> Of what clay enacted,
> Of living alarm,
> A vitalised symbol
> Of earth and of storm,
> Of Chaos contracted
> To intricate form.[4]

Gogarty's work also demonstrates its classical affinities in a penchant for satire and parody, neither of which was important to the revival (with the notable exception of the work of Susan Mitchell), and in an emphasis on Dublin that is voiced in a tone of urbanity quite foreign to the earlier, earthier Dublin poems of Seamus O'Sullivan and James Stephens. The playfulness of Gogarty's poetry distinguishes it further from the revival and much of its aftermath. Gogarty's "Leda and the Swan," for example (Yeats's famous sonnet of the same title came first), uses reductive comedy, along with a parodically complex and inverted syntax, to expose the lack of self-conscious humor in much Irish writing:

> What was it she called him:
>   Goosey-goosey gander?
> For she knew no better
>   Way to call a swan;
> And the bird responding
>   Seemed to understand her,
> For he left his sailing
>   For the bank to waddle on.
>
> Apple blossoms under
>   Hills of Lacedaemon,
> With the snow beyond them
>   In the still blue air,
> To the swan who hid them
>   With his wings asunder,
> Than the breasts of Leda,
>   Were not lovelier.[5]

Nonetheless, for all its formal differences from mainstream revival writing, Gogarty's poetry was very much influenced by romantic thinking. Although he did not start publishing poetry until the late teens—*The Ship* (1918) was his first collection—and although he published his most significant work in the

1920s and 1930s, Gogarty was closer to Yeats's generation than he was to Clarke's; as his memoir, *As I Was Going Down Sackville Street,* attests, he was a prominent figure in Dublin literary circles in the heyday of the revival. The strain of romanticism that colors Gogarty's poetry was not, however, associated specifically with Irish nationalism, political or cultural, and owed more to Wordsworth than it did to the romantic Ireland of Mangan or the early Yeats. Gogarty once said that the mystic and the poet moved "in a region beyond ethics where poetry and religion are one," [6] a statement that reveals the extent to which Gogarty's poetic sensibility was divided between classical and romantic positions—or at home in both. In "High Tide at Malahide," one of his most important poems, Gogarty negotiates between interpreting the Irish land-scape in the specific terms of Irish history and in those of the romantic tran-scendent experience "where poetry and religion are one." The poem takes the form of a meditative lyric set in a symbolically meaningful natural land-scape, and Gogarty uses the incoming tide to suggest the eclipsing of ordinary reality and thought by a profoundly renewing but ultimately unfathomable experience:

> And every axon in my brain
> And neuron takes the tide again,
> Made all the fuller from the tide
> That brims the sands of Malahide;
> But what shall come into it now
> I know not. I await the flow.
> I must abide the cosmic main
> Whose high tide floods the stranded brain;
> For no such miracle is wrought
> On earth like this by taking thought.[7]

At the same time, the poem is acutely aware of a specific history lying behind this landscape, and Gogarty often interrogates conventional, narrowly national-ist readings of that history. At one point, he attributes heroic qualities to the Norman and Norse invaders, evoking a pluralistic history and contemporary culture closer to the vision of George Sigerson's *Bards of the Gael and Gall* than to more exclusivist readings of history, including the Irish-Ireland formula-tions that were so much in force at the time of Gogarty's writing:

> Salt of the earth,
> Salt of the sea,
> Norman and Norse
> And the wild man in me!
> The founders of cities,

The takers of fields,
The heroes too proud to wear armour or shields,
Their blood is in you,
As it cannot but be,
O Townsmen of towns on an estuary![8]

Moving with considerable facility between parody and high seriousness and between classical and romantic modes, Gogarty's writing was informed by an overarching humanism that eventually led him, despite his friendship with Arthur Griffith and his early support of Sinn Fein, to become one of the most outspoken critics of de Valera's Ireland in the 1930s. And although Gogarty's poetry is uneven, marred at times by a tendency to indulge in the ephemeral and at others by an incongruity between classical form and romantic expression, it rests on a fundamental faith in art's moral and social responsibility. That faith is less self-consciously problematic and less sensitive to the complexities of the poet's role in the modern world than is the work of the mature Yeats, but out of that faith Gogarty often makes his most compelling poetry. His well-known lyric "Ringsend" is a monument to Gogarty's humanism and to his view of the poet's function in society:

I will live in Ringsend
With a red-headed whore,
And the fan-light gone in
Where it lights the hall-door;
And listen each night
For her querulous shout,
As at last she streels in
And the pubs empty out.
To soothe that wild breast
With my old-fangled songs,
Till she feels it redressed
From inordinate wrongs,
Imagined, outrageous,
Preposterous wrongs,
Till peace at last comes,
Shall be all I will do,
Where the little lamp blooms
Like a rose in the stew;
And up the back-garden
The sound comes to me
Of the lapsing, unsoilable,
Whispering sea.[9]

Gogarty cut a wide swath in Dublin literary circles in the 1920s and 1930s. By comparison, Thomas MacGreevy (1893–1967) worked in almost complete obscurity; spending only a few years after the establishment of Irish independence in Dublin before moving to London and Paris, publishing just a handful of poems in periodicals in the late 1920s, and then apparently giving up writing poetry after the appearance in 1934 of the only collection of his poetry published in his lifetime, MacGreevy remained far from the limelight in which Gogarty basked. But it is possible to argue that MacGreevy's few ventures into writing poetry about Ireland, by importing into the Irish tradition not only the experimental techniques of modernism but also modernism's general scepticism of romantic aesthetics, ultimately proved to be of more importance in moving Irish poetry beyond the conventions of the literary revival than was the entire substantial body of Gogarty's poetry.

MacGreevy's modernism came principally by way of Eliot, and he especially took to heart Eliot's view that the modern poet had to "dislocate if necessary, language into his meaning." [10] In 1932, while living in Paris, MacGreevy signed a manifesto entitled "Poetry Is Vertical" (other signers included Beckett and Joyce's friend Eugene Jolas), which argued for "the autonomy of the poetic vision" and for a poetic language "which does not hesitate to adopt a revolutionary attitude toward word and syntax, going even so far as to invent a hermetic language, if necessary." [11] MacGreevy's poems rely on free verse— "after Eliot himself, the most perfectly modulated free verse written in the period in England, Ireland, or America," according to Anthony Cronin [12]—and on fragmented syntax, imagism, allusion, and the intersection of realism and mythology. MacGreevy's poems about Ireland interpret the Irish experience in the international context of modernism and, more specifically, of European writing, challenging the inward-looking cultural tendencies of the Irish-Ireland movement as well as the essentially provincial orientation of much of the writing and thinking that came out of the revival. Moreover, the best of Mac-Greevy's Irish poems subvert not only the formal conventions associated with the mainstream tradition of Irish poetry in English but also many of the nationalist cultural and political assumptions that informed the revival and the struggle for political independence.

MacGreevy's general scepticism derived in large part from his experiences in the First World War. MacGreevy joined the British Army as a gunner in 1917, served in the front lines of the Ypres Salient and the Somme, and was wounded twice. As his fine World War I poem "De Civitate Hominum" indicates, the vision of modern man that MacGreevy carried with him from the trenches back to Ireland had little in common with the humanism found in Gogarty or Clarke. Moreover, the sense of disillusionment that generally followed the war was heightened for MacGreevy when he returned to Ireland in 1919 to find the Black and Tans attempting, on behalf of the British government that he had just defended at such risk, to crush the Irish drive for independence. The Anglo-Irish War and the Civil War that followed it are the focus of Mac-Greevy's most accomplished Irish writing, which presents the Irish experience through the lens of the devastating moral and philosophical effects of World War I; more than the work of any other poet of his generation, MacGreevy's poems subject what was happening to Ireland in these tumultuous years to a specifically postwar scepticism. "The Six Who Were Hanged," a poem responding to the execution by the British of six republican prisoners in March, 1921, exemplifies this strategy. By comparing the political martyrs to the thousands who died in the trenches, the poem challenges nationalist notions of political martyrdom and heroism:

> The sky turns limpid green.
> The stars go silver white.
> They must be stirring in their cells now—
>
> Unspeaking likely!
>
> Waiting for an attack
> With death uncertain
> One said little.
>
> For these there is no uncertainty.
>
> The sun will come soon,
> All gold.
>
> *'Tis you shall have the golden throne—*
>
> It will come ere its time.
> It will not be time,
> Oh, it will not be time,
> Not for silver and gold,
> Not with green,
> Till they all have dropped home,
> Till gaol bells all have clanged,
> Till all six have been hanged.
>
> And after?
> Will it be time?[13]

The Eliotic insertion of the line from Mangan's "Dark Rosaleen," perhaps the most famous romantic nationalist poem of the nineteenth century, reverberates with characteristic irony and ambiguity. MacGreevy also inserts into his text phrases from the prayers that were said by the thousands of Irish people who gathered outside Mountjoy Prison that morning. Juxtaposed with a description

of the hangings, these prayers take on an ironic cast that questions the hope
of redemption, both political and personal, that the presence of the crowd
embodies:

> *At the hour of our death*
> At this hour of youth's death,
> *Hail Mary! Hail Mary!*
> Now young bodies swing up.[14]

The execution of Irish nationalists also figures, although less directly, in Mac-
Greevy's most anthologized Irish poem, "Aodh Ruadh Ó Domhnaill." This
poem, which pays homage to Red Hugh O'Donnell, the Prince of Tirconaill,
who went into exile after the Irish defeat at Kinsale in 1601, might be compared
with Mangan's romantic elegy, "Lament for the Princes of Tyrone and Tyrconnell (Buried in Rome)," written from an unreservedly nationalist point of
view and taking the two famous exiled princes as models of inspiration for
nineteenth-century politics. MacGreevy's poem expresses but goes beyond a
Yeatsian lament over the loss of heroism in the modern world, contrasting the
formal burial of O'Donnell with the executions of contemporary nationalists in
a way that calls into question rather than affirms the notion of an unbroken
tradition of heroic political martyrdom, the tradition that Mangan's poem had
helped create:

> Yet when
> Unhurried—
>> Not as at home
>> Where heroes, hanged, are buried
>> With non-commissioned officers' bored maledictions
>> Quickly in the gaol yard—
>
> They brought
> His blackening body
> Here
> To rest
> Princes came
> Walking
> Behind it
>
> All Valladolid knew
> And out to Simancas all knew
> Where they buried Red Hugh.[15]

Although Eliot is the modernist poet who most influenced MacGreevy's
work, the most important Irish writer for him was Joyce. By taking Joyce rather

than Yeats as his Irish mentor, MacGreevy anticipated in another way the efforts of later Irish poets to free their representations of Ireland from the powerful conventions and values of the revival. The influence of both Eliot and Joyce is felt strongly in MacGreevy's most ambitious poem, the lengthy "Crán Tráth na nDeith" ("Dark Time of the Gods"), an Irish *Wasteland* that draws on Eliotic techniques and is structured around a Joycean journey through the streets of Dublin on an ordinary night. Like *The Wasteland* and *Ulysses,* the poem conflates realism with mythology, and popular with high art (two dominant musical motifs are the Dublin street ballad "Cockles and Mussels" and Wagner's *Der Ring des Nibelung.*) Dated Easter, 1923, "Crán Tráth na nDeith" presents images of a city in ruins, physically and spiritually, following the political turbulence that occurred from the Easter Rising through the Civil War. This bleak vision of Dublin just after the establishment of independence, a vision very much at odds with most nationalist views of the time, is significantly conditioned by World War I:

> Wrecks wetly mouldering under rain,
> Everywhere.
> Remember Belgium!
> You cannot pick up the
> Pieces.[16]

As opposed to Yeats's reconstruction of eighteenth-century Anglo-Ireland, MacGreevy presents images of the destruction of Georgian Dublin, in particular the burning of James Gandon's Custom House by the Irish Republican Army in 1921, and the bombardment of the Four Courts by Free State troops in 1922:

> When the Custom House took fire
> Hope slipped off her green petticoat
> The Four Courts went up in a spasm
> Moses felt for Hope
>
> *Folge mir Frau*
> Come up to Valhalla
> To *gile na gile*
> The brightness of brightness
> Towering in the sky
> Over Dublin.[17]

That final verse ironically conflates Wagner's *Das Rheingold* with the eighteenth-century Gaelic vision poem, "Gile na Gile" ("Brightness of Brightness") by Aodhagán Ó Rathaille; the hope of salvation embodied in both works is symbolically subsumed by, or transformed into, the fires of the burning buildings, destroyed by nationalists who bring to an ironic consummation the shining political redemption prophesied in the tradition of Gaelic vision poetry.

MacGreevy left Ireland just after the establishment of independence, moving to London in 1924 and to Paris three years later. There he met Beckett, did some reviewing, wrote a monograph on Eliot, and then, in 1933, decided to return to London, where his *Poems* appeared the following year. His work inspired praise in certain circles—Beckett called his poems "probably the most important contribution to post-war Irish poetry" [18]—but he was very much a marginalized figure in the literary Dublin that he left in 1924 and returned to in 1941. This may account for his silence after *Poems*. Nevertheless, the art that MacGreevy made out of the modern condition of being marginalized and alienated stands as as important achievement in twentieth-century writing, Irish or otherwise.

One Irish poet who worked quite deliberately apart from the modernism of MacGreevy was Austin Clarke (1896–1974). As his friend and fellow poet Robert Farren once put it, Clarke was a "literary separatist," [19] and throughout a long and varied career—his first book was published two years before the publication of Yeats's *The Wild Swans at Coole,* and his last a year before the appearance of Seamus Heaney's fourth collection—Clarke focused almost exclusively on Irish matters. Clarke wrote, moreover, in a style often heavily marked by the Irish-language tradition, and for an Irish audience. "The problems of modernism," Clarke once said, "can have little practical value in this country, where our literary development is so distinctly different." [20] Much of that difference had to do, in Clarke's view, with the Catholic and Gaelic dimensions of Irish culture. No Irish poet before or after Clarke explored Irish Catholicism so thoroughly or so critically; writing from inside his own experience as a middle-class Dublin Catholic, Clarke challenged Irish-Ireland representations of Catholicism, consistently and fiercely attacking what he saw as Jansenist qualities in Irish Catholicism from a humanistic point of view committed to defending sexual, intellectual, and artistic freedom. This focus set Clarke apart from the revival's tendency to ignore the Catholic dimension of Irish culture, while it connected him to Joyce, although in a way very different from the modernist link between Joyce and MacGreevy. Clarke and Joyce came from the same social and religious background, and they shared an extremely sceptical attitude toward it. "The 'Portrait of an Artist' had long since become confused with my own memories or had completed them," Clarke once said in recalling a meeting that he had with Joyce in Paris.[21] Also, few Irish poets managed to infuse so successfully into English verse the formal qualities of poetry written in Irish, or to evoke the graphic, concrete nature of the Irish-language tradition, as opposed both to Celtic Twilight versions produced by the revival and to Irish-Ireland's attempts to appropriate the Gaelic tradition as part of a morally and culturally restrictive view of Irishness.[22]

Clarke's commitment to the Gaelic past was evident at the very beginning of his long career. In the late 1910s and 1920s, he wrote several long poems, or sequences of poems, based on the pre-Christian legendary material that had inspired much of the revival. In this work, Clarke saw himself as offering a corrective to the revival's romanticization of the tradition. "The Celtic Twilight is beautiful in itself," Clarke wrote in 1924, "but it can appear Gaelic only to those—and they are many—who accept with Napoleon the Ossian of Macpherson. The objective manner . . . is as a fact more racial than the shimmering mists of Fiona Macleod." [23] Clarke's early poems based on this pre-Christian material attempt to restore the "objective manner" of the originals, and to counter the revival's tendency to heroicize the characters from these legends in the interests of a specific cultural and aesthetic agenda. Clarke's version of the "pillow-talk" scene that opens the *Táin Bó Cuailgne* demonstrates how Clarke, relying on concrete details and the rhythms of ordinary speech, presents these characters in a human scale, restoring them to their specific historical context:

> Queen Maeve sat up in bed and shook once more
> Her snoring husband:
>   'And I cannot sleep
> An inch now for my head is full of words
> That spoiled the chessboard, held the drinking cups
> Half drained and climbed the more as candlelight
> Ran low and is there any doubt that I
> Had greater wealth when we were wed than you
> Had bargained with my hand—have I not filled
> The west with lowing herds, have I not fleeced
> The hills, have I not brought the middlemen
> From grassing plains to lift a wondering head
> From seaward clouds and count a rout of horses
> Graze beyond swimming and where few island women
> Gallop them, bareback, to the little seas
> Of Connaught? Have I now or have I not?' [24]

Clarke's garrulous Maeve is a long way from Yeats's misty Niamh, with eyes "soft as dew-drops hanging," the heroine of his early long poem *The Wanderings of Osian*. [25] There is also a Rabelesian quality to much of Clarke's early work in this vein, which accurately reflects the candid treatment of sexuality in the originals, while enabling Clarke to critique Jansenist Catholicism and interrogate the tendency in Irish-Ireland formulations of Irish culture to conflate the Gaelic past with the morally conservative and sexually repressive values of the church.

Although Clarke's versions of Ireland's epic literature cleared some poetic

ground away from the influence of the revival, his interest eventually shifted
to medieval Christian Ireland, which he found to hold richer meanings and
implications for his own experience.[26] For Clarke, monastic Ireland offered a
powerful vehicle for critiquing contemporary Catholicism. On one hand, the
medieval church had been a center of art and scholarship, not just for Ireland
but for European civilization as a whole, and Clarke celebrates it with an ironic
awareness of the repressive stance of the contemporary church toward Irish
artists. (The book in which Clarke's interest in Christian Ireland first appears,
Pilgrimage, was published the same year that the Censorship Act was passed.)
On the other hand, in the extreme asceticism of much monastic life, Clarke
found a way to dramatize the conflict between religious discipline and individual freedom. The title poem of *Pilgrimage* celebrates Clonmacnoise, with its
"cloistered scholars,/Whose knowledge of the gospel/Is cast as metal in pure
voices," [27] but also describes, in quite different terms, the penitential pilgrims
at Croagh Patrick:

> Beyond a rocky townland
> And that last tower where ocean
> Is dim as haze, a sound
> Of wild confession rose:
> Black congregations moved
> Around the booths of prayer
> To hear a saint reprove them.[28]

In the 1930s, Clarke developed the confessional lyric as a mode for expressing the conflict between humanism and Irish Catholicism. Many of these
poems, which tend to be denser and more obscure than the monastic poems of
Pilgrimage, appeared in *Night and Morning* (1938), a volume that is particularly concerned with the tension between religious faith and intellectual freedom. These poems recognize that this central conflict cannot be fully resolved,
so they often describe a condition of spiritual and intellectual limbo in which
the poet is unable to accept the anti-humantisitc (and anti-artistic) teachings of
the church but also recognizes that secular humanism, in rejecting the spiritual
values encoded in religion, is less than fully satisfying. The conclusion of
"Tenebrae," which associates the church's doctrines with the darkness in a
church as the ritual candles are extinguished and liberal humanism and reason
with the natural light of day, demonstrates how carefully balanced and emotionally laden is this tension, and with what complexity Clarke explores the Irish
Catholicism of his time:

> An open mind disturbs the soul,
> And in disdain I turn my back

> Upon the sun that makes a show
> Of half the world, yet still deny
> The pain that lives within the past,
> The flame sinking upon the spike,
> Darkness that man must dread at last.[29]

Clarke's interest in Gaelic Ireland went well beyond his early renderings of pre-Christian sagas. Indeed, he spent his entire career negotiating between the Irish-language and English-language traditions, working in particular to impress upon the rhythms and poetic structures of English verse the formal qualities of poetry written in Irish. In this effort, Clarke was carrying forward the antiquarian ambitions of the tradition of translation in Ireland going back to the end of the eighteenth century, but few if any of Clarke's predecessors in that tradition were as successful in expressing the technical qualities and poetic voice of writing in Irish. Clarke was particularly interested, as his lyrics of the 1920s and 1930s demonstrate, in developing assonance as a complement to or replacement for rhyme. "Assonance, more elaborate in Gaelic than in Spanish poetry," Clarke said, "takes the clapper from the bell of rhyme." [30] For example, "The Scholar" is built around a pattern of terminal-medial assonance frequently employed in Irish syllabic verse and capable of producing a distinctly un-English poetic music:

> Summer delights the scholar
> With knowledge and reason.
> Who is happy in hedgerow
> Or meadow as he is?
>
> Paying no dues to the parish,
> He argues in logic
> And has no care of cattle
> But a satchel and stick.[31]

In one of his best-known poems, "The Straying Student" *(Night and Morning)*, Clarke draws on another sound pattern from the Irish, structuring his poem around an abbac pattern of internal assonance:

> On a holy day when sails were blowing southward,
> A bishop sang the Mass at Inishmore,
> Men took one side, their wives were on the other
> But I heard the woman coming from the shore:
> And wild in despair my parents cried aloud
> For they saw the vision draw me to the doorway.[32]

Both these students are emblems of intellectual and artistic freedom, and Clarke is not only attempting to establish a poetic voice with some kind of authenticity in terms of Ireland's Gaelic heritage but also to resist the tendency in the Ireland of his day to identify that heritage with the moral conservatism of modern Irish Catholicism.

F. R. Higgins (1896–1941) shared Clarke's view that the literary revival had emasculated Ireland's Gaelic tradition by translating it into the terms of its own romantic aesthetics and cultural politics. Like Clarke, Higgins admired the vigor, vividness, and "objective manner" of poetry in Irish, and in a note to his second collection of poems, *The Dark Breed* (1927), he specifically distinguished those qualities from the Celtic Twilight mode of the revival, which, he implied, was grounded largely in ignorance:

> The racial strength of a Gaelic aristocratic mind—with its vigorous colouring and hard emotion—is easily recognised in Irish poetry, by those acquainted with the literature of our own people. Like our Gaelic stock its poetry is sun-bred; twilight for it is just the tremulous smoke of one day's fire. Not with dreams but with fire in the mind, the eyes of Gaelic poetry reflect a richness of life and the intensity of a dark people, still part of our landscape.[33]

Whereas Clarke's early work attempted to rewrite the revival's version of the Gaelic tradition's ancient epics, Higgins's corrective to what he saw as the romantic excesses of the revival took the form chiefly of lyrics in which he fused his interest in folk ballads with his view of the realistic, "sun-bred" tradition of writing in Irish. Although his work in this vein was obviously indebted to the poetry of Padraic Colum, Joseph Campbell, and James Stephens, Higgins extended the work of these writers in at least one direction—representations of human sexuality. As Clarke's epics and lyrics insisted on the centrality of sexual freedom and candor in the Gaelic tradition, so the emphasis on eroticism in Higgins's ballads had the effect of redefining the Irish folk tradition away from earlier romantic stereotypes, while implicitly challenging Irish Ireland's conflation of Gaelicism with conservative Catholicism. The exuberant eroticism of a poem such as "A Tinker's Woman" *(The Dark Breed),* is closer to Clarke's work than it is to Colum's or Campbell's:

> You now forget when from the gorse
>   I saw you swim sea water,
> Stark naked I flashed on a tinker's horse
>   Down to the morning water
> And into green seas I took my ride
> Barebacked, horse-swimming I reached your side,
> *Then who but a fool would rob the tide*
>   *And throw away the salmon.*

> Ah, now I know you wrongly thought
> You loved me then, MacDara,
> While peeled to the waist for me you fought
> Some mountainy fellow, MacDara,
> For there on wet grass and stript to my teeth
> I seemed as a sword of light at your feet—
> *Yet who but a fool would keep the sheath*
> *And leave the sword unhandled.*[34]

If Higgins contributed significantly to Yeats's late interest in the folk ballad—and he and Yeats spent much time together in the 1930s—the erotic nature of much of Yeats's late writing might well be indebted to him.

Higgins himself probably owed more than a little to Synge's influence. He certainly followed Synge in taking the west as the center of authentic Irish culture. (Robert Farren called Higgins "the Jack B. Yeats of poetry." [35]) In doing so, Higgins extended rather than radically revised the cultural perspective of the literary revival, at the same time that he accommodated one of the fundamental tenets of the Irish-Ireland movement. For Higgins himself, this attitude represented something of a personal rebellion; his family was Protestant, and his father, an engineer from Co. Meath, was a strict unionist. Inspired by Colum, especially Colum's lyric "a Drover," which he said made him see that "loveliness became possible in daily surroundings," [36] he made himself into a poet of the west and of the native Irish tradition. At its best, his writing in this vein resists the sentimentalism of earlier poetic portrayals of the west. The title poem of *The Dark Breed* is very much aware that the "daily surroundings" for people in the west include poverty and alienation, as they do for Patrick Kavanagh's Co. Monaghan farmers:

> With those bawneen men I'm one,
> In the grey dusk-fall,
> Watching the Galway land
> Sink down in distress—
> With dark men, talking of grass,
> By a loose stone wall,
> In murmurs drifting and drifting
> To loneliness.
>
> . . .
>
> So we, with the last dark men,
> Left on the rock grass,
> May brazen grey loneliness
> Over a poteen still
> Or crowd on the bare chapel floor
> Hearing late Mass,

> To loosen that hunger
> Broken land can never fill.[37]

Even Beckett, who said Higgins was "still victim of the centrifugal daemon," conceded that Higgins's rural poetry had a certain unflinching authenticity: "His verses have . . . a good smell of dung, most refreshing after all the attar of far off, most secret and inviolable rose." [38] Higgins also shared with Clarke an interest in developing assonance as a means of incorporating into English verse some of the formal qualities of poetry in Irish, and he had considerable skill in this, as is evident in a lyric such as "Muineen Water":

> I know a small lake that sails the palest shadows,
> Trailing their frail keels along its waveless sand;
> And when isles of grey turf are sunning in its shallows
> The far hill is a blue ghost on that land.[39]

Nonetheless, Higgins's poetry as a whole, lacking the compelling vision of modern Irish life that drove Clarke's work, never fully escaped from the influence of the revival or, later, from that of Yeats.[40]

Unlike Clarke or Higgins, Robert Farren (1909–1984), a son of the working class who earned a master's degree in Thomistic philosophy, was primarily a religious poet, and his work contributed to the movement of Irish poetry away from the revival by fusing a commitment to Ireland's Gaelic tradition with a fervent belief in Irish Catholicism, a combination that made his work perfectly reflective of Irish-Ireland notions of cultural identity. As Clarke put it, not without a discernible a trace of irony, Farren was "a poet of doctrine, much pleased by all that has been defined for us." [41] Farren's religious faith distinguished his work from the humanism of Clarke, while his interest in the Gaelic tradition, in which he shared Clarke's and Higgins's view of the need to offer a realistic corrective to the romanticism of the revival, set his work apart from earlier Irish poetry expressing Catholic belief, including the asceticism of Lionel Johnson and the mysticism of Katharine Tynan and Joseph Mary Plunkett. Farren's insistence on a necessary relationship between Gaelicism and Catholicism can be seen in "Raftery's Repentance" (from *Time's Wall Asunder,* 1939), in which Farren represents a side of the famous blind Connacht poet not to be found in earlier, Anglo-Irish representations of him, such as Douglas Hyde's or Yeats's. In a note, Farren makes the point that the poem of religious repentance "was a genre to which every Gaelic poet was at some time likely to contribute," and his translation specifically makes of Raftery both a Gaelic poet and a believer:

> Who art in High Heaven, Maker of man,
> whose passionless anger Adam stirred,

> sinner of sinful Adam's clan
> I ask for the pardon Adam heard.
>
> I have grown old and shook down my bloom.
> My hours like grass I have mown away:
> With dram and gossip in tavern-room
> half my Heaven is flown away.
>
> The days go by me: I built no wall,
> and the corn is stolen that you'd have prized.
> Yet, God of Glory, come at my call
> your pelting mercy wets my eyes.
>
> My pulse beats low: to the pulseless earth
> emptied of mirth and song I go.
> I stand on the edge of death in dearth.
> Wine-blood of Christ make the scarlet snow.[42]

In his major poetic work, *The First Exile* (1944), a 4,000-line sequence of lyrics on the religious life of Saint Colmcille, Farren rewrites the Irish epic tradition and the literary revival's notion of romantic heroism into specifically religious terms. At one point, Farren describes in some detail Colmcille's efforts to save the *Táin Bó Cuailgne,* an attempt that serves Farren as a fitting emblem of the absorption of Ireland's pagan culture—the historical ground on which the revival constructed its vision of cultural unity and identity—into its Christian one. This is also the history that Clarke drew on for his collection *Pilgrimage* but, unlike Clarke, Farren is not interested in using Ireland's Christian past as a vehicle for critiquing contemporary Catholicism.

As Clarke recognized, Farren was a gifted translator of poetry in Irish. His work in this vein combines the sensitivity to assonance that characterizes much of Clarke's and Higgins's poetry with specific attention paid to what Clarke called "the systematical alliteration of Gaelic verse." [43] Farren's version of "Úna Bhán" (entitled "Star without Fault" in *Thronging Feet,* 1936) demonstrates how he manipulates assonance, alliteration, and the long flexible line of Mangan and Ferguson to produce a strikingly un-English note:

> 'Tis Úna has hair looped and twisty like horns of the kine,
> her two eyes cup quiet like dew, and drown fire like wine,
> her arms sweep out white as the salmon leap light in the sun.
> O my salt sea of grief! That my life and her life were one.[44]

However accomplished Farren was at this kind of writing, it was his misfortune to be at the end of a well-worn tradition rather than at the beginning of a new one. It was also his misfortune to be facing backward and inward at a time, especially after World War II, when pressures were increasing in Ireland, and particularly among Irish writers, to face forward and outward. Once the very different voices of Patrick Kavanagh and Denis Devlin—not to mention that of Clarke during the second half of his career—had become established, Farren's preoccupation with reconciling Gaelic authenticity and Catholic belief would appear, like much of the Irish-Ireland outlook that it expressed, quaintly irrelevant.

CHAPTER SIXTEEN

NEW PERSPECTIVES AT
MIDCENTURY

For all the new directions charted by Irish poets working in the first two decades after the establishment of Irish independence, much of the poetry of the period was still strongly derivative of the literary revival and marked by a strongly provincial focus. It was not until the 1940s and 1950s that Irish poetry began to disengage itself decidedly from its own considerable recent history, and that Irish writers began to shape a self-consciously modern as well as distinctively Irish poetry. The death of Yeats in 1939 may have had something to do with the sense of liberation that accompanied these changes, as did, more certainly, the end of World War II, which, because of Irish neutrality, had generated a particularly acute sense of Ireland's alienation from Europe. Austin Clarke was, again, an exemplary figure in many of these changes. After a seventeen-year poetic silence, Clarke emerged in the mid-1950s as a public poet in the Swiftian mode, and for the next two decades kept up a relentless barrage of satirical poetry directed against political and social practices that he saw as grounded in anti-humanistic attitudes inspired by the Irish Catholic Church. In this role, which departed markedly from revival poetics, Clarke brought to bear on Irish poetic practice some of the assumptions about the public responsibilities of the poet that had been developing among writers in England and Europe since the 1930s. Clarke also published in this period a long, painfully candid poetic account of a time in his early manhood spent in a mental institution, a poem that recognized the importance of the kind of confessional poetry that was dominating American writing at the time. Thirteen years before Clarke's first collection of satirical poems appeared in 1955, Patrick Kavanagh published "The Great Hunger," which radically challenged not only the revival's romanticization of the Irish peasant but also the cultural idealization of rural life that was central to Irish-Ireland formulations of Irish identity and that de Valera had carried from the early years of independence into the 1940s and 1950s. By focusing on psychological, emotional, and sexual issues in rural Ireland, Kavanagh also modified the long tradition of Irish writing about the land, which had emphasized politics and economics, a shift that reflected modernist preoccupations with psychology and sexuality. Kavanagh also made the problem of the poet in modern Ireland a central theme of his work, and his ceaseless, self-conscious defense of the integrity of the artist, owing much to Yeats, was extremely important for later Irish poets such as Seamus Heaney and Eavan Boland. Although less radically innovative than Kavanagh, Padraic Fallon also was preoccupied, in modernist fashion, with the function of the poet in society and the nature of art, and his work is of particular interest for the ways in which it overtly struggled with the presence of Yeats. Finally, Denis Devlin shifted the ground of Clarke's earlier critique of specific Irish Catholic practices and doctrines to a broader, more widely modernist consideration of Irish Catholicism in the context of the question of religious salvation and meaning in the modern world. Drawing on international rather than nationalist poetic models, Devlin's philosophical approach to his own Catholicism distinguished his work from that of earlier Catholic poets in Ireland, especially from those for whom Catholicism was inseparable from political or cultural nationalism, such as Joseph Plunkett and Robert Farren.

The emergence of Austin Clarke's poetic voice from a seventeen-year silence —a period in which Clarke was active writing plays and, with Robert Farren, establishing and running Dublin's Lyric Theatre—brought to the foreground of modern Irish poetry the figure of the public poet. The assumption that the poet had a responsibility to engage political and social realities, which was central to the development of nationalist poetry in the nineteenth century, had come under significant pressure from the aesthetics of the revival, particularly from Yeats's distrust of overtly political poetry. But with the appearance of Clarke's satirical poems in the 1950s and 1960s, the nationalist agenda that had dominated public poetry in Ireland throughout the nineteenth century was not so much restored as substantially modified to include social issues often neglected by earlier nationalist ideology, and to provide a vehicle for Clarke's social liberalism. "It takes us many years," Clarke wrote in his memoirs *Twice Round the Black Church,* "to learn that the passion for justice and the welfare of all, once it has been aroused, is the deepest one in moral life." [1] Throughout the 1950s and 1960s, in forms ranging from epigrams and occasional lyrics to semi-meditative poems, Clarke exercised that passion, criticizing Ireland as a church-dominated society in which individual freedom was thwarted, social justice ignored, and the principles of nationalism betrayed. These poems carried forward the critique of Irish Catholicism that Clarke had expressed in the historical and confessional lyrics of *Pilgrimage* and *Night and Morning,* but shifted the focus from the personal to the public, from the church's doctrines and teachings to the church's force as a social and political institution. In remaking himself into a public poet concerned with social issues, Clarke was reviving a tradition of Irish poetry that went back to Swift and his circle in the eighteenth century and had been largely submerged since then; in addition, he was marking out a significant path leading away from the romantic aesthetics of the revival.[2]

Many of Clarke's satires took the form of occasional poems: the issuance of a stamp portraying the Madonna and infant Jesus for example, provoked a sharp attack on the church's intervention in the "mother-and-child" scheme of 1951 ("Mother and Child"); a fire in a Co. Cavan orphanage run by the church, and a statement made by a local bishop in response to it, prompted a particularly Swiftian response in "Three Poems about Children":

> Cast-iron step and rail
> Could but prolong the wailing:
> Has not a Bishop declared
> That flame-wrapped babes are spared
> Our life-time of temptation?
> Leap, mind, in consolation
> For heart can only lodge
> Itself, plucked out by logic.
> Those children, charred in Cavan,
> Passed straight through Hell to Heaven.[3]

In part, Clarke abhorred what Irish society had become under this kind of clerical influence because socially conservative religious values betrayed his own nationalist convictions, which were grounded in liberalism. This view called into serious question the Irish-Ireland assumption that nationalism and Catholicism were fundamentally interrelated. In "Celebrations," the opening poem of his collection *Ancient Lights* (1955), Clarke brings to the occasion of the Eucharistic Congress of 1932 his characteristic irony and invective to argue that the new Ireland has exchanged one form of tyranny for another, and that the republican principles of the Easter Rising have been betrayed by the conservative force of a church-dominated society:

> Let ageing politicians pray
> Again, hoardings recount our faith,
> The blindfold woman in a rage
> Condemn her own for treason:
> No steeple topped the scale that Monday,
> Rebel souls had lost their savings
> And looters braved the street.[4]

Clarke's public poetry also included a number of lengthy, less occasional poems that combined satiric invective with reflective subjectivity. The satire in these poems is often directed at the destruction of the environment and at materialism, while their meditative passages explore, among other things, the poet's tenuous position in a society governed by greed. In the best of these, "The Loss of Strength" (*Too Great a Vine*, 1957), Clarke conflates his own declining strength—he had just recovered from a serious illness—with what he saw as the weakening of Irish culture and tradition at the hands of materialism, a point of view obviously indebted to Yeats. The poem opens by counting the costs of "progress":

> Farm-brooks that come down to Rathfarnham
> By grange-wall, tree-stop, from the hills,
> Might never have heard the rustle in barn-dance,
> The sluicing, bolting, of their flour-mills,
> Nor have been of use in the steady reel
> On step-boards of the iron wheel-rim,
> For Dublin crowds them in: they wheeze now
> Beneath new pavements, name old laneways,
> Discharge, excrete, their centuries,
> Man-trapped in concrete, deeper drainage.
> Yet, littling by itself, I found one
> That had never run to town.[5]

That final image of the brook that has escaped destruction represents for Clarke not just nature but also Clarke's slender hopes for the survival of art and humanism in an increasingly materialistic Ireland.

Like Yeats, Clarke enjoyed a period of extraordinary poetic fertility late in his life. Beginning with the publication of *Flight to Africa* in 1963, when he was sixty-seven, Clarke produced, right up to his death in 1974, a greater volume and greater variety of poems than he had during all the previous years. As in much of the poetry that Yeats wrote during the last decade of his life, eroticism figured largely in Clarke's later work, particularly in several narrative poems based on Irish and classical legends. This concern with sexuality represented an extension of a theme that pervades Clarke's writing, embodying, as Yeats's erotic poetry generally did not, a challenge to the puritanical values that Clarke saw the Catholic Church as fostering in modern Ireland. Particularly in those erotic poems that drew on the Gaelic tradition, such as "Phallomeda," "The Healing of Mis," and "The Wooing of Becfola," Clarke called into question the Irish-Ireland insistence on identifying Ireland's Gaelic past with contemporary, puritanical Catholicism. Sexuality was also at the center of Clarke's long confessional poem, *Mnemosyne Lay in Dust* (1966), based on his mental breakdown as a young man, when he spent thirteen months in St. Patrick's Hospital. The poem is specifically interested in the psychological effects of sexual repression, which are documented with startling vividness and intensity. Clarke's critique of Irish Catholicism also informs the many "free variations," as he called them, of Irish poems that he produced in his final years.[6] Clarke's subversive eroticism, as well as his sensitivity to the formal qualities of poetry in Irish, are perhaps most evident in a series of versions of Turlough Carolan's songs published in *Flight to Africa*. Almost every Irish poet working in translation had tried his or her hand at a Carolan song, but one need only compare Clarke's "Mabel Kelly" with earlier translations by Charlotte Brooke, Thomas Furlong, Samuel Ferguson, and George Sigerson to judge the extent of Clarke's authenticity and to see how that authenticity undermines the identification of the Gaelic tradition with Jansenist Catholicism:

>   Lucky the husband
>   Who puts his hand beneath her head.
>   They kiss without scandal
>   Happiest two near feather-bed.
>   He sees the tumble of brown hair
>   Unplait, the breasts, pointed and bare
>   When nightdress shows
>   From dimple to toe-nail,
>   All Mabel glowing in it, here, there, everywhere.[7]

Clarke's version of Aodh Mac Gabhráin's "Pléaráca na Ruarcach," the poem that Swift rendered as "The Description of an Irish Feast," is equally sexual, and equally authentic. Swift's short lines and English rhyme scheme are replaced by the line and stanzaic structure of the original, and by a pattern of assonance that closely follows Mac Gabhráin:

>   Let O'Rourke's great feast be remembered by those
>   Who were at it, are gone, or not yet begotten.
>   A hundred and forty hogs, heifers and ewes
>   Were basting each plentiful day and gallons of pot-still
>   Poured folderols into the mugs. Unmarried
>   And married were gathering early for pleasure and sport.
>   'Your clay pipe is broken.' 'My breeches lost.' 'Look at my skirt torn.'
>   'And where are those fellows who went half under my mantle
>   And burst my two garters?' 'Sure, no one's the wiser.' [8]

It was, ironically enough, Clarke's total commitment both to authenticating Ireland's past and to exposing the failings of the Irish present that ultimately limited his influence on the generation of writers who came after him. Patrick Kavanagh (1904–1967) seemed to these writers a more relevant, because less emphatically Irish, predecessor. Especially since his death in 1967, when writers such as Seamus Heaney and Eavan Boland were just starting to publish, Kavanagh has increasingly been admired by contemporary poets in Ireland as someone who maintained his poetic integrity in the face of various pressures on his work: Yeats's shadow, the legacy of the literary revival, and Irish-Ireland representations of national purpose and identity.[9] For Heaney, who was struggling with the problem of how to accommodate in his art the violence in Northern Ireland during the past quarter-century without betraying his own aesthetic principles, and for Boland, who was seeking to establish her own specifically feminine voice in a tradition with a history of excluding, marginalizing, or co-opting women poets, Kavanagh represented an inspiring model. In effect, Kavanagh attempted to redefine romanticism in Irish writing by divorcing it from all nationalist agendas, be they political, as in much nineteenth-century separatist poetry, or cultural, as in much of the poetry associated with the revival.

Kavanagh himself saw his career as moving through three phases, beginning with poems based on his experiences growing up in rural Co. Monaghan, followed by a more public phase in which he employed satire to attack the literary establishment in Dublin, and concluding with a group of poems in which bitterness was replaced by a return to the relative simplicity and lucidity of his earlier work, a shift apparently precipitated in part by Kavanagh's recovery from surgery for lung cancer in 1955. "We begin by being simple," Kavanagh once said, "and then for years plough through complexities and affectation to come back to where we begin." [10] As the pattern of innocence, experience, and redemption lying behind this comment suggests, Kavanagh was essentially a visionary poet whose work was powerfully shaped by romantic aesthetics.[11] In the preface to his *Collected Poems,* published three years before his death, Kavanagh summed up his view of the poet in highly romantic terms:

> There is, of course, a poetic movement which sees poetry materialistically. The writers of this school see no transcendent nature in the poet; they are practical chaps, excellent technicians. But somehow or other I have a belief in poetry as a mystical thing, and a dangerous thing.[12]

The most significant influence on Kavanagh's poems about rural Ireland is not Yeats or other Irish poets, but Wordsworth, and however realistically these poems may represent the life of the Irish peasant, they are essentially meditative, often highly self-reflexive lyrics in the romantic tradition, poems in which the terrain of Co. Monaghan becomes a vehicle for moments of imaginative transcendence. Part of Kavanagh's achievement lies in his ability to negotiate

between closely observed details, rendered in relatively prosaic, often colloquial language, and moments of visionary intensity, rendered in a highly
charged poetic language that transcends local detail. These two levels of discourse, and two ways of looking at the natural world, the social world, and the
poet's relationship to both, are evident in one of Kavanagh's best-known early
lyrics, "Inniskeen Road: July Evening," a sonnet from *Ploughshares:*

> The bicycles go by in twos and threes—
> There's a dance in Billy Brennan's barn to-night,
> And there's the half-talk code of mysteries
> And the wink-and-elbow language of delight.
> Half-past eight and there is not a spot
> Upon a mile of road, no shadow thrown
> That might turn out a man or woman, not
> A footfall tapping secrecies of stone.
>
> I have what every poet hates in spite
> Of all the solemn talk of contemplation.
> Oh, Alexander Selkirk knew the plight
> Of being king and government and nation.
> A road, a mile of kingdom, I am king
> Of banks and stones and every blooming thing.[13]

"Kerr's Ass," from Kavanagh's last collection, *Come Dance with Kitty Stobling* (1960), while negotiating the same opposition, describes and enacts the
process of artistic creation in a way that clearly reflects Kavanagh's romantic
theory of imagination and memory:

> We borrowed the loan of Kerr's big ass
> To go to Dundalk with butter,
> Brought him home the evening before the market
> An exile that night in Mucker.
>
> We heeled up the cart before the door,
> We took the harness inside—
> The straw-stuffed straddle, the broken breeching
> With bits of bull-wire tied;
>
> The winkers that had no choke-band,
> The collar and the reins . . .
> In Ealing Broadway, London Town
> I name their several names
>
> Until a world comes to life—
> Morning, the silent bog,

And the God of imagination waking
In a Mucker fog.[14]

As both these poems suggest, Kavanagh's romanticism is embodied primarily in the poetic personality, usually depicted as standing apart from what is being described, as in "Iniskeen Road." This emphasis on the poet as romantically alienated from his culture, which owes more than a little to Yeats's representations of the modern artist in Ireland, effectively subverts the traditional fusion of romanticism and nationalism manifest in political terms in much nineteenth-century nationalist verse and in more generally cultural terms in the revival. For Kavanagh, romanticism, far from being inherent in Irish culture or politics, provides a ground for critiquing Irish life. In "The Great Hunger," Patrick Maguire's inability to perceive the spiritual power of the landscape, and accordingly his own spiritual and imaginative possibilities, makes him a tragic figure. The anti-romantic values and conditions of rural Ireland, including the effects of a Jansenist Irish Catholicism, cause this paralyzing blindness; if Maguire "dare not rise to pluck the fantasies/From the fruited tree of Life," it is because when he looks out on the world around him, he sees only "a wet weed twined about his toe." [15] In Kavanagh's view, false romanticizations of Irish rural life mask this failure of true romantic understanding, the cause of the emotional and psychological famine afflicting the modern Irish peasant:

The world looks on
And talks of the peasant:
The peasant has no worries;
In his little lyrical fields
He ploughs and sows;
He eats fresh food,
He loves fresh women,
He is his own master
As it was in the Beginning
The simpleness of peasant life.[16]

For Kavanagh, the possibility of romantic redemption from this unhappy condition lies less in the culture, history, or landscape of Ireland than in the person of the poet who is inevitably alienated from that culture. Kavanagh's poems are obsessed with the nature and function of the artist. Even "The Great Hunger," often read as a realistic account of Irish rural life and a critique of false representations of it, is a decidedly self-conscious, self-reflexive piece of writing. The well-known opening of the poem not only describes the conditions of Maguire's life but also wonders, from the point of view of a distanced poet-observer, about the value of writing the poem. Both the flesh and the word are threatened by the paralyzing clay:

> Clay is the word and clay is the flesh
> Where the potato-gatherers like mechanised scarecrows move
> Along the side-fall of the hill—Maguire and his men.
> If we watch them an hour is there anything we can prove
> Of life as it is broken-backed over the Book
> Of Death? Here crows gabble over worms and frogs
> And the gulls like old newspapers are blown clear of the hedges, luckily.
> Is there some light of imagination in these wet clods?
> Or why do we stand here shivering?[17]

Kavanagh later came to dislike "The Great Hunger," reportedly because it told "the sociological lie, the public lie, like Spender and Day Lewis."[18] By that time, after his brush with death in 1955, Kavanagh's career and life had come full circle, in his view, and he was writing remarkably Wordsworthian poems such as "Canal Bank Walk":

> Leafy-with-love banks and the green waters of the canal
> Pouring redemption for me, that I do
> The will of God, wallow in the habitual, the banal,
> Grow with nature again as before I grew.[19]

Kavanagh's critique of the tendency to romanticize the Irish peasant was a response both to the literary revival and to the cultural politics of de Valera's Ireland.[20] Kavanagh's view of the Irish peasant as repressed and unfulfilled is rooted in his romanticism, but in "The Great Hunger" he also relentlessly documents the specific forces that are responsible for Maguire's spiritual and emotional hunger: "Religion, the fields and the fear of the Lord/And Ignorance giving him the coward's blow"[21]. In this aspect of his work, Kavanagh shared much with Clarke. Maguire's substitution of his mother and the land for a fulfilled sexual relationship, for example ("The twisting sod rolls over on her back"; and "She stayed too long,/Wife and mother in one"[22]), embodies a sexual paralysis that finds echoes in characters like Martha Blake and Maurice Devane in Clarke's work, and both writers portray Irish Catholicism as a force working against human fulfillment and freedom: "The chapel pressing its low ceiling over them."[23] Unlike Clarke, Kavanagh was remarkably silent on more specifically political issues, even those that would seem to have been extremely difficult to ignore. Kavanagh was, after all in his mid- to late teens when the Government of Ireland Act transformed his native Co. Monaghan into a border county and the Anglo-Irish and Civil War were being fought. According to one account, Kavanagh once helped the Irish Republican Army pull down some telegraph wires in Monaghan, and his sympathies lay with the republican side in the Civil War.[24] But there are no traces of this in his poetry. One explanation has to do with Kavanagh's family; Kavanagh's brother, Peter, has described the Kavanagh household in the years between 1918 and 1925 as decidedly apolitical:

> I slept through the so-called War of Independence and even through the Civil War. Fortunately for Patrick he was too young to become involved with either. Not that he would have, had he been older: Father would not have have allowed it. We were never involved in politics.[25]

When Kavanagh did turn to satire, about the same time that Clarke did, his targets were generally literary rather than political or social; indeed, Kavanagh's satires are more usefully read as part of the growth of his poetic mind than as commentary on Irish culture in the 1950s.[26] In any case, Kavanagh eventually abandoned the satirical mode, in part because it seemed to take him outside the province of his true, ineluctably romantic, poetic personality, as he makes clear in a poem with the appropriately Wordsworthian title of "Prelude":

> But satire is unfruitful prayer,
> Only wild shoots of pity there,
> And you must go inland and be
> Lost in compassion's ecstasy,
> Where suffering soars in summer air—
> The millstone has become a star.[27]

Kavanagh's rejection of the satirical mode also represented an abandonment of specifically national issues—what it means to be an Irish poet, for example—and a reaffirmation of his faith in the local and the personal as fit subject matter for art. Kavanagh was consistently suspicious of various constructs of Irishness, most of which he considered at best artificial and at worst destructive of any understanding of the realities of Irish life or of the poetic life. At times, this scepticism seemed to spring from Kavanagh's romantic aesthetics: "Poetry is not Irish or any other nationality; and when writers such as Messrs. Clarke, Farren and the late F. R. Higgins pursue Irishness as a poetic end they are merely exploiting incidental local color." [28] But his hostility to nationalist notions of Irish identity was also capable of generating a shrill nonsense: "there has never been a tradition of Irish poetry in Ireland. . . . it is remarkable that in a thousand years Ireland has not produced a major poet or, indeed, a good minor poet." [29] Whatever the source or validity of these sentiments, much of Kavanagh's significance to the poets who followed in his wake stems from his efforts to resist the powerful tendency to write about the Irish experience in terms of national categories. For Kavanagh, the poet's central struggle was to pursue and preserve his poetic identity and integrity, and it was the local, the parochial, that provided both the most secure ground from which that struggle could be waged, and at the same time, the most powerful source of imaginative inspiration and transcendence. If, as Kavanagh says at the beginning of his poem "Auditors In," the problem that confronts him is "to be eloquent yet sincere," the way to address that problem is to "take yourself in hand/And dig and ditch your authentic land." [30]

As both Kavanagh and Clarke made clear, Ireland's literary past, especially the recent past of the revival, could be as threatening as it was inspiring. Ten years after Yeats's death, Clarke said: "Yeats was rather like an enormous oak-tree, which, of course, kept us in the shade." [31] Padraic Fallon (1905–1974) responded to the pressures of that literary past by making the process of coming to terms with it, especially the presence of Yeats, a central theme of his work. In doing so, Fallon ran certain risks—and his work has been criticized for falling too much under Yeats's shadow—but the thematizing of his relationship to Yeats effectively represented both the extent to which modern Irish poets were necessarily writing out of a considerable anxiety of influence and one way of confronting that anxiety.

The literary relationship between Fallon and Yeats was determined by geography as well as by literary history. Fallon was born and reared in Athenry, Co. Galway—in his own words, "as the crow flies fifteen miles away" [32] from Yeats's tower at Ballylee. But Fallon's experience of that area was decidedly un-Yeatsian. As his son has written, the Fallon family was "typical . . . of the new Ireland which was moving from the land to the town and cities, forming a new bourgeoisie" [33]; his father was a cattle-and-sheep dealer, and the family owned several businesses in the town. Although Fallon was closer to Irish rural and provincial life than Yeats could be, and more knowledgeable about Ireland's Gaelic tradition,[34] the relationship between them as Fallon constructed it in his poems was more complex than this kind of difference might suggest. Fallon found important points of identification with Yeats, whose scepticism and alienation, deepened by the tumultuous events in Ireland in the 1910s and 1920s, provided a position from which Fallon could write about his own post-World War II period, when Ireland seemed even further removed from the heroic Ireland that Yeats saw as having been eclipsed by the greasy tills of middle-class materialism, and when the role of the poet in Irish society seemed problematic, to say the least. In "Yeats's Tower at Ballylee," based on a visit that he made to Thoor Ballylee in 1950, when the Korean War was beginning, Fallon describes Yeats as having been driven to despair by the pressure of events beyond his control, a despair that Fallon, contemplating the start of another war, finds sadly relevant:

> Rain and desolation, isolation
> And fear in civil war can bring a man
> To that harsh point in contemplation
> Where soul no longer sees the sun.
>
> .   .   .
>
> This tower where the poet thought to play
> Out some old romance to the end caught up
> The dream and the dreamer in its brutal way
> And the dream died here upon the crumbling top.
> I know the terror of his vision now.[35]

It has been argued that Yeats's voice prevented Fallon from establishing his own,[36] but at times that voice is deliberately incorporated into Fallon's writing as a means to measure the extent to which his own world has become unpoetic and unheroic.

This kind of sympathy with Yeats is not, however, unqualified in Fallon's work. Fallon's writing about Ireland is particularly conscious of the discontinuous nature of the Irish tradition, and of the tensions between its Gaelic and English components; in this dichotomy, Yeats represents an inevitable and essentially class-determined alienation from the Gaelic roots of Irish culture.[37] In "Yeats at Athenry Perhaps," a poem in which Fallon imagines Yeats as waiting in Athenry for a train to Gort, the distance between Yeats, "an aimless/ Straying gentleman," and "I/The jerseyed fellow driving out the cows"[38] cannot be readily bridged, certainly not by the romantic aesthetics with which Yeats, early in his career, sought to construct a new cultural unity for Ireland:

> I doubt
> He bothered with us, all his sight turned in;
> Some poems come better waiting for a train.
>
> And that winged footprint could have jarred
> The peasant metres of a street given over
> To baker, grocer, butcher and
> The treadmill of the till. . . .
>
> .   .   .
>
> No, he'd have sat down by the line and waited
> Melting his bits of ore or watched the sky
> Jolt from the saltmills of the Atlantic over
> A town that died so often of the rain;
> Why muddy a feathered foot when a great house waited
> Over in Coole among the trees
> (He liked his heraldry alive, well baited)
> With all the amenities for Muse and man,

> Leda's kingbird on a lake, a lawn
> For Juno's peacock, tranquil as a frieze.[39]

Fallon's interest in Ireland's Gaelic tradition is often embodied in his work in the figure of Anthony Raftery (Antoine Ó Reachtabhra), the early nineteenth-century blind Gaelic poet usually seen as the last of the wandering bards in Ireland.[40] Raftery is also an important figure in Yeats's "The Tower," which presents his song about a local girl named Mary Hynes as an example of art's power to create a powerful reality of the imagination. In "Letter from Ballylee," Fallon retells this story, presenting Mary Hynes as a girl violated by one of those hard-riding country gentlemen whom Yeats, in "Under Ben Bulben," recommends to Irish poets following in his wake as a fit subject for art:

> Raftery, a tramp poet,
> Sung for the thatches around the homespun girl
> Whose name was Mary Hynes.
> Later, of course, the beauty was debauched
> By some hard-riding nameless
> Country gentleman,
> And died lost and wrinkled in
> A bog cabin.[41]

If that image suggests that certain kinds of Anglo-Irish writing constitute an aggressive exploitation of the native Gaelic culture, Fallon was also suspicious of efforts to portray the Gaelic tradition as inherently superior to the traditions that modified or displaced it—precisely the point of view on which the cultural politics of the Irish-Ireland movement were based. In "For Paddy Mac," a poem written in memory of his friend and fellow poet Patrick Mac Donogh, Fallon satirizes this kind of stereotyping, while insisting on the impoverished reality that this kind of idealization too often obscures:

> Once, so long ago,
> You used to probe me gently for the lost
> Country, sensing somehow in my airs
> The vivid longlipped peasantry of
> Last century
>
> And those bronze men pushed
> With their diminishing herds far out on
> The last ledge of original earth,
> Formorian types
> In the big one-eyed sky.

. . .

Homer's people,
And wasn't I lucky, born with
Boundaries floating, language still making
Out of the broadlands where my fathers
Tended their clouds of ewes?

Bunkum, Dear P. The thing was gone, or
Never was. And we were the leftovers,
Lord-ridden and pulpit-thumped for all our wild
Cudgels of Gaelic. Ours was Lever's
One-horse country; the bailiff at the bighouse door.

. . .

That was my country, beast, sky, and anger:
For music a mad piper in the mud;
No poets I knew of; or they mouthed each other's words;
Such low powered gods
They died, as they were born, in byres.[42]

Fallon is working here in the realistic, demythologizing manner of Kavanagh, and much of Fallon's work is concerned with portraying realistically the rural Ireland that he knew from his early life. Unlike Kavanagh, however, Fallon was specifically concerned with the political and social issues, including class prejudice, that lay behind this impoverishment. In a poem entitled "Peasantry," Fallon uses broad strokes to define the condition of the Irish peasant in terms of the prejudiced attitudes of landlords, extending the realistic portrayal of the Irish peasant in a poem such as Padraic Colum's "The Plougher" to an analysis of class:

In a thatch
That could be a stable but for the open hearth
A man is born, the tiller of the earth.
Labour there, dumb brothers,
And have no wild itch
To raise yourselves. The world is to your betters.

. . .

Walk the town,
Tiller, interloper, up and down, we
Who live upon you will allow this free,
But close our heavy doors
To any clown
Born to the thatch in the boor-stink of the byres.[43]

Although Fallon was influenced by modernist poetics, as is evident in the form of many of his poems and in his translations of Baudelaire, Mallarmé,

and Rimbaud, modernism was unable, as Seamus Heaney observed, to displace
the "native tin whistle" in his poetry.[44] That tin whistle can also be heard from
time to time in the work of Denis Devlin (1908–1959), but among modern
Irish poets it is Devlin, along with MacGreevy, whose work most effectively
reflects the modernist revolution in poetry. Devlin was particularly influenced
by contemporary French poetry—he took a degree from University College,
Dublin, in 1929 in English and French, and translated the work of a number of
French writers, including Paul Eduord and Paul Valéry—and by American
modernism, especially as it was manifest in the work of the Fugitive poets; in
his career with the Department of Foreign Affairs, he was posted to Washington
during the 1940s, and there met Allen Tate and Robert Penn Warren, a selection
of whose poetry he later edited. More broadly, Devlin's work was profoundly
informed by the modernist vision of the world as a loveless and soulless
wasteland, a vision that had, for Devlin, specifically Irish implications. He saw
Ireland as emotionally and spiritually paralyzed, and, like Clarke, considered
contemporary Irish Catholicism to be a primary cause of this condition. In
"Lough Derg" (Lough Derg and Other Poems, 1946), Devlin portrays the
Lough Derg pilgrims in terms not far from those of Clarke's attacks on the
church's puritanical qualities:

> The poor in spirit on their rosary rounds,
> The jobless with their whiskey-angered eyes,
> The pink bank clerks, the tip-hat papal counts,
> And drab, kind women their tonsured mockery tries,
> Glad invalids on penitential feet.[45]

But whereas Clarke's poetry in this vein is almost always focused on the
specific experience of Irish Catholicism and often on his own Irish Catholic
upbringing, Devlin's writing seeks to place these "poor in spirit" in the wider
context of the spiritual wasteland that is at the center of much modernist
writing. In this regard, it is Eliot, more than any writer in the Irish tradition,
who is crucial to Devlin, and Eliot's influence can be seen plainly in some of
Devlin's writing about Dublin, as in these lines from "Liffey Bridge":

> Trailing behind
> Tired poses
> How they all
> Fulfill their station!
> The young with masks and
> The old with faces
>
> .   .   .
>
> The houses lean
> Against the wind

> Won't you give over?
> Say, what about
> That second coming?[46]

Like Eliot, Devlin was essentially a religious poet; rather than reject Christianity in favor of the secular humanism that motivated Clarke's critique of Irish Catholicism or of the romanticism that informed Kavanagh's portrayal of the empty, church-dominated life of Patrick Maguire, Devlin's poetry seeks to recover Christian faith and express religious ecstasy through the poetic imagination.[47] There is some precedent in the Irish tradition for this kind of writing, such as Lionel Johnson's religious poems, but in postindependence Ireland, with the Irish Catholic Church such a powerful and conservative force, Irish poets writing about Catholicism tended to take aggressively hostile positions, as did Clarke and Kavanagh. For Devlin, the survival of the Christian faith is of paramount importance, and it depends in part on rescuing Christianity from asceticism, on seeing, as he says in a poem entitled "Est Prodest," that God "must be proved in time."[48] In "Meditation at Avila," *(Lough Derg),* Devlin employs the figure of Saint Teresa to represent the Jansenist doctrines that he, like Clarke, finds more destructive than inspiring of religious belief:

> O Santa, Santa Teresa,
> Covetous, burning virgin!
> Scorning to nourish body's
> Farmlands with soul's
> Modulating rains.[49]

Devlin opposes to this asceticism his faith in the presence of the spiritual in the physical, a faith in which soul and flesh can be reconciled. In "Meditation at Avila," Devlin addresses his soul in Wordsworthian terms, celebrating its transcendent powers, but recognizes also that the spiritual can be experienced only through the transient flesh:

> You, at once the radiance and the kindling
> Of dream and deed sown in my travelling.
> What is your word for me?
> I hear: it is the seed, the sap, the fruit
> All flowering in a doomed and sunny moment.[50]

Since the spiritual is present "In love's body,"[51] as Devlin puts it, this religious vision also reconciles the conflict so central in Clarke's work between religion and sexuality.[52] Devlin wrote a considerable amount of love poetry, insisting in it that human love, including sexual passion, was a vehicle for experiencing divine love. In his long philosophical poem "The Heavenly Foreigner" (1950), grounded in the belief that "the world glows with mortal divinity,"[53] the spiritual understanding of the narrator grows out of his love for a woman. In "Est Prodest," Devlin asserts that the only "proof" available to man of the existence of God is the relationship between two lovers:

> Mirrors flashing each other
> That's the only proof
> Let there be no absence
> The only solution
> Is the flesh between mirrors.[54]

Devlin paid a price for writing this kind of dense and often difficult poetry. He has always attracted far fewer readers, at least inside Ireland, than have the more accessible Kavanagh and the more specifically Irish Clarke. Also, Devlin wrote little or no poetry of recognizably political import; as his friend Brian Coffey once remarked, writing poems implied for Devlin "a freedom that neither reasons of state nor policing power can be permitted to restrain or constrain."[55] Even the few poems of Devlin's that might be read as politically revolutionary, such as "Bacchanal" and "Old Jacobin," are political only in the vaguest sense, and have little to do specifically with the Irish situation. Devlin did write one striking elegy on an Irish political figure, "The Tomb of Michael Collins" (*Later Poems [1946–1959]*), a poem rooted in the tradition of political elegy stretching back to Thomas Davis's "Lament for the Death of Eoghan Ruadh O'Neill" in the 1840s. Devlin's poem praises Collins as a man of courage, and its conclusion appeals to the tradition of political martyrdom so prevalent in Irish nationalist writing: "How sometimes death magnifies him who dies,/And some, though mortal, have achieved their race."[56] But the poem as a whole is much more interested in interpreting Collins's death as a moment of transcendence than in placing it in the usual context of nationalist feeling. Earlier in the poem, Devlin interprets one of the most common icons of Irish nationalism in terms of his own spiritual vision:

> There are the Four Green Fields we loved in boyhood,
> There are some reasons it's no loss to die for:
> Even it's no loss to die for having lived;
> It is inside our life the angel happens
> Life, the gift that God accepts or not.[57]

The movement here from the political to the religious reverses the pattern that dominates much nationalist writing in Ireland; even in the work of an intensely religious poet such as Joseph Mary Plunkett, the dark rose that reddens into bloom represents, first and foremost, the spirit of political martyrdom, something for which religious martyrdom, including the death of Christ, serves chiefly as a model. In this way, the "The Tomb of Michael Collins" manifests the tendency in Devlin's work to revise, or extend, the tradition of Irish writing in the interest of concerns that ultimately transcend the Irish situation. As one of Devlin's inheritors, John Montague, once said, Devlin was "the first poet of Irish Catholic background to take the world as his province." [58] As Montague's own work demonstrates, he was not the last.

C O V E R T   V O I C E S :   W O M E N   P O E T S
A F T E R   T H E   R E V I V A L

Irish women poets writing in the eighteenth and nineteenth centuries and
during the years of the literary revival achieved a certain visibility, even if their
work was often subsumed by the various literary or political movements that
both supported and contained them. The poetry of Irish women writing in the
wake of the revival and the establishment of the Irish Free State was much less
widely noticed in its day, and has since been largely forgotten. The relative
silence of the female poetic voice in these years was part of a larger phenomenon. The political, cultural, and religious conservatism that dominated Irish
society in the wake of independence often meant that women were denied
cultural and political influence of all kinds; de Valera's famous vision of Ireland, for example, with its emphasis on the conventional family, Catholicism,
and the traditional rural way of life, had few if any places in it for women
outside the home. The effective absence of women from the mainstream of
Irish poetry in these years, when Irish writing in general was not focused
around well-defined cultural or political movements, also illustrates the extent
to which women writing in Ireland had always been dependent on such male-
controlled enterprise: Swift's literary circle in Dublin in the early decades of the
eighteenth century, the Young Ireland and Fenian movements in the nineteenth
century, and the literary revival at the turn of the twentieth century. Finally,
Irish women writers in the mid-twentieth century were working against well-
established prejudices given authority by an entire tradition of reductive, repressive stereotypes of Irish women, including representations of them as icons of
political or cultural nationalism—the kind of attitudes that poets such as Eavan
Boland, a generation or so later, would find it necessary to deconstruct to
establish their own voices. The results of all this were sadly predictable; even
women writing poetry of a relatively high caliber in these years, and confront-

ing some of the same issues that inform the work of writers such as MacGreevy, Clarke, and Kavanagh, rarely published enough to establish themselves or allow for the development of their art. Nevertheless, much of the poetry written by women in these years is of considerable interest, and it might indeed be argued that women such as Mary Devenport O'Neill, Blanaid Salkeld, Rhoda Coghill, Sheila Wingfield, Máire MacEntee, and Eithne Strong, in part because they worked outside specific political or cultural movements, pointed the way toward the relative independence of position and voice achieved by Ireland's contemporary women poets. Moreover, and possibly for the same reason, Irish women writing at this time tended to be open to experimentation and modernist influences, as in the imagistic work of O'Neill and Wingfield, and unconventional in their views of sexuality and morality in modern Ireland.

Mary Devenport O'Neill (1879–1967) had some connections with the male literary establishment of her day. She married the Galway novelist Joseph O'Neill in 1908, and kept a literary salon in Rathgar for a number of years; she also acted as a consultant to Yeats when he was working on *A Vision* (1925), and saw two of her one-act verse plays produced by Clarke's Lyric Theatre in the 1930s and 1940s.[1] She was, in addition, apparently well versed in modernist poetry, and her work shows signs of a particular interest in imagism.[2] In part because of these influences, O'Neill's writing about Ireland resists, as does the work of Devlin and MacGreevy, the romanticization of Irish experience frequently found among revival poets. In "The Midlands," for example, the ordinary, undramatic landscape of the Irish midlands is presented with imagistic precision as an alternative to the more romantic and conventionally celebrated landscape of the west:

> I've left the mountains
> With the sea behind,
> And come to stop
> Where there are meadows
> With a yellow top
> And separate shadows
> For each blade of grass:
> I see as I pass
> Great smooth cows lumbering home
> Beside canals
> With their long flat waters,
> And then I find
> In the wide sky
> The evening all alone.[3]

In a poem entitled "Galway," the modernist scepticism that informs O'Neill's work in general is applied specifically to the assumption upon which so much

cultural nationalist thinking, especially that of Irish Ireland, was grounded—
that the west of Ireland, always romantically conceived, represented the vital
cultural wellspring of the nation:

> This town is eaten through with memory
> Of pride and thick red Spanish wine and gold
> And a great come and go;
> But the sea is cold,
> And the spare, black trees
> Crouch in the withering breeze
> That blows from the sea,
> And the land stands bare and alone,
> For its warmth is turned away
> And its strength held in hard cold grey-blue stone.[4]

The poetry of Blanaid Salkeld (1880–1959) is formally more conservative
than O'Neill's—Samuel Beckett, in his famously carping essay "Recent Irish
Poetry," said he found much in Salkeld's *Hello Eternity!* "personal and moving, when not rendered blue in the face by the sonnet form"[5]—but it is also
more specifically concerned with the position of the woman writer in postindependence Ireland. Although that interest is sometimes obscured by Salkeld's
vaguely romantic aesthetics[6]—another difference between her and O'Neil—
and sometimes has to be teased out of her work, for Salkeld, the condition of
being a woman poet in Ireland made it necessary to be indirect rather than
direct, covert rather than overt. This is the subtext of her lengthy poem *The
Fox's Covert* (1935). In Salkeld's view, the female poetic imagination is essentially spiritual and semiotic, rather than material and symbolic, and, like the
fox in his covert, survives only by concealment:

> From the cold and wild merman I have concealed well,
> Motherly-wise.
> A small flame-holiness, male envy cannot quell.
> I feared much for the germ, faint-quickening so deep,
> And coiled about with day's coarse circumstance. As sweep
> Of furious floods gave tongue, I sighed a wordless spell
> Through my Apollo-drunken veins, through my heart's shell—
> Shielding the prize![7]

Later in the poem, this argument is cast in specifically Irish terms, with the
woman poet seen as under the possessive thumb of the predominantly male
Irish literary tradition:

> . . . 'Twas my enclosure, that small
> Untidy garden; but down in the valley's dream,
> A man draws up blithe trout from a shadow-swayed stream.
> Blooded silver will fade, the light, the curlew-call:
> Regret, regret. He stamps his wet boots in my hall—
> Owning my world.[8]

Salkeld might be said here to be rewriting Yeats's Connemara fisherman in feminist terms.

Salkeld was conscious of the poetic and subversive potential of the marginalized: "No doubt,/The Lost have epic history to tell," as she puts it in "Delerium," one of those sonnets in *Hello Eternity!* that apparently annoyed Beckett so much.[9] For Salkeld herself, however, the potential was not fully realized. *Hello Eternity!* and *The Fox's Covert* were published in the 1930s, when Salkeld was in her fifties, and there is one book in the 1940s and another in the 1950s, neither of them at all up to the standard of the earlier work. This decline in the quality of her work no doubt reflects the difficulties facing women poets in Ireland in general in these years, but Salkeld's sense of herself as an Irish poet was complicated by her background. She was born in Chittagong, India (now Pakistan), of Irish parents (her father was in the Indian medical service). Although she spent much of her childhood in Ireland, she married an English member of the Indian Civil Service, and moved back to Bombay as a young woman. Widowed at the age of twenty-eight, she returned to Ireland, joined the Abbey Theatre company, and started writing plays and poems. But her view of her Irishness was always somewhat ambiguous, and much of her poetry about Ireland carries the mark of the exile: "I was, babe and child,/ From that ancestral fount—amid the antic Forces of alien peoples, far exiled." [10] In a poem entitled "Even the Carrollers," from *Hello Eternity!*, her sense of being imaginatively exhausted is specifically related to this sense of alienation from the mainstream of Irish writing, the product of her background as well as her sex.

> I hate verse. I have lost faith. To the sky,
> Even the carollers sing cold to-night,
> Precise and stiff—their measure of delight.
> I know but emptiness and liberty.
> My craft grown old and crazy, I still ply
> Unwilling oar. No harbour is in sight.
> I shall not ride at anchor off the bight
> Of Innisfail, nor catch the beacon's eye.
> Unstable, dark, my rough inheritance—
> Mapped out by Fate's insoluble mistrust.[11]

The subversive potential of writing from the position of what Salkeld calls "The Lost" is at the center of the poetry of Rhoda Coghill (1903–). Coghill's work is remarkably divided between conventional descriptive poems in the mode of the English Georgian poets and highly unconventional poems that explore the dark underside of human consciousness, usually identified with female perception and experience, and express a specifically feminine sense of alienation and marginalization. There is no precedent in Irish poetry written by women for a poem like Coghill's "Dead" (*The Bright Hillside,* 1948), although it anticipates some of the poems about female consciousness written by Eavan Boland in the early 1980s:

> I was the moon.
> A shadow hid me
> and I knew what it meant
> not to be at all.
> The moon in eclipse is sad,
> and sinless.
> There is no passion in her plight.
> Cold, unlighted,
> moving in trance,
> she comes to her station
> or passes again to her place;
> uncovers her loneliness:
> eyeless behind no eyelids
> has neither sleeping nor waking,
> no body, parts, nor passions,
> no loving, perceiving,
> having, nor being;
> moves only in a wayless night;
> and drifting, as a ship without direction,
> sinks to a forgotten depth,
> among weeds,
> among stones.[12]

A number of Coghill's poems portray male attitudes as threatening and destructive, while asserting the need for female independence, as in "The Young Bride's Dream":

> I wonder will he still be gentle
> When I am fastened safe to his side?
> Will he buy grandeur to cover my beauty,
> And shelter me like a bird that he'd hide

In a quiet nest, and show me great courtesies,
And make me queen of his body and all that he is?

Or curse me, use me like a chance woman,
A servant, a girl that he'd hire at a fair?
Bid me rip my fine gown to a hundred pieces,
Make rags of it then, for the floors and the stair?
I had warning, last night, in a dream without reason or rhyme;
But the words may be true ones: *"Obedience is ice to the wine."*[13]

Like many of the women writers working at this time, Coghill came to poetry late—she was forty-five when *The Bright Hillside,* her first collection of poems, was published—and did not publish enough to allow any development in her work. Her second, and last, book of poems, *Time Is a Squirrel,* published in 1956, is a much less compelling and innovative collection than is *The Bright Hillside.* And she had another career; after taking a degree in music from University College, Dublin, she studied piano under Arthur Schnabel in Berlin, and became a concert pianist.

Sheila Wingfield (1906–1992) was born in England, and her marriage to the Viscount of Powerscourt did not exactly place her at the center of Irish culture in the years following the establishment of the Free State. Moreover, what is arguably her best book, *Beat Drum, Beat Heart* (1946), a long poem about World War II that Herbert Read called "the most sustained meditation on war that has been written in our time," [14] had nothing to do with Ireland. But her work as a whole was more concerned with representing the social and cultural realities of modern Ireland, albeit from the position of an outsider, than was that of the Dublin-born Coghill, and her poems about Ireland are of particular interest in part because, like the work of Mary Devenport O'Neill, they brought to bear on the Irish situation the formal techniques of imagism and the sceptical vision of modernism. Although Wingfield is said to have known nothing of Ezra Pound when she published her first book of poems in 1938,[15] the influence of imagism is plainly evident throughout her work, and she once described her "poetic outlook" in these terms: "What is personally felt must be fused with what is being, and has been, felt by *others.* But always in terms of the factual. Nothing wordy or disembodied will do." [16] This distrust of subjectivity well suited an Englishwoman writing about Ireland, and Wingfield's poems on the subject are heavily marked by both an imagistic clarity and a definite distance. Although Wingfield's outsider status at times blinded her to the realities of Irish life, her anti-subjective aesthetics tended to counter any tendency to romanticize the Irish experience. Her poem "Beggarman" (*The Leaves Darken,* 1964) combines the urban realism of Seamus O'Sullivan and James Stephens with a modernist sense of alienation that owes something to Eliot:

Grincing on a yellow fiddle
In a town where gulls
And grime mix in the air's
Familiar chime

For priest and bookie, Dooley's Bar,
Swans and sticks and dead old
Buckets on the Liffey
Mud—he knows

Men turn their head away when walking
Past, and flush in the cold,
As if their breath or blood
Had a catarrh.[17]

Occasionally, Wingfield goes beyond this kind of objective descriptive writing. Her poem "Clonmacnoise," which bears comparison with Austin Clarke's "Pilgrimage" and T. W. Rolleston's "The Dead at Clonmacnoise," effectively and compactly conveys a sense of spiritual satisfaction drawn from the Irish landscape:

Along the gently
Sloping riverbanks
Of Shannon with its placid flow
And all its wildfowl,
Why should the ruins
Of Clonmacnois,
Pillaged by savages
When most renowned and holy—
Why do its ravages,
In fact,
Make the heart easy
With high calm, tact
And harmony?[18]

Although Wingfield's class background might be said to have prevented her from writing about this medieval center of Irish Christianity so important to Irish Catholicism with the same intimacy and personal relevance as Clarke, her poem represents an attempt to understand what that intimacy and relevance might be like, and so to reach across the sectarian and cultural barriers that divided Wingfield from the Ireland in which she lived.

Most of the poetry that Máire MacEntee (1922–) has written is in Irish, but she did publish one volume of translations from the Irish, *A Heart Full of Thought* (1959), which identified sexual passion as a central theme in the tradition of writing in Irish. In this regard, MacEntee's translations can be associated with Clarke's "free translations" of the 1960s and 1970s, and so with the effort to challenge Irish-Ireland assumptions about the relationship between Gaelicism and Jansenist Catholicism. Although her work in this vein is somewhat less graphic than is Clarke's, MacEntee's insistent focus on sexuality, including sexual desire outside marriage, as in "Duibhe Id Mhailghibh," is potentially as subversive as are Clarke's eroticized versions of "Mabel Kelly" and "The Healing of Mis":

> Black eye-brow and the cheek an ember glowing,
> Blue eye beneath the glossy head of hair,
> Wind-ruffled now—O Lad, 'tis easy knowing
> Whom women's glances follow at the fair.
>
> And she whose wedded eye dares not to linger,
> Shaking the loosened locks about her face,
> Lifts up the silken lattice with a finger,
> To gaze her fill, unguessed at by disgrace.[19]

MacEntee's use of flexible rhythms and assonantal sound patterns, possibly owing something to the long line of Ferguson and Mangan, effectively reflects some of the formal qualities in Irish verse, as is evident in the concluding quatrain of a seduction poem entitled "Mo-Chion Dár Lucht Abarthaigh":

> Lady my wits are astray and I may not recover
> For the light of your delicate face where the warm blushes hover—
> My grief on the day when the tale-bearing rabble discover
> That binding our names in disgrace does not make me your lover.[20]

Eithne Strong (1923–) also writes in both languages, but her significance for modern Irish poetry lies chiefly in her uninhibited and unconventional exploration in her writing in English of female perception and experience. Although she started publishing poetry in Irish in the 1940s, she did not publish her first collection of poems in English, *Songs of Living,* until 1961, after raising nine children. With the exception of some of Rhoda Coghill's poems, *Songs of Living* stands decidedly apart from the tradition of Irish poetry written by women, apparently more influenced in its style and its representation of female psychology by the work of the American poet Sylvia Plath than by that of any earlier Irish poet. In this regard, Strong's work, like some of Coghill's, anticipates the poetry in the 1980s of Irishwomen such as Eavan Boland and Medbh McGuckian; indeed, Strong herself has continued to publish poetry in this vein into the 1990s. Strong's poem "Symbols," from *Songs of Living,* might be read as a defense of her poetic vision and interests:

If I come out of the mists now
and speak of incapacity
do not turn
to look upon the sea-wet stone.
Do not talk of the sun
and yellow sand.
More than the tangled trees
and dark sea-moss
is the tangled dark of my imprisoning.

            .   .   .

Turn over the wet sea-stone
so let out the buried dead
to stalk abroad
over the wind-stript void.[21]

There certainly are signs of Plath in "A Woman Unleashed," a poem that examines male stereotypes of women based on fear, while presenting as well vivid images of female power:

Swift breed of sin
all the lightning fire
hell in the breast
a witch's sabbath
all the cauldron of gluttony and lust.

            .   .   .

Standing alone
victor of magnificence;
thickening red of blood upon a knife.
Queen of blood.

And so alone
all saffron-red
between the blood of earth and sky.[22]

Although specifically Irish matters are not to be found on the surface of Strong's poems—another way in which she parts company from most Irish women poets of the nineteenth century and the literary revival—the kind of imaginative, usually specifically female, power that Strong celebrates is often portrayed as pre-linguistic and druidic, and in this way she effectively rewrites nationalist icons reductively identifying Ireland as female (Cathleen ní Houlihan, the Shan Van Vocht) into a more profound relationship between Ireland's ancient past and the female imagination, connected to semiotic rather than symbolic ways of experiencing and describing reality. In "Synthesis—Achill

1958," the landscape of western Ireland becomes a manifestation of a druidical, imaginative power that enables the poem's narrator to discover her own poetic abilities and responsibilities:

> But I must go alone
> and put my head low upon the heather
> to find my strength.
>
> Old druid hills
> gird black the sunset sky.
> Old, old strength of immemorial earth
> lies quiet beneath my tangled heart.
>
> .   .   .
>
> Hear the inner, inner pulse
> go slow,
> slower,
> quiet,
> still.
> Wait for the inward silence.
> Now
> the naked heart.
>
> The hills abide in ancient strength
> against the endless sea.
> Old druid hills bide dark
> against the western light.
>
> And I
> must bear witness to this midnight tryst.[23]

"A Druid land, a Druid tune,"[24] as Yeats once said, but Strong revises this concept which provided Yeats with a justification for romanticizing the Irish past into a metaphor for the female, the unapprehended, the "inner, inner pulse" to which her art, like that of a number of women poets in her wake, was so sensitively and so subversively tuned.

THE NORTH

The late eighteenth-century Ulster poets James Orr and William Drennan often wrote out of an acute consciousness of the distinctive culture of their region, but they were, first and foremost, nationalists, and their work clearly belongs to the tradition of nationalist writing in Ireland more than to any specifically Ulster tradition. Although Samuel Ferguson, in the nineteenth century, wrote poems set in his native Belfast that draw on Ulster legends and folklore, the bulk of his work, especially his translations from the Irish, depends on and expresses national rather than regional concepts of cultural identity. Ethna Carbery and Alice Milligan wrote in the context of the specifically nationalist cultural vision of the literary revival, although they both had deep roots in Ulster. By redrawing the political geography of Ireland, and so the context for nationalist thinking, the Government of Ireland Act of 1920 changed all that, promoting if not requiring a well-defined and quite self-conscious sense of regional identity among northern writers, while at the same time underscoring the many and various ambiguities and complexities that came with the territory. By the 1940s, John Hewitt was arguing that the concept of an Ulster regionalism could produce the kind of cultural revival, on a more limited scale, that had been the aim of Yeats and his followers. In his essay "Regionalism: The Last Chance" (1947), Hewitt argued that Ulster (not just Northern Ireland), considered as a region, could "command the loyalty of every one of its inhabitants" and produce "a culture and an attitude individual and distinctive."[1] While this argument echoed the broader cultural aims of the revival, it also implicitly conceded what partition had made painfully clear: that those aims had not been fully realized. Hewitt's poetry embodied many of the insecurities and ambiguities that the regional writer, as he conceived of him, was inevitably heir to. Not only was Hewitt writing from within a country politically separated from the rest of Ireland, and deeply, even violently, divided within itself, but also, because of his planter ancestry, he felt alienated from the Catholic, Gaelic culture that he understood to be essential to Irish identity, and so to his own.[2] For Louis MacNeice, this sense of an unstable cultural identity complicated significantly the condition of poetic limbo, divided between the Irish and the English traditions, that informed much of his work. Less at home in a divided homeland than Hewitt, and in fact living most of his adult life outside Ireland, MacNeice wrote about Ireland from a position of exile that was greatly intensified by his sense of himself as an exile within Ireland as well as from it. The work of northern poets in this century has also been distinctively marked by a regionally generated concern with religion and religious difference. Although in theory Hewitt's regionalism crossed sectarian lines, Hewitt's nonconformist upbringing was no less central to his art than Austin Clarke's Catholic upbringing was to his. For W. R. Rodgers, a Calvinist background that might also be compared to the puritanical qualities of Clarke's Jansenist Catholicism produced a poetic response very different from the ironies of exile in MacNeice or the Augustan understatement in Hewitt. The extravagant and erotic lyricism of Rodgers's work can be read as an attempt to liberate himself from the constrictions of his upbringing, leading him away from the reserved discourse associated with Ulster Protestantism and toward a relatively exuberant, uninhibited discourse associated with the Gaelic tradition. All these midcentury northern writers, and the poetic strategies that they employed to negotiate the complexities of their cultural positions, anticipate the emergence later in the century, in the midst of widespread sectarian violence in the north, of a group of extraordinarily gifted poets (including Seamus Heaney, Michael Longley, Derek Mahon, John Montague, and Paul Muldoon) engaged, in one way or another, with the troubled history of Ulster.[3]

"I wish one could either *live* in Ireland or *feel oneself* in England." So wrote Louis MacNeice (1907–1963) to a friend in 1948.[4] This remark says much about MacNeice's ambiguous sense of himself as an Irishman living in England and writing poetry that had more to do with English culture than with Irish, but it tells only part of the story. MacNeice was born in Belfast and reared in Carrickfergus, where his father was an Anglican rector (he later was made a bishop), but his family originally came from the west. Ireland represented for MacNeice both a state of oppression and bitterness that seemed inimical to his poetic ambitions and a romantic world of imaginative possibility that offered a mesmerizing alternative to the drab, materialistic realities of mid-century England. This bifurcated perception depended on MacNeice's sense of Ireland as divided; on the whole, it was Ulster Protestantism and Belfast industrialism that MacNeice saw as inhibiting and destructive, while he admired the rest of the island, especially the west, through Arnoldian lenses. "Even in those early sunlit days there was a kind of tension in the household which, I think, arose in part from the fact that neither our mother nor Louis nor myself felt that we belonged properly to the Ulster community in which we were living," his sister once said. "It [the west] became for us both a 'many-coloured land' and a kind of lost Atlantis where we thought that by right we should be living, and it came to be a point of honour that we did not belong to the North of Ireland. We were in our minds a West of Ireland family exiled from our homeland." [5] MacNeice's writing about Ireland was considerably less interested in promoting cultural regionalism than was Hewitt's, and it constituted a small portion of his work as a whole; there are almost no poems about Ireland after the mid-1940s, when Hewitt was just starting to publish. Yet MacNeice's Irish poetry embodies a consciousness of the north as a distinct region, divided from the rest of Ireland by politics, economics, religion, and culture, and deeply divided within itself by the same issues.

Much of MacNeice's early writing about his Ulster background was bitterly critical; indeed, MacNeice's poems of the 1930s are the first to depict industrial Belfast in anti-Edenic terms that define northern culture as different from or even inimical to Irish culture. "Carrickfergus" (1937), for example, presents a radically different view of industrial Ulster than Samuel Ferguson's celebratory poem about nineteenth-century Belfast, "The Forging of an Anchor":

> I was born in Belfast between the mountains and the gantries
> To the hooting of lost sirens and the clang of trams:
> Thence to Smoky Carrick in Country Antrim
> Where the bottle-neck harbour collects the mud which jams
>
> The little boats beneath the Norman castle,
> The pier shining with lumps of crystal salt;
> The Scotch Quarter was a line of residential houses
> But the Irish Quarter was a slum for the blind and halt.
>
> The brook ran yellow from the factory stinking of chlorine,
> The yarn-mill called its funeral cry at noon;
> Our lights looked over the lough to the lights of Bangor
> Under the peacock aura of a drowning moon.[6]

In another early poem, "Belfast" (1931), MacNeice presents the Ulsterman and the Ulster landscape as agents of spiritual and imaginative death at the hands of materialism and political fanaticism:

> The hard cold fire of the northerner
> Frozen into his blood from the fire in his basalt
> Glares from behind the mica of his eyes
> And the salt carrion water brings him wealth.

Down there at the end of the melancholy lough
Against the lurid sky over the stained water
Where hammers clang murderously on the girders
Like crucifixes the gantries stand.[7]

This despairing view of the north is also marked in MacNeice's work by a strong streak of fatalism that may owe something to MacNeice's strict religious upbringing, much of it at the hands of a mother's helper who, as MacNeice wrote in his unfinished autobiography, *The Strings Are False,* "brought Hell home to me."[8] MacNeice's critique of Ireland sees violence and cruelty as endemic to the culture; as his Irish character Ryan, in "Eclogue from Iceland" (1936), says: "I come from an island, Ireland, a nation/Built upon violence and morose vendettas."[9] In *Autumn Journal* (1939), these qualities are related specifically to an indigenous religious bigotry:

And the voodoo of the Orange bands
     Drawing an iron net through darkest Ulster,
Flailing the limbo lands—
     The linen mills, the long wet grass, the ragged hawthorn.
And one read black where the other read white, his hope
     The other man's damnation:
Up the Rebels, To Hell with the Pope,
     And God Save—as you prefer—the King or Ireland.[10]

The assumption that violence is inherent in the culture ultimately limits Mac-Neice's critique of Ulster, discouraging analysis of the historical and cultural causes of the attitudes that he describes. As Anthony Cronin has argued, Mac-Neice's poems about Ireland in general never quite escape being "touristy,"[11] and the tourist's-eye view of Ulster often includes violence and sectarian hatred as part of the scenery.

The other way of seeing Ireland, as the "many-coloured land" of imaginative possibility and liberation, owes something to MacNeice's reading of Yeats (he published a critical study, *The Poetry of W. B. Yeats,* in 1941),[12] but it also embodies specifically regional perceptions. While MacNeice saw Belfast as the city of deterministic Protestantism and destructive industrialism and viewed England as the locus of materialism, Dublin and the west of Ireland represented a poetic, pastoral alternative that was necessary to his artistic imagination. In the 1940s MacNeice became increasingly interested in mythology, especially the Irish legend of St. Brandan's voyage. This story appealed to him in part because it embodied the idea of exile, and in part, as is evident in the poem "Western Landscape" (1945), because it embodied the possibility of a Yeatsian transcendence:

O Brandan, spindrift hermit, who
Hankering roaming un-homing up-anchoring
From this rock wall looked seawards to
Knot the horizon round your waist,
Distil that distance and undo
Time in quintessential West.[13]

A romantic hymn of praise to Ireland, "Western Landscape" is written with an unbridled lyricism notably unlike the language of invective that dominates MacNeice's earlier writing about the north. Characteristically, however, the poem also remains aware of the possibility that all that the west represents to MacNeice may be illusory and misleading: "the kiss of the past is narcotic," and "the western climate is Lethe." [14] Ireland's western landscape may carry within it the potential, rooted in the dark mysteries of mythology and ancient history, for imaginative vitality, and Dublin, with its "greyness run to flower," [15] may offer an alluring alternative to the hard realities of Belfast or London, but the clear-eyed realism and scepticism that dominate MacNeice's imagination are never completely absent, even when that imagination is embracing, as in "Dublin," the Ireland that MacNeice finds so appealing:

But oh the days are soft,
Soft enough to forget
The lesson better learnt,
The bullet on the wet
Streets, the crooked deal,
The steel behind the laugh,
The Four Courts burnt.[16]

Here MacNeice, largely because of his Ulster experience, parts company with the romantic aesthetics and vision of the literary revival. Of Yeats, MacNeice said, "His lights are not ours," [17] and about Thomas Moore and James Clarence Mangan, he was much less reserved: "The more self-conscious nineteenth-century Irish poets writing in English were also more vulgar. There we get the pineapple sweetness of Moore and the thump and swagger and syrupy self-pity of Mangan." [18]

In 1934, at the age of twenty-six, MacNeice wrote a farewell poem to Ireland. "Valediction" expresses some of the same relentlessly unforgiving attitudes toward the Ulster of his upbringing that are to be found in other early poems, and it was apparently written out of a determination to leave behind him the "drug-dull fatalism" of the north.[19] But the poem nonetheless conveys a self-conscious ambiguity that argues against such single-minded views, and that defines MacNeice's position as an Irish poet:

I can say Ireland is hooey, Ireland is
A gallery of fake tapestries,
But I cannot deny my past to which my self is wed,
The woven figure cannot undo its thread.[20]

In an essay entitled "Planter's Gothic," John Hewitt (1907–1987) recalled discovering one day a planter's Gothic tower built around the stump of a round tower. "It is the best symbol I have yet found," he said, "for the strange textures of my response to this island of which I am a native. It may appear Planter's Gothic, but there is a round tower somewhere inside, and needled through every sentence I utter."[21] It is also significant for Hewitt that this tower-within-a-tower, representing the complex relationship between Ireland's different traditions—and so different in its implications from Yeats's Norman keep in Co. Galway—was found in Ulster. In Hewitt's view, the most likely means to reconciling Ireland's differing traditions, to seeing them as interrelated rather than diametrically opposed to one another, was the idea of the region, an area small enough to generate a loyalty capable of transcending cultural, religious, and political prejudices. As he put it in his essay, "Regionalism: The Last Chance," published in 1947:

Ulster, considered as a region and not as the symbol of any particular creed, can, I believe, command the loyalty of every one of its inhabitants. . . .out of that loyalty to our place, rooted in honest history, in familiar folkways and knowledge, phrased in our own dialect, there shall emerge a culture and an attitude individual and distinctive.[22]

When sectarian violence began in Belfast and Derry in the late 1960s, if not before, it became obvious to everyone, including Hewitt, that this position, embodying a pluralist rather than nationalist or unionist perspective, could not be realized. The poetry that this position has inspired is, however, not at all enslaved to the theory. Indeed, Hewitt's poems about Ireland are most compelling when they depart from the rather uncritical optimism of Hewitt's regionalism, and recognize, often with considerable candor and conviction, the very tensions and complexities that have undermined the prospects for reconciliation that the theory advanced. Hewitt's poetry is also of interest in that it represents, as MacNeice's does not, the view from inside the planter tradition, and from someone who spent most of his adult life in the north, not in exile.[23] Born in Belfast and educated at Queen's University, Hewitt worked for twenty-seven years for the Belfast Museum and Art Gallery; in 1957 he moved to Coventry to take up the post of director of the Herbert Art Gallery and Museum, but he returned to Belfast upon his retirement in 1972 and remained there until his death fifteen years later.

Hewitt greatly admired the work of William Allingham, especially Allingham's long poem *Laurence Bloomfield in Ireland*. In Allingham, Hewitt found
another Ulster poet committed to the idea that poetry should engage economic
and social issues and convinced that economic and social progress was most
likely to be effected through a change in the attitudes of individuals, an assumption that underlies Hewitt's theories of regionalism. Also, Allingham was alienated by religion and class from the people that he wrote about, and alienated
within the Protestant minority by "his unorthodox theological and political
ideas," as Hewitt put it.[24] A descendent of seventeenth-century planter stock,
Hewitt found himself decidedly outside the Gaelic, Catholic tradition; he also
felt marginalized within Ulster Protestantism because of his relatively tolerant
views on sectarian difference.[25] The best of Hewitt's poetry is written out of
this acute sense of alienation, embodying with clarity and force the cultural
insecurity and ambiguity of postpartition Ulster. His poem "The Colony,"
which Hewitt once described as "the definitive statement of my realisation that
I am an Ulsterman," [26] strikes precisely the precarious balance between guilt,
hope of reconciliation, and determination to be integrated into the colonized
culture that informs much of Hewitt's writing. The poem is written in the voice
of an unusually sensitive Roman colonizer of England reflecting on the native
population, but its implications for the twentieth-century colonizing English
and colonized Irish are perfectly clear, and the measured, reasonable tone of
the speaking voice is characteristic of Hewitt's writing:

> I find their symbols good, as such, for me,
> when I walk in dark places of the heart;
> but name them not to be misunderstood.
> I know no vices they monopolise,
> if we allow the forms by hunger bred,
> the sores of old oppression, the deep skill
> in all evasive acts, the swaddled minds,
> admit our load of guilt—I mourn the trees
> more than as symbol—and would make amends
> by fraternising, by small friendly gestures,
> hoping by patient words I may convince
> my people and this people we are changed
> from the raw levies which usurped the land,
> if not to kin, to co-inhabitants,
> as goat and ox may graze in the same field
> and each gain something from proximity;
> for we have rights drawn from the soil and sky;
> the use, the pace, the patient years of labour,
> the rain against the lips, the changing light,
> the heavy clay-sucked stride, have altered us;

> we would be strangers in the Capitol;
> this is our country also, nowhere else;
> and we shall not be outcast on the world.[27]

Despite this determination to be accepted as an Irishman and to use his "patient words" to bridge the gap between colonized and colonizer, Hewitt's poetry candidly and self-consciously confronts the difficulties of his project. In "Once Alien Here," from *No Rebel Word* (1948), he represents his family as having earned over the centuries a respected place in Ireland, but the poem is acutely aware of the tentative character of the colonizer's claims and of the obstacles to finding an appropriate discourse for presenting his position:

> So I, because of all buried men
> in Ulster clay, because of rock and glen
> and mist and cloud and quality of air
> as native in my thought as any here,
> who now would seek a native mode to tell
> our stubborn wisdom individual,
> yet lacking skill in either scale or song,
> the graver English, lyric Irish tongue,
> must let this rich earth so enhance the blood
> with steady pulse where now is plunging mood
> till thought and image may, identified,
> find easy voice to utter each aright.[28]

Hewitt identifies "this rich earth" of rural Ireland specifically with Gaelic culture and tradition and urban Ireland with himself, resulting in an ironic pastoral through which he explores the tensions that threaten his vision of reconciliation.[29] In "The Glens" (1942), the native culture of the wild glen country is seen as inevitably separate from the townbred poet:

> Not these my people, of a vainer faith
> and a more violent lineage. My dead
> lie in the steepled hillock of Kilmore
> in a fat country rich with bloom and fruit.
>
>   .   .   .
>
> My days, the busy days I owe the world,
> are bound to paved unerring roads and rooms
> heavy with talk of politics and art.
> I cannot spare more than a common phrase
> of crops and weather when I pace these lanes
> and pause at hedge gap spying on their skill
> so many fences stretch between our minds.

> I fear their creed as we have always feared
> the lifted hand against unfettered thought.
> I know their savage history of wrong
> and would at moments lend an eager voice,
> if voice avail, to set that tally straight.[30]

The prim understatement of a phrase such as "set that tally straight," or the cultural assumptions inherent in phrases such as "vainer faith" and "more violent lineage," affirm Hewitt's cultural distance from that "savage history of wrong," and so involuntarily keep open the cultural gap that he is working to close. On the other hand, Hewitt's sobriety and modesty, so different from the unbridled poetic voices associated with the neo-romantic movement flourishing in English poetry in the 1940s, speak eloquently for the conviction that the poet has a responsibility to engage in civic, social discourse, and for the more specific belief that Hewitt's own poetry, by carefully incorporating and speaking for Catholic and Protestant traditions in Ireland, could foster attitudes among his readers that might well lead to cultural and even political reconciliation of some kind. It is an Augustan view of the poet, something that had all but disappeared from Irish writing in the powerful fusion of nationalism and romanticism that dominated Irish thinking in the nineteenth and early twentieth centuries. Although the events of the last part of the twentieth century in Northern Ireland have proved Hewitt's theories of regionalism to be somewhat naive, the very violence of those events may be said to have made that measured voice of reason all the more appealing, if not necessary. As Michael Longley, a contemporary northern poet indebted to Hewitt on this ground, has said, Hewitt was a poet who "held out the creative hand rather than the clenched fist [and] made himself heard in a land of bellowers without raising his voice." [31]

It would be unfair to describe the poetry of W. R. Rodgers (1909–1969) as poetic "bellowing," but the linguistic exuberance and extreme pitch of lyricism that characterize his work mark it off sharply from both the reasoned sobriety of Hewitt and the self-conscious irony of MacNeice. "Everyone should read him," Stephen Spender once said, "because he is a poetic phenomenon." [32] Rodgers's unqualifiedly romantic aesthetics, which had more to do with neo-romanticism in England in the 1940s than with the tradition of Irish romanticism, tend to obscure the complex, specific issues associated with being a northern poet in postpartition Ireland, the issue that so engaged Hewitt and MacNeice in their different ways. Nonetheless, Rodgers's work represents a response to and expression of some of the cultural pressures that have so powerfully shaped poetry in the north since partition. For one thing, Rodgers's Ulster presbyterian background was a significant force in his writing. Born in Belfast and educated at Queens University and the Presbyterian Theological

College, Rodgers was ordained a presbyterian minister at the age of twenty-six, and spent eleven years as a minister in Co. Armagh before resigning and moving to London. The strong streak of sensuality that runs through his poetry was in large part a reaction against the puritanical strictures of his religious upbringing, in much the same way that Austin Clarke's was a rejection of Jansenist Catholicism.[33] The lengthy title poem of *Europa and the Bull* (1952) is Rodgers's most sustained and explicit work in this vein, but the use of metaphoric as well as mythical modes to celebrate the erotic is common in his lyrics as well, perhaps best represented by "The Net," from that collection:

> Ah, shifty as the fin
> Of any fish this flesh
> That, shaken to the shin,
> Now shoals into your mesh,
> Bursting to be held in;
> Purse-proud and pebble-hard,
> Its pence like shingle showered.
>
> Open the haul, and shake
> The fill of shillings free,
> Let all the satchels break
> And leap about the knee
> In shoals of ecstasy.
> Guineas and gills will flake
> At each gull-plunge of me.[34]

Rodgers's poetry is grounded in the sense that language itself is highly sensual, as opposed to seeing language as an instrument of moral and religious instruction, a view that Rodgers knew first-hand from his experience as a minister. In the hands of the poet, language can realize feelings and states of experience lying beyond rationality and social convention, including conventional religious doctrine. "There is a power of words that is imprisoned," Rodgers once said, "and like underground water-springs they are bursting to be let out."[35]

Rodgers's lyricism can also be interpreted in more broadly cultural terms as a rejection of a specifically Ulster language and outlook in favor of a more uninhibited discourse associated with the Gaelic dimension of Irish culture: a rejection, one might say, of the northern voice of Hewitt and a yearning for the southern and western Ireland that appealed so powerfully to MacNeice. In the epilogue to a lengthy, uncompleted poem, "The Character of Ireland," Rodgers defines the difference between the north and the south in explicitly linguistic terms that reveal the cultural significance of his own poetic style:

I am Ulster, my people an abrupt people
Who like the spiky consonants in speech
And think the soft ones cissy; who dig
The *k* and *t* in orchestra, detect sin
In sinfonia, get a kick out of
Tin cans, fricatives, fornication, staccato talk,
Anything that gives or takes attack,
Like Micks, Tagues, tinkers' gets, Vatican.
An angular people, brusque and Protestant,
For whom the word is still a fighting word,
Who bristle into reticence at the sound
Of the round gift of the gab in Southern mouths.[36]

At times, Rodgers's proclivity for the "round gift of the gab" carried him too far, producing verse that reads like a parody of Dylan Thomas and manifesting what one critic has called "verbal irresponsibility."[37] But at his best, Rodgers was capable of an intensity and vividness rarely to be found in the work of other northern poets. Not surprisingly, Rodgers's romantic aesthetics led him to celebrate the poetic imagination, as in "The Swan," a poem that shares certain symbolic valences with Yeats but also compellingly evokes the being of the swan itself through a Lawrentian sympathy and a striking use of rhythm and imagery:

Into abashed confusions of ooze
It dips, and from the muddy fume
The silver and flute-like fishes rise
Endlessly up through all their octaves of gloom

To where the roofed swan suavely swings
Without qualm on the quivering wave
That laves it on, with elbowing wings held wide
Under its eyes' hugged look and architrave.[38]

This kind of writing does not evoke the kind of cultural or political analysis to be found in the work of Hewitt and MacNeice. Indeed, Rodgers's romanticism often seems to assume a threatening tension between poetry and the world of social and political reality. Nevertheless, the very intensity with which Rodgers attempts to transcend rather than confront the religious, social, and political realities of his native Ulster calls attention to the extent to which his work was shaped by the complex, often constraining pressures of those realities —realities that have inspired increasingly varied kinds of poetic expression as the political divisions within the north, and between the north and the rest of Ireland, have stubbornly continued to dominate Irish life in the closing decades of the twentieth century.

CHAPTER NINETEEN

TOWARD CONTEMPORARY POETRY

Although a distinctively contemporary Irish poetry began developing only in the late 1960s, several new poetic voices, preoccupied with the position of the Irish poet in the postwar world and anticipating in many ways the poetry of the last quarter of the century, emerged in Ireland in the 1950s and early 1960s. Richard Murphy, Thomas Kinsella, and John Montague were all born after the establishment of Irish independence; by the time they began writing, the romantic poetics and politics of the revival years were at least two generations away, and the role of the Irish poet had changed, as Montague put it, into "the struggle with casual/Graceless unheroic things,/The greater task of swimming/ Against a slackening tide." [1] In large part because of this change, some of the work of these poets in the 1950s and 1960s was relatively interior in focus, more interested in individual consciousness than in the political, social, and cultural issues that had so engaged earlier figures such as Clarke and Kavanagh as well as most of the writers associated with the revival. "The most sensitive individuals," Kinsella wrote in 1960, "have been shaken loose from society into disorder." [2] These writers have also tended to be more responsive to developments in poetry outside Ireland, especially in America, than were many of their predecessors. Nevertheless, all three have been profoundly engaged by their relationship to the Irish tradition, but tend to regard the past less as a basis for inspiration or liberation than as what Seamus Deane has called "a maiming influence," [3] a broken and divisive history that the Irish poet cannot avoid in his effort to write his way out of an unstable present and into a meaningful future. Murphy's position as an Anglo-Irish Protestant writing in the 1960s more or less insured that his relationship to Irish history would be marked by sober realism and resignation rather than romantic affirmation. Yeats's vision of a culturally privileged Anglo-Irish tradition seemed, by Murphy's time, considerably more wishful than it had been when Yeats, in 1925, told the Irish Senate that the Anglo-Irish were "one of the great stocks of Europe," [4] and Murphy's writing works hard to deheroicize the class that Yeats had done so much to recreate as the locus of art and civilization in Ireland. Of these three poets, Kinsella has been the most influenced by British and American modernism—"the Irish Eliot," as one critic has called him [5]—and the most overtly preoccupied with the devastating cultural and psychological effects of World War II. But behind Kinsella's sense of the modern world as fragmented lies the fractured tradition of Irish literature, a past that Kinsella has described as "mutilated." [6] For Kinsella, the modern Irish poet's attempt to establish a cultural and personal identity must be made against the background of this difficult history. For Montague, the divided and divisive history of Ireland is firmly grounded in place, particularly the Co. Tyrone of his upbringing, and his intense exploration of the history, personal and political, of his region significantly extends the tradition of Irish writing about locality, going back to Goldsmith in the eighteenth century.

The first book of poems that Richard Murphy (1927–) published, *The Archaeology of Love* (1955), had more to do Greece and Mediterranean culture than with Ireland. But in the late 1950s, Murphy started working on a long poem about his Ascendancy grandmother, and on another about a fishing disaster off the west coast of Ireland in 1927. In 1963, *Sailing to an Island* appeared, containing both these poems and a number of others that established Murphy as a new voice in Irish poetry. His central preoccupation, as was evident in "The Woman of the House" and "The Cleggan Disaster," was history; as Murphy said at the end of "The Last Galway Hooker," from *Sailing to an Island,* a poem that recounts the modern state's history from the Civil War to the emergence of the "new Ireland" in the late 1950s and early 1960s, his intention was "to prolong/For a while the spliced yards of yesterday." [7] But for Murphy, the Irish poet's charge goes beyond preserving remnants of the past in the face of short-sighted modernization and beyond reviving the past as part of a cultural revolution such as the literary revival; rather, the modern poet in Ireland must, in Murphy's view, demythologize and deheroicize history, must rescue the Irish past from the dangerous distortions and prejudices upon which so much of the Irish present has been constructed.

The Irish past that Murphy seeks to rewrite in this fashion is principally that of his own class. Murphy was born into an Anglo-Irish family in Co. Galway, and educated at a Protestant boarding school in Dublin and at Oxford; his grandfather, like Yeats's, was a Church of Ireland rector. Writing very much in the wake of Yeats, Murphy works against Yeats's tendency to represent the Anglo-Irish as a cultural aristocracy under siege from a materialist, philistine society, acknowledging instead that the heyday of the Ascendancy is beyond recovery and attempting to humanize rather than heroicize his ancestors. [8] Murphy's representation of the Anglo-Irish also makes room for a consciousness of colonial guilt that is rare in Yeats's portrayal of the class. All these attitudes are embodied in Murphy's affectionate but unflinchingly candid portrait of his grandmother, especially the madness that afflicted her during her declining years:

> 'The house in flames and nothing is insured!
> Send for the doctor, let the horses go.
> The dogs are barking again. Has the cow
> Calved in the night? What is that great singed bird?
>
> 'I don't know who you are, but you've kind eyes.
> My children are abroad and I'm alone.
> They left me in this gaol. You all tell lies.
> You're not my people. My people have gone' [9]

In this poem, Murphy in effect rewrites Yeats's portraits of Lady Gregory and Coole Park; the "Beloved books that famous hands have bound" [10] are recast, for example, as images of decay:

> Lever and Lover, Somerville and Ross
> Have fed the same worm as Blackstone and Gibbon,
> The mildew has spotted *Clarissa's* spine
> And soiled the *Despatches of Wellington.* [11]

Murphy is also capable of describing his class with a self-reflexive comic irony. His poem "Christening," from *The Battle of Aughrim* (1968), is written in a voice that Yeats, in his heroic formulation of the Anglo-Irish, could not afford to adopt:

> A side-car creaks on the gravel drive,
> The quality arrive.
> With Jordan water
> They mean to give me a Christian start.
>
> Harmonium pedals squeak and fart.
> I'm three weeks old.
>
> It's a garrison world:
> The good are born into the Irish gentry.
>
> What do they hope my use of life will be?
> Duty.
>
> Fight the good fight:
> Though out of tune, if loud enough, it's right.

. . .
Two clergy christen me: I'm saved from Rome.
The deaf one has not heard my name,

He thinks I am a girl.
The other bellows: "It's a boy, you fool!" [12]

The candid objectivity in Murphy's portrayal of the Anglo-Irish is also found in his writing about the native Irish, particularly the fishermen of the west of Ireland. In poems such as "The Cleggan Disaster" and "The Last Galway Hooker," Murphy in effect reconstructs in human rather than mythic or aesthetic terms Yeats's Connemara fisherman, that "wise and simple man" who, for Yeats, "is but a dream." [13] At the same time, he implicitly calls into question attempts in Irish-Ireland thinking to give special status to the west for political and cultural purposes. Murphy's work is also characterized by an ironic awareness of the impossibility of his being able to write with authenticity about a culture that is to him always alien. In the title poem of *Sailing to an Island*, the narrator's attempt to land at Clare Island, "its crags purpled by legend" and stories of "the hot O'Malleys,/Daughters of Granuaille," [14] inevitably fails; the boat is driven to Inishbofin, where Murphy is made to feel his cultural alienation. While this kind of self-doubting irony departs from the self-confidence that marked much of the writing associated with the revival, it anticipates the self-questioning ironies that govern the tone of much contemporary Irish poetry.

For Murphy, history is the ground upon which Ireland's two traditions meet, and it therefore provides a potential means of understanding more profoundly the relationship between them. But history is also vulnerable to dangerous interpretations that justify and motivate prejudice. Murphy's most sustained attempt at deconstructing this kind of history is his sequence of lyrics about the Battle of Aughrim, "the last decisive battle in Irish history," as Murphy describes it in a note,[15] and a powerfully symbolic moment in both nationalist and unionist versions of the past. Explaining his intentions in writing *The Battle of Aughrim* (1968), Murphy said:

I was trying to get clear a division in my mind between England and Ireland —between an almost entirely English education, an English mind and Irish feeling. I tried to reconcile these two by focussing on the battle (in which my ancestors fought on both sides), finding out all I could, what it was really about and what people thought it was about; putting in different points of view, the errors and atrocities of which myths are made, and drawing up an evaluation of what the religious conflict meant: what it meant in the past and how the past is still influencing us.[16]

By building his poem around the self-interested betrayal of the Irish cause by a colonel on the Irish side, Murphy's poem resists the tendency to heroicize either side of the conflict, at the same time that it goes to considerable lengths to depict the battle itself as an unheroic disaster of confusion, prejudice, and futility:

> Twenty thousand soldiers on each side,
> Between them a morass
> Of godly bigotry and pride of race,
> With a causeway two abreast could cross.
>
> In opposite camps our ancestors
> Ten marriages ago,
> Caught in a feud of absent kings
> Who used war like a basset table
> Gambling to settle verbal things,
> Decide if bread be God
> Or God a parable,
> Lit matches, foddered horses, thirsted, marched,
> Halted, and marched to battle.[17]

The Battle of Aughrim also frames the account of the battle with poems set in the present, thereby insisting in its structure on the contemporary force of history. Murphy, like Yeats, laments a present so ready to ignore or dispense with the past, usually for self-interested, materialistic purposes, but he is even more concerned about the construction of present-day attitudes and prejudices on highly subjective readings, or misreadings, of history. The Orange marches are an obvious example of this, and Murphy sees the marches as resulting from interpretations of history that join the past and the present in a continuum defined by hatred:

> In bowler hats and Sunday suits,
> Orange sashes, polished boots,
> Atavistic trainbands come
> To blow the fife and beat the drum.
>
> Apprentices uplift their banner
> True blue-dyed with "No Surrender!"
> Claiming Aughrim as if they'd won
> Last year, not 1691.[18]

If, as Murphy says elsewhere in *The Battle of Aughrim,* "The past is happening today," it happens through memory and imagination; the Battle of Aughrim, he says, "Has a beginning in my blood." [19] So, as Murphy conceives it, the poet's responsibility to the present mandates a responsible representation of the past.

Yeats and the literary revival demonstrated how the Irish past could be reconstructed in the interests of a vision of cultural unity, even if that vision was never fully realized outside the writing that it inspired. The early work of Thomas Kinsella (1928–) demonstrated how that same past, conceived as fragmented and discontinuous because of the replacement of Irish by English as the dominant language of the culture, could be read as defining a modern, specifically postwar vision of cultural and personal alienation. For Kinsella, part of Yeats's significance for succeeding generations of Irish poets was that he failed to heal the breach in the Irish tradition: as Kinsella said in his influential essay, "The Irish Writer" (1966), Yeats "had a greatness capable, perhaps, of integrating a modern Anglo-Irish culture, and which chose to make this impossible by separating out a special Anglo-Irish culture from the main unwashed body." [20] This failure is powerful evidence for Kinsella of the force of disjunction in Irish writing, and that disjunction is the central preoccupation of his art.

In the spirit of earlier translators from the Irish, Kinsella has done much to make the Irish-language tradition available to readers of English. His version of the *Táin Bó Cuailnge* (1969) and his translations of Irish lyric poetry in *An Duanaire 1600–1900: Poems of the Dispossessed* (1981) significantly extended into modern Irish literature the translation enterprise of the nineteenth century and the revival. But Kinsella's work in literature written in Irish has served only to increase his sense of alienation from it. As a twentieth-century Irish poet whose chosen medium is English, Kinsella has found himself, he once said, standing "on one side of a great rift" and feeling "the discontinuity in myself." [21] Kinsella responded to this situation by rejecting the kind of cultural nationalism and emphasis on Irishness that had informed so much Irish poetry written earlier in the century. In "The Irish Writer," he argued against national feeling as a useful ground for poetry: "A man in his life shares more with all men than he does with any class of men—in eating, sleeping, loving, fighting, dying; he may lack the sense of tradition and still have most of human experience." [22] In this regard, Kinsella was influenced by American poets such as William Carlos Williams, Ezra Pound, Robert Lowell, and Theodore Roethke, an influence reflected in Kinsella's moving to the United States in 1965, first to become writer-in-residence at Southern Illinois University and then, in 1970, professor of English at Temple University.[23] Nonetheless, Kinsella's deeply troubling perception of the Irish tradition as discontinuous is arguably the most powerful force at work in his poetry of the 1950s and 1960s, informing his sense of the modern poet's isolation and alienation and his view of the human condition in general in the wake of two world wars. "I am certain," Kinsella wrote to conclude "The Irish Writer," "that a great part of the significance of my own past, as I try to write my poetry, is that that past *is* mutilated." [24]

In a world in which disorder and meaninglessness are perceived as inevitable, the poet's responsibility, as Kinsella sees it, is to conduct a constant search for order and meaning, for ways of establishing identity and integrity, cultural and psychological, in the face of the flux of experience and the nightmare of history. "I believe the significant work begins in eliciting order from actuality," Kinsella said in an interview. "We're surrounded and penetrated by squalor, disorder and the insignificant, and I believe the artistic impulse has a great deal to do with our trying to make sense out of that." [25] This effort to construct meaning in the face of chaos is the driving force of Kinsella's art. The journey and the search are common motifs in Kinsella's early poems, and his narrators are often observers seeking some kind of hold on the flux that surrounds them. The poet, as Kinsella defines him in the long title poem to his collection *Nightwalker* (1968), is a "Watcher in the tower" (a reference to Joyce, an important figure for Kinsella), who scans "A rich darkness/Alive with signals." [26] The pressures of disorder, particularly of World War II and the holocaust, are considerable. As dramatized in this passage from "Nightwalker," based on Kinsella's experience in the Civil Service, they inevitably intrude upon the poetic imagination:

> —Two young Germans I had in this morning
> Wanting to transfer investment income;
> The sister a business figurehead, her brother
> Otterfaced, with exasperated smiles
> Assuming—pressing until he achieved—response.
> Handclasp; I do not exist; I cannot take
> My eyes from their pallor. A red glare
> Plays on their faces, livid with little splashes
> Of blazing fat. The oven door closes. [27]

Images from World War II also accompany the narrator of the title poem of *Downstream* (1962) as he drifts down a river and the flux of the passing landscape is mirrored in his shifting memories. Kinsella also insists in this poem on making connections between the Irish experience and that of Europe as a whole. It ends, after a brief, transitory moment of transcendence in observing the stars, with an image that defines precisely Kinsella's aesthetics:

> The slow, downstreaming dead, it seemed, were blended
> One with those silver hordes, and briefly shared
> Their order, glittering. And then impended

> A barrier of rock that turned and bared
>> A varied barrenness as toward its base
>> We glided—blotting heaven as it towered—
>
> Searching the darkness for a landing place.[28]

While the fragmented Irish tradition provided a paradigm for Kinsella's perception of postwar alienation, Kinsella's early poetry at times offered a specific critique of modern Irish society. In "A Country Walk" *(Downstream),* another poem in which the narrator is an observer passing through a landscape and preoccupied with memory, Irish history is deheroicized, as it is in Murphy's work. Romantic nationalism is described as "the phantom hag,/Timeless Rebellion," who brings about the meaningless death of a young man, and leads only to the divisiveness of the Civil War and the subsequent self-interested materialism of postindependence Ireland:

> They turned the bloody corner, knelt and killed,
> Who gather still at Easter round his grave,
> Our watchful elders. Deep in his crumbled heart
> He takes their soil, and chatting they return
> To take their town again, that have exchanged
> A trenchcoat playground for a gombeen jungle.[29]

Contemporary Ireland is portrayed as an unheroic wasteland, and Yeats's litany of heroes in "Easter 1916" is transformed by Kinsella's irony into an image of middle-class materialism and loveless religion:

> Around the corner, in an open square,
> I came upon the sombre monuments
> That bear their names: MacDonagh & McBride,
> Merchants; Connolly's Commercial Arms . . .
>
> .   .   .
>
> I turned away. Down the sloping square
> A lamp switched on above the urinal;
> Across the silent handball alley, eyes
> That never looked on lover measured mine
> Over the Christian Brothers' frosted glass
> And turned away.[30]

The terms of this critique are those employed by other postrevival poets, most notably Clarke, with whom Kinsella also shares a commitment to Ireland's Gaelic tradition and to writing about urban Dublin. (Kinsella edited a selection of Clarke's poems published in 1976.) But behind Kinsella's corrosive view of

Ireland at mid-century lies neither the humanism of Clarke nor the romanticism of Kavanagh, but rather a profound despair that belongs specifically to a European generation that came of age amid the horrors of the World War II, and that gives Kinsella's work its distinctive aura of desiccation and darkness.

While for Murphy Irish history must be deheroicized and for Kinsella it must be understood as a paradigm for postwar alienation, for John Montague (1929–   ) history needs to be localized. From his first collection of poems, *Forms of Exile* (1958) through his important book-length sequence, *The Rough Field* (1972), Montague focused insistently on the Co. Tyrone of his upbringing (he was born in Brooklyn, but was sent to rural Tyrone at the age of four to live with his aunts), investigating its past as a means of understanding the present. In this regard, Montague's work belongs to the tradition of Irish poetry centered on locality—Goldsmith's deserted village in Co. Roscommon, Allingham's tenant farms in Co. Donegal, Kavanagh's bleak hills in Co. Monaghan —a tradition that Montague himself, in an essay on Goldsmith, described as rooted in the "agrarian problem." [31] But for Montague, the landscape of Co. Tyrone is less a vehicle for exploring Ireland's agrarian problems than it is a rich reservoir of history, like the bogland in Seamus Heaney's poems, a text that the poet must learn to read if he is to become what, in Montague's view, the Irish poet should be: a spokesman for his community and therefore his nation, "a tribal consciousness," as he once put it.[32]

The tribe for which Montague speaks is essentially Gaelic, and the tradition that interests him is that of Gaelic Ulster,[33] a focus that not only differentiates Montague's preoccupation with locality from the nonsectarian regionalism of Hewitt but also dictates that the governing themes of Montague's work will be loss and dislocation, as they are, for much the same reasons, in Kinsella's less localized poetry. These themes are also be be found in the tradition of Irish poetry about the land: Goldsmith's village is deserted, Allingham's peasants are in desperate economic straits, and Kavanagh's farmers are suffering from ruin and paralysis. But for Montague, the crucial deprivation is cultural rather than political, economic, or psychological, the "lost/syllables of an old order," as he says in *The Rough Field* (1972).[34] In Montague's writing, the Tyrone landscape becomes indeed a text expressing cultural loss:

> Like shards
> Of a lost culture, the slopes
> Are strewn with cabins, deserted
> In my lifetime. . . .
>   .   .   .
> The whole landscape a manuscript
> We had lost the skill to read.[35]

Bitterness and anger are inevitable responses to this kind of devastation: "the vomit surge/of race hatred,/the victim seeing the oppressor." [36] Yet for Montague, the poet's responsibility is less to engender righteous rage in the tradition of much nineteenth-century nationalist writing than it is to read the landscape of loss thoroughly in an effort to recover what can be recovered and understand what can be understood.[37] This enterprise does not, however, offer much hope, as the "Old Rhyme" that Montague uses to introduce one section of *The Rough Field* suggests: "who ever heard/Such a sight unsung/As a severed head/With a grafted tongue" [38]—an even less encouraging image of Irish art than Joyce's cracked looking-glass of a servant.

Localizing history also means seeing the past in personal, human, unheroic terms, as opposed to the national, often mythic terms of the literary revival. At times, Montague engages in a satiric debunking of romanticized Ireland, as in "The Siege of Mullingar, 1963," a parody of Yeats's "September 1913" that dismisses both the revival's Ireland and de Valera's Irish Ireland that followed in its wake, while expressing reservations about the unheroic present that has replaced both:

> At the Fleadh Cheoil in Mullingar
> There were two sounds, the breaking
> Of glass, and the background pulse
> Of music. Young girls roamed
> The streets with eager faces,
> Shoving for men. Bottles in
> Hand, they rowed out a song:
> *Puritan Ireland's dead and gone,*
> *A myth of O'Connor and O'Faolain.*[39]

Montague also rewrites nationalist icons into a human scale, something in the manner of Murphy. His "Sean Bhean Bhocht" is an old neighbor woman whom Montague recalls from his childhood, and who graphically embodies not the heroic, potentially liberating past of nationalist rhetoric, but history as a burden and form of death:

> Eyes rheumy with racial memory;
> Fragments of bread soaked in brown tea
> And eased between shrunken gums.
> Her clothes stank like summer flax;
> Watched all day as she swayed
> Towards death between memories and prayers
> By a farmer's child in a rough play-box.[40]

With *The Rough Field,* written in part in response to the sectarian violence that began in Northern Ireland in the late 1960s, Montague's fusion of past and present, public and private, national and local is most effectively realized. Relying on a subversion of conventional literary categories—it mixes historical documents, family lore, folk art, political propaganda, and lyric poetry—the book negotiates between a maimed past and a divided present, attempting to read each in terms of the other and so to reveal history as a human construct that reinforces and indeed engenders the attitudes and prejudices of the present, the same theme that governs Murphy's book-length poetic exploration of the Battle of Aughrim. Because of its concern with the north and its innovative interrogation of historical stereotypes as well as poetic conventions, *The Rough Field* is situated on the boundary between modern and contemporary Irish poetry. The year of its publication, 1972, marked a turning point in the transition between modern and contemporary Ireland; not only was it the worst year of the violence in the north, including Bloody Sunday of January 30, but also in that year, in two separate referenda, the people in the twenty-six counties voted overwhelmingly to join the European Economic Community and narrowly to remove from de Valera's 1937 Constitution the reference to the special position in Irish society held by the Catholic Church.[41] But *The Rough Field* might be taken as marking the end of modern Irish poetry and the beginning of contemporary Irish poetry, and so as a fitting conclusion to a history of Irish poetry in English, for still another reason. In the "Epilogue" to the sequence, Montague describes himself as a traveler in the tradition of Goldsmith, the Irish exile adrift in the diaspora, haunted by images of his homeland and seeking a way back. Much Irish poetry has been written on the theme of exile, and indeed the Irish poet himself, whether he is writing from inside Irish society or from outside it, might well be represented by the figure of a traveler. For Montague, what the exile and the poet are searching for—if not a way back, then a way of establishing a personal and cultural sense of who they are—is always just out of reach, always already changed into something else by the time they get close to it:

> Harsh landscape that haunts me,
> well and stone, in the bleak moors of dream
> with all my circling a failure to return
> to what is already gone.[42]

It is this sense of ambiguity and discontinuity, of the poet as inevitably decentered, living in exile, doomed to be simultaneously at home and homeless, that, more than anything else, characterizes Irish poetry written in English from the beginning of the eighteenth century to the end of the twentieth. The Ireland that Swift both loathed and defended, the Protestant Ascendancy in its heyday, was already gone at the moment of its greatest authority, and Swift's position as an Anglo-Irish writer driven by love-hate relationships with both England and Ireland was defined by ambiguity and instability, to say the least. No less ambiguous was Goldsmith's position of literal as well as literary exile later in the eighteenth century, and, as Goldsmith well knew, the "sweet Auburn" of his imagination was already gone even as he remembered and memorialized it. The same might be said of the Irish-language tradition that inspired the art of poetic translation in the nineteenth century; indeed, the very need for such an enterprise affirmed that the language and its literature were, just as Mangan, Ferguson, and others set out to save them, beyond saving. Thomas Davis's vision of an Ireland that would transcend sectarian differences in the interests of the nationalist cause was also more phantom than fact at the time that he and other Young Ireland poets and writers were trying to create it, having already expired in the failure of the rising of 1798. And finally, the entire effort of the Irish literary revival at the turn of the century rested on a vision of cultural unity that could be realized only in the writing that it inspired. Nevertheless, if the fundamental condition of writing Irish poetry in English seems to be one of a constant and inevitably unfulfilled search for an ever-elusive identity and meaning—as Kinsella said, "Searching the darkness for a landing place" that, as Montague would add, is "already gone"—the poetry itself has endured, leaving a record not just of two-and-a-half centuries of Irish culture, valuable as that is, but, at its best, masterful images of the human effort to create order out of chaos, truth out of ambiguity, art out of life.

SOME OBSERVATIONS
ON CONTEMPORARY POETRY
IN IRELAND

The last quarter of the twentieth century in Ireland has witnessed something of a second literary renaissance, complete with a Nobel-prize-winning poet.[1] Although by definition literary history must stop short of the contemporary—and this study concludes in the early 1970s—some observations on the relationship between the poetry being written in contemporary Ireland and the tradition of Irish poetry in English are in order. It is all too easy to read the work of contemporary Irish poets as responding principally to the pressures of contemporary events: to see recent political poetry as shaped chiefly by the sectarian violence that has plagued Northern Ireland since the late 1960s; to relate the emergence of a new kind of Irish poetry written by women to the rise of feminism generally and to the increased attention paid in Irish public life to domestic and personal as well as traditional political issues; and to interpret the increasingly cosmopolitan quality of Irish poetry as reflecting the steadily growing importance of Ireland's relationship to Europe in the twenty-five years since the nation voted to join the European community as well as the markedly increased cultural traffic between Ireland and the United States. All these developments, however, have significant roots in the history of Irish poetry. Moreover, many of the issues that contemporary poets see as central to their work—the poet's relevance for and responsibility to contemporary political and social life, and the ground of poetic authority in general—have often demanded some kind of engagement, even if a subversive one, with the tradition of Irish poetry that stands behind them. By considering the work of a few representative writers rather than trying to offer a comprehensive account of contemporary Irish poetry, this essay will attempt to establish how contemporary poetry in Ireland has grown out of a complex, often troubling, but almost always productive interaction with its history.

Seamus Heaney's writing about Northern Ireland—part of a significant body of contemporary Irish poetry, including work by writers as different as Derek Mahon, Michael Longley, Paul Muldoon, Tom Paulin, Medbh McGuckian, and Ciaran Carson—has self-consciously represented itself as an intersection between the poet and the past. In the face of criticism about his failure to take an unambiguous stand on the conflict, the most eloquent of it coming from Heaney himself,[2] Heaney has sought to create an imaginative space in which the historical forces behind the conflict, often read and misread in ways that fuel sectarian and political animosities, can be better understood. This ambition has a significant poetic history behind it. In some of his early poems, Heaney explores linguistic differences between the two main traditions in the north as a vehicle for uncovering the historical grounds of the conflict, and for suggesting ways in which political and religious differences could be addressed if not resolved at the level of culture.[3] This strategy, particularly its faith in the political efficacy of cultural exchange, is deeply rooted in the history of Irish poetry, most evident perhaps in the translation enterprise of the late-eighteenth and nineteenth centuries and in the agenda of the literary revival in its earliest, most sanguine stages. Charlotte Brooke's hope, expressed in her preface to the first significant collection of translations from the Irish, *Reliques of Irish Poetry* (1789), that the muses of Irish and English poetry might prove "sweet ambassadresses of cordial union"[4] might almost be taken as a gloss on a Heaney poem such as "A New Song":

> But now our river tongues must rise
> From licking deep in native haunts
> To flood, with vowelling embrace,
> Desmesnes staked out in consonants.[5]

Also, Heaney's focus in his early work on his native Co. Derry draws significantly on the example of Patrick Kavanagh, an influence that Heaney has cited many times. It is also one that carries definite political implications in the work of a northern Catholic who began establishing his reputation amid the worst of the northern violence. Writing in 1975, Heaney said that Kavanagh's trust in what he called the parochial had demonstrated to him the poetic possibilities in "raising the inhibited energies of a subculture to its power of a cultural resource."[6] Ten years later, Heaney interpreted that influence in notably political terms that reveal as much about his own early work as about Kavanagh's:

Over the border, into a Northern Ireland dominated by the noticeably English accents of the local BBC, he broadcast a voice that would not be cowed into accents other than its own. Without being in the slightest way political in its intentions, Kavanagh's poetry did have a political effect. Whether he wanted it or not, his achievement was inevitably co-opted, north and south, into the general current of feeling which flowed from and sustained ideas of national identity, cultural otherness from Britain and the dream of a literature with a manner and a matter resistant to the central Englishness of the dominant tradition.[7]

In a lecture given in 1974, two years after Bloody Sunday, Heaney spelled out his idea of the Irish poet as cultural archeologist, a view closely related to the theories of cultural preservation and recovery that informed much nineteenth- and early twentieth-century Irish poetry in English. Poetry, Heaney said, leads to both "revelation of the self to the self" and "restoration of the culture to itself."[8] Both these ambitions have been immensely complicated for Heaney by the violence in the north. Heaney's bog poems of the early and mid-1970s, using images of victims of ancient fertility rites and violence preserved in the bogs of Jutland to represent what Heaney called "an archetypal pattern"[9] of violence carried out in the name of one presumably redemptive cause or another, draw on and extend traditional theories of cultural restoration to address the issues at stake in the conflict in the north. While these images enabled Heaney to examine more or less critically certain political attitudes, particularly those associated with political martyrdom, at the same time they left him open to the charge of essentializing the violence.[10] The best of these poems, however, are characteristically self-conscious about their own limitations and vulnerabilities, especially their tendency to participate more readily in what Heaney has called the "religious intensity of the violence" than to encourage "the perspectives of a humane reason."[11] At the end of "Punishment," Heaney's speaker recognizes a division in himself between the morally minded citizen, "who would connive/in civilized outrage" and the poet, "the artful voyeur" who would "understand the exact/and tribal, intimate revenge."[12] Moreover, halfway through *North* (1975), Heaney abandons the bog as a vehicle for writing about Northern Ireland in favor of a more direct, autobiographical voice and, in his later work, various dramatic personae.

One effect of this change in strategy has been to increase Heaney's concern with issues of poetic authority and responsibility, often at the expense of analzying the violence itself and its causes and effects. In this regard, Heaney's most important ancestor is Yeats, not Kavanagh. Yeats's obsessive interrogation of his own poetic practices and theories, particularly in relation to the political violence of his own day, stands behind much of Heaney's relentless investigation of his position as a northern-born Irish poet writing amid the violence in contemporary Northern Ireland. And Yeats's tendency to aestheticize the political issues and violence of his Ireland stands behind Heaney's reading of the conflict in the north, especially from *Field Work* (1979) on, in ways that seem interested at least as much in aesthetic as in political concerns. Although Yeat's confidence in art's power to transcend if not transform culture is less available to a contemporary poet such as Heaney, confronted with a conflict that has demonstrated, among other things, that Yeats's literary revival deferred rather than resolved problems of cultural difference that it addressed, Yeats's transformation of the Easter Rising into the "terrible beauty" of "Easter 1916" significantly informs Heaney's important poem, "Casualty." The killing in the wake of Bloody Sunday of a fisherman whom Heaney had known since boyhood is self-consciously transformed into a celebration of poetic power and independence:

> I missed his funeral,
> Those quiet walkers
> And sideways talkers
> Shoaling out of his lane
> To the respectable
> Purring of the hearse . . .
> They move in equal pace
> With the habitual
> Slow consolation
> Of a dawdling engine,
> The line lifted, hand
> Over fist, cold sunshine
> On the water, the land
> Banked under fog: that morning
> I was taken in his boat,
> The screw purling, turning
> Indolent fathoms white,
> I tasted freedom with him.
> To get out early, haul
> Steadily off the bottom,
> Dispraise the catch, and smile
> As you find a rhythm
> Working you, slow mile by mile,
> Into your proper haunt
> Somewhere, well out, beyond . . .[13]

For Eavan Boland, the Irish poet's relationship to politics depends crucially on an element that she sees as excluded from the tradition in which a writer such as Heaney is self-consciously working. In Boland's view, it is virtually impossible to write a truly radical political poem if the author remains oblivious to the repressive force of Irish poetry in relation to gender; whatever the poet's views on traditional political issues, to write from such a position is to be, Boland says, "unquestioning of inherited authority."[14] The rise of women to a central position in Irish poetry over the past quarter-century—"women have

moved from being the objects of Irish poems to being the authors of them," as
Boland has put it[15]—represents therefore a radicalizing of Irish poetry that
goes beyond questions of gender. Moreover, as Boland has consistently argued,
this change has come about through an essentially subversive engagement with
the male-dominated tradition of Irish poetry, which, by casting women largely
as nationalist icons and symbols, effectively marginalized them from sources
of political, social, and economic power at the same time that it dangerously
oversimplified nationalism.

Boland recognizes that there have been women poets of significance in that
tradition, but in her view they were usually appropriated by relatively monolithic, and male-determined, cultural and political agendas—a phenomenon
that this history has described, especially in reference to nineteenth-century
political poetry and much of the work of the literary revival. What is missing
from most of the earlier writing by Irish women, Boland says, is the actual
experience of women, "an expressed poetic life which would have dignified
and revealed mine."[16] The effort to deconstruct and repossess that tradition
has required, to begin with, writing poems about realities excluded from it,
establishing, for example, the acceptability of the female body and female
sexuality as subjects for Irish poems. This was the effect of Boland's two highly
controversial collections, *In Her Own Image* (1980) and *Night Feed* (1982), for
which Boland turned for models to contemporary American poets such as
Sylvia Plath and Adrienne Rich. At the level of aesthetics as well as sexuality,
the poems in these volumes are bluntly, graphically radical. "Tirade for the
Mimic Muse" identifies the tradition of Irish poetry with a prostitute in a voice
calculated to shock and subvert:

> I've caught you out. You slut. You fat trout.
> So here you are fumed in candle-stink.
> Its yellow balm exhumes you for the glass.
> How you arch and pout in it!
> How you poach your face in it!
> Anyone would think you were a whore—
> An ageing out-of-work kind-hearted tart.
> I know you for the ruthless bitch you are:
> Our criminal, our tricoteuse, our Muse—
> Our Muse of Mimic Art.[17]

More recently, Boland has focused on victims of Irish history, less as symbolic
representations of the marginalized position of women in Irish culture than as
a means of exposing the ways in which the tradition of Irish poetry has betrayed
the distinctive experiences of women, usually in the name of nationalism, and
as a means of recovering that tradition for contemporary women. Boland's

"Mise Eire" takes its title from a well-known nationalist poem by the Easter Rising poet Patrick Pearse, and Boland's poem interrogates the tradition that Pearse's poem represents by linking Boland's rejection of it ("I won't go back to it—//my nation displaced/into old dactyls") to its exploitation of women and their suffering, figured in images of a prostitute—a radical rewriting of the nationalist icon of virginal Ireland being raped by corrupted England—and of a woman emigrant:

> No. I won't go back.
> My roots are brutal:
>
> I am the woman—
> a sloven's mix
> of silk at the wrists,
> a sort of dove-strut
> in the precincts of the garrison—
>
> who practises
> the quick frictions,
> the rictus of delight
> and gets cambric for it,
> rice-coloured silks.
>
> I am the woman
> in the gansy-coat
> on board the "Mary Belle",
> in the huddling cold,
>
> holding her half-dead baby to her
> as the wind shifts East
> and North over the dirty
> water of the wharf
>
> mingling the immigrant
> guttural with the vowels
> of homesickness . . .[18]

The long tradition of Irish poetry about emigration has been of particular interest to Boland, in part because of her own experience—she spent most of her childhood outside Ireland. More important, her poems about emigration subvert traditionally sentimentalized and nationalist representations of exile at the same time that they argue that an understanding of how the past has been misrepresented can enable Irish women to empower themselves in the present. As she says in "The Emigrant Irish": "By their lights now it is time to/imagine how they stood there, what they stood with,/that their possessions may become our power." [19]

The idea that the way to write women's voices and experiences into Irish poetry is to engage rather than reject the tradition that excluded them is itself derivative of that tradition, as Boland has acknowledged. For Boland, Kavanagh is an important predecessor in this regard, an Irish poet who had to write the realities of the life that he knew into a tradition that had betrayed those realities by representing rural Ireland in symbolic terms dictated by one kind of nationalist agenda or another; like Irish women, Boland has said, Kavanagh "was part of the iconic structure of the Irish poem long before he became its author." [20] More broadly, modern Irish poets working in Yeats's considerable wake had to repossess the Yeatsian poem and its representations of certain aspects of the Irish experience. As Boland said in a recent interview, she has come to see her work—and the same might be said of the work of many other contemporary Irish women, such as Nuala Ní Dhomhnaill, Medbh McGuckian, Eiléan Ní Chuilleanáin, and Paula Meehan, to name only the most prominent —as "a continuation, a broadening out, of something that had been happening in Irish poetry for quite a while." [21] But it also might be argued, as Boland has also done, that the repossession of the Irish poetic tradition undertaken in the past twenty-five years by women is a more radical, and ultimately more important, rewriting of the past than those that have preceded it. Not only has it given power and voice to a significant range of Irish experience hitherto absent from Irish poetry, but it has also exposed the dangers inherent in the kind of romantic nationalism that has informed Irish writing and thinking at least since the early years of the nineteenth century. As Richard Kearney has argued, the mythologizing of women in the Irish tradition occurred alongside the promulgation of definitions of the Irish nation that were equally unrealistic [22]; to expose the fallacies of one kind of mythologizing is, therefore, to expose the fallacies of the other. The result is a new view of women and of the nation, as well as a new kind of poetry. "When the history of poetry in our time is written," Boland has said, "women poets will be seen to have re-written not just the poem, not just the image. . . . They will have altered the cartography of the poem. The map will look different." [23]

The work done in translation during the past quarter-century has also helped change the map of Irish poetry to accommodate contemporary experience. Departing from the long tradition of translation as an enterprise committed to cultural recovery and preservation, and therefore a relatively conservative force in Irish writing, much contemporary translation has taken for its texts the work of contemporary poets writing in Irish, affirming the relevance of poetry in Irish to contemporary culture. [24] It is significant that the most prominent contemporary poet writing in Irish is Nuala Ní Dhomhnaill, who shares many of Boland's feminist values as well as her attitudes toward the tradition of Irish writing. [25] Nor is it surprising that Ní Dhomhnaill is the most widely translated of contemporary poets writing in the language, or that her translators include so many contemporary Irish poets whose own work in English is concerned with the kinds of issues regarding poetic authority and the poet's relationship to the Irish poetic tradition raised by Boland's work: Michael Hartnett (who writes in both languages), John Montague, Michael Longley, Paul Muldoon, Medbh McGuckian, and Ciaran Carson. Moreover, the work of these translators often draws heavily on colloquial diction, idioms, and speech rhythms, effectively recentering poetry written in Irish, and the translation enterprise along with it, in contemporary culture. Muldoon is probably the raciest of Ní Dhomhnaill's translators; in his version of "An Crann," he translates the opening line "Do tháinig bean an leasa" ("a woman of the fairy mound came") as "There came this bright young thing," and "Bhí an gomh dearg air" ("the red venom was on him") as "he lost the rag." The chief effect of his translation, entitled "As for the Quince," is to emphasize the way in which Ní Dhomhnaill's poem seeks to subvert romantic representations of women in certain versions of Irish fairylore, such as those that dominated the early years of the literary revival:

> There came this bright young thing
> with a Black & Decker
> and cut down my quince-tree.
> I stood with my mouth hanging open
> while one by one
> she trimmed off the branches.
>
> When my husband got home that evening
> and saw what had happened
> he lost the rag,
> as you might imagine.
> 'Why didn't you stop her?
> What would she think
> if I took a Black & Decker
> round to her place
> and cut down a quince-tree
> belonging to her?
> What would she make of that?'
>
> Her ladyship came back next morning
> while I was at breakfast.
> She enquired about his reaction.
> I told her straight
> that he was wondering how she'd feel
> if he took a Black & Decker
> round to her house
> and cut down a quince-tree of hers,
> etcetera etcetera.

'O,' says she, 'that's very interesting.'
There was a stress on the 'very'.
She lingered over the 'ing'.
She was remarkably calm and collected.

These are the times that are in it, so,
all a bit topsy-turvy.
The bottom falling out of my belly
as if I had got a kick up the arse
or a punch in the kidneys.
A fainting-fit coming over me
that took the legs from under me
and left me so zonked
I could barely lift a finger
till Wednesday.

As for the quince, it was safe and sound
and still somehow holding its ground.[26]

The sense of being displaced that has inspired much of Boland's writing about the position of women in the Irish tradition is also central to the work of Derek Mahon; indeed, homelessness is arguably the most important theme in Mahon's work. Moreover, more than any other Irish poet of his cosmopolitan generation, Mahon is as at home in the world of continental or American writing as in that of the tradition of Irish poetry. There are, of course, precedents in that tradition for the tendency to define Irish writing in an international rather than a strictly national context. Mahon's considerable interest in French literature—in Camus, Moliére, Racine, Rimbaud, Tristan Corbière, Phlippe Jaccottet, and Gerard de Nerval—can be seen as an extension of Yeats's early efforts to import continental literary theories and practices into the writing of the Irish literary revival; it also draws on the substantial links between Irish poetry and continental modernism forged by later writers such as Denis Devlin, Thomas MacGreevy, and Brian Coffey. And the intersection between Mahon's work and modern American poetry owes something to the work in the 1950s and 1960s of Thomas Kinsella and John Montague. Mahon's more radical, distinctly postmodern embrace of homelessness, however, represents not just an extension of the tradition of Irish poetry but also a subversive engagement with it. Much of Mahon's work can be seen as rewriting the nostalgia for Ireland as a lost Eden in the long tradition of nationalist writing about exile and emigration into a Joycean critique of Irish culture enabled by distance, and, more broadly, into an affirmation of exile and centrifugality as constitutive of the postmodern sensibility. Indeed, one effect of Mahon's work in this vein has been to recenter the exile tradition in Irish writing; Mahon's recent long poem about New York City, "The Hudson Letter," arguably belongs as much to American poetry, specifically the tradition of New York poetry represented by Walt Whitman and Hart Crane, as it does to Irish poetry.

Boland has described Mahon as "more expert on distance than on engagement." [27] If the idea of distance is central to Mahon's view of postmodern man —"distance is the vital bond," as he once put it[28]—his sceptical, at times adversarial attitude toward his native Northern Ireland seems to have been very much encouraged by his separation from it. (He has lived outside the north for most of his adult life). At times, especially when confronted with the intensity of religious prejudice that lies behind the violence in the north, Mahon has written of his Northern Protestant background with a bitterness reminiscent of some of Yeats's writing about the Irish Catholic middle class. More characteristically, however, his poetry about the north is marked by a sense of ambiguity and guilt not unlike that found in much of Heaney's writing. In "Afterlives," Mahon describes a return to Belfast that leaves him feeling as Heaney once described himself, "lost,/Unhappy and at home," [29] a reversal of Mahon's usual position of feeling more or less at home in being lost:

> And I step ashore in a fine rain
> To a city so changed
> By five years of war
> I scarcely recognize
> The places I grew up in,
> The faces that try to explain.
>
> But the hills are still the same
> Grey-blue above Belfast.
> Perhaps if I'd stayed behind
> And lived it bomb by bomb
> I might have grown up at last
> And learnt what is meant by home.[30]

This complex response to his northern background owes something to the work of Louis MacNeice, and Mahon has frequently acknowledged the debt. As a displaced northerner who often wrote out of a cosmopolitan, modernist sense of alienation, MacNeice has also served Mahon as a model in his engagement with the broader, postmodern implications of his embrace of distance. " 'A tourist in his own country', it has been said, with the implication that this is somehow discreditable," Mahon has written of MacNeice. "But of what sensitive person is the same not true? The phrase might stand, indeed, as an epigraph for Modern Man." [31] But Mahon's view of the periphery as the only certainty, and his corresponding distrust of home or center, also critically engages the tradition of Irish poetry on several fronts. For one thing, it reverses the romantic-nationalist assumptions on which the tradition of exile writing has been constructed, assumptions that idealize home—that is, Ireland—as the only substantial ground, the position from which all experience, personal and political, is to be measured. Mahon's aggressive internationalism also implicitly calls into question the provincial focus that has traditionally dominated Irish writing, and, more specifically, Yeatsian notions of community and rootedness that lay behind the literary revival, not to mention a considerable amount of Irish writing in its wake.[32] In "The Hudson Letter," writing about Ireland from his usual distance, and from the position of a father separated from his children, Mahon evokes one of Yeats's most famous affirmations of these qualities, "A Prayer for My Daughter," as a way of critiquing conservative and nationalist notions of Irish community, and of affirming the need for a different kind of mythology in the contemporary world:

> Sometimes, as I sit in the Knickerbocker or stand up there
> in Columbia University like Philby in Red Square,
> I blush like a traitor; but what kind of a traitor?
> A traitor to the past? To a country not our own?
> To the land of fiscal rectitude and spiritual desolation?
> The 'family values' brigade? The conservative task-force?
> The gene militia? The armies of the unborn?
> I know 'our loyalty to unhappiness', of course,
> 'the feeling that this is where we really belong';
> and yet, across 3,000 miles of water
> and five time-zones, my prayer for my own daughter
> would be, not innocence and ceremony
> exactly, but a more complicated grace,
>
>   .   .   .
>
> some rich myth of reconciliation
> as if a statue moved and began to live—
> for I like to think all this is a winter's tale
> around a hearth (but whose?)[33]

In the same poem, it is Yeats's father, living out his years in voluntary exile in New York, not Yeats himself, with whom Mahon expresses an affinity:

> Now, to 'Yeats, Artist and Writer', may we add
> that you were at home here and in human nature?
> —But also, in your own words, lived and died
> like all of us, then as now, 'an exile and a stranger'?[34]

Finally, Mahon's poetry calls into question the emphasis in Irish writing on the importance of place and locality. In this regard, Mahon's view that, as he once put it, "Irish poetry in the 20th century, like poetry everywhere, has been increasingly centrifugal" departs radically from the archeological aesthetics that drive much of Heaney's early work and from the affirmation of locality inherited by Heaney and other contemporary Irish poets from Kavanagh.[35] This scepticism about Irish notions of place and community also represents another way in which Mahon's work questions the relevance of the attitudes and values embedded in the Irish tradition for a postmodern world defined by high technology and instantaneous global communication, aspects of contemporary life increasingly represented in Mahon's work.

Like Boland, Mahon often writes from the point of view of history's victims. But for Mahon these figures—the departed emigrant family in "A Garage in Co. Cork," the lost people represented by the mushrooms in "A Disused Shed in Co. Wexford," the ghostly victims of a British massacre during the Elizabethan wars in "Rathlin"—suggest not only marginalized or silenced voices that Irish poetry has an obligation to represent but also the precariousness of life on the margins. As such, they inject ambiguity and scepticism into Mahon's view of homelessness as a meaningful center, and therefore into his own position and authority as a postmodern poet; as he puts it in "The Hudson Letter," "there's something missing here/in this autistic slammer." [36] This doubt about the efficacy of his position as a writer is also evident in Mahon's fondness for the verse-letter; poems such as "Beyond Howth Head," "The Sea in Winter," "The Globe in North Carolina," "The Yaddo Letter," and "The Hudson Letter" are one-sided dialogues, messages sent blindly across great distances.

Mahon's poetic tribute to MacNeice—the words of one Irish poet bound up in the multiple ambiguities that have been part of the condition of the Irish poet writing in English since the days of Swift's worried self-dramatizations to another Irish poet who wrote out of a similar position—might be taken both as an acknowledgement of the difficulties inherent in that condition and as a celebration of the Irish poet's ability to create his art from them:

> Locked in the winter's fist, these hills are hard
> As nails, yet soft and feminine in their turn
> When fingers open and the hedges burn.
> This, you implied, is how we ought to live—
> The ironical, loving crush of roses against the snow,
> Each fragile, solving ambiguity. So
> From the pneumonia of the ditch, from the ague
> Of the blind poet and the bombed-out town you bring
> The all-clear to the empty holes of spring,
> Rinsing the choked mud, keeping the colours new.[37]

As this history has consistently argued, Irish poetry's "fragile, solving ambiguity," not to mention its potential for making the hedges burn, has depended significantly on its ability to negotiate between a complex and divided past—one constituted and complicated in part by the tradition of poetry itself—and a present very much shaped by that past, to insist on the necessity for historical continuity, however disrupted or unstable the tradition being continued might seem to be, and so on the need for the past to be continuously repossessed and reinvented by the present.

Notes

Part One. The Eighteenth Century

Introduction

1. Upon a House Shaken by the Land Agitation," *The Green Helmet and Other Poems* (1910); rpt. *The Variorum Edition of the Poems of W. B. Yeats,* ed. Peter Allt and Russell K. Alspach (New York: Macmillan, 1957), p. 264. The most thorough study of the realities of the Anglo-Irish Ascendancy is W. J. McCormack, *Ascendancy and Tradition in Anglo-Irish Literary History from 1789 to 1939* (Oxford: Clarendon Press, 1985.)

2. Norman Vance, *Irish Literature: A Social History: Tradition, Identity and Difference* (Oxford: Basil Blackwell, 1990), pp. 65–66.

3. Seamus Deane, *A Short History of Irish Literature* (London: Hutchinson, 1986), found this disjunction particularly evident in the writings of Swift and Burke, who, he said, "inaugurated a tradition in which language is rarely reconciled to fact, but is instead always in the condition of transcending or humiliating fact" (p. 36).

Chapter One. Swift and His World

1. Swift was not, of course, the first poet writing in English about Ireland. Parts of Spenser's poetic canon certainly pertain to Ireland, for example, and Naham Tate (1652–1715), a Dubliner by birth, was a prolific poet, although little of his work concerns Ireland.

2. Denis Florence McCarthy, *The Poets and Dramatists of Ireland* (Dublin: James Duffy, 1846), p. 130.

3. Quoted in David Nokes, *Jonathan Swift, A Hypocrite Reversed: A Critical Biography* (Oxford: Oxford University Press, 1985), pp. 373–74.

4. Samuel Johnson, *The Lives of the Poets,* vol. 2 (Dublin: Whitestone, 1781), p. 482.

5. Ibid., p. 440.

6. From a letter by Swift to Charles Wogan, July-August, 1732; quoted in *The Field Day Anthology of Irish Writing,* ed. Seamus Deane, vol. 1 (Derry: Field Day Publications, 1991), p. 990.

7. Johnson, *Lives of the Poets,* p. 481.

8. Ibid., p. 474.

9. As Nokes put it, "Swift tantalized himself and the world by rejecting the fruit which gossips everywhere believed him to be enjoying"; Nokes, *Jonathan Swift,* p. 259.

10. According to Nokes: "In reality, Ireland in 1719 had become a colony in all but name; and it was a colonial system that the *Drapier's Letters* were written to challenge. But like all conservatives, even the most radical, Swift could not avow so revolutionary an intention, and preferred to argue instead in terms of precedent and tradition"; Ibid., p. 286.

11. Johnson, *Lives of the Poets,* p. 447.

12. *The Poems of Jonathan Swift,* vol. 1, ed. Harold Williams, 2d ed. (Oxford: Clarendon Press, 1958), p. 137.

13. Ibid., p. 203.

14. Jonathan Swift, "Some Observations upon a Paper, Call'd, the Report of the Committee," in *The Drapier's Letters and Other Works 1724–1725,* ed. Herbert Davis (Oxford: Basil Blackwell, 1941), p. 31.

15. Jonathan Swift, *Irish Tracts: 1720–1723 And Sermons,* ed. Louis Landa (Oxford: Basil Blackwell, 1948), p. 21.

16. Swift, *Poems,* vol. 2, p. 484.

17. Ibid., vol. 1, pp. 236–37.

18. Ibid., p. 237.

19. Ibid., vol. 3, p. 772.

20. Ibid., pp. 770–71.

21. Ibid., p. 856. Williams glosses "mundungus" as "rank tobacco."

22. Ibid., vol. 2, p. 567.

23. Ibid., p. 571.

24. Robert Welch, in *A History of Verse Translation from the Irish: 1789–1897* (Gerrards Cross, England: Colin Smythe, 1988), said of the origins of this poem: "According to an account in *Swiftiana* (1804), Swift met the Gaelic poet Hugh MacGowran, who wrote 'Pléaráca na Ruarcach'('O'Rourke's Feast'), at a country house in County Cavan. There he heard the poem sung to Carolan's music and liked it so much that he asked MacGowran for a literal version. From this version he made his 'Description of an Irish Feast' (1720)" (p. 17).

25. Austin Clarke, "O'Rourke's Feast," in *Flight to Africa* (1963), is discussed in Chapter 16 of this book. Thomas Kinsella, in *The Dual Tradition: An Essay on Poetry and Politics in Ireland* (Manchester: Carcanet Press, 1995), argued that Swift's version of this poem provides "the first full occurence of the stage Irishman" (p. 36).

26. Swift, *Poems,* vol. 1, p. 246.

27. Ibid., pp. 244–45.

28. Ibid., vol. 3, pp. 789–90.

29. Ibid., vol. 2, pp. 420–21.

30. Jonathan Smedley, *Gulliveriana: or, a Fourth Volume of Miscellanies* (London: J. Roberts, 1728), p. 77–78.

31. Nokes argued that Swift's religious views were more a matter of practicality than of a deep-seated belief in God and the redemption. Swift's religious writings, Nokes said, reveal "the tormented pessimism of an orthodox clergyman who cannot really believe in God"; Nokes, *Jonathan Swift,* p. 101.

32. "His Grace's Answer to Jonathan," *Poems of Jonathan Swift,* vol. 2, p. 361.

33. *A Miscellaneous Collection of Poems, Songs and Epigrams. By Several Hands,* ed. T. M Gent, 2 vols. (Dublin: A. Rhames, 1721), vol. 1, p. 129.

34. Both these volumes include the work of other writers, but most of the poems in them are attributed to Winstanley.

35. *Poems, Written Occasionally by John Winstanley . . . Interspers'd with Many Others. By Several Ingenious Hands,* 2 vols. (Dublin: S. Powell, 1742), vol. 1, pp. 194–95.

36. "The Life of Dr. Parnell" (1770), in *Collected Works of Oliver Goldsmith,* ed. Arthur Friedman, vol. 3 (Oxford: Clarendon Press, 1966), p. 422.

37. Johnson, *Lives of the Poets,* vol. 3, p. 31.

38. Thomas Parnell, *Poems on Several Occasions* (London: B. Lintot, 1722), p. 18.

39. Goldsmith, *Collected Works,* vol. 3, p. 415.

40. Ibid., p. 426.

41. Parnell, *Poems on Several Occasions,* pp. 153, 155–56.

42. Thomas Parnell, *Poetical Miscellanies,* ed. Richard Steele, 2d ed. (London: J. Tonson, 1727), p. 101.

43. Introduction to *Poems by Thomas Parnell,* ed. Lennox Robinson (Dublin: Cuala Press, 1927), n. p.

44. *The Poems of Alexander Pope,* ed. John Butt (New Haven: Yale University Press, 1963), p. 394.

45. Matthew Concanen, *Poems Upon Several Occasions* (Dublin: A. Rhames, 1722), pp. 34–5.

46. Concanen, *Poems upon Several Occasions,* p. 74.

47. Matthew Pilkington, *Poems on Several Occasions* (Dublin: 1730; London: T. Woodward, Charles Davis, and W. Bowyer, 1731), p. 9.

48. Earl of Orreny, quoted in Iris Barry, "Introduction," *Memoirs of Laetitia Pilkington, 1712–1750* (London: Routledge, 1928), p. 1.

49. Jonathan Swift, quoted in [Mary Barber], *Poems on Several Occasions* (London: C. Rivington, 1735), p. vi.

50. Jonathan Swift, quoted in Barry, "Introduction," *Memoirs,* p. 9.

51. There is some dispute as to Barber's birthdate. Anne M. Brady and Brian Cleeve, *A Biographical Dictionary of Irish Writers* (Mullingar, Ireland Lilliput Press, 1985), p. 6, *The Field Day Anthology of Irish Writing,* ed. Deane, vol. 1 p. 494, and *The Oxford Companion to Irish Literature,* ed. Robert Welch (Oxford: Clarendon Press, 1996), p. 32, all place it at 1690. Patrick Fagan, *A Georgian Celebration: Irish Poets of the Eighteenth Century* (Dublin: Branar, 1989), p. 43, says that the date is not certain, but estimates it to be 1685.

52. *Correspondence of Mary Granville/Mrs Delany,* ed. Lady Llanover, vol. 3, first series (London, 1861), p. 327, quoted in Fagan, *A Georgian Celebration,* p. 44.

53. Barber, *Poems on Several Occasions,* p. 3.

54. Ibid., p. 58.

55. Ibid., pp. 59–60.

56. Ibid., p. 138.

57. Ibid., pp. 33–34.

58. Ibid., p. xxv.

59. Ibid., p. 142. Several of Grierson's poems were published posthumously in Barber's book.

60. *Memoirs of Mrs Laetitia Pilkington* (Dublin and London: R. Griffiths, 1748), vol. 1, p. 50.

61. Pilkington, *Memoirs,* p. 105.

62. Ibid., p. 238.

63. Ibid., p. 241.

64. Ibid., p. 297.

65. [Dorothea Du Bois,] *Poems on Several Occasions. By a Lady of Quality* (Dublin, 1764), p. 135. I am indebted to Andrew Carpenter for acquainting me with Du Bois's work.

66. [Du Bois,] *Poems on Several Occasions,* pp. 85–86.

67. Ibid., p. 4.

Chapter Two. Divergent Directions: Beyond and Within the Pale

1. There is some dispute as to Whyte's birth date and date of death. According to *The Field Day Anthology,* ed. Seamus Deane, vol. 1 (Derry: Field Day Publications, 1991), he was born circa 1700 (p. 498). Patrick Fagan, *A Georgian Celebration: Irish Poets of the Eighteenth Century* (Dublin: Branar, 1989), says he may have born in the early 1680s (p. 32). *The Field Day Anthology* and *The Oxford Companion to Irish Literature,* ed. Robert Welch (Oxford: Clarendon Press, 1996), put his death at 1755, while Fagan says it occurred in 1752 or 1753.

2. Laurence Whyte, *Poems on Various Subjects, Serious and Diverting* (Dublin: S. Powell, 1740), pp. 69–70.

3. This hypothesis has been suggested by Fagan, *A Georgian Celebration,* p. 33.

4. Laurence Whyte, *Poems on Various Subjects,* p. 158. "Sweet Bocci" refers to Lorenzo Bocchi, an Italian musician.

5. Ibid., p. 159.

6. Ibid., p. vii.

7. Ibid., p. 92.

8. Ibid.

9. Laurence Whyte, "To the Rev. Dr. *Jonathan Swift,* Dean of St. *Patrick's,* Dublin, on the Publishing of a New Edition of His Works in Four Volumes," *Poems on Various Subjects,* p. 181.

10. *The Field Day Anthology,* ed. Deane, vol. 1, places Dunkin's birth "about 1709" (p. 495); Fagan, *A Georgian Celebration,* says he was born in 1706 or 1707 (p. 108); Anne M. Brady and Brian Cleeve, *A Biographical Dictionary of Irish Writers* (Mullingar Ireland, Lilliput Press, 1985), place his birth in 1709 (p. 66).

11. Jonathan Swift, letter to John Barber, January 17, 1737–38, quoted in *The Field Day Anthology,* ed. Deane, vol. 1, p. 396.

12. William Dunkin, *Select Poetical Works,* vol. 1 (Dublin: W. G. Jones and S. Dowell, 1769), p. 157.

13. Dunkin, *Select Poetical Works,* vol. 1, p. 21.

14. Ibid., pp. 63–65.

15. Ibid., vol. 2 p. 27.

16. *The Irish Hudibras, or Fingallian Prince, Taken from the Sixth Book of Virgil's Aeneaids, and Adapted to the Present Time* (London: Richard Baldwin, 1689), p. 35. "Cronans" comes from the Irish "cronán," meaning "humming, droning, or purring."

17. *Irish Hudibras,* p. 16.

18. Ibid., pp. 108–9.

19. W. M., *Hesperi-neso-Graphia: or, a Description of the Western Isles. In Eight Cantos* (Dublin: Theo. Jones, 1735), pp. 4–5. This poem has variously, but inconclusively, been attributed to William Moffett and to William Jones. Another version of the poem in the National Library in Dublin is William Moffett, *The Irish Hudibras. Hesperi-neso-graphia: or, a Description of the Western Isles* (London: J. Reason, 1755). *The Field Day Anthology,* ed. Deane, vol. 1 p. 440, dates the poem circa 1716.

20. *Hesperi-neso-Graphia,* p. 9.

21. Ibid., p. 21.

22. *The Petition of Murrough O Connor to the Provost and Senior Fellows of Trinity College, near Dublin. To which are added: I. An Eclogue, in Imitation of the First Eclogue of Virgil . . . II. Two Dialogues between Murrough O Connor and his Friend . . . III. The County of Kerry. A Poem* (Dublin, 1740), pp. 24–25.

23. *Petition of Murrough O Connor,* p. 14.

Chapter Three. Goldsmith and the Beginnings of Romanticism

1. Oliver Goldsmith to Henry Goldsmith, January 1759, quoted in W. J. McCormick, "Goldsmith, Biography and the Phenomenology of Anglo-Irish Literature," in *The Art of Oliver Goldsmith,* ed. Andrew Swarbrick (London: Vision Press, 1984), p. 176.

2. Samuel Johnson, quoted in "Introduction" to *Goldsmith: The Gentle Master,* ed. Sean Lucy (Cork: Cork University Press, 1984), p. 9.

3. Oliver Goldsmith to Henry Goldsmith, January 1759, quoted in McCormick, "Goldsmith," p. 176.

4. Goldsmith quoted in Roger McHugh and Maurice Harmon, *Short History of Anglo-Irish Literature* (Totowa, N. J.: Barnes and Noble, 1982), p. 61.

5. Oliver Goldsmith, "A Description of the Manners and Customs of the Native *Irish," The Weekly Magazine,* December 29, 1759; rpt. in *Collected Works of Oliver Goldsmith,* ed. Arthur Friedman vol. 3 (Oxford: Clarendon Press, 1966), p. 25.

6. The work that represents a partial exception to this attitude is Laurence Whyte's "The Parting Cup," discussed earlier; Goldsmith may well have been familiar with this poem since Goldsmith's native Lissoy is only a few miles from Whyte's native Ballymore.

7. Seamus Deane, for example, in *The Field Day Anthology,* vol. 1, said that for Goldsmith, Ireland was less a political and social reality than "the occasion for a nostalgia" (p. 660). Noting that Yeats included Goldsmith among the important figures in his conservative reconstruction of the eighteenth century, Deane said that Goldsmith offered Yeats "a pastoral version of Ireland to support the notion of the Anglo-Irish honeymoon which had intervened between the seventeenth century wars and the rise of nationalism in the nineteenth century" (p. 660).

8. Goldsmith, *Collected Works,* vol. 4, pp. 248–49.

9. Ibid., pp. 249–50.

10. Ibid., pp. 263–64. As Donald Davie argued, these lines constitute a "caustic indictment of the world of 'free enterprise', unstructured and unrestricted competitiveness, the morality of the market—in ideas, in status, and in feelings, as well as commodities"; Davie, "Notes on Goldsmith's Politics," in *The Art of Oliver Goldsmith,* ed. Swarbrick, p. 86.

11. Goldsmith, *Collected Works,* vol. 4, p. 264.

12. Ibid., p. 267.

13. John Montague, "Exile and Prophecy: A Study of Goldsmith's Poetry," in *Goldsmith: The Gentle Master,* ed. Lucy, p. 63.

14. Quoted in John Montague, "The Sentimental Prophecy: A Study of *The Deserted Village,"* in *The Art of Oliver Goldsmith,* Swarbrick, p. 102.

15. Montague, "The Sentimental Prophecy," p. 103.

16. Goldsmith, *Collected Works,* vol. 4, p. 299.

17. Ibid., p. 301.

18. Oliver Goldsmith, "The Revolution in Low Life," *Lloyd's Evening Post,* June 14–16, 1762; rpt. in Goldsmith, *Collected Works,* vol. 3, p. 195.

19. Goldsmith, quoted in McHugh and Harmon, *Short History of Anglo-Irish Literature,* p. 61.

20. Rev. Edward Mangin, *Essay on Light Reading* (1808); quoted in Montague, "The Sentimental Prophecy," p. 91.

21. Goldsmith, *Collected Works,* vol. 4, p. 296.

22. Oliver Goldsmith to Henry Goldsmith, quoted in Frank O' Connor, *A Short History of Irish Literature: A Backward Look* (1966; New York: Capricorn Books,1967), p. 124.

23. O'Connor, *Short History,* p. 124.

24. Goldsmith, *Collected Works,* vol. 4, p. 297.

25. Roger McHugh, "Anglo-Irish Poetry 1700–1850," in *Irish Poets in English,* ed. Sean Lucy (Cork: Mercier Press, 1973), p. 82.

26. Samuel Whyte, *The Shamrock: or Hibernian Cresses* (Dublin: R. Marchbank, 1772), p. 421.

27. Whyte, *Shamrock* p. 11.

28. Ibid., p. 12.

29. Ibid.

30. Samuel Whyte, *Poems on Various Subjects,* 3d ed., rev. Edward Anthenry Whyte (Dublin: Robert Marchbank, 1795), p. 257.

31. Samuel Whyte, "Impromptu, Written on the Back of a Trencher in the Cottage at the Crooked Wood, County Westmeath, August, 1773," *Poems on Various Subjects,* p. 188.

32. "Thomas Dermody," in *The Cabinet of Irish Literature,* ed. Charles A. Read, vol. 2 (London: Blackie and Son, 1879), p. 58. In a poem entitled "The Pursuit of Patronage," Dermody invites the comparison, citing Chatterton as an example of a brilliant young poet—"All untaught genius breathing from his breast"—destroyed by economic want; Dermody, *(The Harp of Erin, containing the Poetical Works of the Late Thomas Dermody,* ed. James G. Raymond, 2 vols. London: Richard Phillips, 1807), vol. 1, p. 47.

33. Dermody, *Harp of Erin,* vol. 1, p. 91.

34. James Grant Raymond, Introduction to *Harp of Erin,* p. ix.

35. Dermody, *Harp of Erin,* vol. 1, p. 20.

36. Ibid., pp. 15–16.

37. Ibid., p. 132.

38. Ibid., p. 84.

39. Ibid., vol. 2, p. 267.

40. Ibid., vol. 1, p. 246.

41. Ibid., p. 247.

Chapter Four. Political Poetry at the End of the Century

1. Mary O'Brien, *The Political Monitor; or Regent's Friend* (Dublin: William Gilbert, 1790), pp. 31–32.

2. Edward Lysaght, *Poems* (Dublin: Gilbert and Hodges, 1811), p. 19.

3. Lysaght, *Poems,* p. 52.

4. Ibid., pp. 87–88.

5. Ibid., p. 92.

6. *The Posthumous Works of James Orr,* ed. A. M'Dowell (Belfast: Francis D. Finlay, 1817), p. 75.

7. Orr, *Poems on Various Subjects* (Belfast: Smyth and Lyons, 1804; rpt. Belfast: William Mullan, 1936), pp. 167–68.

8. Orr, *Poems on Various Subjects,* p. 168.

9. Ibid., pp. 52–53.

10. In *Irish Literature: A Social History* (Oxford: Basil Blackwell, 1990), Norman Vance said that Drennan "was the most effective literary exponent of the radical nationalist possibilities within Irish Presbyterianism" (p. 88).

11. The poem's title is given as "Wake. 1797." in Drennan, *Fugitive Pieces, in Verse and Prose* (Belfast: F. D. Finlay, 1815), p. 79.

12. Drennan, *Fugitive Pieces,* p. 79.

13. Ibid., pp. 80–81. As Norman Vance argued in *Irish Literature: A Social History,* the poem resists "wallowing in martyr's blood," and instead advances "an Enlightenment confidence that order and justice will eventually prevail over primal chaos" (p. 99).

14. Terence Brocon, *Northern Voices: Poets from Ulster* (Dublin: Gill and Macmillan, 1975), p. 25.

15. *Fugitive Pieces,* p. 114.
16. Ibid., p. 115.

Epilogue. The Other Ireland

1. Henry Brooke, "The Farmer's Letter to the Protestants of Ireland" (1745); quoted in *The Field Day Anthology of Irish Writing,* ed. Seamus Deane, 1 vol. (Derry: Field Day Publishing, 1991), p. 900.

2. Charlotte Brooke, *Reliques of Irish Poetry: Consisting of Heroic Poems, Odes, Elegies, and Songs* (Dublin: George Bonham, 1789), p. 250.

3. *Poems of Sir Samuel Ferguson,* ed. Alfred Percival Graves (Dublin: Talbot Press, [1917]), pp. 48–49.

4. Brooke, *Reliques of Irish Poetry,* pp. vii–viii.

5. As Declan Kiberd argued: "Her call to the English reader . . . is a warning that they must blend the Gaelic tradition with the English, if they wish to administer a united and peaceful land. It remarkably anticipates the 'union of hearts' policy of Matthew Arnold in the 1860s and it is not coincidence that both calls were issued by enlightened unionists when Ireland was on the verge of rebellion." Kiberd, "The Perils of Nostalgia: A Critique of the Revival," in *Literature and the Changing Ireland,* ed. Peter Connolly (Gerrards Cross, England: Colin Smythe, 1982), p. 17.

6. Mangan, "Dark Rosaleen," *Poems of James Clarence Mangan,* ed. D. J. O'Donoghue (Dublin: M. H. Gill, 1922), p. 5.

Part Two. The Nineteenth Century

Introduction

1. Theobold Wolfe Tone, Diary, July 13, 1792, quoted in Robert Welch, *A History of Irish Verse Translation from the Irish, 1789–1897* (Gerrards Cross, England: Colin Smythe, 1988), p. 45.

2. As Robert Welch put it: "Swift, the dissenting Republicans, the men of 1798, these were now a world away. . . . What was present and defined, with a very secure sense of its legitimacy, was the modern British Empire, into which Irishmen, somehow, would have to be translated." Welch, "Constitution, Language and Tradition in Nineteenth-Century Irish Poetry," in *Tradition and Influence in Anglo-Irish Poetry,* eds. Terence Brown and Nicholas Grene (Totowa, N.J.: Barnes and Noble, 1989), p. 29.

3. As David Lloyd put it, "the theme of identity saturates the discursive field, drowning out other social and cultural possibilities"; Lloyd, *Anomalous States: Irish Writing and the Post-Colonial Movement* (Durham, N.C.: Duke University Press, 1993), p. 3. Declan Kiberd said: "The colonialist crime was the violation of the traditional community; the nationalist crime was often a denial of the autonomy of the individual." Kiberd, *Inventing Ireland: The Literature of the Modern Nation* (London: Jonathan Cape, 1995), p. 292.

4. Seamus Deane made this point, adding: "Such a literature demanded, therefore, that the poet manifest some contact with an aspect of that essence." *The Field Day Anthology of Irish Writing,* ed. Seamus Deane, vol. 2 (Derry: Field Day Publishing, 1991), p. 4.

5. Deane argued that the motto of *The Nation*—"To create and foster public opinion, and make it racy of the soil"—represents the founders' "concern for Irish identity in the past as well as the present—'the soil' of Ireland is its timeless symbol"; *The Field Day Anthology,* ed. Deane, vol. 1, p. 1176.

6. Charles Gavan Duffy, ed. *The Ballad Poetry of Ireland,* 40th ed. (Dublin: James Duffy, 1869), p. 25.

Chapter-Five. Ireland in Transition: Thomas Moore

1. An elaborate, although not particularly compelling, argument along these lines is made by Patrick Rafroidi, *Irish Literature in English: The Romantic Period (1789–1850),* vol. 1 (Atlantic Highlands, N.J.: Humanities Press, 1972, 1980). According to Rafroidi, "the first body of poetry that is wholly Romantic and national came from Thomas Moore" (p. 11).

2. *The Poetical Works of Thomas Moore, Collected by Himself,* vol. 4 (Boston: Houghton Mifflin, 1856), p. 196.

3. Thomas Moore, quoted in Stopford A. Brooke, "Thomas Moore," in *A Treasury of Irish Poetry in the English Tongue,* ed. Stopford A. Brooke and T. W. Rolleston (1900; New York: Macmillan, 1905), p. 38.

4. Moore, *Poetical Works,* vol. 4, p. 82.

5. William Hazlitt, quoted in Terence deVere White, *Tom Moore: The Irish Poet* (London: Hamish Hamilton: 1977), p. 74. Thomas Kinsella, in *The Dual Tradition: An Essay on Poetry and Politics in Ireland* (Manchester: Carcanet Press, 1995), described Moore's poetry in general as "a development of the stage Irishman, with the capering verbal and the sentiments adjusted to the drawing room" (p. 49). On the other hand, Terry Eagleton, in *Heathcliff and the Great Hunger: Studies in Irish Culture* (London: Verso, 1995), argued that Moore's poetry, precisely because it "aspires to the condition of music," reflects perfectly the romantic quality of nationalism, "a spiritual principle before it is a political programme": "The music of Moore's lyrics is the untranslatable spirit of the nation, a distilled essence of national yearning which resists verbal embodiment" (pp. 230–31).

6. Moore, quoted in *The Field Day Anthology,* ed. Deane, vol. 1, p. 1053.

7. Seamus Deane, *The Field Day Anthology,* vol. 1, p. 1053.

8. Moore, *Poetical Works,* vol. 4, p. 102.

9. Thomas Moore, Appendix to "Intolerance: A Satire" (1808), quoted in *The Field Day Anthology,* ed. Deane, vol. 1, p. 1057.

10. As Deane said, Moore's *Irish Melodies* have "a quality of feeling that catholic emancipation could not appease"; *The Field Day Anthology,* ed. Deane, vol. 1, p. 1055.

11. Moore, *Poetical Works,* vol. 4, p. 70.

12. Ibid., p. 162.

13. Ibid., p. 64.

14. Ibid., p. 65.

15. Robert Emmett, quoted in *The Field Day Anthology,* ed. Deane, vol. 1, p. 1059.

16. Moore, *Poetical Works,* vol. 4, p. 49.

17. Ibid., p. 49.

18. Ibid., p. 72.

19. Ibid., pp. 72–73.

20. Ibid., p. 73.

21. Ibid.

22. "Oh! blame not the bard," Moore, *Poetical Works,* vol. 4, p. 74.

Chapter Six: Ireland Translated

1. Cathal G. Ó Háinle, "Towards the Revival: Some Translations of Irish Poetry: 1789–1897," in *Literature and the Changing Ireland,* ed. Peter Connolly (Gerrards Cross, England; Colin Smythe, 1982), p. 37.

2. As David Lloyd argued in *Nationalism and Minor Literature: James Clarence Mangan and the Emergence of Irish Cultural Nationalism* (Berkeley: University of California Press, 1987), the specifically nationalist concept of Ireland as a spiritual state or essence, as in the Young Ireland phrase "the spirit of the nation," rests on an assumption that that essence can be located in the nation's language (p. 66).

3. Charlotte Brooke, *Reliques of Irish Poetry: Consisting of Heroic Poems, Odes, Elegies, and Songs* (Dublin: George Bonham, 1789), pp. vii–viii.

4. In *A Short History of Irish Literature* (London: Hutchinson, 1986), Seamus Deane argued that the Protestant ascendancy needed to see the Irish language as "the symbol of a lost culture rather than a reminder of a rebellious one" (p. 63). In *Heathcliff and the Great Hunger: Studies in Irish Culture* (London: Verso, 1995), Terry Eagleton said that translation was, in effect, "an act of hegemony": "By rendering the Gaelic text in an English language at once civil and faithful, the political union of Britain and Ireland is reenacted at the level of poetic discourse" (p. 99).

5. "Aileen Aroon," *The Poetical Works of Gerald Griffin* (Dublin: James Duffy, 1854), pp. 113–4.

6. Mary Balfour, *Hope, a Poetical Essay; with Various Other Poems* (Belfast: Smyth and Lyons, 1810), p. 173.

7. Balfour *Hope,* p. 43.

8. James Hardiman, Introduction to *Irish Minstrelsy, or Bardic Remains of Ireland; with English Poetical Translations,* vol. 1, ed. James Hardiman (London: Joseph Rubins, 1831), p. i.

9. James Hardiman, quoted in Robert Welch, *A History of Verse Translation from the Irish, 1789–1897* (Gerrards Cross, England; Colin Smythe, 1988), p. 76.

10. Anon. [Samuel Ferguson], "Hardiman's Irish Minstrelsy.—No. III," *Dublin University Magazine,* 4:22 October, 1834), 453.

11. Ibid., p. 455.

12. Ibid., p. 453.

13. Thomas Furlong, "The Spint of Irish Song," in *The Field Day Anthology of Irish Writing,* ed. Seamus Deane (Derry: Field Day Publications, 1991), vol. 2, p. 17.

14. Furlong, "Roisin Dubh," *Irish Minstrelsy,* ed. Hardiman, vol. 1 p. 255.

15. Ibid., p. 49.

16. *Poems of Sir Samuel Ferguson,* ed. Alfred Percival Graves (Dublin: Talbot Press, [1917]), p. 53.

17. Sean Ó Tuama and Thomas Kinsella, eds., *An Duanaire 1600–1900: Poems of the Dispossessed* (Mountrath: Dolmen Press, 1981), p. 278.

18. Thomas Furlong, "Cashel of Munster," *Irish Minstrelsy,* ed. Hardiman, vol. 1, p. 239.

19. Anon., "Preface" to Thomas Furlong, *The Misanthrope; with Other Poems* (Dublin: W. Underwood, 1821), p. iv.

20. Thomas Furlong, *The Doom of Derenzie; A Poem* (London: Joseph Rubins, 1829), p. 14.

21. Charles Gavan Duffy, ed. *The Ballad Poetry of Ireland,* 40th ed. (Dublin: James Duffy, 1869], p. 149.

22. There is some confusion over Callanan's Christian name. According to most records, his name was Jeremiah Joseph Callanan. But he apparently also was known as James Joseph Callanan, and has been referred to as Jeremiah John Callanan.

23. George Sigerson, "Jeremiah Joseph Callanan," in *A Treasury of Irish Poetry in the English Tongue,* ed. Stopford A. Brooke and T. W. Rolleston (1900; London: Macmillan, 1905), p. 93. In the twentieth century, Geoffrey Taylor credited Callanan with being "the first to transmute not only the verbal meaning but also the rhythms, something of the emotional charge, and the alien spirit of the [Irish] poems in English"; Taylor, *Irish Poets of the Nineteenth Century* (London: Routledge and Kegan Paul, 1951), p. 59. Patrick C. Power said of Callanan: "One can scarcely call his translations anything else except a reincarnation of the old poems in a different

language"; Power, *The Story of Anglo-Irish Poetry (1800–1922)* (Cork: Mercier Press, 1967), p. 64.

24. J. J. Callanan, quoted in *The Poems of J. J. Callanan* (Cork: Daniel Mulcahy, 1861), p. xiii.

25. J. J. Callanan to Thomas Crofton Croker, quoted in Welch, *A History of Verse Translation*, p. 61.

26. J. J. Callanan, *Poems*, p. 102.

27. W. B. Yeats, *Reveries over Childhood and Youth* (1914); rpt. in *The Autobiography of W. B. Yeats* (New York: Collier Books, 1965), p. 67.

28. J. J. Callanan, *Poems*, p. 4.

29. Ibid., p. 22.

30. Ibid., p. 66.

31. Ibid.

32. Ibid.

33. Ibid., p. 67.

34. Ibid., p. 103.

35. Ibid., p. 106.

36. Ibid.

37. Ibid., p. 112.

38. Ibid., p. 115.

39. Ibid.

40. Duffy, *Ballad Poetry of Ireland*, p. 118.

41. James Clarence Mangan, *Autobiography*, ed. James Kilroy (Dublin: Dolmen Press, 1968), p. 13.

42. *The Poetical Works of Thomas Moore*, vol. 4 (Boston: Houghton Mifflin, 1856), p. 81.

43. *Poems of James Clarence Mangan*, ed. D. J. O'Donoghue (Dublin: M. H. Gill, 1922), pp. 4–5.

44. Mangan, *Autobiography*, p. 23.

45. Charles Gavan Duffy, "Personal Memories of James C. Mangan," *Dublin Review*, no. 142 (1908), p. 278.

46. Mangan, *Autobiography*, p. 26.

47. Henry J. Donoghy, *James Clarence Mangan* (New York: Twayne, 1974), p. 28.

48. W. B. Yeats, "Clarence Mangan," *Irish Fireside*, March 12, 1887; rpt. in W. B. Yeats, *Uncollected Prose*, vol. 1, ed. John P. Frayne (New York: Columbia University Press, 1970), p. 118.

49. *Poems of Mangan*, p. 124. John Mitchel, writing with his usual abandon, describes the experience this way: "As a beautiful dream she entered into his existence once for all: as a tone of celestial music she pitched the key-note of his song; and sweeping over all the chords of his melodious desolation you may see that white hand"; John Mitchel, *Poems of Mangan*, p. xxxii.

50. *Poems of Mangan*, pp. 122–23.

51. Ibid., p. 152.

52. Ibid., p. 9.

53. Ibid., p. 11.

54. Ferguson, "Hardiman's Irish Minstrelsy.—No. III," p. 457.

55. *Poems of Mangan*, p. 9. Welch, in comparing these two translations, pointed out that whereas Ferguson's poem focuses on the affection that O'Hussey feels for Maguire as an example of the capacity for loyalty among the Irish, Mangan's poem is full of an energy that is "disruptive, anarchic, explosive"; Robert Welch, *Irish Poetry from Moore to Yeats* (Totowa, N.J.: Barnes and Noble, 1980), pp. 113–13.

56. In *Nationalism and Minor Literature*, Lloyd made this argument: "the implications of his peculiar modes of translation . . . suggest the problematic nature of nationalist theories of translation as a mode of assimilating the Gaelic to the English" (p. 77). Also, Seamus Deane

argued in *The Field Day Anthology of Irish Writing,* vol. 2: "By making the possibility of translations problematic, he questions the very basis of Irish cultural nationalism, which, after all, assumes the translatability of Irish spirit into English words" (p. 6).

57. Duffy, "Personal Memories of James C. Mangan," p. 287.

58. James Clarence Mangan to John Mitchel, 1848, quoted in Duffy, "Personal Memories," p. 291.

59. *Poems of Sir Samuel Ferguson,* p. 46.

60. *Poems of Mangan,* p. 27.

61. Ibid.

62. Ibid.

63. Mangan, *Autobiography,* p. 28.

64. *Poems of Mangan,* p. 16.

65. Ibid., p. 17.

66. Ibid., p. 24.

67. Ibid., p. 172.

68. Edward Walsh to John O'Daly, 1844, quoted in Edward Walsh, *Irish Popular Songs,* 2d ed. (Dublin J. M'Glashan, 1883), p. 38.

69. John Mitchel, quoted in *The Cabinet of Irish Literature,* ed. Charles A. Read, vol. 3 (London: Blackie and Son, 1879), p. 146.

70. *Poems of Mangan,* p. 53. "Shane Bwee" is an Anglicization of "Seán Buí," or "Yellow John," a derogatory term for the English.

71. Edward Walsh, *Reliques of Irish Jacobite Poetry,* 2d ed. (Dublin: John O'Daly, 1866), p. 53.

72. Walsh, *Irish Popular Songs,* pp. 10–11.

73. Walsh, *Reliques of Irish Jacobite Poetry,* p. 73.

74. John Mitchel, quoted in *Cabinet of Irish Literature,* ed. Read, vol. 3, p. 146.

75. Duffy, *Ballad Poetry of Ireland,* pp. 119–20.

76. Walsh, *Irish Popular Songs,* pp. 12, 29.

77. Walsh, *Reliques of Irish Jacobite Poetry,* p. 49.

78. Walsh, *Irish Popular Songs,* p. 77. Robert Farren, who called "Have You Been at Carrick?" Walsh's best poem, said of his translations: "He appreciated several of the formal virtues of his originals, determined to reproduce them in translating, and did, in fact, do this thing, in a certain degree. That is, he fits the words always to the tune, as Moore did, arriving as did Moore, Callanan and Ferguson at the long, sinuous line; and he 'vowels' well, employing cross-rhyme and assonance." Farren, *The Course of Irish Verse* (New York: Sheed and Ward, 1947), p. 29.

79. Duffy *Ballad Poetry of Ireland,* p. 66.

80. Farren, *Course of Irish Verse,* p. 29.

81. Deane's *A Short History of Irish Literature,* described Ferguson in these terms: "A nationalist who was a unionist, a Protestant preaching intellectual freedom to the Papists whom he held in contempt, a utilitarian who wished to revive a version of romantic Ireland, a believer in the people who defended the supremacy of a caste" (pp. 7–8.)

82. Quoted in M. A. G Ó Tuathaigh, "Sir Samuel Ferguson—Poet and Idealogue," in *Samuel Ferguson: A Centenary Tribute,* ed. Terence Brown and Barbara Hayley (Dublin: Royal Irish Academy, 1987), p. 40.

83. Sir Aubrey de Vere (1788–1846), the father of the poet Aubrey de Vere (1814–1902), was another.

84. Samuel Ferguson, "To Clarence Mangan," *Dublin University Magazine,* 29:174 (June 1847), 623.

85. Samuel Ferguson, "A Dialogue between the Head and Heart of an Irish Protestant (1833); quoted in Malcolm Brown, *Sir Samuel Ferguson* (Lewisburg, Pa.: Bucknell University Press, 1973), p. 40.

86. Samuel Ferguson, "Hardiman's Irish Minstrelsy—No. I," *Dublin University Magazine,* 3:16 (April 1834), 457.

87. This has been pointed out by Ó Tuatheigh, "Sir Samuel Ferguson," pp. 32–34.

88. *An Duanaire, 1600–1900,* ed. Ó Tuama and Kinsella, p. 278.

89. *Poems of Ferguson,* p. 53.

90. Thomas Furlong, "Cashel of Munster," in *Irish Minstrelsy,* ed. Hardiman, vol. 1, p. 239.

91. Ferguson, "Hardiman's Irish Minstrelsy—No. I," p. 453.

92. See Epilogue to part I of this study. In the 1960s, Austin Clarke published several "free translations" of Carolan's songs, and Ferguson's pioneering work is plainly evident in Clarke's versions.

93. Samuel Ferguson, "The Forging of an Anchor," in Duffy, ed., *Ballad Poetry of Ireland,* p. 209. This poem is not included in Graves's edition of the *Poems of Ferguson.*

94. *Poems of Ferguson,* pp. 66–67.

95. W. B, Yeats, "The Poetry of Sir Samuel Ferguson—I," *Irish Fireside* (Oct. 9, 1886); rpt. in Yeats, *Uncollected Prose,* vol. 1, p. 82.

96. *Poems of Ferguson,* p. 62.

97. Terence Brown, *Northern Voices: Poets from Ulster* (Dublin: Gill and Macmillan, 1975), argued that "The Fairy Thorn" "is strangely sensual, druidic in a way that makes Yeats's early exercises in the same mode seem literary and artificial" (p. 40).

98. Samuel Ferguson, quoted in Brown, *Sir Samuel Ferguson,* pp. 79–80.

99. Samuel Ferguson, quoted in Barbara Hayle, "Introduction to *Samuel Ferguson: A Centenary Tribute,* ed. Brown and Hayley, p. 13.

100. Duffy, ed., *Ballad Poetry of Ireland,* pp. 197–8.

101. *Poems of Ferguson,* p. xxvi.

102. Ibid., pp. 201–2.

103. Ibid., p. 114.

104. Ferguson "Conary," *"Poems of Ferguson,"* p. 191, and *Congal,* in *Poems of Ferguson,* p. 250.

105. *Poems of Ferguson,* p. 162.

106. Lady Wilde, quoted in Brown, *Sir Samuel Ferguson,* p. 95.

107. These departures have been pointed out by Peter Denman, "Ferguson's *Congal:* Claiming an Epos?" in *Samuel Ferguson: A Centenary Tribute,* ed. Brown and Hayley, p. 53.

108. *Poems of Ferguson,* pp. 273–74.

109. Brooke, *Reliques of Irish Poetry,* p. 7.

Chapter Seven. Ireland Anglicized

1. George Darley, *The Errors of Ecstasie: A Dramatic Poem* (London: Whittaker, 1822), p. v.

2. Claude Colleer Abbott, *The Life and Letters of George Darley: Poet and Critic* (Oxford: Clarendon Press, 1928), p. 5.

3. George Darley, quoted in Graham Greene, "George Darley," in Greene, *The Last Childhood and Other Essays* (New York: Viking, 1952), p. 144.

4. *The Complete Poetical Works of George Darley,* ed. Ramsay Colles (London: George Routledge, 1908), p. 474.

5. Greene, "George Darley," *The Last Childhood,* p. 150.

6. *Nepenthe* (London, 1835), p. 17.

7. *Nepenthe,* p. 69.

8. In an 1893 essay titled "Nationality and Literature," Yeats referred to "our best writers, De Vere, Ferguson, Allingham, Mangan, Davis, O'Grady," and in an 1894 review, Yeats de-

scribed Ferguson, Mangan, Allingham, and de Vere as "the masters of Irish song." *Uncollected Prose* by W. B. Yeats, ed. John P. Frayne (New York: Columbia University Press, 1970), pp. 273, 333.

9. Yeats, "Irish National Literature, III" (*Bookman,* September, 1895); rpt. *Uncollected Prose,* p. 381.

10. William Wordsworth, quoted in *A Treasury of Irish Poetry,* ed. Stopford A. Brooke and T. W. Rolleston (1900; New York: Macmillan, 1905), p. 509.

11. Aubrey de Vere, quoted in Robert Welch, *Irish Poetry from Moore to Yeats* (Totowa, N.J.: Barnes and Noble, 1980), p. 156.

12. Aubrey de Vere, Feb. 12, 1866, quoted in Wilfried Ward, *Aubrey de Vere: A Memoir* (London: Longmans, Green, 1904), p. 284.

13. Aubrey de Vere, *Inisfail: A Lyrical Chronicle of Ireland* (London: Burns and Oates, 1877), pp. 334–35.

14. De Vere, *Inisfail,* p. 333.

15. De Vere, "Preface" to *Inisfail; A Lyrical Chronicle of Ireland* (Dublin: James Duffy, 1863), p. 26.

16. De Vere, *Inisfail* (1863), p. 35.

17. Ibid., pp. 66–67.

18. Ibid., pp. 146–47.

19. In his preface to *The Foray of Queen Maeve,* de Vere referred to O'Grady's "brilliant bardic 'History of Ireland,' " and added: "How entirely early Irish legends are susceptible of a high poetic rendering in our own day can be doubted by no one who has read the poems founded on them which we owe to the genius of Sir Samuel Ferguson." De Vere, "Preface" to *The Foray of Queen Maeve and Other Legends of Ireland's Heroic Age* (London: Kegan, Paul, Trench, 1882), p. xxiv. O'Grady's *History of Ireland's Heroic Period* was published in 1878 and 1880; Ferguson's *Lays of the Western Gael* was published in 1865, and his *Congal* in 1872.

20. Yeats, "Irish National Literature, III," *Uncollected Prose,* p. 381.

21. Anon., "Thomas Caulfield Irwin," in *Treasury of Irish Poetry,* p. 219.

22. Geoffrey Taylor, ed., *Irish Poets of the Nineteenth Century* (London: Routledge and Kegan Paul, 1951), p. 149.

23. John O'Donovan, letter to Samuel Ferguson, quoted in *Treasury of Irish Poetry,* ed. Brooke and Rolleston, p. 218.

24. Thomas Caulfield Irwin, *Sonnets on the Poetry and Problems of Life* (Dublin: M. G. Gill, 1881), p. 79.

25. Thomas Caulfield Irwin, Preface to *Irish Poems and Legends; Historical and Traditionary* (Glasgow: Cameron and Ferguson, 1869), p. v.

26. Irwin, *Irish Poems and Legends,* pp. 50–51.

27. In *Irish Poets of the Nineteenth Century,* Taylor argued that Irwin's poems on Swift alone "ought to have kept his memory alive among his compatriots" (p. 151).

28. Irwin, *Irish Poems and Legends,* p. 108.

29. Ibid., p. 111.

30. William Butler Yeats, "A Poet We Have Neglected," *United Ireland,* Dec. 12, 1891; rpt. *Uncollected Prose,* p. 209.

31. *William Allingham: A Diary,* ed. H. Allingham and D. Radford (London: Macmillan, 1907), p. 1.

32. *Allingham: A Diary,* p. 19.

33. Tennyson, quoted in *The Poems of William Allingham,* ed. John Hewitt (Dublin: Dolmen Press, 1967), pp. 18–19.

34. William Butler Yeats, "A Poet We Have Neglected," *Uncollected Prose,* p. 212.

35. Aubrey de Vere, quoted in Terence Brown, *Northern Voices: Poets from Ulster* (Dublin: Gill and Macmillan, 1975), p. 47.

36. Malcolm Brown, *The Politics of Irish Literature* (Seattle: University of Washington Press, 1972), p. 316.

37. William Allingham, *Laurence Bloomfield in Ireland: A Modern Poem* (London and Cambridge: Macmillan, 1864), p. 4.

38. Allingham, *Laurence Bloomfield,* pp. 94–5.

39. Ibid., p. 77.

40. Seamus Deane, ed., *The Field Day Anthology of Irish Writing,* vol. 2 (Derry: Field Day Publishing., 1991), p. 8.

41. William Allingham, quoted in Alan Warner, *William Allingham: An Introduction* (Dublin: Dolmen Press, 1971), p. 20.

42. *William Allingham: A Diary,* p. 91.

43. William Allingham, *Songs Ballads and Stories* (London: George Bell, 1877), p. 18.

44. Allingham, *Songs Ballads and Stories,* pp. 146–49.

45. Ibid., p. 141.

46. Yeats, "A Poet We Have Neglected," *Uncollected Prose,* p. 209.

47. John Francis O'Donnell *Poems* (London: Ward & Downey, 1891), pp. 212–13.

48. O'Donnell, *Poems,* p. 214.

49. Ibid., p. 126.

Chapter Eight. Ireland Politicized

1. Thomas D'Arcy McGee, "The Dead Antiquary O'Donovan," *The Poems of Thomas D'Arcy McGee* (New York: D. J. Sadlier, 1869), pp. 451, 454.

2. Seamus Deane, *The Field Day Anthology of Irish Writing,* vol. 2 (Derry: Field Day Publications, 1991), argued, for example, that the Young Ireland movement was unable to respond effectively to the famine because its notion of national identity repudiated precisely what Ireland needed at the time—industrialism and utilitarianism (p. 117).

3. Norman Vance, *Irish Literature: A Social History* (Oxford: Basil Blackwell, 1990), also pointed out that the "patriotic antiquarian endeavor to secure national possessions from the ravages of time is paralleled in the writing of commemorative elegy" (p. 158).

4. John Mitchell, "Introduction" to Thomas Davis, *Essays Literary and Historical: Centenary Edition,* ed. D. J. O'Donoghue (Dundalk: Dundalgen Press, 1914), p. xix.

5. Charles Gavan Duffy, quoted in J. M. Hone, *Thomas Davis* (London: Gerald Duckworth; Dublin: Talbot Press, 1934), p. 78.

6. Mitchell, "Introduction" to Davis, *Essays Literary and Historical,* p. xix.

7. Seamus Deane, *A Short History of Irish Literature* (London: Hutchinson, 1986), observed: "Like Ferguson, Davis believed 'culture' to be the central agency in the formation of a new politics. But he returned again and again to the notion that cultural separation from imperial and industrial England was a precondition of success in the enterprise. . . . this was an important and new note" (p. 76).

8. Quoted in *Thomas Davis: Selections from His Prose and Poetry,* ed. T. W. Rolleston (Dublin: Talbot Press, 1914), p. vi.

9. *Thomas Davis: Selections from His Prose and Poetry,* p. 83.

10. Charles Gavan Duffy, quoted in *Thomas Davis: The Memories of an Irish Patriot: 1840–1846* (London: Kegan, Paul, Trencher, Trübner, 1890), p. 222.

11. Mitchell, "Introduction" to Davis, *Essays Literary and Historical,* p. xix.

12. *Deane, Short History of Irish Literature,* p. 77.

13. Thomas Davis, quoted in Patrick Rafroidi, *Irish Literature in English: The Romantic Period (1789–1850),* vol. 1 (Atlantic Highlands, N. J.: Humanties Press, 1972), pp. xxvi–xxvii.

14. Dean, *Short History of Irish Literature,* p. 78.

15. *Thomas Davis: Selections from His Prose and Poetry,* p. 334.

16. In *Irish Literature,* Vance argues that most nineteenth-century writers "set about trying to write themselves into significant relationship with the past, and past writing, as a way of establishing or affirming identity. Past ages, particularly the seventeenth and eighteenth centuries, were not so much revisited as recreated" (p. 120).

17. *Thomas Davis: Selections from His Prose and Poetry,* p. 307.

18. Ibid., p. 319.

19. Thomas Davis, "The Speeches of Grattan," *Thomas Davis: Selections from His Prose and Poetry,* p. 124.

20. *Thomas Davis: Selections from His Prose and Poetry,* p. 332.

21. Ibid., p. 333.

22. D. J. O'Donoghue, "Preface" to Davis, *Essays Literary and Historical,* p. ix.

23. *The Spirit of the Nation; or, Ballads and Songs by the Writers of "The Nation"* (Dublin: James Duffy, 1866), p. 31.

24. *Spirit of the Nation,* p. 30.

25. *Thomas Davis: Selections from His Prose and Poetry,* p. 318.

26. William Bulter Yeats, 1914, *rpt. in W. B. Yeats and Thomas Kinsella, Davis, Mangan, Ferguson? Tradition and the Irish Writer* (Dublin: Dolmen Press, 1970), p. 19.

27. Yeats, 1914, in *Davis, Mangan, Ferguson?,* ed. Yeats and Kinsella, pp. 15–6.

28. Denis Florence McCarthy, *Poems* (Dublin: M. H. Gill, 1882), p. 230.

29. Denis Florence McCarthy, *Irish Legends and Lyrics* (Dublin: McGlashan and Gill, 1858), pp. 119–20.

30. Denis Florence McCarthy, "Introduction" to *The Poets and Dramatists of Ireland,* ed. McCarthy (Dublin: James Duffy, 1846), p. 16.

31. McCarthy, *Poems,* p. 19.

32. Ibid., p. 30.

33. Ibid., p. 31.

34. Thomas D'Arcy McGee, quoted in Malcolm Brown, *The Politics of Irish Literature* (Seattle: University of Washington Press, 1972), p. 175.

35. *Poems of McGee,* p. 345.

36. In *Irish Literature,* Vance said: "His literary nationalism froze into a self-sufficient Celto-centric myth constantly reiterated to provide a largely artificial identity for first-and second-generation Catholic Irishness in the new world" (p. 162).

37. *Poems of McGee,* p. 117.

38. Ibid., pp. 119–20.

39. Ibid., p. 177.

40. Deane argued that the rise to prominence of popular political verse in the nineteenth century represented a deliberate attempt at "the raising of the national consciousness," and that the process of publishing and distributing such poetry became, for the first time, "organized as a political practice." *The Field Day Anthology,* ed Deane, vol. 2, p. 77.

41. Casey's popularity has continued on into the twentieth century; his poems were republished in 1933 (*The Rising of the Moon, and Other Ballads, Songs, and Legends* [Dublin: M. H. Gill, 1933]), and a critical study, written in Irish and including a selection of his poetry and prose, appeared in 1981 (M. F. Ó Donnchú, *Leo: Saol agus Saothar an Fhile: Seán Aogánach Ó Cathasaigh* [Dublin: Foilsacháin Náisiúnta Teoranta, 1981]).

42. *London Literary Review,* quoted in John K. Casey (Leo), *The Rising of the Moon, and Other Ballads, Songs, and Legends* (Glasgow: Cameron and Ferguson, 1869), p. 8.

43. John Keegan Casey, "Agitation," rpt. in Ó Donnchú, *Leo,* p. 143.

44. John Keegan Casey, "The Influence of National Poetry," rpt. in Ó Donnchú, *Leo,* pp. 131–32.

45. "In *Politics and Irish Literature,* Brown said:" In the patriots' songbook the Fenians made only the one memorable addition, John Casey's 'The Rising of the Moon' " (p. 182).

46. Casey, *Rising of the Moon,* p. 66.

47. Ibid., p. 57.

48. Casey, "Goldsmith," *Rising of the Moon,* p. 63.

49. Ibid., p. 73.

50. David Lloyd, *Anomalous States: Irish Writing and the Post-Colonial Movement* (Durham, N.C.: Duke University Press, 1993), argued this point, saying that "the identity of the individual, his integrity, is expressed by the degree to which that individual identifies himself with and integrates his differences in a national consciousness" (p. 151).

51. Lord Dufferin wrote: "Dead bodies had lain putrefying in the midst of the sick remnants of their families, none strong enough to remove them, until the rats and decay made it difficult to recognize that they had been human beings"; quoted in Harold Nicolson, *Helen's Tower* (London: Constable, 1937), p. 71.

52. Lady Dufferin, *Songs, Poems, and Verses,* 2d ed. (London: John Murray, 1894), pp. 105–6.

53. Dufferin, *Songs, Poems, and Verses,* pp. 188–9.

54. Ibid., p. 126.

55. Cecil Francis Alexander, *Poems* (London: Macmillan, 1896), p. 150.

56. Alexander, *Poems,* p. 168.

57. Ibid., p. 171.

58. John K. Casey, "The Influence of National Poetry," rpt. in Ó Donnchú, *Leo,* p. 136. Richard Ellmann, *Oscar Wilde* (New York: Knopf, 1988), produced convincing evidence for fixing Lady Wilde's birthdate in 1821 (p. 7). It has also been placed as early as 1820 and as late as 1826.

59. Lady Wilde was, in the words of Terence de Vere White, "a highly emotional woman to whom drama was the breath of life"; White, *The Parents of Oscar Wilde: Sir William and Lady Wilde* (London: Hudder and Stoughton, 1967), p. 103.

60. See the discussion of Thomas Davis earlier in this chapter for the details of this story, related in Yeats and Kinsella, *Davis, Mangan, Ferguson?,* p. 19.

61. Lady Wilde quoted in Horace Wyndham, *Speranza: A Biography of Lady Wilde* (London and New York: T. V. Boardman, 1951), p. 199.

62. Lady Wilde's disillusionment with the Young Ireland rebellion had less to do with the cause or the leaders of the rising than it did with the general lack of support for it. "I do not blame the leaders in the least," she said, "in Sicily or Belgium they would have been successful." Lady Wilde, quoted in de Vere White, *The Parents of Oscar Wilde,* p. 110.

63. *Poems by Speranza (Lady Wilde)* (Dublin: James Duffy, 1864), p. 73.

64. Lady Wilde, "Jacta Alen Est," Quoted in Wyndham, *Speranza,* p. 199.

65. *Poems by Speranza (Lady Wilde),* 4th ed. (Glasgow: Cameron and Ferguson, n. d.), p. iii.

66. *Poems by Speranza,* p. 6.

67. Ibid., pp. 8,10.

68. Lady Wilde, quoted in Wyndham, *Speranza,* p. 64.

69. Martin MacDermott, quoted in Wyndham, *Speranza,* p. 15.

70. Quoted in Wyndham, *Speranza,* p. 15.

71. A. M. Sullivan, *New Ireland* (1877), quoted in *The Cabinet of Irish Literature,* ed. Charles A. Read, vol. 4 (London: Blackie and Son, 1879), p. 146.

72. *Poems by "Eva" of "The Nation"* (San Francisco: P. J. Thomas, 1877), p. 13.

73. *Poems by "Eva,"* p. 24.

74. Ibid., p. 10.

75. Ibid., p. 74.

76. John K. Casey, "The Influence of National Poetry," rpt. in Ó Donnchú, *Leo,* p. 136.

77. Ellen Mary Downing, "The Old Church at Lismore," quoted in Thomas Markham, *Ellen Mary Downing: "Mary of the Nation"* (Dublin: Catholic Truth Society, n. d.), p. 26.

78. T. W. Rolleston, "Introductory Notice" to Ellen O'Leary, *Lays of the Country, Home and Friends* ed. Rolleston (Dublin: Sealy, Bryers and Walker, 1891), p. xii.

79. William Butler Yeats, "Reveries over Childhood and Youth" (1914), rpt. in *The Auto-biography of William Butler Yeats* (New York: Collier Books, 1965), p. 63.

80. Charles Gauan Duffy, "A Celtic Singer," in O'Leary, *Lays of Country,* p. xxix.

81. O'Leary, *Lays of Country,* pp. 7–8.

Part Three. The Literary Revival

Introduction

1. "It was the death of Parnell that convinced me that the moment had come for work in Ireland," Yeats wrote in a letter, "for I knew that for a time the imagination of young men would turn from politics"; *The Letters of W. B. Yeats,* ed. Allan Wade (New York: Macmillan, 1951), p. 193. Among critics who cite O'Grady's *History of Ireland* as the starting point of the revival is Ernest Boyd, who called O'Grady "the father of the revival" in *Ireland's Literary Renaissance* (1916; New York: Alfred A. Knopf, 1922), p. 26.

2. F. S. L. Lyons, *Culture and Anarchy in Ireland: 1890–1939* (Oxford: Clarendon Press, 1979), argued that the "marriage between Catholicism and Gaelicism was fatal to the hopes of the Protestant Anglo-Irish protagonists of cultural fusion"; because the forces of Catholicism and Gaelicism were aligned chiefly against the English, Yeats and his associates "were incidental casualties, the walking wounded of a war in which the enemy was always England" (p. 82).

3. Declan Kiberd, *Inventing Ireland: The Literature of the Modern Nation* (London: Jonathan Cape, 1995), argued that Yeats worked "mightily to keep open this gap between 'Catholic' and 'national' feeling. On it the very notion of a cultural renaissance depended" (p. 23).

4. David Cairns and Shaun Richards, *Writing Ireland: Colonialism, Nationalism and Culture* (Manchester: Manchester University Press, 1988), argued that the Anglo-Irish version of Celt-icism, by emphasizing the "virtues of the tribal society. . . enabled the elision of the contempo-rary leaders of the people-nation, the Catholic bourgeoise, by offering a reprise of an idealized Gaelic tribal society, based on identifying the warrier chiefs with the Anglo-Irish and the Chief's followers with the peasants, denying the Catholic bourgeoise a role" (p. 50).

5. Stopford A. Brooke, quoted in Wayne E. Hall, *Shadowy Heroes: Irish Literature of the 1890s* (Syracuse: Syracuse University Press, 1980), p. 39.

6. David Lloyd, *Anomalous States: Irish Writing and the Post-Colonial Movement* (Durham: Duke University Press, 1993), argued that part of the distaste for the Catholic middle class expressed in the literary revival was based on identifying that class with "the effects of commer-cialization on Irish culture, effects that are grasped in nationalist terms as the inroads of angliciza-tion" (p. 132).

7. W. B. Yeats, "To Ireland in the Coming Times," *The Countess Kathleen and Various Legends and Lyrics* (London: 1892); rpt. in *The Variorum Edition of the Poems of W. B. Yeats,* ed. Peter Allt and Russell K. Alspach (New York: Macmillan, 1957), p. 139. Seamus Deane, *A Short History of Irish Literature* (London: Hutchinson, 1986), made the argument about the revival's tendency to identify its own leaders with the epic heroes: "Since the death of Parnell, modern Irish wriitng has been fond of providing us with the image of the hero as artist surrounded by the philistine or clerically-dominated mob. This is a transposition of the political theory of aristocracy into the realm of literature and it has had, since Yeats, a very long run in Irish writing" (p. 31).

8. A. E. [George Russell], quoted in Phillip L. Marcus, *Yeats and the Beginning of the Irish Renaissance,* 2d ed. (Syracuse: Syracuse University Press, 1987), pp. 186–87.

9. W. B. Yeats, "Ireland and the Arts" (1901), *Essays and Introductions* (New York: Collier, 1961), p. 206.

10. W. B. Yeats, *The Trembling of the Veil* (1922); rpt. in *The Autobiography of William Butler Yeats* (New York: Collier Books, 1965), p. 190.

11. A. E. [George Russell], "The Iron Age," *Collected Poems* (London: Macmillan, 1919), p. 268.

12. As Kiberd noted in *Inventing Ireland,* "it was the grand destiny of Yeats's generation in Ireland to make Ireland once again interesting to the Irish" (p. 3).

13. W. B. Yeats, "Poetry and Tradition," *Essays and Introductions,* p. 260.

Chapter Nine. Translation: Gael, Gall, and Peasant

1. Dedication page of George Sigerson, *Bards of the Gael and Gall: Examples of the Poetic Literature of Ireland* (London: T. Fisher Unwin, 1897).

2. George Sigerson, "Irish Literature: Its Origin, Environment, and Influences," in Charles Gavan Duffy, George Sigerson, and Douglas Hyde, *The Revival of Irish Literature* (London: T. Fisher Unwin, 1894), p. 71.

3. Sigerson, "Preface" to *Bards of Gael and Gall,* p. 76.

4. Ibid., pp. 185, 187.

5. Ibid., p. 189.

6. Ibid., p. 21.

7. Ibid., p. 22.

8. Ibid., p. 96.

9. Ibid., p. 120.

10. Douglas Hyde, "George Sigerson," in *A Treasury of Irish Poetry in the English Tongue,* ed. Stopford A. Brooke and T. W. Rolleston (1900; New York: Macmillan, 1905) p. 331. Robert Welch, *A History of Verse Translation from the Irish, 1789–1897* (Gerrards Cross, England: Colin Smythe, 1988), was more direct: "Prosody intoxicated Sigerson and he frequently mistook it for poetry" (p. 163).

11. Seamus Deane, *The Field Day Anthology of Irish Writing,* vol. 2 (Derry: Field Day Publications, 1991), made this argument about Sigerson's influence. Norman Vance, *Irish Literature: A Social History* (Oxford: Basil Blackwell, 1990), said that Sigerson "argues not for the splendid isolation of the Gael but for the splendid permeation" of Gaelic with European cultures (p. 173).

12. Douglas Hyde, *Abhráin Grádh Chúige Connacht: Love Songs of Connacht* (London: T. Fisher Unwin; Dublin: Gill and Son, 1893), n.p.

13. Hyde, *Love Songs,* pp. 29, 43, 9.

14. Hyde *Abhráin Diadha Chúige Connacht: The Religious Songs of Connacht,* vol. 1 (London: T. Fisher Unwin; Dublin: M. H. Gill, 1906), p. 219.

15. Hyde, *Love Songs,* p. 141.

16. Hyde, *Religious Songs,* vol. 2, pp. 227, 281, 283.

17. Seamus Deane, *A Short History of Irish Literature* (London: Hutchinson; Notre Dame: University of Notre Dame Press, 1986), said that Hyde became "the unwitting sponsor of a theory of both cultural and political separateness," adding: "By preaching the de-anglicization of Irish culture, he managed to persuade his audience that Irish independence was a political as well as a linguistic ideal" (p. 28).

18. Douglas Hyde, TK, in Duffy, Sigerson, and Hyde, *Revival of Irish Literature,* p. 159.

19. Douglas Hyde, quoted in Gareth W. Dunleavy, *Douglas Hyde* (Lewisburg, Pa: Bucknell University Press, 1974), p. 30.

20. In *Anomalous States,* Lloyd argued that in Hyde's work "Irish folk culture is transformed into an ahistorical ground on which the defining differences of 'Irishness' can be established over against the homogenizing/hydbridizing influence of 'Anglicization'" (p. 103). Declan Kiberd, "The Perils of Nostalgia: A Critique of the Revival," in *Literature and the Changing Ireland,* ed. Peter Connolly (Gerrards Cross, England: Colin Smythe, 1982), portrayed Hyde as socially and politically regressive: "He never said anything in favour of Home Rule and he ended his career as he began it, a golf-playing, grouse-shooting Anglo-Irishman" (p. 11).

21. David Cairns and Shaun Richards, *Writing Ireland: Colonialism, Nationalism and Culture* (Manchester: Manchester University Press, 1988), argued that Hyde's program for reviving the language was particularly amenable to the Anglo-Irish as "the image of a nation defining itself in terms of the past and seeing modernity as a threat to its ancestral integrity" (p. 65).

22. W. B. Yeats, quoted in Mícheál Ó Laodha, Introduction to *Love Songs of Connacht* (Shannon: Irish University Press, 1968), p. ix.

23. W. B. Yeats, quoted in Lester Conner, "The Importance of Douglas Hyde to the Irish Literary Renaissance," in *Modern Irish Literature: Essays in Honor of William York Tindall,* ed. Raymond J. Porter and James D. Brophy (New York: Iona College Press, 1972), p. 97.

24. Hyde, *Love Songs,* n.p.

Chapter Ten. Celticism and Romanticism

1. Terry Eagleton, *Heathcliff and the Great Hunger: Studies in Irish Culture* (London: Verso, 1995), said on this point: "The Yeats-sponsored view that politics yielded ground to culture after the fall of Parnell, while one sees what it means, betrays a narrowly parliamentarian view of politics and a curiously depoliticized notion of culture" (p. 232).

2. This view is still very much alive; Seamus Deane described Lionel Johnson, for example, as "an honorary Irishman," whose "contribution to Irish poetry is important only as a reminder of the appeal of Ireland as a minority cause to the intellectuals and writers of the decadent era"; *Field Day Anthology of Irish Writing,* ed. Deane, vol. 2 (Derry: Field Day Publications, 1991), p. 720.

3. Lionel Johnson, quoted in Phillip L. Marcus, *Yeats and the Beginning of the Irish Renaissance,* 2d ed. (Syracuse: Syracuse University Press, 1987), p. 172.

4. Ernest Boyd, *Ireland's Literary Renaissance* (1916; New York: Alfred A. Knopf, 1922), p. 158.

5. W. B. Yeats, "Dr. Todhunter's Irish Poems," review of *The Banshee* (*United Ireland,* January 23, 1892); rpt. *Uncollected Prose by W. B. Yeats,* ed. John P. Frayne, vol. 1 (New York: Columbia University Press, 1970), p. 216.

6. John Todhunter, *The Banshee and Other Poems* (London: Kegan Paul, Trench, 1888), pp. 3–4.

7. Todhunter, *Banshee,* p. 84.

8. Ibid., pp. 85–86.

9. John Todhunter, "Under the White-Boy Acts, 1800, An Old Rector's Story," *Poems and Ballads of Young Ireland* (1888; Dublin: M. H. Gill, 1903), pp. 5–7. This poem was not included in *The Banshee.*

10. The theory was spelled out primarily in William Larminie, "The Development of English Metre," *The Contemporary Review,* no. 66 (November 1894), pp. 717–36.

11. A. E. [George Russell], "William Larminie," *A Treasury of Irish Poetry in the English Tongue,* ed. Stopford A. Brooke and T. W. Rolleston (1900; New York: Macmillan, 1905), p. 476.

12. William Larminie, *Fand and Other Poems* (Dublin: Hodges, Figgis, 1892), p.19.

13. Larminie, *Fand,* n. p.

14. Ibid., pp. 28–29.

15. T. W. Rolleston, "To John O'Leary," preface poem to *Poems and Ballads of Young Ireland,* p. 2. The poem was reprinted in T. W. Rolleston, *Sea Spray: Verses and Translations* (Dublin:Maunsel, 1909)

16. Rolleston, *Sea Spray: Verses and Translations,* p. 9.

17. Rolleston, *Sea Spray,* 15–16.

18. Ibid., p. 12.

19. Ibid., p. 47.

20. Lionel Johnson, "Poetry and Patriotism," 1894, quoted in Marcus, *Yeats and the Beginning of the Irish Renaissance,* p. 173.

21. For more on this aspect of Johnson's work, see Wayne E. Hall, *Shadowy Heroes: Irish Literature of the 1890s* (Syracuse: Syracuse University Press, 1980), pp. 53–54.

22. Lionel Johnson, *Poems* (London: Elkin Mathews, 1895), p. 12.

23. Johnson, *Poems,* p. 51.

24. As Hall said in *Shadowy Heroes,* Johnson "combined the vague, narcotic religiosity of the Pre-Raphaelites with a distanced asceticism and emotional neutrality" (p. 176).

25. W. B. Yeats, *The Trembling of the Veil* (1922); rpt. in *The Autobiography of William Butler Yeats* (New York: Macmillan, 1965), p. 148.

26. Lionel Johnson *Ireland: with Other Poems* (London: Elkin Mathews, 1897), p. 1.

27. Johnson, *Ireland,* p. 5.

28. Lionel Johnson quoted in W. B. Yeats, *Trembling of the Veil,* p. 203.

29. W. B. Yeats, "In Memory of Major Robert Gregory," *The Wild Swans at Coole* (1919); in *The Variorum Edition of the Poems of W. B. Yeats,* ed. Peter Allt and Russell K. Alspach (New York: Macmillan, 1957) p. 324.

30. W. B. Yeats, "Ireland and the Arts" (1901), *Essays and Introductions* (New York: Collier, 1961), p. 204.

31. A. E. [George Russell], quoted in Marcus, *Yeats and the Beginning of the Irish Renaissance,* p. 192.

32. A. E. [George Russell] to W. B. Yeats, 1900, quoted in Roger McHugh and Maurice Harmon, *Short History of Anglo-Irish Literature* (Totowa, N.J.: Barnes and Noble, 1982), p. 134.

33. John Eglinton, William Larminie, A. E., and W. B. Yeats, *Literary Ideals in Ireland* (London: T. Fisher Unwin 1899), p. 53.

34. A. E. [George Russell], ed., *New Songs: A Lyric Selection* (Dublin: O'Donoghue; London: A. H. Bullen, 1904), p. 5. John Eglinton once said that the major event of 1891, for A. E., was not the death of Parnell but that of Madame Blavatsky; quoted in Marcus, *Yeats and the Beginning of the Irish Renaissance,* p. 181).

35. A. E. [George Russell], "Nationality and Imperialism," in *Ideals in Ireland,* ed. Lady Gregory (London: Unicorn, 1901), p. 15.

36. W. B. Yeats, "Lionel Johnson," in *Treasury of Irish Poetry,* ed. Brooke and Rolleston, p. 466.

37. A. E. [George Russell], *Collected Poems* (London: Macmillan, 1913, 1919), p. 9.

38. Yeats, for example, in reviewing A. E.'s first collection, *Homeward: Songs by the Way* (1894), for the most part admiringly, said that "certain rhymes are repeated too often, the longer lines tumble now and then, and here and there a stanza is needlessly obscure"; W. B. Yeats, quoted in Marcus, *Yeats and Beginning of the Irish Renaissance,* p. 77. Robert Farren, in *The Course of Irish Verse in English* (New York: Sheed and Ward, 1947), said flatly, "A.E. the poet was incurious in matters of craft" (p. 81).

39. A. E. [George Russell], *Collected Poems,* p. 106.

40. Ibid., pp. 150–51.

41. A. E. [George Russell], quoted in Richard J. Loftus, *Nationalism in Modern Anglo-Irish Poetry* (Madison: University of Wisconsin Press, 1964), p. 100.

42. A. E., *Collected Poems* (London: Macmillan, 1935), p. 352.

43. This effort has been described by F. S. L. Lyons, *Culture and Anarchy in Ireland: 1890–1939* (Oxford: Clarendon Press, 1979), pp. 163–67.

44. A. E. [George Russell], "Nationality and Cosmopolitanism in Literature," *Literary Ideals in Ireland,* ed. Eglinton et al., p. 83.

Chapter Eleven. Celticism and Feminism

1. W. B. Yeats, quoted in David Perkins, *A History of Modern Poetry: From the 1890s to the High Modernist Mode* (Cambridge, Mass.: Belknap Press, 1976), p. 581.

2. W. B. Yeats, quoted in Matthew Russell, Introduction to *Rose Kavanagh and Her Verses* (Dublin: M. H. Gill, 1909), pp. 13–14.

3. *Rose Kavanagh and Her Verses,* pp. 35–36.

4. Katharine Tynan, quoted in *Rose Kavanagh and Her Verses,* p. 15.

5. *Rose Kavanagh and Her Verses,* pp. 33–35.

6. Ibid., pp. 37–38.

7. Ibid., p. 54.

8. W. B. Yeats, quoted in Phillip L. Marcus, *Yeats and the Beginning of the Irish Renaissance,* 2d ed. (Syracuse: Syracuse University Press, 1987), p. 134.

9. W. B. Yeats, quoted in Marcus, *Yeats and the Beginning of the Irish Rennaissance,* p. 143.

10. W. B. Yeats, quoted in Roger McHugh and Maurice Harmon, *Short History of Anglo-Irish Literature* (Totowa, N.J.: Barnes & Noble, 1982), p. 135.

11. Katharine Tynan, *Ballads and Lyrics* (London: Kegan, Paul, Trench, Trubner, 1891), p. 2.

12. Katharine Tynan, *Experiences* (London: A. H. Bullen, 1908), p. 23.

13. Tynan, *Ballads and Lyrics,* pp. 92–3.

14. *Uncollected Prose by W. B. Yeats,* ed. John P. Frayne, vol. 1 (New York: Columbia University Press, 1970), p. 370.

15. Ernest Boyd's *Ireland's Literary Renaissance* (1916; New York: Barnes and Noble, 1922), said that Hopper's work was "flagrantly imitative" (p. 195), and Roger McHugh and Maurice Harmon's *Short History of Anglo-Irish Literature* referred to her as "that shameless borrower of his [Yeats's] themes and phrases" (p. 135). In Hopper's defense, it should be said that although there are certainly some striking echoes between her work and Yeats's early poems, this is also true of other writers, such as Katherine Tynan, who were working in the early days of the revival and came under the powerful influence of Yeats.

16. W. B. Yeats, "The Symbolism of Poetry" (1900), *Essays and Introductions* (New York: Collier, 1961), p. 164.

17. Nora Hopper, *Ballads in Prose* (London: John Lane, 1894), p. 63.

18. Hopper, *Ballads in Prose,* p. 51.

19. W. B. Yeats to Katherine Tynan, 1906, quoted in *Uncollected Prose by W. B. Yeats,* ed. John P. Frayne and Colton Johnson, vol. 2 (New York: Columbia University Press, 1976), p. 124.

20. Padraic Fallon, Introduction to *The Poems of Emily Lawless* (Dublin: Dolmen Press, 1965), p. 8.

21. Emily Lawless, *The Inalienable Heritage* (London: Richard Clay, 1914), p. 73.

22. According to Fallon's Introduction to *Poems of Emily Lawless,* Lawless's ancestry can be traced back to the Wild Geese (p. 8).

23. Emily Lawless, *With the Wild Geese* (London: Isbister, 1902), pp. 3–4.

24. Lawless, *With the Wild Geese,* pp. 7–9.

25. *Thomas Davis: Selections from His Prose and Poetry* (Dublin: Talbot Press, 1914), p. 330.

26. Lawless, *With the Wild Geese,* p. 27.

27. *The Collected Poems of Dora Sigerson Shorter* (New York and London: Harper Brothers, 1907), p. 68.

28. Sigerson, *Collected Poems,* p. 122.

29. Boyd, *Ireland's Literary Renaissance,* p. 205.

30. Sigerson, *Collected Poems*, pp. 249–50.

31. Seamus MacManus, "Preface" to Ethna Carbery, *The Four Winds of Eirinn*, ed. Seamus MacManus (Dublin: M. H. Gill, 1902), p. vi.

32. These prose pieces were published as *In the Celtic Past* (1904).

33. Ethna Carbery, *Four Winds of Eirinn*, p. 9.

34. Alice Milligan, *Hero Lays* (Dublin: Maunsel, 1908), p. 10.

35. Milligan, *Hero Lays*, p. 77.

36. Ibid., p. 28.

37. Ibid., p. 43.

38. See Terence Brown, *Northern Voices: Poets from Ulster* (Dublin: Gill and Macmillan, 1975), pp. 58–64, for a discussion of this aspect of Milligan's work.

39. Milligan, *Hero Lays*, pp. 36–37.

40. Moira O'Neill, *Songs of the Glens of Antrim* (1901; Edinburgh and London: William Blackwood, 1918), n. p.

41. Brown, *Northern Voices*, p. 70.

42. O'Neill, *Songs of the Glens*, pp. 21–22.

43. Ibid., pp. 4–6.

44. Ibid., p. 8.

45. A. E. [George Russell], ed., *New Songs: A Lyric Selection* (Dublin: O'Donoghue; London: A. H. Buller, 1904) p. 5.

46. Ella Young, *Flowering Dusk: Things Remembered Accurately and Inaccurately* (New York: Longman, Green, 1945), p. 65.

47. Young, *Flowering Dusk*, p. 132.

48. *Poems by Ella Young* (Dublin: Maunsel, 1906), p. 18.

49. *Poems by Ella Young*, p. 17.

50. Boyd, *Ireland's Literary Renaissance*, p. 255.

51. Susan Mitchell to Seamus O'Sullivan, quoted in Richard M. Kain, *Susan L. Mitchell* (Lewisburg, Pa.: Bucknell University Press, 1972), p. 48.

52. Kain, *Susan L. Mitchell*, pp. 52–53.

53. Susan Mitchell, *The Living Chalice and Other Poems* (1908; Dublin and London: Maunsel, 1913), p. 39.

54. Mitchell, *Living Chalice*, p. 18.

55. Susan Mitchell, *Aids to the Immortality of Certain Persons in Ireland* (Dublin: New Nation Press, 1908), p. 32.

56. Mitchell, *Aids to Immortality*, p. 35.

57. Ibid., pp. 15–16.

58. Ibid., pp. 25–26.

59. Katharine Tynan, quoted in Esther Roper, Introduction to *Poems of Eva Gore-Booth* (London: Longmans, Green, 1929), p. 18.

60. A. E. [George Russell], Quoted in Roper, Introduction to *Poems of Eva Gore-Booth*, pp. 16–17.

61. *Poems of Eva Gore-Booth*, p. 244.

62. "Weariness," *Poems of Eva Gore-Booth*, p. 115.

63. *Poems of Eva Gore-Booth*, p. 407.

64. Ibid., pp. 196–97.

65. Ibid., p. 194.

66. Ibid., p. 409.

Chapter Twelve. Early Yeats

1. W. B. Yeats, ed., *A Book of Irish Verse* (London: Methuen, 1900), p. xxiv
2. Yeats, ed., *Book of Irish Verse,* pp. 13–14.
3. As Declan Kiberd put it in *Inventing Ireland: The Literature of the Modern Nation* (London: Jonathan Cape, 1995): "As a poet, he [Yeats] invents an ideal Ireland in his imagination, falls deeply in love with its form and proceeds to breathe it, Pygmalion-like, into being. It is hard, even now, to do full justice to the audacity of that enterprise" (p. 202).
4. G. J. Watson, *Irish Identity and the Literary Revival: Synge, Yeats, Joyce and O'Casey* (London: Croom Helm, 1979), saw Yeats's chief significance in terms of Irish culture, describing his work as representing "a considerable effort to purify Irish nationalism from within, to broaden its base from the narrowly politically to the wider cultural" (p. 100).
5. Edward Said, *Culture and Imperialism* (New York: Random House, 1993), redefined this conflict in terms of English versus Irish culture, and concluded that the tension drove Yeats to an apolitical aestheticism: "For Yeats the overlapping he knew existed of his Irish nationalism with the English cultural heritage, which both dominated and empowered him, was bound to cause tension, and one may speculate that it was the pressure of this urgently political and secular tension that caused him to try to resolve it on a 'higher,' that is, nonpolitical level" (p. 227).
6. W. B. Yeats, "The Literary Movement in Ireland" (1899), *Ideals in Ireland,* ed. Lady Gregory (London: Unicorn, 1901), pp. 97–98.
7. W. B. Yeats, "Ireland and the Arts" (1901), *Essays and Introductions* (New York: Collier, 1961), p. 210.
8. W. J. McCormack, *Ascendancy and Tradition in Anglo-Irish Literary History from 1789 to 1939* (Oxford: Clarendon Press, 1985), made this point: "Not only is Yeats's work a multifarious act of self-making and autobiography but the ramifications of the endeavour aspire to create a new history in which that undertaking appears exemplary, necessary, and accomplished" (p. 297).
9. W. B. Yeats, *The Countess Kathleen and Various Legends and Lyrics* (1892; rpt. in *The Variorum Edition of the Poems of W. B. Yeats,* ed. Peter Allt and Russell K. Alspach (New York: Macmillan), pp. 138–39.
10. As Seamus Deane put it in *Celtic Revivals: Essays in Modern Irish Literature 1800–1980* (Winston-Salem, N.C.: Wake Forest University Press, 1985): "Ireland was, for him, a revolutionary country for the very reason that it was, in the oldest sense, a traditional one. . . . Irish politics enacted for him the great cultural battle of the era between Romantics and Utiliterians" (p. 39).
11. W. B. Yeats to Lady Gregory, *Dramatis Personae, 1896–1902;* rpt. in *The Autobiography of William Butler Yeats* (New York: Collier Books, 1965), p. 289.
12. Yeats, "The Literary Movement in Ireland," p. 106.
13. Ibid.
14. W. B. Yeats, "The Celtic Element in Literature" (1897), *Essays and Introductions,* pp. 186–87.
15. W. B. Yeats, "The Circus Animals' Desertion," *Last Poems and Two Plays* (1939; rpt. *Variorum Edition),* p. 629.
16. W. B. Yeats, *Poems* (1895; rpt. *Variorum Edition),* p. 16.
17. W. B. Yeats, "Fergus and the Druid," *Countess,* rpt. *Variorum Edition,* p. 103.
18. Yeats, "The Literary Movement in Ireland," p. 91.
19. Yeats, *Countess;* rpt. *Variorum, Edition,* p. 117.
20. Yeats, *Countess;* rpt. *Variorum Edition,* pp. 100–101.
21. W. B. Yeats, "The Symbolism of Poetry" date?, *Essays and Introductions,* p. 155.
22. Ibid., p. 164.

23. W. B. Yeats, "King Goll," in *Poems and Ballads of Young Ireland* (1888; Dublin: M. H. Gill, 1903) p. 44.

24. Yeats, "King Goll," in *Poems and Ballads, of Young Ireland,* p. 44.

25. Writing of Yeats's early poems based on pre-Christian legends, Watson said in *Irish Identity:* "These poems are remarkable chiefly in the very absence from them of the strident, hectoring tone of militant nationalism" (p. 94).

26. W. B. Yeats, "The Stolen Child," in *Poems and Ballads of Young Ireland,* p. 12.

27. Ibid., p. 12.

28. W. B. Yeats, *Wind Among the Reeds;* rpt. *Variorum Edition,* p. 161.

29. Ibid.

30. Yeats, "The Symbolism of Poetry," p. 163.

31. Yeats, *Wind Among the Reeds,* rpt. *Variorum Edition,* pp. 151–52.

32. Ibid., pp. 150–51.

33. Yeats, *Countess;* rpt. *Variorum Edition,* pp. 91–92.

34. W. B. Yeats to Alice Milligan, 1894, quoted in John Kelly, "Choosing and Inventing: Yeats and Ireland," in *Across a Roaring Hill: The Protestant Imagination in Modern Ireland,* ed. Gerald Dawe and Edna Longley (Belfast: Blackstaff Press, 1985), p. 12.

35. Yeats, "Ireland and the Arts," p. 203.

36. W. B. Yeats, quoted in Ian Jack, "Yeats: Always an Irish Writer," *The Poet and His Audience* (Cambridge: Cambridge University Press, 1984), p. 154.

Chapter Thirteen. Other Visions and Revisions

1. John M. Synge, *Poems and Translations* (Dundrum: Cuala Press, 1909), p. 14.

2. John M. Synge to Stephen MacKenna, 1907, quoted in G. J. Watson, *Irish Identity and the Literary Revival: Synge, Yeats, Joyce, and O'Casey* (London: Croom Helm, 1979), p. 39. Watson said that Synge was never able to expunge "that residue of quasi-artistocratic contempt for 'the natives' " (p. 38).

3. Seamus Deane argued that Synge's plays constitute an "analysis of a dying culture," in which "the gestures of freedom are made at the expense of the community, because they are not possible in and through it"; Deane, *A Short History of Irish Literature* (London: Hutchinson, 1986), p. 152. Watson concluded: "In the end, as his background made almost inevitable, Synge found it more congenial to imagine not the typical Irishman, but the unusual, isolated Irishman"; Watson, *Irish Identity,* p. 85.

4. In *Irish Identity,* Watson argued that Synge's anomalous "community" on Aran grew out of a need to replace the Anglo-Irish community, against which he rebelled, and the Catholic middle-class community, which he could not abide, and that this limited his ability to represent the national consciousness (p. 42).

5. Synge, *Poems and Translations,* p. 29.

6. Synge, "Preface" to *Poems and Translations,* pp. 1–2.

7. W. B. Yeats, *Essays and Introductions* (New York: Collier, 1961), p. 308.

8. J. M. Synge, *Collected Works: Vol. 1: Poems,* ed. Robin Skelton (London: Oxford University Press, 1962), pp. 56–57.

9. Synge, *Collected Works,* p. 56.

10. This point has been made by Robin Skelton in *The Writings of J. M. Synge* (New York: Bobbs-Merrill, 1971), p. 163.

11. In *Synge and the Irish Language* (Totowa, N.J.: Rowan and Littlefield, 1979), Declan Kiberd also convincingly established the extent of Synge's knowledge of the language. Indeed, Kiberd argues that Synge is himself not only a "great Anglo-Irish writer" but also "a vital artist in the Gaelic tradition" (p. 16). In *A Short History of Irish Literature* (London: Hutchinson,

1986), Seamus Deane said of Synge's language: "English had never been so effectively de-Anglicized" (p. 151).

12. Synge, *Collected Works*, p. 49.

13. See Watson, *Irish Identity*, pp. 46–7. In *A Short History*, Deane said that the Aran Islands constituted for Synge a landscape and culture "as stark, lonely and vital as his own sensibility" (p. 151).

14. Synge, *Poems and Translations*, p. 20.

15. W. B. Yeats, "J. M. Synge and the Ireland of His Time" (1910), *Essays and Introductions*, p. 319.

16. Declan Kiberd, *Inventing Ireland: The Literature of the Modern Nation* (London: Jonathan Cape, 1995), made this point: "what Pearse did was no different from what had been done by men like Yeats and Synge: he moved from faith in 'the Kingdom of God' to faith in 'the king-dom of Ireland', employing the language of the former to launch his crusade for the latter" (p. 211).

17. David Cairns and Shaun Richards, *Writing Ireland: Colonialism, Nationalism and Culture* (Manchester: Manchester University Press, 1988), pp. 104–5.

18. Thomas MacDonagh, "Preface" to *Literature in Ireland: Studies Irish and Anglo-Irish* (Dublin: The Talbot Press, 1916), p. viii.

19. Thomas MacDonagh, quoted in Johann A. Norstedt, *Thomas MacDonagh: A Critical Biography* (Charlottesville: University Press of Virginia, 1980), p. 70.

20. *The Poetical Works of Thomas MacDonagh*, ed. James Stephens (London: T. Fisher Unwin, 1916), pp. 65–66.

21. A stanza from "An Bonnán Buí," by Cathal Buí Mac Giolla Ghunna, illustrates some of these patterns:

> A bhonnáin bhuí, is é mo chrá do luí
> is do chnámha críon tar éis a gcreim,
> is chan díobháil bídh ach easpa dí
> d'fhág tú 'do luí ar chúl do chinn;
> is measa liom féin ná scrios na Traí
> thú bheith sínte ar leacaibh lom,
> is nach ndearna tú díth ná dolaidh is tír
> is nárbh fhearr leat fíon ná uisce poill.

An Duanaire 1600–1900: Poems of the Dispossessed, ed. Seán Ó Tuama, trans. Thomas Kinsella (Mountrath: Dolmen Press, 1981), p. 132.

22. MacDonagh, *Poetical Works*, pp. 68–69.

23. Richard J. Loftus, *Nationalism in Modern Anglo-Irish Poetry* (Madison University of Wisconsin Press, 1964), p. 128.

24. Thomas MacDonagh, *An Macaomh*, I, 1 (1909), quoted in Loftus, pp. 131–2.

25. As Loftus argued, "MacDonagh simply could not convert Christ, as Plunkett did, into a God of vengeance; for him Christ remained a figure of gentle love"; Loftus, *Nationalism in Modern Anglo-Irish Poetry*, p. 158.

26. MacDonagh, *Poetical Works*, p. 128.

27. W. B. Yeats, "Easter 1916," *The Variorum Edition of the Poems of W. B. Yeats*, ed. Peter Allt and Russell K. Alspach (New York: Macmillan, 1957), p. 392.

28. Seamus Deane argued that through Pearse, "catholicism and nationalism formed an alli-ance which peripheralized secular republicanism"; Deane, *Field Day Anthology of Irish Writing* (Derry: Field Day Publications, 1991), vol. 2 p. 211.

29. *Collected Works of Padraic H. Pearse* (Dublin: Maunsel and Roberts, 1922), p. 44.

30. *The Literary Writings of Patrick Pearse: Writings in English*, ed. Séamus Ó Buachalla (Dublin and Cork: Mercier Press, 1979), p. 28.

31. *Collected Works of Padraic H. Pearse*, p. 339. In *Nationalism in Modern Anglo-Irish Poetry*, Loftus said that in this poem Pearse "gives to the cause of revolution an implied reli-

gious sanction by taking his theme, imagery, and even rhythm from the Old Testament" (p. 146).

32. Seamus Deane, "Pearse: Writing and Chivalry," in *Celtic Revivals: Essays in Modern Irish Literature,* ed. Seamus Deane (Winston-Salem, N.C.: Wake Forest University Press, 1985), described Pearse as "a strictly utilitarian writer" who "wrote to teach and move his audience" (p. 74).

33. *Collected Works of Padraic M. Pearse,* pp. 312–13.

34. Ibid., pp. 324–25.

35. *Literary Writings of Patrick Pearse,* pp. 40–41.

36. Geraldine Plunkett, "Foreward" to *The Poems of Joseph Mary Plunkett* (Dublin: Talbot Press, 1916), pp. x–xi.

37. As William Irwin Thompson put it, in *The Imagination of an Insurrection: Dublin, Easter 1916: A Study of an Ideological Movement* (New York: Oxford University Press, 1967): "As Yeats went to Swedenborg, so Plunkett went to St. John of the Cross" (p. 134).

38. *Poems of Joseph Mary Plunkett,* p. 52.

39. Ibid., pp. 59–60.

40. Ibid., p. 86.

41. Ibid., p. 69.

42. A. E. [George Russell], quoted in Ernest Boyd, *Ireland's Literary Renaissance* (1916; New York: Alfred A. Knopf, 1922), p. 258. Boyd himself described O'Sullivan as "unexcelled as a painter of soft-toned pictures pervaded by the quiet of evening solitude" (p. 257) and as "the typical disciple of A. E." (p. 259). A. Norman Jeffares, *Anglo-Irish Literature* (New York: Schocken Books, 1982), characterized O'Sullivan's poetry as "the epitome of the Celtic Twi-light" (p. 163). Robert Farren, *The Course of Irish Verse in English* (New York: Sheed and Ward, 1947), said that O'Sullivan's poems exhibit "a possibly more delicate melody than A.E.'s, and less earthy passion that Yeats's" (p. 86). And Padraic Colum, in an introduction to a collection of O'Sullivan's poems, argued that O'Sullivan's writing is "in subject and music, far removed from the work-a-day world"; quoted in Liam Miller, ed., *Retrospect: The Work of Seamus O'Sullivan 1879–1958 and Estella F. Solomons 1882–1968* (Dublin: Dolmen Editions, 1973), p. 52.

43. Seamus O'Sullivan, *Poems* (Dublin: Maunsel, 1912), p. 2.

44. O'Sullivan, *Poems,* pp. 4–5.

45. Austin Clarke, *Poetry in Modern Ireland* (Cork: Mercier Press, 1951), p. 21.

46. O'Sullivan, *Poems,* p. 3.

47. Ibid., p. 21.

48. Ibid., pp. 18–19.

49. Padraic Colum, "The Poet: Seamus O'Sullivan," in *Retrospect,* ed. Miller, p. 90.

50. In a broadcast done in 1943, Campbell said: "I grew up with three languages: a legacy from father's side of the family of a memory of Border Gaelic, the Chaucer-cum-Burns of Co. Down, the class English of my schoolbooks, and the literature I read"; quoted in Norah Saunders and A. A. Kelly, *Joseph Campbell: Poet and Nationalist: 1879–1944* (Dublin: Wolfhound Press, 1988), p. 32.

51. Joseph Campbell, quoted in Saunders and Kelly, *Joseph Campbell,* p. 36.

52. Seamus Deane, *The Field Day Anthology of Irish Writing,* vol. 2, p. 723.

53. Joseph Campbell, *Irishry* (Dublin: Maunsel, 1913), p. 74.

54. Joseph Campbell, *The Mountainy Singer* (Dublin: Maunsel, 1909), p. 1. This poem was first published in *The Nationalist,* November 9, 1905.

55. As Seamus Deane put it in *The Field Anthology of Irish Writing:* "In Campbell, in Colum, and sometimes in Higgins, there is an intimacy with the popular folk poetry and songs that lends to some of their best efforts the impersonal quality of the broadsheet poem—precisely the kind of thing that Allingham and Davis, in their different ways, had sought in the previous century" (vol. 2, p. 723).

56. Saunders and Kelly argued that Campbell never wavered in his belief in "an undivided Republic", and that when he left Ireland for the United States in 1925, he did so because "his Republican hopes were dashed"; Saunders and Kelly, *Joseph Campbell,* p. 8.

57. Joseph Campbell, *The Rushlight* (Dublin: Maunsel, 1906), p. 20.

58. Joseph Campbell, *The Gilly of Christ* (Dublin: Maunsel, 1907), pp. 2–3.

59. Campbell, *Rushlight,* p. 21.

60. Saunders and Kelly, *Joseph Campbell,* p. 32.

61. Joseph Campbell, quoted in Saunders and Kelly, *Joseph Campbell,* p. 33. Farren, in *The Course of Irish Verse,* said that Campbell was influenced by Blake, and that he "believed, like A. E., in the poet as seer" (p. 94).

62. Boyd, in *Ireland's Literary Renaissance,* said of Campbell's portraits in *Irishry,* "behind the humble ploughers, fiddlers and shepherds, Campbell sees the kings and warriors of old. As he views the Irish scene he is conscious of a continuity of tradition and spirit, which attaches the people to distant origins of which they know perhaps nothing but what is revealed by some remnant of the past, surviving in legend or a phrase" (p. 280).

63. Campbell, *Irishry,* pp. 66–67.

64. Ibid., p. 79.

65. Padraic Colum, quoted in Jeffares, *Anglo-Irish Literature,* p. 271.

66. Padraic Column, review of Hyde's *Love Songs of Connacht, The Nationalist,* October 5, 1905, quoted in Saunders and Kelly, *Joseph Campbell,* p. 36.

67. Padraic Colum, *The Poet's Circuits: Collected Poems of Ireland* (London: Oxford University Press, 1960), p. 15.

68. Thomas McDonagh, *Literature in Ireland,* p. 176.

69. Padraic Colum, *Wild Earth and Other Poems* (1916; New York: Macmillan, 1922), p. 26.

70. Padraic Colum, *Old Pastures* (New York: Macmillan, 1930), p. 10

71. Padraic Colum, *Wild Earth. A Book of Verse* (Dublin: Maunsel, 1907), p. 17.

72. Colum, *Wild Earth,* p. 1.

73. Ibid., pp. 3–4.

74. Sanford Sterlicht, *Padraic Colum* (Boston: Twayne, 1985), pp. 54–63.

75. Augustine Martin, *James Stephens: A Critical Study* (Totowa, N.J.: Rowan and Littlefield, 1977), argued about *Insurrections:* "There is a recurrent note of rebellion against society. . . . In counterpoint with the social protest there is a persistent, various and often ambiguous complaint lodged with God for his role in the sorry scheme of things" (p. 15).

76. *In Ireland's Literary Renaissance,* Boyd said of Stephens: "His insurgency is shown . . . in a general determination to see life stripped of conventionalised romance" (pp. 269–70).

77. James Stephes, quoted in Jeffares, *Anglo-Irish Literature,* p. 175.

78. James Stephens, *Insurrections* (1909; Dublin: Maunsel, 1912), pp. 8–9.

79. Stephens, *Insurrections,* p. 9.

80. See Martin, *James Stephens,* p. 86.

81. Stephens, *Insurrections,* pp. 18–19.

82. Ibid., p. 7.

83. Ibid., pp. 21–23.

84. Martin, *James Stephens,* concluded that Stephens's poems from the Irish focus on aspects of the personalities behind the poems that bring him close to his own themes "of social complaint, more especially the poet's complaint against a materialistic society which shows no respect for his ministry" (p. 114). Indeed, Martin said, the strength of these poems lies in Stephens's ability to find a style "which would not betray the historical situations of the originals and at the same time reconstitute them as modern poems" (pp. 114–25).

85. James Stephens, *Reincarnations* (New York: Macmillan, 1918), p. 71.

86. Thomas Kinsella, in *An Duanaire*, ed. Ó Tuama and Kinsella, p. 109.

87. Stephens, *Reincarnations*, pp. 47–8.

88. James Stephens, quoted in Martin *James Stephens*, p. 115.

89. In *James Stephens*, Martin argued that the influence of the Georgians "was to divert him from those themes—and their attendant technical challenges—which had made his early poetry most strikingly original: his doubts, his defiances, his questioning of social and religious orthodoxies" (p. 94).

90. Francis Ledwidge to Lord Dunsany, 1916, quoted in Seamus Heaney, Introduction to *Francis Ledwidge: Selected Poems*, ed. Dermot Bolger (Dublin: New Island Books, 1992), p. 18. Heaney, whose interest in Ledwidge is explained by a shared feeling for rural landscapes—Heaney's Co. Derry and Ledwidge's Co. Meath—and by a shared pressing awareness of cultural division, described Ledwidge's ambiguous position in his poem "In Memoriam Francis Ledwidge," *Field Work* (New York: Farrar Straus Giroux, 1976).

91. Francis Ledwidge, *Songs of the Fields* (London: Herbert Jenkins, 1916,1918), p. 51.

92. Francis Ledwidge, *Last Songs* (London: Herbert Jenkins, 1918), p. 29. In *The Course of Irish Verse*, Farren said that Ledwidge "had little more than the landscape of Meath to make him an Irish poet" (p. 116).

93. Francis Ledwidge, *Songs of Peace* (London: Herbert Jenkins, 1917), p. 88.

94. James Stephens, Preface to *Poetical Works of Thomas MacDonagh*, p.ix.

Part Four. Poetry in Modern Ireland

Introduction

1. W. B. Yeats, "The Man and the Echo," *Last Poems and Two Plays* (Dublin: Cuala Press, 1939); rpt. in *The Variorum Edition of the Poems of W. B. Yeats*, ed. Peter Allt and Russell K. Alspach (New York: Macmillan, 1957), p. 632.

2. Benedict Kiely, *Modern Irish Fiction: A Critique*, quoted in Augustine Martin, "Inherited Dissent: The Dilemma of the Irish Writer," *Studies*, 54: 213 (1965), 7.

3. F. S. L. Lyons, *Ireland Since the Famine* (London: Weidenfeld and Nicolson, 1971), pp. 91–92. Terry Eagleton, in *Heathcliff and the Great Hunger: Studies in Irish Culture* (London: Verso, 1995), argued that the Rising was "a watershed between two strains of nationalism—between the Romantic, idealist, traditionalist version of the creed which carried out the insurrection, much of it with Anglo-Irish roots, and the modernizing, Catholic, petty-bourgeois variety which reaped the fruits of it" (p. 276).

4. Seamus Deane, *The Field Day Anthology of Irish Writing*, vol. 3 (Derry: Field Day Publications, 1991), p. 90.

5. Robert Greacen, quoted in Dillon Johnston, *Irish Poetry after Joyce* (Mountrath: Dolmen Press, 1985), p. 7.

6. W. B. Yeats, "Poetry and Tradition" (1907) *Essays and Introductions* (New York: Collier Books, 1968), p. 260.

7. Terence Brown, *Ireland: A Social and Cultural History, 1922–79* (Glasgow: Fontana, 1981), p. 195.

8. John Montague, quoted in Johnston, *Irish Poetry after Joyce*, p. 14.

9. Sean O' Faolain, quoted in Brown, *Ireland: A Social and Cultural History*, p. 201.

10. Anthony Cronin, quoted in Brown, *Ireland: A Social and Cultural History*, p. 227.

11. R. F. Foster, *Modern Ireland 1600–1972* (London: Penguin, 1988), p. 581.

12. As Seamus Deane put it in "Irish Poetry and Irish Nationalism," in *Two Decades of Irish Writing: A Cultural Survey*, ed. Douglas Dunn (Chester Springs, Pa: Dufour, 1975), modern Irish poets "found themselves in a culture which could no longer convert its brilliantly re-created past

to any conceivable future" (p. 18). Robert F. Garratt, in *Modern Irish Poetry: Tradition and Continuity from Yeats to Heaney* (Berkeley: University of California Press, 1986), argued that the modern Irish poem "accepts discontinuity as a dominant feature of his cultural past" (p. x).

Chapter Fourteen. Yeats

1. W. B. Yeats, "Ireland and the Arts" (1901), *Essays and Introductions* (New York: Collier Books, 1968), p. 210.

2. Yeats, "Ireland and the Arts," p. 203.

3. W. B. Yeats, "Preface" to *A Book of Irish Verse,* ed. W. B. Yeats (London: Methuen, 1900), pp. xiii-xiv. The preface is dated 1899.

4. In *Irish Identity and the Literary Revival: Synge, Yeats, Joyce and O'Casey* (London: Croom Helm, 1979), G. J. Watson said: "Yeats loved Irish nationalists as heroic losers, but Irish nationalists as potential winners—and politician-winners at that—was a different matter" (p. 104).

5. W. B. Yeats, "J. M. Synge and the Ireland of His Time" (1910), *Essays and Introductions.* See R. F. Foster, "Good Behaviour: Yeats, Synge and Anglo-Irish Etiquette," in Foster, *Paddy and Mr Punch: Connections in English and Irish History* (1993; London: Penguin, 1995), pp. 195–211, on the relationship between Yeats and Synge, and specifically on this essay.

6. W. B. Yeats, "J. M. Synge and The Ireland of His Time," *Essays and Introductions,* p. 313.

7. W. B. Yeats, *Michael Robartes and the Dancer* (1921); rpt. in *The Variorum Edition of the Poems of W. B. Yeats,* ed. Peter Allt and Russell K. Alspach (New York: Macmillan, 1957), p. 394.

8. W. B. Yeats, "J. M. Synge and The Ireland of His Time," *Essays and Introductions,* p. 339.

9. Yeats, *Variorum Edition,* p. 290.

10. Ibid., pp. 289–90. Terry Eagleton, in *Heathcliff and the Great Hunger: Studies in Irish Culture* (London: Verso, 1995), interpreted Yeats's conservatism in terms of the radical right associated with modernism: "The radical right finds conventional middle-class society supremely distasteful, and confronts it with a critique far more searching and fundamental, if also a good deal more wrong-headed, than anything a liberal realism can muster. . . . Yeats is the supremely fine poet he is, not despite his politics but in some measure because of them" (p. 301).

11. Yeats, *Variorum Edition,* p. 392.

12. W. B. Yeats, "The Tragic Theatre" (1910), *Essays and Introductions,* p. 241. Declan Kiberd, *Inventing Ireland: The Literature of the Modern Nation* (London: Jonathan Cape, 1995), said that the 1916 rebels "staged the Rising as street theatre and were justly celebrated in metaphors of the drama by Yeats" (p. 203).

13. Yeats, *Variorum Edition,* p. 394.

14. Eagleton, in *Heathcliff and the Great Hunger,* says that "Easter 1916" "imitates the action of the Rising itself, which proclaims into being something which plainly does not exist. . . . Yeats's own creative act is an instance of Benjamin's anti-historicist consciousness, blasting the Rising out of the continuum of history as the British have just blasted the rebels out of it" (pp. 307–8).

15. Yeats, *Variorum Edition,* p. 420.

16. Ibid., pp. 423–24, 427.

17. Ibid., p. 425.

18. In *Irish Identity and the Literary Revival,* Watson argued that Yeats's disillusionment with the Irish Catholic middle class did not lead to a withdrawal from his interest in remaking Irish

culture, but rather to the creation of two mythologies proposed as counters to utilitarian materialism: "the mythology of the great individual, the hero, and the mythology of the cultural aristocracy" (p. 107).

19. In *Heathcliff and the Great Hunger,* Eagleton said that Yeats saw the Big House as "a kind of Romantic symbol all in itself, a place where material opulence is justified as a medium of spirit" (p. 69).

20. Yeats, *Variorum Edition,* p. 264.

21. Eagleton argued that the empowerment of the Irish tenantry, by depriving nationalism of its primary economic issue, effectively refocused the movement on the issue of political separatism, at the same time that it strengthened the "self-assurance" of the tenantry, and so the prospects of a nationalist revolution; Eagleton, *Heathcliff and the Great Hunger,* pp. 96–97.

22. Yeats, *Variorum Edition,* p. 264.

23. W. B. Yeats, *The Wild Swans at Coole* (1919); rpt. in Yeats, *Variorum Edition,* p. 328.

24. Ibid., p. 328.

25. W. B. Yeats, "The Tower," *The Tower* (1928); rpt. in Yeats, *Variorum Edition,* p. 414.

26. Yeats, *Variorum Edition,* p. 326.

27. Ibid., pp. 327–28. In *Ireland: A Social and Cultural History,* Brown argued: "It was Yeats's genius to realize that at the moment of Anglo-Irish collapse he could so celebrate a class that its demise would be seen not simply as a fact of history but as an event that threatened the death of culture" (p. 133).

28. W. G. Yeats, *Winding Stair* (1933); rpt. in Yeats, *Variorum Edition,* p. 475.

29. W. B. Yeats, "Coole Park, 1929," *Winding Stair;* rpt. in Yeats, *Variorum Edition,* p. 489.

30. Yeats, *Variorum Edition,* pp. 491–92.

31. W. J. McCormack, in *Ascendancy and Tradition in Anglo-Irish Literary History from 1789 to 1939* (Oxford: Clarendon Press, 1985), demonstrated various ways in which Yeats ignored or departed from the historical realities surrounding the development of the Anglo-Irish Ascendancy. "Not only is Yeats's work a multi-farious act of self-making and autobiography but the ramifications of that endeavour aspire to create a new history in which that undertaking appears exemplary, necessary, and accomplished" (p. 297). In *Inventing Ireland,* Declan Kiberd argued that Goldsmith, Swift, Sheridan, and Berkeley "were each of them impeccable representatives of the Irish Protestant middle class: hard-working men who lived by the pen and who felt, if anything, a very unYeatsian contempt for the idleness and mendacity of the rural ascendancy" (p. 449).

32. W. B. Yeats, "Bishop Berkeley" (1931), *Essays and Introductions,* p. 402.

33. Yeats, *Winding Stair;* rpt. in Yeats, *Variorum Edition,* pp. 480–81.

34. Yeats's friendship with F. R. Higgins in the 1930s had much to do with his renewed interest in the traditional ballad.

35. W. B. Yeats, *New Poems* (1938); rpt. in Yeats, *Variorum Edition,* p. 586.

36. Thomas Kinsella, "The Irish Writer," in Thomas Kinsella and W. B. Yeats, *Davis, Mangan, Ferguson? Tradition and the Irish Writer* (Dublin: Dolmen Press, 1970), p. 62.

37. W. B. Yeats, "A General Introduction for My Work" (1937), *Essays and Introductions,* p. 519.

38. Norman Vance, *Irish Literature: A Social History* (Oxford: Basil Blackwell, 1990), p. 215.

Chapter Fifteen. Exits from the Revival

1. George Russell, Preface to *The Collected Poems of Oliver St. John Gogarty* (New York: Devin-Adair, 1954), p. 10.

2. Oliver St. John Gogarty, quoted in James F. Carens, *Surpassing Wit: Oliver St. John Gogarty, His Poetry and His Prose* (New York: Columbia University Press, 1979), p. 22.

3. A. Norman Jeffares, in *Anglo-Irish Literature* (New York: Schocken Books, 1982), said that Gogarty "exhibited an insouciantly classical control in his poetry" (p. 146). Roger McHugh and Maurice Harmon, in *Short History of Anglo-Irish Literature* (Totowa, N.J.: Barnes and Noble, 1982), argued that Gogarty was "well versed in the classics and learned from them a discipline of form which controlled his natural vivacity" (p. 217).

4. *Collected Poems of Gogarty*, p. 49.

5. Ibid., p. 147.

6. Oliver St. John Gogarty, quoted in Carens, *Surpassing Wit*, p. 51.

7. *Collected Poems of Gogarty*, p. 85.

8. Ibid., p. 86.

9. Ibid., p. 102.

10. T. S. Eliot, "The Metaphysical Poets" (1921); rpt. in *Selected Essays*, 3d ed. (New York: Harcourt Brace Jovanovich, 1951, p. 290.

11. "Poetry Is Vertical" (1932), quoted in Thomas MacGreevy, *Collected Poems*, ed. Thomas Dillon Redshaw (Dublin: Raven Arts Press, 1971), p. 73.

12. Anthony Cronin, *Heritage Now: Irish Literature in the English Language* (New York: St. Martin's Press, 1982), p. 157.

13. *Collected Poems of Thomas MacGreevy*, ed. Susan Schreibman (Dublin: Anna Livia Press, 1991), p. 7.

14. *Collected Poems of MacGreevy*, p. 8.

15. Ibid., p. 35.

16. Ibid., p. 15.

17. Ibid., p. 19.

18. Samuel Beekett, "Recent Irish Poetry" (1934), in *The Field Day Anthology of Irish Writing*, ed. Seamus Deane, vol. 3 (Derry: Field Day Publications, 1991), p. 247.

19. Robert Farren, *The Course of Irish Verse in English* (New York: Sheed and Ward, 1947), p. 150.

20. M. D. [Maurice Devane, pseud. for Clarke], review of *Horizon: A Review of Literature and Art*, ed. Cyril Connolly, *The Dublin Magazine*, new series 17, no. 2 (April–June 1942), 66.

21. Arthur Clarke, *Twice Round the Black Church: Early Memories of Ireland and England* (London: Routledge and Kegan Paul, 1962), p. 16.

22. Thomas Kinsella, *The Dual Tradition: An Essay on Poetry and Politics in Ireland* (Manchester: Carcanet Press, 1995), said that Clarke "was not the only Irish writer who wanted to write intricately in the Gaelic manner, but he was the only one to make this element a part of his poetic nature" (p. 95).

23. Austin Clarke, "The Poetry of Herbert Trench," *The London Mercury*, 10:56 (1924), 159.

24. Austin Clarke, "The Cattledrive in Connaught" (1925), *Collected Poems*, ed. Liam Miller (Dublin: Dolmen Press, 1974), p. 135.

25. W. B. Yeats, *The Wanderings of Oisin and Other Poems* (1889); rpt. in *The Variorum Edition of the Poems of W. B. Yeats*, ed. Peter Allt and Russell K. Alspach (New York: Macmillan, 1957), p. 3.

26. Terence Brown, while acknowledging the importance of this moment, reads it in terms of a shift in Irish consciousness: "In such a transition, undoubtedly rooted in Clarke's own personality, one may perhaps detect a more general intimation of the failing powers of the mythological and heroic vision in the 1920s in the depressed aftermath of the civil war." Brown, *Ireland: A Social and Cultural History, 1922–79* (Glasggow: Fontana, 1981), p. 81.

27. Clarke, *Collected Poems*, p. 153. Clarke's reconstruction of Clonmacnoise might be compared with that of T. R. Rolleston's revival lyric, "The Dead at Clonmacnoise," which emphasizes the pagan dimension of the place.

28. Clarke, *Collected Poems*, p.154.

29. Ibid., p. 183.

30. Ibid., p. 547.

31. Ibid., p. 162. The poem on which this is based, "Beatha an Scoláire," uses a different pattern of assonance from that employed by Clarke. The first stanza is:

> Aoibhinn beatha an scoláire
> > bhíos ag déanamh a léighinn;
> is follas díbh, a dhaoine,
> > gurab dó is aoibhne in Éirinn.

An Duanaire Poems of the Dispossessed, ed. Seán Ó Tuama; trans. Thomas Kinsella (Mountrath: Dolmen Press, 1981), p. 16.

32. Clarke, *Collected Poems*, p. 188.

33. F. R. Higgins, *The Dark Breed* (London: Macmillan, 1927), p. 66.

34. Higgins, *Dark Breed,* pp. 26–27.

35. Farren, *Course of Irish Verse,* p. 135.

36. F. R. Higgins, quoted in W. R. Rodgers, ed., *Irish Literary Portraits* (New York: Taplinger, 1973), p. 172.

37. Higgins, *Dark Breed,* pp. 2–3.

38. Samuel Beckett, "Recent Irish Poetry," p. 246.

39. F. R. Higgins, *The Gap of Brightness* (London: Macmillan, 1940), p. 15.

40. Robert F. Garratt, in *Modern Irish Poetry: Tradition and Continuity from Yeats to Heaney* (Berkeley: University of California Press, 1986), said that Higgins's poetry "shows the debilitating effects of tradition and a strong mentor" (p. 70).

41. Austin Clarke, *Poetry in Modern Ireland* (Cork: Mercier Press, 1951), p. 60.

42. Robert Farren, *Selected Poems* (New York: Sheed and Ward, 1951), p. 45.

43. Clarke, *Poetry in Modern Ireland,* p. 62.

44. Ferran, *Selected Poems,* p. 12.

Chapter Sixteen. New Perspectives at Midcentury

1. Austin Clarke, *Twice Round the Black Church: Early Memories of Ireland and England* (London: Routledge and Kegan Paul, 1962), p. 121.

2. Maurice Harmon, "New Voices in the Fifties," in *Irish Poets in English,* ed. Sean Lucy (Cork and Dublin: Mercier Press, 1973), said that although Clarke's early poems of religious anguish had little interest for poets emerging in the 1950s, those poets "could see that his satirical engagement with contemporary Irish life encompassed the contexts of their lives" (pp. 191–92). In *Ireland: A Social and Cultural History, 1922–1979* (Glasgow: Fontana, 1981), Terence Brown noted the influence of Clarke's public poetry: "A sceptical, radical mind found expression in a body of verse that a younger generation in the 1960s was to find invigorating" (p. 228).

3. Austin Clarke, *Ancient Lights* (1955); rpt. in Austin Clarke, *Collected Poems,* ed. Liam Miller (Dublin: Dolmen Press, 1974), p. 197.

4. Clark, *Collected Poems,* p. 195.

5. Ibid., p. 212.

6. Ibid., p. 554.

7. Ibid., p. 295. Sigerson's version (*Bards of the Gael and Gall,* 2d ed. [New York: Charles Scribner's, 1907], pp. 256–58), is among the better attempts, before Clarke's, to render this poem into English:

> No song the sweetest,
> No music meetest,

But she sings its melody, full, soft, and true;
    Her cheek the rose a-blowing,
    With comrade lily glowing,
Her glancing eyes, like opening blossoms blue.
And a bard has sung how herons keen
On hearing her victor-voice slumber serene.
    Her eyes of splendour
    Are wells of candour.—
Here's thy health, go leór, a stór, our beauty bright queen!

In *A Penny in the Clouds: More Memories of Ireland and England* (London: Routledge and Kegan Paul, 1968), Clarke said that Sigerson's translations in *Bards of the Gael and Gall* were "already old-fashioned, since the poet in his literary version used double rhyme and jingling internal rhyme" (p. 42).

8. Clarke, *Collected Poems,* p. 300.

9. Anthony Cronin, in *Heritage Now: Irish Literature in the English Language* (New York: St. Martin's Press, 1982), argued that at the center of Kavanagh's work is the need to "make clear that the ultimate self is incorruptible; and, however aberrant, has maintained its integrity and refusal to compromise" (p. 190). Seamus Heaney, "From Monaghan to the Grand Canal: The Poetry of Patrick Kavanagh," in: *Preoccupations: Selected Prose, 1968–1978* (London: Faber and Faber, 1980), said: "Kavanagh's proper idiom is free from the intonations typical of the Revival poets. His imagination has not been tutored to 'sweeten Ireland's wrong', his ear has not been programmed to retrieve in English the lost music of verse in Irish. The 'matter of Ireland', mythic, historical or literary, forms no significant part of his material" (p. 115).

10. Patrick Kavanagh, quoted in Dillon Johnston, *Irish Poetry after Joyce* (Mountrath: Dolmen Press, 1985), p. 135.

11. Brendan Kennelly, "Patrick Kavanagh," in *Irish Poets in English,* ed. Sean Lucy (Cork and Dublin: Mercier Press, 1973), argued that as a visionary poet, Kavanagh is to be associated chiefly with Blake and Yeats (p. 181). Heaney, "From Monaghan to the Grand Canal," said that even Kavanagh's poems about rural life are less realistic representations than poems that "aspire to visionary statement" (p. 119).

12. Patrick Kavanagh, "Preface" to *Collected Poems* (1964; New York: Norton, 1973), p. xiii.

13. Kavanagh, *Collected Poems,* p. 19.

14. Ibid., p. 135.

15. Ibid., p. 40.

16. Ibid., p. 52.

17. Ibid., p. 34.

18. Patrick Kavanagh, quoted in Anthony Cronin, *Dead as Doornails* (Dublin: Poolbeg Press, 1980), p. 78.

19. Kavanagh, *Collected Poems,* p. 150.

20. John Ryan, in *Remembering How We Stood: Bohemian Dublin at the Mid-Century* (Dublin: Gill and Macmillan, 1975), described Kavanagh as "the last poet to work from the enormous reserves of experience that the enraged, brutalizing, backbreaking, emasculating toil of the small farmer provides" (p. 155). In *Ireland: A Social and Cultural History,* Terence Brown wrote of "The Great Hunger": "Kavanagh's poem is an outraged cry of anger, an eloquently bleak riposte from the heart of the rural world to all those polemicists, writers and demagogues who in de Valera's Ireland sought to venerate the countryman's life from the study or political platform" (p. 187).

21. Kavanagh, *Collected Poems,* p. 40.

22. Ibid., pp. 36, 38.

23. Ibid., p. 45.

24. Darcy O'Brien, *Patrick Kavanagh* (Lewisburg, Pa.: Bucknell University Press, 1975), pp. 36–37.

25. Peter Kavanagh, *Sacred Keeper: A Biography of Patrick Kavanagh* (The Curragh: Goldsmith Press, 1979), p. 24. Seamus Heaney, "The Placeless Heaven: Another Look at Kavanagh," in *The Government of the Tongue: Selected Prose, 1978–1987* (New York: Farrar, Straus and Giroux, 1988), claimed that Kavanagh's writing had a political effect, quite apart from his intentions: "Over the border, into a Northern Ireland dominated by the noticeably English accents of the local BBC, he broadcast a voice that would not be cowed into accents other than its own. . . . Whether he wanted it or not, his achievement was inevitably co-opted, north and south, into the general current of feeling which flowed from and sustained ideas of national identity, cultural otherness from Britain" (pp. 9–10).

26. In *Heritage Now,* Cronin argued that Kavanagh's satires are best understood as representations of the forces that he saw as threatening his poetic integrity, although he also sees them as constituting a "chapter in the moral history of his country. . . the chapter relating specifically to a new phenomenon, the 'art-loving', liberal middle classes of independent Ireland" (p. 192).

27. Kavanagh, *Collected Poems,* p. 132.

28. Patrick Kavanagh, quoted in Robert F. Garratt, *Modern Irish Poetry: Tradition and Continuity from Yeats to Heaney* (Berkeley: University of California Press, 1986), p. 142.

29. Patrick Kavanagh, "From Monaghan to the Grand Canal," in Kavanagh, *Collected Prose* (1967), quoted in *Poetry and Ireland Since 1800: A Source Book,* ed. Mark Storey (London and New York: Routledge, 1988), pp. 192, 198.

30. Kavanagh, *Collected Poems,* pp. 123–24.

31. Austin Clarke (1949), quoted in W. R. Rodgers, ed., *Irish Literary Portraits* (London: British Broadcasting Corp., 1972), p. 19.

32. Padraic Fallon, "Yeats at Athenry Perhaps," *Collected Poems,* ed. Brian Fallon (Oldcastle, Co. Meath: Gallery Press, 1990), p. 112.

33. Brian Fallon, "Afterword" to *Collected Poems,* p. 265.

34. Brian Fallon, in "Afterword," also argued that Fallon's understanding of myth was different from Yeats's notion of myth as embodying universal truth: "While he had a mystical streak, it is not Platonic or transcendental; it is more a kind of psychic energy rooted in the earth" (pp. 268–69).

35. Fallon, *Collected Poems,* pp. 43–44.

36. Robert Garratt took this view in *Modern Irish Poetry* (pp. 68 ff.). Donald Davie, "Austin Clarke and Padraic Fallon," in *Two Decades of Irish Writing: A Survey,* ed. Douglas Dunn (Chester Springs, Pa.: Dufour, 1975), said that "the heroic cadences of the great ventriloquist overwhelm Fallon and push him into unintended parody" (p. 55).

37. Declan Kiberd, in *The Field Day Anthology of Irish Writing,* vol. 3 (Derry: Field Day Publications, 1991), associates Fallon with George Sigerson's *Bards of the Gael and Gall,* calling him "the poet of the 'other' Revival, the revival of the Gael rather than the revival of the Celt" (p. 1309). In his "Afterward" to Fallon's *Collected Poems,* Brian Fallon remarked that for Fallon, Yeats "remained the Irish Protestant burgher in his frock coat, the visitor to the Big House hunting for copy among the local peasantry" (p. 268).

38. Fallon, *Collected Poems,* p. 112.

39. Ibid., pp. 112, 114.

40. Brian Fallon's "Afterword" described Fallon as "a countryman by background and ancestry who grew up in a world where the tramp-poet Raftery was still a fairly recent memory, and Gaelic folk-song was a living tradition and not an archive culture"; Fallon, *Collected Poems,* p. 268.

41. Fallon, *Collected Poems,* p. 119.

42. Ibid., pp. 133–34.

43. Ibid., p. 75. Brian Fallon's "Afterword" says that Fallon saw the struggle for Irish

independence "as a land war and a class struggle, fought primarily against the Anglo-Irish ruling and landowning class rather than against England"; Fallon, Collected Poems, p. 265.

44. Seamus Heaney, Introduction to Fallon, *Collected Poems,* p. 14.

45. *Collected Poems of Denis Devlin,* ed. J. C. C. Mays (Winston-Salem, N.C.: Wake Forest University Press, 1989), pp. 132–34.

46. *Collected Poems of Devlin,* pp. 57–58.

47. As the poet Michael Smith said, "Denis Devlin, having absorbed an incredible range of European influences both of the past and the present, set himself the task of exploring the possibilities of spiritual and religious salvation in the modern world"; quoted by Brian Coffey, "Denis Devlin: Poet of Distances," in *Place Personality and the Irish Writer,* ed. Andrew Carpenter (Gerrards Cross England, Colin Smythe, 1977), p. 151. In *A Short History of Irish Literature* (London: Hutchinson, 1986), Seamus Deane described Devlin's poetry as "metaphysical in the symbolist mode," and therefore a rare instance of specifically Christian poetry "in a country where the traditional modern relationship between poetry and belief has been fraught with tension and suspicion" (p. 232).

48. *Collected Poems of Devlin,* p. 151.

49. Ibid., pp. 163–64.

50. Ibid., p. 164.

51. Ibid., p. 165.

52. Terence Brown, in *The Field Day Anthology,* vol. 3, argued: "Devlin seeks to reconcile flesh and spirit in an understanding of sexual love and thereby to sustain a Christian tradition profoundly under threat in a modern world of political and philosophical nihilism" (p. 132). Deane's *Short History* said that Devlin's work rebukes the conflict in Clarke's work between "the prescriptions of religion and the desires of the body and the imagination" (p. 231).

53. *Collected Poems of Devlin,* p. 273.

54. Ibid., p. 153.

55. Brian Coffey, "Denis Devlin: Poet of Distances," p. 141.

56. *Collected Poems of Devlin,* pp. 284–5.

57. Ibid., p. 283.

58. John Montague, "The Impact of International Modern Poetry on Irish Writing Today," in *Irish Poets in English,* ed. Lucy, pp. 148–49.

Chapter Seventeen. Covert Voices: Women Poets after the Revival

1. A. A. Kelly, ed., *Pillars of the House: An Anthology of Verse by Irish Women from 1690 to the Present* (Dublin: Wolfhound, 1987), p. 94.

2. The one volume of poems to Mary Devenport O'Neill's credit, *Prometheus and Other Poems,* was published in 1929, one year before Denis Devlin and Brian Coffey brought out their first modernist collection, *Poems.*

3. Mary Devenport O'Neill *Prometheus and Other Poems* (London: Jonathan Cape, 1929), p. 27.

4. O'Neill, *Prometheus,* p. 40.

5. Samuel Beckett, "Recent Irish Poetry" (1934), in *The Field Day Anthology of Irish Writing,* ed. Seamus Deane, vol. 3 (Derry: Field Day Publications, 1991), p. 247.

6. Roger McHugh and Maurice Harmon, in *A Short History of Anglo-Irish Literature* (Totowa, N.J.: Barnes and Noble, 1982), describe Salkeld's poetry as "impressionist realism" (p. 222).

7. Blanaid Salkeld, *The Fox's Covert* (London: J. M. Dent, 1935), p. 8.

8. Salkeld, *Fox's Covert,* p. 17.

9. Blanaid Salkeld, *Hello, Eternity!* (London: Elkin Mathews and Marrot, 1933), p. 48.

10. Salkeld, "There's None Shall Say," *Hello Eternity!,* p. 60.

11. Salkeld, *Hello Eternity!*, p. 55.

12. Rhoda Coghill, *The Bright Hillside* (Dublin: Hodges, Figgis, 1948), p. 26.

13. Coghill, *Bright Hillside*, p. 18.

14. Herbert Read, quoted in G. S. Fraser, "Preface" to Sheila Wingfield, *Collected Poems: 1938–1983* (London: Enitharmon Press, 1983), p. xiii.

15. G. S. Fraser, "Preface" to Wingfield, *Collected Poems*, p. xv.

16. Sheila Wingfield, quoted in Fraser, "Preface" to *Collected Poems*, p. xvi.

17. Wingfield, *Collected Poems*, p. 120.

18. Ibid., p. 133.

19. Máire MacEntee, *A Heart Full of Thought* (Dublin: Dolmen Press, 1959), p. 8.

20. MacEntee, *Heart Full of Thought*, p. 10.

21. Eithne Strong, *Songs of Living* (Monkstown: Runa Press, 1961), p. 52.

22. Strong, *Songs of Living*, p. 10.

23. Ibid., pp. 66–67.

24. W. B. Yeats, "To Ireland in the Coming Times," *The Variorum Edition of the Poems of W. B. Yeats,* ed. Peter Allt and Russell K. Alspach (New York: Macmillan, 1957), p. 139.

Chapter Eighteen. The North

1. John Hewitt, "Regionalism: The Last Chance" (1947), in *Ancestral Voices: The Selected Prose of John Hewitt,* ed. Tom Clyde (Belfast: Blackstaff Press, 1987), p. 125.

2. John Wilson Foster, " 'The Dissidence of Dissent': John Hewitt and W. R. Rodgers," in *Across the Roaring Hill: The Protestant Imagination in Modern Ireland,* ed. Gerald Dawe and Edna Longley (Belfast: Blackstaff Press, 1985), asserted, "Hewitt is conscious of having an alien heritage in his own country, and is yet determined to have it recognized that it *is* his own country" (p. 142).

3. Thomas Kinsella, *The Dual Tradition: An Essay on Poetry and Politics in Ireland* (Manchester: Carcanet Press, 1995), argued against seeing these poets in the context of a poetry of the north: "Poetry in Northern Ireland, far from constituting a renaissance, has responded to nothing and contributed nothing to the situation" (p. 117). Kinsella is highly suspicious of the concept of a distinctive northern poetry, saying that the phrase "is a journalistic entity rather than a literary one" (p. 114).

4. Louis MacNeice, quoted in Peter McDonald, *Louis MacNeice: The Poet in His Contexts* (Oxford: Clarendon Press, 1991), p. 205.

5. Quoted in Terence Brown, *Northern Voices: Poets from Ulster* (Dublin: Gill and Macmillan, 1975), p. 100.

6. *The Collected Poems of Louis MacNeice,* ed. E. R. Dodds (London: Faber and Faber, 1966, 1979), p. 69.

7. *Collected Poems of MacNeice*, p. 17.

8. Louis MacNeice, *The Strings Are False: An Unfinished Autobiography* (New York: Oxford University Press, 1966), pp. 41–42.

9. *Collected Poems of MacNeice*, p. 41.

10. Ibid., p. 132.

11. Anthony Cronin, *Heritage Now: Irish Literature in the English Language* (New York: St. Martin's Press, 1982), p. 200.

12. Terence Brown, "Louis MacNeice's Ireland," in *Tradition and Influence in Anglo-Irish Poetry,* ed. Terence Brown and Nicholas Grene (Totowa, N.J.: Barnes and Noble, 1989), p. 88.

13. *Collected Poems of MacNeice,* p.256.

14. Ibid., p. 255.

15. "Dublin," *Collected Poems of MacNeice,* p. 164.

16. *Collected Poems of MacNeice,* p. 164.

17. Louis MacNeice, quoted in *The Poetry of W. B. Yeats* (New York: Oxford University Press, 1941), p. 197.

18. Louis MacNeice, qouted in *Poetry of W. B. Yeats,* p. 55.

19. *Collected Poems of MacNeice,* p. 53.

20. Ibid., pp. 52–53.

21. John Hewitt, "Planter's Gothic," quoted in Frank Ormsby, Introduction to *The Collected Poems of John Hewitt,* ed. Ormsby (Belfast: Blackstaff Press, 1991), p. vii.

22. John Hewitt, "Regionalism: The Last Chance," p. 125.

23. In *The Dual Tradition,* Kinsella said that Hewitt's work is "valuable for its complete presentation, in a determined pentameter, of the colonial mentality" (p. 118).

24. John Hewitt, *Ancestral Voices,* p. 18.

25. Norman Vance, in *Irish Literature: A Social History* (Oxford: Basil Blackwell, 1990), described Hewitt's position as a "painful, sometimes arrogant, loneliness as a leftist secular Protestant in conservative Ulster" (p. 227).

26. John Hewitt, "No Rootless Colonist" (1972), in *Ancestral Voices,* p. 154.

27. *The Collected Poems of John Hewitt,* ed. Frank Ormsby (Belfast: Blackstaff Press, 1991), p. 79.

28. *Collected Poem of Hewitt,* p. 21.

29. Terence Brown, "The Poetry of W. R. Rodgers and John Hewitt," in *Two Decades of Irish Writing: A Survey,* ed. Douglas Dunn (Cheshire: Carcanet, 1975), said that Hewitt writes "in terms of ironic pastoral, recognizing his own alienation" (p. 90).

30. *Collected Poems of Hewitt,* p. 310.

31. Michael Longley, quoted in Ormsby, Introduction to *Collected Poems of Hewitt,* p. xxiii.

32. Stephen Spender, quoted in Foster, "The Dissidence of Dissent," p. 139.

33. In "The Poetry of W. R. Rodgers and John Hewitt," Terence Brown argued that many of Rodgers's poems "dramatize not only human conflict but suggest breaking through puritan inhibitions and self-protective prudence to sexual and emotional risks and satisfactions" (p. 86). In *Northern Voices,* Brown also described *Europa and the Bull* as an attempt "to use poetry to write himself out of the ministry, with its requirements in the service of Calvin's God, into a romantic faith in the richness and fundamental unity of life's possibilities" (p. 120).

34. W. R. Rodgers, *Collected Poems* (London: Oxford University Press, 1971), p. 84.

35. W. R. Rodgers, quoted in Brown, "The Poetry of W. R. Rodgers and John Hewitt," p. 83.

36. Rodgers, *Collected Poems,* p. 147.

37. Brown, *Northern Voices,* p. 114.

38. Rodgers, *Collected Poems,* p. 77.

Chapter Nineteen. Toward Contemporary Poetry

1. John Mountague, "Speech for an Ideal Irish Election," *Collected Poems* (Old Castle, C. Meath, Gallery Press, 1985), p. 200.

2. Thomas Kinsella, quoted in Maurice Harmon, "New Voices in the Fifties," in *Irish Poets in English,* ed. Sean Lucy (Cork: Mercier Press, 1973), p. 189.

3. Seamus Deane, "John Montague: The Kingdom of the Dead," in *Celtic Revivals: Essays in Modern Irish Literature, 1800–1980* (1985; Winston-Salem, N.C.: Wake Forest University Press, 1987), p. 152.

4. W. B. Yeats, quoted in A. Norman Jeffares, *A Commentary on the Collected Poems of W. B. Yeats* (Stanford, Calif.: Stanford University Press, 1968), p. 265.

5. Declan Kiberd, *The Field Day Anthology of Irish Writing,* vol. 3 (Derry: Field Day Publications, 1991), p. 1341.

6. Thomas Kinsella, "The Irish Writer" (1966), in W. B. Yeats, and Thomas Kinsella, *Davis, Mangan, Ferguson? Tradition and the Irish Writer* (Dublin: Dolmen Press, 1970), p. 66.

7. Richard Murphy, *Sailing to an Island* (London: Faber and Faber, 1963), p. 20.

8. In *Irish Literature: A Social History* (Oxford: Basil Blackwood, 1990), Norman Vance called Murphy "the finest, perhaps the last literary representative of stubborn Anglo-Ireland" (p. 216).

9. Richard Murphy, "The Woman of the House," *Sailing to an Island,* p. 40.

10. W. B. Yeats, "Coole Park and Ballylee, 1931," *The Variorum Edition of the Poems of W. B. Yeats,* ed. Peter Allt and Russell K. Alspach (New York: Macmillan, 1957), p. 491.

11. Murphy, *Sailing to an Island,* p. 39.

12. Richard Murphy, *New Selected Poems* (1985; London: Faber and Faber, 1989), p. 53.

13. W. B. Yeats, "The Fisherman," *Variorum Edition,* pp. 347–8.

14. Murphy, *Sailing to an Island,* p. 13.

15. Murphy, *New Selected Poems,* p. 45.

16. Richard Murphy, quoted in Maurice Harmon, "Introduction: The Poet and His Background" to *Richard Murphy: Poet of Two Traditions,* ed. Harmon (Dublin: Wolfhound Press, 1978), p. 8.

17. Richard Murphy, "Legend,"*New Selected Poems,* p. 55.

18. Richard Murphy, "Orange March," *New Selected Poems,* p. 49.

19. Richard Murphy, "History," *New Selected Poems,* p. 54.

20. Thomas Kinsella, "The Irish Writer," p. 64.

21. Ibid., p. 59.

22. Ibid., pp. 65–66.

23. The influence of Williams, Pound, Lowell, and Roethke on Kinsella was discussed by Dillon Johnston in *Irish Poetry after Joyce* (Mountrath: Dolmen Press, 1985), pp. 104–5. Robert F. Garratt, in *Modern Irish Poetry: Tradition and Continuity from Yeats to Heaney* (Berkeley: University of California Press, 1986), argued that Kinsella's commitment to modernism represented "a purgation of revivalism" (p. 171).

24. Kinsella, "The Irish Writer," p. 66.

25. Thomas Kinsella, quoted in Johnston, *Irish Poetry after Joyce,* p. 104. Seamus Deane, in *A Short History of Irish Literature* (London: Hutchinson, 1986), described Kinsella's work as dramatizing "the confrontation between poetry as a system of order and history as a spectacle of disorder" (p. 235).

26. Thomas Kinsella, *Poems, 1956–1973* (Winston-Salem, N.C.: Wake Forest University Press, 1979), p. 108.

27. Kinsella, *Poems, 1956–1973,* p. 105.

28. Ibid., p. 61.

29. Ibid., pp. 55–56.

30. Ibid., p. 56.

31. John Montague, "The Sentimental Prophecy: A Study of *The Deserted Village,*" in *The Art of Oliver Goldsmith,* ed. Andrew Swarbrick (London: Vision Books, 1984), p. 93.

32. John Montague, quoted in Johnston, *Irish Poetry after Joyce,* p. 193.

33. Terence Brown, in *Northern Voices: Poets from Ulster* (Dublin: Gill and Macmillan, 1975), said that the tradition that Montague "espouses, defiantly, assuming its importance, is a Gaelic 'hidden Ulster'—intuitively apprehended in childhood" (p. 155).

34. John Montague, *The Rough Field* (Dublin: Dolmen Press, 1972), p. 39.

35. Montague, *The Rough Field,* pp. 34–35. As Terry Eagleton put it in *Heathcliff and the Great Hunger: Studies in Irish Culture* (London: Verso, 1995): "Irish literary landscapes are often enough decipherable texts rather than aesthetic objects, places made precious or melancholic by the resonance of the human" (p. 6).

36. Montague, *The Rough Field,* p. 45.

37. Seamus Deane, "Irish Poetry and Irish Nationalism," in *Two Decades of Irish Writing: A Critical Survey,* ed. Douglas Dunn (Cheshire: Carcanet, 1975), argued that Montague's poetry is powerfully informed by the "conviction of the importance of writing as a means to recover that loss both for himself and for the community he represents" (p. 15).

38. Montague, *The Rough Field,* p. 31.

39. John Montague *Collected Poems* (Liverpool: Gallery Books, 1995), p. 67.

40. Ibid., p. 190.

41. R. F. Foster chose 1972 as the year with which to conclude his history, *Modern Ireland: 1600–1972* (London: Penguin, 1988).

42. Montague, *The Rough Field,* p. 83.

Epilogue. Some Observations on Contemporary Poetry

1. Declan Kiberd, *Inventing Ireland: The Literature of the Modern Nation* (London: Jonathan Cape, 1995), argued that a second renaissance is under way in contemporary Ireland, under conditions very like those that prevailed during the first one, including "a highly-educated young population, whose intellectual ambitions often exceeded the available career opportunities" (p. 613). When the Nobel Prize for 1995 was announced, Seamus Heaney observed that his success should be seen in the context of all the poetry being written in contemporary Ireland.

2. As Kiberd put it in, *Inventing Ireland,* "the worst that can be said against Heaney always turns out to have been said already of himself by the artist within the poems" (pp. 594–95).

3. Kiberd, *Inventing Ireland,* p. 592.

4. Charlotte Brooke, "Preface" to *Reliques of Irish Poetry: Consisting of Heroic Poems, Odes, Elegies, and Songs* (Dublin: George Bonham, 1789), p. vii.

5. Seamus Heaney, *Wintering Out* (London: Faber and Faber, 1972), p. 33.

6. Seamus Heaney, "From Monaghan to the Grand Canal: The Poetry of Patrick Kavanagh," in *Preoccupations: Selected Prose, 1968–1978* (London: Faber and Faber, 1980), p. 116.

7. Seamus Heaney, "The Placeless Heaven: Another Look at Kavanagh," *The Government of the Tongue: Selected Prose, 1978–1987* (New York: Farrar, Straus and Giroux, 1988), pp. 9–10.

8. Seamus Heaney, "Feeling into Words" (1974), in *Preoccupations,* p. 41.

9. Heaney, "Feeling into Words,", p. 57.

10. The most detailed criticism of Heaney's bog poems is made by David Lloyd, " 'Pap for the Dispossessed': Seamus Heaney and the Poetics of Identity," in Lloyd, *Anomalous States: Irish Writing and the Post-Colonial Moment* (Durham, N.C.: Duke University Press, 1993), pp. 13–40.

11. Heaney, "Feeling into Words," pp. 56–57. Seamus Deane, "Seamus Heaney: The Timorous and the Bold," in Deane, *Celtic Revivals: Essays in Modern Irish Literature, 1880–1980* (Winston-Salem, N.C.: Wake Forest University Press, 1985), said that Heaney's "dilemma is registered in the perception that the roots of poetry and of violence grow in the same soil; humanism, of the sort mentioned here, has no roots at all" (pp. 180–81).

12. Seamus Heaney, *North* (London: Faber and Faber, 1975), p. 38.

13. Seamus Heaney, *Field Work* (New York: Farrar Straus Giroux, 1979), pp. 23–24.

14. Eavan Boland, *Object Lessons: The Life of the Woman and the Poet in Our Time* (Manchester: Carcanet Press, 1995), p. 200.

15. Boland, *Object Lessons,* p. 126.

16. Ibid, p. 134.

17. Eavan Boland, *Selected Poems* (Manchester: Carcanet Press, 1989), p. 31.

18. Eavan Boland, *The Journey* (Manchester: Carcanet Press, 1986), pp. 10–11.

19. Boland, *The Journey,* p. 54.

20. Boland, *Object Lessons,* p. 198.

21. Jody Allen-Randolph, "An Interview with Eavan Boland," *Irish University Review,* 23:1 (Spring/Summer 1993), 121.

22. As Richard Kearney put it in *Myth and Motherland* (Derry: Field Day Publication's, 1984): "Women became as sexually intangible as the ideal of national independence became politically intangible. They became aspirations rather than actualities" (p. 20). Boland, *Object Lessons,* said, "if there really was an emblematic relation between the defeats of womanhood and the suffering of a nation, I need only prove the first in order to reveal the second. If so, then Irishness and womanhood, those tormenting fragments of my youth, could at least stand in for each other" (p. 148).

23. "Interview with Eavan Boland," p. 130.

24. Important translations have been done by contemporary poets in the tradition of cultural recovery: Thomas Kinsella's *Táin Bó Cuailigne* and his versions of lyric poems in *An Duanaire, 1600–1900: Poems of the Dispossessed;* and Seamus Heaney's *Sweeney Astray.*

25. Ní Dhomhnaill has argued, for example, that "at its deepest level . . . the Irish poetic tradition is sexist and masculinist to the core"; Nuala Ní Dhomhnaill, "The Hidden Ireland: Woman's Inheritance," in *Irish Poetry since Kavanagh,* ed. Theo Dorgan (Dublin: Four Courts Press, 1996), p. 114.

26. Nuala Ní Dhomhnaill, "An Crann," trans. Paul Muldoon, "As for the Quince," in *The Penguin Book of Contemporary Irish Poetry,* ed. Peter Fallon and Derek Mahon (London: Penguin; New York: Viking Penguin, 1990), pp. 405–6.

27. Eavan Boland, "Compact and Compromise: Derek Mahon as a Young Poet," *Irish University Review,* 24:1 (Spring/Summer 1994), 64.

28. Derek Mahon, "The Sea in Winter," *Selected Poems* (London: Penguin; Oldcastle, Co. Meath: Gallery Press, 1991), p. 115.

29. Seamus Heaney, "The Tollund Man," *Wintering Out,* p. 48.

30. Derek Mahon, *Selected Poems,* p. 51.

31. Derek Mahon, "MacNeice in England and Ireland," in *Time Was Away: The World of Louis MacNeice,* ed. Terence Brown and Alec Reid (Dublin: Dolmen Press, 1974), p. 117.

32. Brian Donnelly made this argument in his introduction to an issue of *Irish University Review* on Derek Mahon (24:1, Spring/Summer 1994), 2. In *Celtic Revivals,* Seamus Deane said that "Mahon does not enjoy or seek a sense of community with the kind of Ireland which is so dominant in Irish poetry" (p. 159).

33. Derek Mahon, *The Hudson Letter* (Oldcastle, Co. Meath: Gallery Press, 1995), pp. 53–4.

34. Mahon, *Hudson Letter,* p. 74.

35. Derek Mahon, quoted in Hugh Haughton, " 'Even now there are places where a thought might grow': Place and Displacement in the Poetry of Derek Mahon," in *The Chosen Ground: Essays on the Contemporary Poetry of Northern Ireland,* ed. Neil Corcoran (Chester Springs, Pa.: Dufour, 1992), p. 92. Haughton pointed out how Mahon's work differs from Heaney's (pp. 93–94).

36. Mahon, *The Hudson Letter,* p. 37. In *Celtic Revivals,* Deane related this quality in Mahon's work to the violence in the north: "Homelessness has become a matter of sorrow now that the ruin of home has become a matter of fact" (p. 161). Maurice Riordan, "An Urbane Perspective: The Poetry of Derek Mahon," in *The Irish Writer and the City,* ed. Maurice Harmon (Gerrards Cross, England Colin Smythe, 1984), said that the speaker in many of Mahon's poems, "instead of consolidating his sense of self by reference to his environment, experiences only self-doubt and epistemological uncertainty" (p. 173).

37. Derek Mahon, "In Carrowdore Churchyard," *Selected Poems,* p. 11.

BIBLIOGRAPHY

This list includes relevant contemporary collections and principal modern editions.

The Eighteenth Century

Barber, Mary (1690–1757)
  Poems on Several Occasions. London: C. Rivington, 1734.
  The Poetry of Mary Barber. Lewiston, N. Y.: Edwin Mellen Press, 1992.

Brooke, Charlotte (1740–1793)
  Reliques of Irish Poetry: Consisting of Heroic Poems, Odes, Elegies, and Songs. Dublin:
     George Bonham, 1789.

Concanen, Matthew (1701–1749)
  A Match at Foot-ball. Dublin, 1720; London, 1721.
  Poems upon Several Occasions. Dublin: A. Rhames, 1722.

Dermody, Thomas (1775–1802)
  The Harp of Erin. Ed. James G. Raymond. 2 vols. London: Richard Phillips, 1807.

Drennan, William (1754–1820)
  Fugitive Pieces, in Verse and Prose. Belfast: F. D. Finlay, 1815.
  Glendalloch, and Other Poems. Dublin: W. Robertson, 1859.

Du Bois, Dorothea (1728–1774)
  Poems on Several Occasions. Dublin, 1764.

Dunkin, William (c.1709–1765)
  Select Poetical Works. 2 vols. Dublin: W. G. Jones and S. Powell, 1769–1770.

Goldsmith, Oliver (1728–1774)
  Collected Works of Oliver Goldsmith. Vol. 4 (Poems). Ed. Arthur Friedman. Oxford:
     Clarendon Press, 1966.

Grierson, Constantine (c.1704–1733)

Poems by Eminent Ladies [Includes poems by Grierson]. Ed. George Colman and Bonnell Thornton. 2 vols. London, 1755.

Lysaght, Edward (1763–1810)

Poems. Dublin: Gilbert and Hodges, 1811.

O'Brien, Mary (fl.1783–1810)

The Political Monitor; or Regents' Friend. Dublin: William Gilbert, 1790.

Orr, James (1770–1816)

Poems on Various Subjects. Belfast: Smyth and Lyons, 1804.
The Posthumuous Works of James Orr. Ed. A. M'Dowell. Belfast: Francis D. Finlay, 1817.

Parnell, Thomas (1679–1718)

Poems on Several Occasions. London: B. Lintot, 1722.
Collected Poems of Thomas Parnell. Ed. Claude Rawson and F. P. Lock. Newark: University of Delaware Press; London and Toronto: Associated University Presses, 1989.

Pilkington, Laetitia (1712–1750)

Memoirs of Mrs Laetitia Pilkington [Includes Pilkington's poems]. 3 vols. Dublin and London: R. Griffiths, 1748–1754.
Memoirs of Laetitia Pilkington. Athens: University of Georgia Press, 1996.

Pilkington, Matthew (c.1701–1744)

Poems on Several Occasions. Dublin: G. Faulkner, 1730.

Smedley, Jonathan (1671–c.1729)

Poems on Several Occasions. London, 1721, 1730.
Gulliveriana, or a Fourth Volume of Miscellanies. London: J. Roberts, 1728.

Swift, Jonathan (1667–1745)

The Poems of Jonathan Swift. Ed. Harold Williams. 3 vols. Oxford: Clarendon Press, 1937, 1958.

Whyte, Laurence (c.1700–c.1753)

Poems on Various Subjects, Serious and Diverting. Dublin: S. Powell, 1740.

Whyte, Samuel (1733–1811)

The Shamrock: or Hibernian Cresses. Dublin: R. Marchbank, 1772.
A Collection of Poems on Various Subjects. Dublin: Robert Marchbank, 1792.

Winstanley, John (c.1677–1750)

Poems, Written Occasionally by John Winstanley . . . Interspers'd with Many Others. By Several Ingenious Hands. 2 vols. Dublin: S. Powell, 1742, 1751.

The Nineteenth Century

Alexander, Cecil Francis (1818–1895)

Poems. London: Macmillan, 1896.

Allingham, William (1824–1889)

Poems. London: Chapman and Hall, 1850.
Day and Night Songs. London: G. Routledge, 1854.

Lawrence Bloomfield in Ireland: A Modern Poem. London and Cambridge: Macmillan, 1864.
Songs Ballads and Stories. London: George Bell, 1877.
Irish Songs and Poems. London: Reeves and Turner, 1887.

Balfour, Mary (1780–1819)

Hope, a Poetical Essay; with Various Other Poems. Belfast: Smyth and Lyons, 1810.

Callanan, J. J. (1795–1829)

The Recluse of Inchidony. London: Hurst, Chance, 1830.
The Poems of J. J. Callanan. Cork: Daniel Mulcahy, 1847, 1861.

Casey, John Keegan (1846–1870)

A Wreath of Shamrocks: Ballads, Songs, and Legends. Dublin: Robert S. McGee, 1866.
The Rising of the Moon, and Other Ballads, Songs, and Legends. Glasgow: Cameron and Ferguson, 1869.

Darley, George (1795–1846)

The Errors of Ecstatsie. London: G. and W. B. Whittaker, 1822.
Nepenthe. London, 1835.
The Complete Poetical Works of George Darley. Ed. Ramsey Colles. London: George Routledge, 1908.

Davis, Thomas (1814–1845)

The Poems of Thomas Davis. Dublin: James Duffy, 1846.

De Vere, Aubrey (1814–1902)

The Sisters, Inisfail, and Other Poems. London: Green, Longman and Roberts; Dublin: McGlashan and Gill, 1861.
Inisfail; A Lyrical Chronicle of Ireland. Dublin: James Duffy, 1863.
The Foray of Queen Maeve and Other Legends of Ireland's Heroic Age. London: Kegan Paul, Trench, 1882.
The Poetical Works of Aubrey de Vere. 6 vols. London: Kegan Paul, Trench (vols. 1–3); Macmillan (vols. 4–6), 1884–1898.

Downing, Ellen Mary Patrick (1828–1869)

Ellen Mary Downing: "Mary of the Nation." Ed. Thomas Markham. Dublin: Catholic Truth Society, n.d.

Dufferin, Lady (1807–1867)

Songs, Poems, & Verses. London: John Murray, 1894.

Ferguson, Samuel (1810–1886)

Lays of the Western Gael. London: Bell and Daldy, 1865.
Congal. Dublin: Sealy; London: George Bell, 1872.
Poems. Dublin: William McGee; London: George Bell, 1880.
Lays of the Red Branch. London: T. Fisher Unwin; Dublin: Sealy, Bryers and Walker, 1897.
Poems of Sir Samuel Ferguson. Ed. Alfred Percival Graves. Dublin: Talbot Press, [1917].

Furlong, Thomas (1794–1827)

The Misanthrope; with Other Poems. Dublin: W. Underwood, 1821.
The Doom of Derenzie: A Poem. London: Joseph Robins, 1829.

Irwin, Thomas Caulfield (1823–1892)

Versicles. London and Dublin: W. M. Hennessey, 1856.
Poems. Dublin: McGlashan and Gill, 1866.
Irish Poems and Legends; Historical and Traditionary. Glasgow: Cameron and Ferguson, 1869.
Songs and Romances. Dublin: M. H. Gill, 1878.
Pictures and Songs. Dublin: M. H. Gill, 1880.
Sonnets on the Poetry and Problems of Life. Dublin: M. H. Gill, 1881.
Poems, Sketches, and Songs. Dublin: M. H. Gill, 1889.

Kelly, Mary (c.1825–1910)

Poems. By 'Eva' of 'The Nation.' San Francisco: P. J. Thomas, 1877; Dublin: M. H. Gill, 1909.

MacCarthy, Denis Florence (1817–1882)

Ballads, Poems, and Lyrics, Original and Translated. Dublin: James McGlashan, 1850.
The Bell-founder. London: D. Bogue, 1857.
Underglimpses. London: D. Bogue, 1857.
Irish Legends and Lyrics. Dublin: McGlashan and Gill, 1858.
Poems. Dublin: M. H. Gill, 1882.

Mangan, James Clarence (1803–1849)

The Collected Poems of James Clarence Mangan. Ed. Augustine Martin. Dublin: Irish Academic Press, 1996.

McGee, Thomas D' Arcy (1825–1868)

The Poems of Thomas D'Arcy McGee. London and New York: J. Sadlier, 1869.

Moore, Thomas (1779–1852)

Irish Melodies. 10 vols. Dublin: William Power (vols. 1–6); London: James Power, 1808–1834.
The Poetical Works of Thomas Moore, Collected by Himself. 10 vols. London: Longmans, 1841.

O'Donnell, John Francis (1837–1874)

Poems. London: Ward and Downey, 1891.

O'Leary, Ellen (1831–1889)

Lays of Country, Home and Friends. Dublin: Sealy, Bryers and Walker, 1890.

Walsh, Edward (1805–1850)

Reliques of Irish Jacobite Poetry. Dublin: Samuel J. Machen, 1844.
Irish Popular Songs. Dublin: J. McGlashan, 1847.

Wilde, Lady (1821–1896)

Poems by Speranza. Dublin: James Duffy, 1864.

The Literary Revival

Campbell, Joseph (1879–1944)

The Rushlight. Dublin: Maunsel, 1906.
The Gilly of Christ. Dublin: Maunsel, 1907.
The Man-Child. Loch Press, 1907.

The Mountainy Singer. Dublin: Maunsel, 1909.
Irishry. Dublin and London: Maunsel, 1913.
Earth of Cualann. Dublin and London: Maunsel, 1917.

Carbery, Ethna (1866–1902)

The Four Winds of Eirinn. Ed. Seamus MacManus. Dublin: M. H. Gill, 1902, 1905, 1918.

Colum, Padraic (1881–1972)

Wild Earth: A Book of Verse. Dublin: Maunsel, 1907, 1922.
Dramatic Legends and Other Poems. London: Macmillan, 1922.
Creatures. New York: Macmillan, 1927.
Old Pastures. New York: Macmillan, 1930.
Poems. London: Macmillan, 1932.
The Collected Poems of Padraic Colum. New York: Devin-Adair, 1953.
The Poet's Circuits: Collected Poems of Ireland. London: Oxford University Press, 1960.

Gore-Booth, Eva (1870–1926)

Poems. London: Longmans, 1898.
The One and the Many. London: Longmans, 1904.
Unseen Kings. London: Longmans, Green, 1904.
The Egyptian Pillar. Dublin: Maunsel, 1907.
The Agate Lamp. London: Longmans, 1912.
The Perilous Light. London: Erskine MacDonald, 1915.
Broken Glory. Dublin and London: Maunsel, 1918.
The Shepherd of Eternity. London: Longmans, 1925.

Hopper, Nora (1871–1906)

Ballads in Prose. London: John Lane, 1894.
Under Quicken Boughs. London: John Lane, 1896.
Songs of the Morning. London: Grant Richards, 1900.
Aquamarines. London: Grant Richards, 1902.
Collected Poems. London: Alston Rivers, 1906.

Hyde, Douglas (1860–1949)

Abhráin Grádh Chúige Connacht: Love Songs of Connacht. London: T. Fisher Unwin; Dublin: Gill and Son, 1893.
Abhráin atá Leagtha ar an Reactúire, or, Songs Ascribed to Raftery. Dublin: Gill and Macmillan, 1903.
Abhráin Diadha Chúige Connacht: The Religious Songs of Connacht. 2 vols. London: T. Fisher Unwin; Dublin: M. H. Gill and Son, 1906.

Johnson, Lionel (1867–1902)

Poems. London: Elkin Mathews, 1895.
Ireland: with Other Poems. London: Elkin Mathews, 1897.
The Collected Poems of Lionel Johnson. Ed. Ian Fletcher. New York and London: Garland, 1982.

Kavanagh, Rose (1859–1891)

Rose Kavanagh and Her Verses. Ed. Matthew Russell. Dublin: M. H. Gill, 1909.

Larminie, William (1849–1900)

Glanlua. London: Kegan Paul, 1889.
Fand and Other Poems. Dublin: Hodges, Figgis, 1892.

Lawless, Emily (1845–1913)

With the Wild Geese. London: Isbister, 1902.
The Poems of Emily Lawless. Ed. Padraic Fallon. Dublin: Dolmen Press, 1965.

Ledwidge, Francis (1887–1917)

Songs of the Fields. London: Herbert Jenkins, 1916.
Songs of Peace. London: Herbert Jenkins, 1917.
Last Songs. London: Herbert Jenkins, 1918.
The Complete Poems of Francis Ledwidge. London: Herbert Jenkins, 1919.

MacDonagh, Thomas (1878–1916)

April and May. Dublin: Sealy, Bryers, 1903.
Through the Ivory Gate. Dublin: Sealy, Bryers, 1903.
Songs of Myself. Dublin: Hodges, Figgis, 1910.
Lyrical Poems. Dublin: Irish Review, 1913.
The Poetical Works of Thomas MacDonagh. Ed. James Stephens. London: T. Fisher Unwin, 1916.

Milligan, Alice (1866–1953).

Hero Lays. Dublin: Maunsel, 1908.
Poems by Alice Milligan. Ed. Henry Mangan. Dublin: M. H. Gill, 1954.

Mitchell, Susan (1866–1926)

Aids to the Immortality of Certain Persons in Ireland. Dublin: New Nation Press, 1908; Dublin and London: Maunsel, 1913.
The Living Chalice and Other Poems. Dublin: Maunsel, 1908, 1913.

O'Neill, Moira (c.1897–1955)

Songs of the Glens of Antrim. Edinburgh and London: William Blackwood, 1900.
More Songs of the Glens of Antrim. Edinburgh and London: William Blackwood, 1921.
Collected Poems of Moira O'Neill. Edinburgh and London: William Blackwood, 1933.

O'Sullivan, Seamus (1879–1958)

The Twilight People. Dublin: Whaley; London: A. H. Bullen, 1905.
Verses Sacred and Profane. Dublin: Maunsel, 1908.
The Earth Lover. Dublin: New Nation Press, 1909.
Poems. Dublin: Maunsel, 1912.
An Epilogue to the Praise of Angus. Dublin and London: Maunsel, 1914.
The Rosses. Dublin: Maunsel, 1918.
The Lamplighter. Dublin: Orwell Press, 1929.
Poems 1930–1938. Dublin: Orwell Press, 1938.
Collected Poems. Dublin: Orwell Press, 1940.

Pearse, Patrick (1879–1916)

Collected Works of Padraic H. Pearse: Plays, Stories, Poems. Dublin and London: Maunsel, 1917.

Plunkett, Joseph Mary (1887–1916)

The Circle and the Sword. Dublin: Maunsel, 1911.
The Poems of Joseph Mary Plunkett. Dublin: Talbot Press; London: T. Fisher Unwin, 1916.

Rolleston, T. W. (1857–1920)

Sea Spray: Verses and Translations. Dublin: Maunsel, 1909.

Russell, George ("A.E.") (1867–1935)

Homeward: Songs by the Way. Dublin: Whaley, 1894.
The Earth Breath. New York and London: J. Lane, 1897.
The Nuts of Knowledge. Dundrum: Dun Emer Press, 1903.
The Divine Vision. London and New York: Macmillan, 1904.
By Still Waters. Dundrum: Dun Emer Press, 1906.
Collected Poems. London: Macmillan, 1913, 1919, 1926, 1935.
Enchantment. London: Macmillan, 1930.
Vale. London: Macmillan, 1931.
The House of the Titans. London: Macmillan, 1934.

Sigerson, Dora (1866–1918)

Verses. London: E. Stock, 1893.
Ballads and Poems. London: J. Bowden, 1899.
The Collected Poems of Dora Sigerson Shorter. New York and London: Harper Brothers, 1907.
Sixteen Dead Men and Other Poems of Easter Week. New York: Mitchell Kennedy, 1919.
The Tricolour. Poems of the Irish Revolution. Dublin: Maunsel and Roberts, 1919.

Sigerson, George (1836–1925)

Bards of the Gael and Gall. London: T. Fisher Unwin, 1897.

Stephens, James (1882–1950)

Insurrections. Dublin: Maunsel, 1909.
The Hill of Vision. Dublin: Maunsel, 1912.
Songs from the Clay. London: Macmillan, 1915.
Reincarnations. London: Macmillan, 1918.
Collected Poems. London: Macmillan, 1926, 1954.
Strict Joy. London: Macmillan, 1931.

Synge, John M. (1871–1909)

Poems and Translations. Dundrum: Cuala Press, 1909.
Collected Works: Volume 1: Poems. Ed. Robin Skelton. London: Oxford University Press, 1962.

Todhunter, John (1839–1916)

The Banshee. London: Kegan, Paul, Trench, 1888; Dublin: Sealy, Bryers and Walker, 1891.
Three Irish Bardic Tales. London: J. M. Dent, 1896.

Tynan, Katharine (1861–1931)

Shamrocks. London: Kegan, Paul, Trench, 1887.
Ballads and Lyrics. London: Kegan, Paul, Trench, Trübner, 1891.
Cuckoo Songs. London: Elkin Mathews and John Lane, 1894.
The Wind in the Trees: A Book of Country Verse. London: Grant Richards, 1898.
Poems. London: Lawrence and Bullen, 1901.
Innocencies: a Book of Verse. Dublin: Maunsel; London: A. H. Bullen, 1905.
Twenty One Poems by Katherine Tyrian. Ed. W. B. Yeats. Dundrum: Dun Emer Press, 1907.

Experiences. London: A. H. Bullen, 1908.
New Poems. London: Sidgwick and Jackson, 1911.
Irish Poems. London: Sidgwick and Jackson, 1913.
Collected Poems. London: Macmillan, 1930.

Yeats, W. B. (1865–1939)

The Collected Poems of W. B. Yeats. New York and London: Macmillan, 1933, 1950, 1956.
The Variorum Edition of the Poems of W. B. Yeats. Ed. Peter Allt and Russell K. Alspach. New York: Macmillan, 1957.
W. B. Yeats. The Poems. A New Edition. Ed. Richard J. Finneran. NewYork and London: Macmillan, 1983.

Young, Ella (1865–1951)

Poems by Ella Young. Dublin: Maunsel, 1906.
The Rose of Heaven. Dublin: Candle Press, 1920.
The Weird of Fionavar. Dublin: Talbot Press; London: T. Fisher Unwin, 1922.

Poetry in Modern Ireland

Clarke, Austin (1896–1974)

The Vengeance of Fionn. Dublin and London: Maunsel, 1917.
The Sword of the West. Dublin and London: Maunsel and Roberts, 1921.
The Cattledrive in Connaught. London: Allen and Unwin, 1925.
Pilgrimage. London: Allen and Unwin, 1929.
Night and Morning. Dublin: Orwell Press, 1938.
Ancient Lights. Dublin: Bridge Press, 1955.
Too Great a Vine. Dublin: Bridge Press, 1957.
The Horse-eaters. Dublin: Bridge Press, 1960.
Later Poems. Dublin: Dolmen Press, 1961.
Flight to Africa. Dublin: Dolmen Press, 1963.
Mnemosyne Lay in Dust. Dublin: Dolmen Press, 1966.
Old-fashioned Pilgrimage. Dublin: Dolmen Press, 1967.
The Echo at Coole. Dublin: Dolmen Press, 1968.
Collected Poems. Ed. Liam Miller. Dublin: Dolmen Press, 1974.

Coghill, Rhoda (1903–)

The Bright Hillside. Dublin: Hodges, Figgis, 1948.
Time Is a Squirrel. Dublin: Dolmen, 1956.

Devlin, Denis (1908–1959)

Poems (by Brian Coffey and Denis Devlin). Dublin: A. Thom, 1930.
Intercessions. London: Europa Press, 1937.
Lough Derg. New York: Reynal and Hitchcock, 1946.
Collected Poems of Denis Devlin. Winston-Salem, N.C.: Wake Forest University Press, 1989.

Fallon, Padraic (1905–1974)

Collected Poems. Ed. Brian Fallon. Old Castle, Co. Meath: Gallery Press; Manchester: Carcanet Press, 1990.

Farren, Robert (1909–1984)

Thronging Feet. London: Sheed and Ward, 1936.
Time's Wall Asunder. London: Sheed and Ward, 1939.
The First Exile. London: Sheed and Ward, 1944.
Rime, Gentlemen, Please. London: Sheed and Ward, 1945.

Gogarty, Oliver St. John (1878–1957)

The Ship. Dublin: Talbot Press, 1918.
An Offering of Swans. Dublin: Cuala Press, 1923
Wild Apples. Dublin: Cuala Press, 1928, 1930.
Others to Adorn. London: Rich and Cowan, 1938.
Elbow Room. Dublin: Cuala Press, 1939.
The Collected Poems of Oliver St. John Gogarty. London: Constable, 1951.

Hewitt, John (1907–1987)

The Collected Poems of John Hewitt. Ed. Frank Ormsby. Belfast: Blackstaff Press, 1991.

Higgins, F. R. (1896–1941)

Island Blood. London: John Lane, 1925.
The Dark Breed. London: Macmillan, 1927.
Arable Holdings. Dublin: Cuala Press, 1933.
The Gap of Brightness. London: Macmillan, 1940.

Kavanagh, Patrick (1904–1967)

Ploughman. London: Macmillan, 1936.
The Great Hunger. Dublin: Cuala Press, 1942.
A Soul for Sale. London: Macmillan, 1947.
Come Dance with Kitty Stobling. London: Longmans Green, 1960.
The Complete Poems of Patrick Kavanagh. New York: Kavanagh Hand Press, 1972, 1996.

Kinsella, Thomas (1928–)

Poems. Dublin: Dolmen Press, 1956.
Another September. Dublin: Dolmen Press, 1958.
Downstream. Dublin: Dolmen Press, 1962.
Wormwood. Dublin: Dolmen Press, 1966.
Nightwalker. Dublin: Dolmen Press, 1968.
The Collected Poems, 1956–1994. London and New York: Oxford University Press, 1996.

MacEntee, Máire (1922–)

A Heart Full of Thought. Dublin: Dolmen Press, 1959.

MacGreevy, Thomas (1893–1967)

Poems. London: William Heinemann, 1934.
Collected Poems of Thomas MacGreevy. Ed. Susan Schreibman. Dublin: Anna Livia Press, 1991.

MacNeice, Louis (1907–1963)

The Collected Poems of Louis MacNeice. Ed. E. R. Dodds. London: Faber and Faber, 1966, 1979.

Montague, John (1929–)

Forms of Exile. Dublin: Dolmen Press, 1958.
Poisoned Lands. London: Macgibbon and Kee, 1961.
A Chosen Light. London: Macgibbon and Kee, 1967.
Tides. Dublin: Dolmen Press, 1970.
The Rough Field. Dublin: Dolmen Press, 1972.
Collected Poems. Old Castle, Co. Meath: Gallery Press; Winston-Salem, N. C.: Wake Forest University Press, 1995.

Murphy, Richard (1927–)

Sailing to an Island. London: Faber and Faber, 1963.
The Battle of Aughrim. London: Faber and Faber; New York: Knopf, 1968.
High Island. London: Faber and Faber, 1974.

O'Neill, Mary Devenport (1879–1967)

Prometheus and Other Poems. London: Jonathan Cape, 1929.

Rodgers, W. R. (1909–1969)

Awake! London: Secker and Warburg, 1941.
Europa and the Bull. London: Secker and Warburg, 1952.
Collected Poems. London: Oxford University Press, 1971.

Salkeld, Blanaid (1880–1959)

Hello, Eternity! London: Elkin Mathews and Marrot, 1933.
The Fox's Covert. London: J. M. Dent, 1935.
The Engine Is Left Running. Dublin: Gayfield, 1937.
Experiment in Error. Aldington: Hand and Flower Press, 1955.

Strong, Eithne (1923–)

Songs of Living. Monkstown: Runa Press, 1961.
Sarah, in Passing. Dublin: Dolmen Press, 1974.

Wingfield, Sheila (1906–1992)

Poems. London: Cresset Press, 1938.
Beat Drum, Beat Heart. London: Cresset Press, 1946.
A Cloud across the Sun. London: Cresset Press, 1949.
The Leaves Darken. London: Weidenfeld and Nicholson, 1964.
Collected Poems: 1938–1983. London: Enitharmon Press, 1983.

Selected Anthologies

A Miscellaneous Collection of Poems, Songs and Epigrams. By Several Hands. 2 vols. Dublin: A. Rhames, 1721.
Irish Minstrelsy, or Bardic Remains of Ireland; with English Poetical Translations. Ed. James Hardiman. 2 vols. London: Joseph Rubins, 1831.
The Spirit of the Nation; or, Ballads and Songs by the Writers of "The Nation". Dublin: James Duffy, 1843.
The Ballad Poetry of Ireland. Ed. Charles Gavan Duffy. Dublin: James Duffy, 1845.
The Cabinet of Irish Literature. 4 vols. Ed. Charles A. Read. London: Blackie and Son, 1879.
Poems and Ballads of Young Ireland. Dublin: M. H. Gill, 1888.
A Book of Irish Verse. Ed. W. B. Yeats. London: Methuen, 1895.

A Treasury of Irish Poetry in the English Tongue. Ed. Stopford A. Brooke and T. W. Rolleston. London and New York: Macmillan, 1900.

Irish Literature. 10 vols. Ed. Justin McCarthy. New York: Bigelow, Smith, 1904.

New Songs: A Lyric Selection. Ed. A. E. [George Russell]. Dublin: O'Donoghue; London: A. H. Bullen, 1904.

An Anthology of Irish Verse. Ed. Padraic Colum. New York: Boni and Liveright, 1922, 1948.

1000 Years of Irish Poetry. Ed. Kathleen Hoagland. New York: Devin-Adair, 1947.

Irish Poets of the Nineteenth Century. Ed. Geoffrey Taylor. London: Routledge and Kegan Paul, 1951.

The Penguin Book of Irish Verse. Ed. Brendan Kennelly. London: Penguin Books, 1970, 1981.

The Faber Book of Irish Verse. Ed. John Montague. London: Faber, 1974.

Irish Poetry after Yeats. Ed. Maurice Harmon. Portmarnock: Wolfhound, 1979.

An Duanaire 1600–1900: Poems of the Dispossessed. Ed. Seán Ó Tuama; trans. Thomas Kinsella. Mountrath: Dolmen Press, 1981.

Pillars of the House: An Anthology of Verse by Irish Women from 1690 to the Present. Ed. A. A. Kelly. Dublin: Wolfhound, 1987.

A Georgian Celebration: Irish Poets of the Eighteenth Century. Ed. Patrick Fagan. Dublin: Branar, 1989.

The Field Day Anthology of Irish Writing. 3 vols. Ed. Seamus Deane. Derry: Field Day Publications, 1991.

INDEX